D1259271

Rhetoric
and
Philosophy

Rhetoric
and
Philosophy

Edited by
Richard A. Cherwitz
The University of Texas at Austin

With a Foreword by
Henry W. Johnstone, Jr.
The Pennsylvania State University

LEA LAWRENCE ERLBAUM ASSOCIATES, PUBLISHERS
1990   Hillsdale, New Jersey   Hove and London

Copyright © 1990 by Lawrence Erlbaum Associates, Inc.
All rights reserved. No part of this book may be reproduced in
any form, by photostat, microform, retrieval system, or any other
means, without the prior written permission of the publisher.

Lawrence Erlbaum Associates, Inc., Publishers
365 Broadway
Hillsdale, New Jersey 07642

Library of Congress Cataloging-in-Publication Data

Rhetoric and philosophy / edited by Richard A. Cherwitz ; with a
  foreword by Henry W. Johnstone, Jr.
      p. cm.
  Includes bibliographical references and indexes.
  ISBN 0-8058-0413-7
  1. Rhetoric—Philosophy. 2. Philosophy—History. I. Cherwitz,
Richard A.
PN175.R4 1990   90-42339
808′.001—dc20   CIP

Printed in the United States of America
10 9 8 7 6 5 4 3 2 1

To N. L. C. and R. P. H.

Contents

Contributors

Richard A. Cherwitz is Associate Professor and Director of Graduate Studies in the Department of Speech Communication at The University of Texas at Austin. He earned his PhD in 1978 in Rhetorical Studies from the University of Iowa. Recipient of the Speech Communication Association's 1978 Karl R. Wallace Memorial Award, Dr. Cherwitz is the co-author of *Communication and Knowledge: An Investigation in Rhetorical Epistemology* (University of South Carolina Press, 1986). His articles and reviews appear in *The Quarterly Journal of Speech, Philosophy and Rhetoric, Communication Quarterly, Pre/Text,* and *The Journal of the American Forensics Association.* Dr. Cherwitz's research has dealt with rhetoric and epistemology, political mythology, rhetorical effects, and a variety of associated topics.

James Arnt Aune received his BA from St. Olaf College in 1975, and his MA (1977) and PhD (1980) from Northwestern University. He has taught at Tulane University, the University of Virginia, and is currently Associate Professor of Speech–Theatre at St. Olaf College, Northfield, Minnesota. Dr. Aune has published articles exploring the relationships among rhetoric, literary theory, and political philosophy. He is at work on a book entitled, *Marxism, Rhetoric, and Political Judgment.*

Barry Brummett is Associate Professor of Speech Communication at the University of Wisconsin-Milwaukee. He earned his PhD from the University of Minnesota in 1978. Dr. Brummett's research interests are in rhetorical theory and criticism. His many articles have appeared in *The Quarterly Journal of Speech, Philosophy and Rhetoric,* and *Critical Studies in Mass Communication.*

James W. Hikins is Assistant Professor of Speech Communication at The Ohio State University. Previously an Assistant Professor of Communication at Tulane University, Dr. Hikins' articles appear in *The Quarterly Journal of Speech, Central States Speech Journal,* and *The Southern Speech Communication Journal.* He is the co-author of *Communication and Knowledge: An Investigation in Rhetorical Epistemology* (University of South Carolina Press, 1986). In addition to rhetorical epistemology, his research has focused on contemporary political communication, classical rhetorical theory, and 19th century theories of rhetoric.

Michael J. Hyde (PhD, Purdue University) is Associate Professor of Communication Studies at Northwestern University. Previously an Assistant Professor of Speech Communication at The University of Alabama, Tuscaloosa, Dr. Hyde is the editor of and a contributor to *Communication, Philosophy and the Technological Age* (University of Alabama Press, 1982/1986). His numerous essays and critical reviews appear in such academic journals as *The Quarterly Journal of Speech, Man & World, Communication, Philosophy and Rhetoric, Communication Quarterly,* and *The International Journal of Oral History.* Professor Hyde is a past National Fellow of The W. K. Kellogg Foundation and a recipient of national and state research grants for his work in "the rhetoric of medicine."

Henry W. Johnstone, Jr. is Professor Emeritus of Philosophy at The Pennsylvania State University. He is the co-founder and editor of *Philosophy and Rhetoric.* Professor Johnstone's work has appeared in *The Quarterly Journal of Speech, Revue Internationale de Philosophie, Journal of Philosophy, Philosophy and Rhetoric, Dialectica,* and *Philosophy and Phenomenological Research.* He is the author of *Philosophy and Argument, The Problem of the Self, Validity and Rhetoric in Philosophical Argument* and co-author of *Philosophy, Rhetoric, and Argumentation.*

John R. Lyne (PhD, University of Wisconsin, 1978) is Associate Professor of Communication Studies at the University of Iowa. He teaches courses in rhetorical theory and argument. Professor Lyne's scholarly articles and essays have appeared in *The Quarterly Journal of Speech, Communication Quarterly, Central States Speech Journal,* and a number of books. He has been a regular contributor to the SCA/AFA summer conference on argument at Alta, Utah. A book, *Gene Talk,* co-authored with biologist Henry Howe, is forthcoming from the University of Wisconsin Press.

James A. Mackin, Jr. is Assistant Professor of Communication at Tulane University, where he teaches courses in rhetorical criticism and in classical, modern, and contemporary rhetorical theory. He received his PhD from The University of Texas in 1989. Dr. Mackin's most recent research is dedicated to finding a commensurate ground for public moral argument in a pluralistic society; as part of this project, Dr. Mackin has been conducting an inquiry into the role of rhetorical criticism in public moral argument.

Michael McGuire (PhD, Iowa, 1975) is Professor of Communication Studies at the University of Nevada, Las Vegas. He has also held positions at the University of Georgia, California State University, Long Beach, the University of California, Davis, the University of Marburg, and the University of Erlangen. His publications on rhetorical theory and criticism have appeared in *Philosophy & Rhetoric, The Quarterly Journal of Speech, Communication Monographs, Communication Education, Sprache and Sprechen,* and a number of books and other journals.

C. Jack Orr is Associate Professor of Communication at West Chester State University. He holds a PhD in Speech Communication from Temple University and an MA in Philosophy of Religion from Northwestern University. Dr. Orr's articles have appeared in *The Quarterly Journal of Speech, Communication Monographs, Communication Education,* and *Central States Speech Journal.* In addition to critical rationalism, he is interested in the relationship between Buber's dialogical philosophy and equity theory, and the quest for identity as a rhetorically generative event.

Foreword

Henry W. Johnstone, Jr.

This book explores alternative ways in which the attempt has been made to find a philosophical grounding for rhetoric.

Throughout the period since 1952, when I first became associated with people in the field now usually referred to as "Speech Communication," I have noticed that practitioners of this field, especially those concerned with rhetoric, have continued to feel a need for philosophical grounding.

There has been a succession of ways in which theorists of Speech have sought to satisfy this need. At first they proceeded in total independence and indeed ignorance of the studies that their colleagues in Philosophy were engaged in. They put their own seal of approval on works most professional philosophers regarded as worthless, such as Count Korzybski's *Science and Sanity* and the writings of S.I. Hayakawa; they blithely taught their own philosophy courses using works like these as textbooks. Indeed, they even taught their own courses in logic (non-Aristotelean, of course), unaware, it seems, that they were bound to wind up losing this battle for turf. I mention these early days characterized by confusion and lack of communication only to illustrate the fact that these Speech people were groping in their own way toward a legitimate goal—the goal of discovering and articulating the philosophical foundations of the authenticity of their own enterprise.

In speaking of the need for philosophical grounding, I mean something beyond the interest in the rhetorical theories of Plato and Aristotle and in the relations between these theories and the philosophies of Plato and Aristotle that has been characteristic of students of classical rhetoric for a long time. The outcome of that interest has mainly taken the form of historical conclusions rather than a recommendation of philosophical principles on which the enterprise of speech, especially in the form of rhetoric, might be grounded. To be sure, there have been Platonists and Aristotelians among students of Plato and Aristotle. Were they claiming to have discovered philosophical groundings for their own profession? I do not believe that such partisans were as much concerned with the *metaphysical* foundations of the enterprise that now goes under the name of Speech Communication as with finding a basis in human nature for carrying out the tasks traditionally associated with rhetoric.

At the time of which I am speaking — the decade of the 1950s — there were in fact some professional philosophers examining rhetoric, the activity that primarily concerned Speech people seeking philosophical foundations; the best example is Richard McKeon. But I do not recall any professional philosophers for whom there was any real enthusiasm in Speech departments before the publication of Stephen Toulmin's *The Uses of Argument* in 1958. Even then, there was a considerable time-lag before a Toulmin-bandwagon developed in Speech; it was roughly after the book had been reviewed in every relevant philosophical journal, and philosophers were beginning to interest themselves in other matters, that Toulmin began to be used as a textbook in courses on rhetoric and argumentation. This lag has characterized other Speech philosopher bandwagons as well; witness the recent interest in works of Habermas long since read and digested by his colleagues in Philosophy.

An important moment in the history of the interaction between rhetoricians and philosophers was the appearance on the American scene, in 1962, of Chaim Perelman. This appearance was largely engineered by Robert Oliver, then head of the Speech Department at The Pennsylvania State University. In my opinion, Perelman advanced few, if any, original philosophical ideas. The philosophical position he did take was a form of what will be described on the following pages as "pragmatism," but Perelman did not go much further in articulating a pragmatic position than to quote occasionally from Charles Sanders Peirce. Yet he did occupy an important role in relation to the quest for foundations to which rhetoricians were committed; he was perceived as a professional philosopher concerned with a fundamental classification of rhetorical strategies. It was not so much that the philosophical presuppositions of this concern were taken to be at issue in Perelman's enterprise; it was just that attention was finally being paid to a professional philosopher doing serious work in rhetoric as a technē, or at least as a technique.

Robert Oliver must have particularly felt the need to foster the articulation of the philosophical foundations of his own field, for in 1964 he sponsored a conference of Philosophers and Speech people at The Pennsylvania State University to explore this theme. An aftermath of this conference was the foundation in 1968 of the journal *Philosophy and Rhetoric*.

Beginning with Volume I, No. 1, the masthead of this journal began with the sentence *"Philosophy and Rhetoric* concerns itself with rhetoric as a philosophical concept."* These words were modified in later years, but their intent has so far remained unchanged throughout the career of the journal. This intent is tantamount to the encouragement of a quest for the philosophical foundations of rhetoric. Obviously not all of the articles have been concerned specifically with this quest, but most of them have dealt in some fashion with philosophical issues surrounding activities of concern to Speech Communication departments. Speaking from a biased point of view—I have been editor of *Philosophy and Rhetoric* on two separate occasions—the journal seems to me to have been influential in increasing the number of Speech people who see the philosophical authentication of their own field as a legitimate inquiry. In recent years, other journals have also contributed to this movement; for example, the *Rhetoric Society Quarterly* and the new Dutch-Belgian journal *Argumentation. Informal Logic,* issued in Canada, is also helpful in this regard, although I don't think many rhetoricians or other members of the Speech Communication profession have yet begun to turn to it for help. Throughout the entire period in question, and before it, the *Quarterly Journal of Speech* has been helping to raise consciousness regarding the philosophical principles undergirding the field.

Many more people in Speech are now interested in professionally acceptable philosophy than were in 1952, but not always for the right reasons. I find many students of Speech Communication—especially graduate students—who seem to have chosen their major at least partly in the belief that it is *"philosophy without tears."* They take an interest in philosophical issues—as undergraduates they may even have majored in philosophy—but they are unable or unwilling to do the work or hard thinking that worthwhile philosophical studies demand. Archimedes, asked by a king to explain geometry, is said to have replied *"*There is no royal road to geometry.*"* There is similarly no easy road to philosophy. The illusion that there is has been partly fostered, I am afraid, by standards of scholarly work in Speech Communication departments that are in some respects so relaxed that they offer no incentive to the student to rise to the level of serious philosophizing. I am thinking particularly of logic and languages. Logic ought surely to be indispensable to the methodology of Speech as well as constituting part of its subject matter; a Speech student ought to be able both to distinguish the canons of logical validity from the methods of rhetoric and to use these canons in conducting his own research. And the study of languages other than English offers liberation from the otherwise inevitable predicament of being misled by translators, even the most competent and best-intentioned ones. To study logic and languages is work; it evokes the tears that are a necessary accompaniment of serious work in philosophy. "Philosophy without tears" is not philosophy at all; the phrase is an oxymoron.

I make these remarks only to suggest that the increased interest in philosophy during the past few decades among the members of the Speech community has had a negative side as well as a positive one. This book is a brilliant illustration of the positive side. It makes a point inaccessible to those who wish to escape the work of serious philosophy. Part of the motivation underlying their unwillingness to cope with what is difficult in philosophy is the desire simply to be told which position is true, and to settle for that. If one could, without effort, discover the one verity underlying rhetoric—as well as everything else—what could more properly exemplify "Philosophy without tears"? The problem is that when one comes to apply serious thought to philosophical matters, one perceives that there is no single verity. The discovery that there are *types* of philosophy, each emerging from the critique of others, is reserved for those willing to contribute their tears to the project. The most important contribution of this book, in my opinion, is just the recognition that there is a variety of ways in which rhetoric could be undergirded, none altogether without defect. This is the *hard* road to philosophy. That this road can be taken by a group of authors largely from Speech Communication shows that this field is coming of age in at least one important respect.

Unless there is a recognition that different thinkers can have good reasons to adhere to different types of philosophy there will always be serious problems of communication among the thinkers—problems tending toward hostility and even approaching violence. Thus the Deconstructionist may strike the Realist as crazy or worse. When this happens, the breakdown can usually be attributed to the Realist's failure to identify his opponent as the advocate of a serious and plausible position. One of the main points of studying types of philosophy is to enable people to identify others whom they hear using language that seems strange, and making claims that seem unintelligible.

The study of types not only offers the identification of alien philosophical positions but also suggests their justification. The Realist can end up seeing the Deconstructionist not only as a fellow human with concerns similar in principle to his own, but also as having reasons for taking the position he does. He comes to see the arguments—even in the case of positions which, like Deconstructionism, do not explicitly argue. Ths is not to say that the gap between the two positions will or can ever be narrowed, or even that it ought to be. Ultimately, the significance of there being a plurality of possible groundings of the rhetorical enterprise resides just in the tensions among them. The reader of this book will do well to attend carefully to these tensions.

ACKNOWLEDGMENTS

The undertaking and completion of this project have given me pause to reflect about all of those persons who have played a vital role in my personal and professional development. I am indebted and grateful to many people. To my Dean, Robert C. Jeffrey, who 12 years ago had enough faith to hire a somewhat naive, but hungry, young scholar. To my Chair, Mark Knapp, whose ability to listen without judging helps me work through the daily frustrations that go with simultaneously wearing the hats of scholar, teacher, and administrator. To my friend and colleague, Roderick Hart, who constantly has his eye on the "rhetorical" and who, through example, regularly demonstrates what it means to achieve scholarly excellence. To my current and former graduate students—Rudolph Busby, Earl Croasmun, Tommy Darwin, Jim Hikins, Bill Keith, Dick Lesicko, Jim Mackin, Ken Mihalik, Don Nobles, Kerry Riley, Jon Swanson, and Ken Zagacki—who have participated in the philosophical conversation that is the subject of this book. To my teacher, Douglas Ehninger, who gave me the opportunity and motivated me to enter the conversation; his sensibilities shall remain forever embedded in my memory. I am indebted to Tommy Darwin, who, in addition to carefully proofreading and preparing an index for this book, is a source of philosophical stimulation. Finally, and most especially, I am grateful to Nancy, who always understands: her goodness and love nourish me.

Chapter 1

The Philosophical Foundations of Rhetoric

Richard A. Cherwitz

Since the 5th century B.C. there has been a fascination with "rhetoric," a concept encompassing the manner in which humans symbolically influence one another. Throughout the ensuing centuries, thinkers have attempted to refine understanding of the nature, scope, and function of the rhetorical art. To be sure, definitions of rhetoric, although varied, have focused attention on an important aspect of human thought and behavior, namely, the way the content and form of language affects individual experience and social order.

Beginning with one of the earliest, systematic, and extended treatments of the subject and continuing through the 20th century, let us consider some representative definitions of rhetoric: rhetoric is the art of "enchanting the soul with words" (Plato, *Phaedrus,* p. 261a); rhetoric is an art whose function is to discover "in the particular case what are the available means of persuasion" (Cooper, *The Rhetoric of Aristotle,* p. 1355b); rhetoric involves the "application of reason to imagination for the better moving of the will" (Dick, 1955, p. 309); rhetoric is "the rationale of informative and suasory *in* discourse" (Bryant, 1973, p. 14); and rhetoric may be described broadly as the study of "all of the ways in which men may influence each other's thinking and behavior through the strategic use of symbols" (Ehninger, 1972, p. 3). Although these and other definitions are suggestive of the varied purposes, functions, processes, ends, and effects of communication, they all underscore the centrality of "persuasion" to rhetoric.

Regardless of one's definition or theoretical orientation, it would be hard to deny the pervasiveness of persuasion in society. After all, what human enterprise does not involve symbolic influence? All human activity, unin-

1

tentionally or by design, contains a rhetorical component. Whether our interest is in making ethical judgments, articulating the preferability of a particular philosophical, scientific, or historical theory vis-à-vis another, or in gaining followers for a political, social, or religious cause, rhetoric abounds. Although the motive for engaging in these or other activities may not always *explicitly* be to persuade, this fact cannot obfuscate the existence and importance of symbolic influence; in each of the aforementioned cases we can discover the presence of a rhetor (speaker or writer) utilizing a wide array of symbolic tools (verbal and nonverbal) to communicate a message to an audience. The fact that the intent of rhetors in each of these instances is not identical is unimportant. It might be, for example, that some of these rhetors desire conversion or change in audience attitudes, beliefs, and values, whereas some seek modifications in human behavior, and still others wish only to obtain the understanding of those with whom they communicate. Yet in every case the dynamic relationships among rhetor, message, and auditor indicate the potential for, if not the fact of, symbolic influence. In short, our ability or inability to discern the intent or outcomes of messages is not germane to detection of the rhetorical.

It is not surprising, therefore, that throughout history scholars interested in comprehending human symbolic influence have written treatises explicating the role of rhetoric in and the relationship of rhetoric to such activities as politics, philosophy, science, religion, and literature. However, it is only of late that we have begun to recognize how essential rhetoric is to the functioning of these other enterprises. In the last 10 years alone countless numbers of books and essays have emerged from a variety of academic disciplines — all arguing for the significance of rhetoric in human affairs. Explication of rhetoric in the late 20th century is an interdisciplinary quest. For example, at major centers of learning throughout the United States today, scholars from various parts of campus routinely convene to explore what has been termed "the rhetoric of inquiry" — the common denominator and essential core undergirding all human efforts to know (Lyne, 1985; McCloskey, 1985; Nelson & Megill, 1986; Simons, 1985, 1989). Economists, philosophers, historians, political scientists, accountants, mathematicians, and others are beginning to notice that it is the discipline and subject matter of rhetoric that contains many of the principles and concepts endemic to and accounting for all academic inquiries. Rather than remaining preoccupied with the methodological and ideological differences traditionally separating disciplines and resulting in battles over academic turf, increasingly principles and methods uniting all domains of knowledge acquisition are sought. And within rhetoric we may have discovered the glue binding together the many seemingly disparate, academic ventures; for regardless of content and methodology, we now realize that knowledge is discovered by or created through the machinery of human symbol use (Brummett, 1976; Cherwitz, 1977; Cherwitz & Hikins, 1986; Scott, 1967, 1976). Sharp distinctions between content and form, and invention and disposition no longer can be maintained (Johnstone, 1969). To speculate about human symbol use, therefore, is to make comment not only about how we communicate, but about how we inquire and come to know.

Admittedly, recognition of the ubiquitous and interdisciplinary properties of rhetoric is enlightening. Cognizant of the rhetorical fact that communicators of our day (whether they be politicians, theologians, scientists, or philosophers) inherently reside within the tenuous and often unstable world of ideas, surely we must be humbled. Discerning the rhetorical forces at work in all varieties of conduct and inquiry underscores the habitual problem of locating certainties as a basis for action, and reminds us of the virtue of tolerance. But if symbolic influence is indeed "a" or even "the" basis for all human thought and action, then the use or conscious choice of a rhetorical theory will have consequences and implications for one's understanding and evaluation of the world. To say that rhetoric is a fundamental part of all activity, from trivial to serious, does not mean, for example, that we will arrive at and share the same understandings and evaluations. How the art of rhetoric is conceived, what theoretical assumptions are made about its operation and scope, and what is posited as rhetoric's relationships to the other essential dimensions and components of human activity will affect our understandings and evaluations. Thus, at a time when the vocabulary for analyzing the many different activities of life is so fulsomely rhetorical, it is necessary to make clear not only the different possible conceptions of rhetoric, but the rationales for choosing among them.

Rhetoric and Philosophy represents an attempt to do just that. This collection of essays begins with a two-part question:

1. If common sense and experience suggest that symbolic influence is both pervasive and important to understanding the world in which we live, then what are some of the possible conceptions and theories of rhetoric we might choose from to explain the art's pervasiveness and potential impact?
2. If there are many potential conceptions of the nature, scope, and function of rhetoric, then what is to account for differences among them, and what method can be used for choosing or preferring one conception over another?

To answer these questions requires philosophical analysis. Thus, *Rhetoric and Philosophy* is not a case study of actual specimens of rhetorical discourse; its objective is not *criticism*. Nor is this book an investigation of chronological developments in rhetorical theory or an interpretive account of the views espoused by rhetorical theorists of the past and present; *history* is not a goal. Our concerns are *conceptual* and *theoretical;* for one cannot accomplish the tasks of rhetorical criticism and history, or perhaps such projects will be of diminished worth, without first canvassing the landscape of available theories of rhetoric and articulating the philosophical assumptions attendant to choosing among them.

Put simply, one of the central claims of this book is that rhetoricians are, or at least on occasion must be, philosophers. The reader should note that the term "philosopher" is used here to underscore (as the degree title Ph.D. — Doctorate of Philosophy — designates) how all serious inquiries are at root philosophical. The term is not intended to suggest that rhetoricians are professional philosophers. The fundamental questions raised by rhetoricians have been and will always be about the world of prudential conduct. From its inception rhetoric has been a discipline devoted to a study of *praxis.* But, as the essays in this volume attest, any academic consideration of rhetorical praxis must commence with and end in *theory;* scholars in rhetoric, like scholars in any area of study, seek to account for and make sense out of the world — in this case, the rhetorical world. And it is this habit of accounting and making sense that is the cornerstone of theory. Yet the demands for generalization incumbent upon theory cannot be met exclusively through an analysis of actual events, rhetorical or otherwise. After all, how those events are viewed, that is, what methodologies are employed and how those methodologies are used to examine and analyze the data of the rhetorical world is as much the product of antecedent theories as it is the result of methodological rigor and painstaking efforts to be obedient to the details of the world scrutinized.

If at least a part of our theory is antecedent to rhetorical analysis, and if that theory can affect the outcome of analysis, then we must ask: What is the source of such theory and how can one be made conscious of and choose among competing theories? The answer, of course, is that in order to compare and choose one must ask philosophical questions, think philosophically, and employ philosophical methods of analysis. To do this will in turn require us to make our assumptions explicit, examine the consequences entailed by those assumptions and, in the spirit of dialectic, interact argumentatively with others. To say that a rhetorician must be a philosopher, then, is to suggest what should be obvious: a complete and thorough understanding of the *practice* of human symbolic influence involves the critical inspection of and inquiry into the *theoretical* presuppositions of rhetoric.

Yet there may be a more fundamental sense in which rhetoric is and must be philosophical. Rhetoricians, like all scholars, must introduce a technical vocabulary as part of their theorizing. Whenever such terminology is offered, the first question asked will always be Socratic: What is it? History reminds us that, whether the focus of analysis is ordinary language or the more erudite and specialized jargon comprising academic explanation, humans inherently must grapple with the philosophical issues of definition and interpretation. To raise and answer the question of "what is it" is to engage in philosophical analysis. Avoiding or circumventing this question prevents or restricts the kind of clarity and knowledge necessary for informed scholarly inquiry.

Nowhere is the importance of philosophical activity more apparent than in academic studies of rhetoric. Regardless of what rhetorical phenomena are investigated or the rhetorical methods utilized, conclusions will always be about human agents, symbol systems, audiences, and the place of each in the world. It seems inconceivable that generalizations could be made about any of these constructs or the interrelationships among them without presuming or advancing philosophical claims. To make comment on the properties of the symbol system comprising a communicator's message, for instance, is to raise serious philosophical questions about *meaning* and interpretation. Similarly, to delineate the effects of rhetorical discourse (and in so doing ascertain the relationships among rhetor, message, and auditor) is to broach the traditional philosophical question of what is *reality*. Moreover, to determine how speakers and writers build arguments for consideration of their audiences is to wrestle with the philosophical problem of *certainty* and the related question of whether and how we can *know*.

It is important to note that such issues, whether presumed as a basis for conducting rhetorical analysis (antecedent theory) or taken as a part of the theoretical conclusions derived from rhetorical study, are quintessentially *philosophical*. And because they are philosophical, they cannot be discussed rigorously and comprehensively in the absence of philosophical analysis. An analogy will serve to illustrate. Just as science cannot and does not retreat to methodological arguments as the basis for establishing certitude, so too rhetoric cannot hide within the logic of its analytic systems as the basis for advancing larger knowledge claims; for the methodologies and logic of rhetoric, like those of science or any discipline, are themselves predicated upon philosophical assumptions. One cannot use the rules of a particular methodology as a way of validating the methodology itself. In arguing for the viability of knowledge about rhetoric, therefore, one must raise and endeavor to answer philosophical questions. When that is done, researchers necessarily will stand back from their data and methods, articulating the assumptions made and the arguments underpinning them; and to accomplish this feat will require investigators to think and speak *philosophically*.

At this point the reader may feel uncomfortable with an insistence that rhetoricians frequently must operate in the realm of the philosophical. This claim, some might retort, is at best arguable. Yet to attempt refutation, as have many rhetoricians (including several contributors to this volume), is itself a philosophical act. After all, even many familiar pronouncements—for example, that rhetoric must be "resituated at the end of philosophy" (Schrag, 1985, pp. 164–174), or that traditional philosophy is of little value to understanding the practical world of the rhetorical (this seems to be the upshot of Fisher, 1987), or that philosophy is not foundational and should be de-centered (Derrida, 1981; Heidegger, 1973), or that traditional philosophical questions are problematic, unanswerable, or misleading (Rorty, 1979)—are themselves philosophical contentions. Conclusions of this sort cannot be articulated, defended, or evaluated in the absence of philosophical argument and a philosophical context. Like all other propositions of a larger order, these claims must be argued and secured explicitly. Hence, whatever our view of rhetoric and its relationship to other human activities, there will come a time when we must don our philosophical hat and critically inspect rhetoric's theoretical tenets and the presuppositions anchoring them.

Rhetoric and Philosophy is premised on the claim that all theories of rhetoric are ultimately shaped by a particular philosophical worldview; one cannot understand differences and similarities among theories of rhetoric without first discerning their philosophical moorings. Each of the contributors to this book illustrates how one's choice of a philosophical system—a set of first principles—constrains and occasions the development of rhetorical theory. Our thesis is that all theories of rhetoric are an outgrowth of a particular intellectual climate; that is, one's theory of human symbolic influence is predicated upon a specific understanding of philosophical problems. Hence, differences among rhetorical theories may be explained by the differing views held about the world and how humans apprehend that world. The argument within each chapter proceeds inductively, showing how particular beliefs about, for example, ontology (the study of what is), epistemology (the study of how we come to know what is), and the issue of whether those questions (ontology and epistemology) should be raised or can be answered, lead to unique theories of the nature, scope, and function of rhetoric.

Although previous work in rhetoric focuses on the historical development of thought and deals predominantly with key thinkers in rhetorical theory (Ehninger, 1972; Foss, Foss, & Trapp, 1985; Golden, Berquist, & Coleman, 1989; Johannesen, 1971), few efforts have been made to understand the concept comparatively and at an ideational level. The purpose of this book is to take some of the major philosophical starting places (regardless of when in history they may have been conceived or by whom they may have been advocated) that have shaped and perhaps *can* shape views of rhetoric, showing how the choice of such philosophical premises makes a difference in conceiving what rhetoric is, how it operates, and how it can be critiqued. Although such premises issue from a vast literature in philosophy and elsewhere, *interpretation of theorists and texts is not the driving force of the book*. Frankly, many philosophers eschew the use of labels and may comfortably reside in more than one school of thought. Consequently, this book should not be read as a referendum on any particular philosopher or rhetorician.

Nevertheless, it is possible to identify a number of categories of thought that potentially impact rhetoric. The philosophical beginning places for rhetoric to be treated are: *realism, relativism, critical rationalism, idealism, materialism, existentialism, deconstructionism,* and *pragmatism*. The first four (realism, relativism, critical rationalism, and idealism) seem to fit within what has been described as the Anglo-American tradition of philosophy. The next three (materialism, existentialism, and deconstructionism) derive more from Continental philosophical thought of the 19th and 20th centuries. The final beginning place for rhetoric, pragmatism, has roots in both the Continental and Anglo-American traditions.

It should come as no surprise that no one of these worldviews is entirely discrete; some represent critical reactions to previous philosophies and a few are even premised and build upon other schools of thought. Our task is to show both the existence of overlap, as well as identifiable differences regarding how each philosophy views the nature of human beings, language, and knowledge, and how such differences create possibilities for understanding rhetoric.

Several disclaimers regarding the goal of the book and the rationale for selecting the eight schools of thought will help place the significance of this project in perspective. First, as noted above, we do not pretend to assume that the chosen philosophical beginning places for rhetoric are discrete or constitute the only way to divide the rhetorical/philosophical pie. Readers will discover quickly that the eight worldviews are not all mutually incompatible with one another. Although some major differences exist and these dissimilarities constrain how rhetoric is viewed, it may be possible to construct a theory of rhetoric incorporating tenets from more than one philosophical school. Our argument, then, is not that the eight categories are self-contained, nor is it that there are only eight ways to think about human symbolic influence. Rather, our claim is that housed within these representative philosophical positions are certain fundamental questions and suggested answers that have bearing on theorizing about rhetoric. By appreciating both the nuances of each approach, as well as the shared properties among them, we are in a better position to think *heuristically* about rhetoric.

Like all philosophical exercises, the value of this undertaking is rooted not in a definitive outcome or *product,* but in the importance of *process.* Our claim is that, by going through the sometimes arduous and tedious process of participating in the philosophical conversation, we will better be able to make conscious, informed, and reflective decisions about rhetorical theory; and in the end, this will facilitate more accessible and productive defenses of chosen theories of rhetoric. Simply stated, the *legitimacy* of the rhetorical enterprise is linked inextricably to theoretical choices and the philosophical manner in which those choices are obtained and defended.

Admittedly, the task of determining which philosophical schools of thought to consider was difficult. Readers should understand that at the outset of this project many alleged philosophical positions were discarded. Our primary goal was to include those beginning places that representatively covered the entire philosophical spectrum. The eight positions chosen, therefore, reflect not only a wide array of possibilities, but some of the more divergent and controversial philosophies advanced throughout history. Secondarily, our intent was to choose philosophical foundations for rhetoric that were already rooted in the long and rich tradition of the discipline. Finally, we made choices cognizant of the fact that philosophy is not equated and should not be confused with *ideology* or *modes of discursive (literary or rhetorical) analysis.* For this reason, absent from this book is an *explicit* discussion of such quasi-philosophies as feminism and structuralism. Several other views were not chosen (e.g., Marxism, skepticism, empiricism, hermeneutics, and semeiotics) because they were judged to be smaller parts of the larger philosophical worldviews discussed.

In placing the content of this book in perspective, one also should realize that our declaration that theories of rhetoric are ultimately grounded in a set of philosophical options should *not* be interpreted to mean that the line of influence (from philosophy to rhetoric) is unilateral. As already suggested, the importance of rhetoric can be gleaned, among other ways, by recognizing its presence in all human affairs and modes of conduct. Even philosophical activity, it might be argued, is influenced by the dynamic relationships among rhetor, message, and auditor. Theories of rhetoric, then, may have the potential to give back to and inform the functioning of the philosophical enterprise. This potential has not gone unnoticed by rhetoricians and philosophers (Carleton, 1975; Johnstone, 1969, 1973; Natanson, 1962). In reviewing these essays, readers will discover that several contributors have commented on the capacity of rhetoric to offer insights into the "doing of philosophy." Although not always stated, many of the arguments marshalled throughout are indicative of the *symbiotic* relationship between rhetoric and philosophy.

Before inspecting each of the philosophical worldviews, a final point must be made. Throughout history, and particularly in the late 20th century, rhetoricians have been concerned with the issue of legitimacy. It could be hypothesized that many recent discussions of rhetoric have been influenced, if not motivated, by a worry about what place rhetoric (as discipline) occupies alongside the other arts and sciences. Since the time of Plato, rhetoricians have struggled with the questions of whether or not rhetoric has a subject matter rightly its own, and whether casual and pedestrian observations regarding its misuse and malpractice inevitably lead to an inferior position for rhetoric within the academy.

The argument made in various ways throughout these pages, and perhaps in contradistinction to popular conceptions, is that rhetoric is already a legitimate art. The fact that human symbolic influence, as noted above, is pervasive and inescapably intertwined with the workings of all modes of inquiry, should be sufficient to establish this conclusion. Moreover, because the question of legitimacy is bound up in a philosophical defense of rhetorical theory, the eight position statements represent the many different ways in which the legitimacy of the rhetorical enterprise can be secured. As a result, readers will observe that no one of the eight philosophical starting points necessarily privileges the discipline of rhetoric. The contributors to this book make evident that none of the available philosophical worldviews is inherently anti-rhetorical; an anti-rhetorical view can be sustained only when the term "rhetoric" is used pejoratively. Each chapter, in its own way, allows us to witness the ubiquitous and purposeful nature of rhetoric.

Consider, for example, the issues of ontology and epistemology—two of the major problems raised in philosophical analysis and for which spirited disagreement exists. The contributors to *Rhetoric and Philosophy* provide very different responses to these problems. But the differing arguments made about such notions as "truth", "reality," and "knowledge" do not automatically prohibit a positive and constructive conception of rhetoric. For regardless of whether truth is taken to be independent of humans and somehow discoverable, or conceived as humanly constructed, or seen perhaps as beyond human awareness, it is still the case that humans engage in rhetorical activity for the purpose of coming to grips with their world and behaving in it. Thus, although each philosophy harbors distinct implications for how we understand the function, operation, and role of rhetoric, none sounds rhetoric's death knell. Surely we can disagree about the exact nature of human symbol use. No doubt we can argue about just how instrumental a role symbolic influence plays in the myriad human activities. And most assuredly we can have different opinions about whether all or some rhetorical practice is unethical and/or unproductive. But we cannot deny rhetoric's existence and widespread use. This fact should hardly be surprising; for no matter what one's philosophy, how could it be argued that symbol use is not an important and vital part of what it means to be human?

Let us now preview the eight philosophical worldviews. Each contributor was assigned a philosophical school of thought. Readers should be aware that authors were not selected because they necessarily advocated a particular position; authors had as their goal only to show what is entailed and meant by a specific philosophy and what possibilities such a view holds for rhetoric. Hence, each author: (a) lays out and explains the tenets of one of the philosophical beginning points for rhetoric; (b) details the theory or theories of rhetoric occasioned by that philosophy; (c) explains the uniqueness and usefulness of the proposed theory of rhetoric; and (d) compares, contrasts, and integrates that view of rhetoric with other relevant positions contained within the book.

Part one of all chapters is devoted to definition and principle: authors spell out, often through operational definition, what their assigned philosophy is and what central claims anchor it. Accordingly, the first section is not written as a literature review; our objective was to do more than provide a history of selected theorists who might fall within a given school of thought. Instead, authors ask: What would it mean for one to accept the tenets of a particular philosophical position? For instance, what would one have to believe in order to be a "pragmatist"?

In the second section of every chapter the question of what difference the philosophy makes for our understanding of what rhetoric is and how it operates is discussed. Since many of the philosophical schools of thought currently do not enjoy popularity, part two of each essay gives us the opportunity to observe that there are important and constructive possibilities for rhetoric issuing from acceptance of *any* of the philosophical worldviews. As already emphasized, one of the primary motivations for this project is our belief that rhetoric is not limited to any one philosophical starting point. After all, philosophical "isms" may come and go; although a given position could now enjoy currency and another be seen as "dead," there will always come a time when this philosophical state of affairs is reversed. Accepting one philosophical perspective over another, therefore, is a matter of preference. And as section two of every essay suggests, a part of our preference ultimately comes down to what the various philosophical alternatives can tell us about the nature of human symbol use. As is the case for part one, analysis is not restricted or limited to what rhetoricians have already said about the philosophy under discussion. Focus is on a wide range of possibilities. In this spirit, authors ask: If one accepts a philosophy, what potential avenues are there for viewing the rhetorical enterprise? For viewing the relationship of rhetoric to the other arts and sciences? For appraising actual instances of rhetorical discourse? That is, how could we conceive of rhetoric and view its contribution to human thought and understanding given a particular philosophical beginning place?

The final portion of each chapter is more loosely structured. Using whatever methods and resources of argument seemed appropriate, contributors endeavored to highlight the strengths and weaknesses of their assigned philosophy/rhetoric. Most of the authors compared and contrasted their school of thought with others developed in the book. Readers will note, however, that not all of the contributors juxtaposed their position with all of the others. The decision of what comparisons and contrasts to draw was a function of the specific characteristics of the philosophy being examined. For example, some of the schools of thought seem more prone to comparison with others because they are part of the same conversation. In addition, comparison and contrast was most useful among radically opposed perspectives. Nevertheless, contained within each author's third section are the needed argumentative resources to help readers choose from the available philosophical beginning places for rhetoric.

In chapter 2 of this book James Hikins tells us that philosophical *realism* can be defined as exhibiting two distinct and interrelated emphases: from the standpoint of metaphysics, the world — or at least significant portions of it — exists independent of human attitudes, beliefs, values, and behaviors (including, of course, communication); and from an epistemological purview, the world can be, at least in part, known to humans. Hikins offers us an historical survey of the various formulations of realism. His basic claim is that to understand realism one must examine the many arguments lodged against it; this is a necessary move, declares Hikins, given the fact that realism enjoys presumption in the world of praxis as well as in the world of philosophy.

After establishing the basic tenets of realism, Hikins explores several quite diverse schools of realist thought, including pedestrian realism, formal realism, representative realism, critical realism, and appearance realism. The principal claims of each of these views serves as a point of departure for the second section of Hikins' chapter, where he indicates the implications of realism for theories of rhetoric. His contention is not only that rhetoric operates within a realistic context (i.e., the concepts traditionally at the heart of persuasion assume and are premised upon realism), but that realism offers the best theoretical grounds for explaining rhetorical phenomena.

Hikins argues that rhetoric is a fundamental part of our endeavors to understand and discover the world (real) independent of discourse. He claims that humans are conscious, intention-imbued entities invested with the ability to know at least some aspects of the natural world in which they reside. In addition, humans are invested with the ability to communicate knowledge through symbol usage; a realist rhetorical theory would hold that symbol systems have the capacity to embody the physical as well as nonphysical aspects of reality. Because reality is at least in part knowable, symbolic influence has as its subject the way humans weave knowledge, in the guise of facticity, into their efforts to gain the adherence of others—

even on contingent issues where the ultimate truth is as yet unattainable. Because rhetoric is inextricably tied to reality, concludes Hikins, we are assured of the availability of objective criteria to compose and evaluate rhetorical practice. In short, rhetoric's grounding in reality and fundamental relationship to the process of knowing that reality make evident the inherent connection of rhetoric to the other arts and sciences.

The basic position of philosophical *relativism,* according to Barry Brummett (chap. 3), is that human reality is socially and symbolically constructed. He argues that relativism is based on several presuppositions. To begin with, the social and the symbolic are linked, continuous, and inseparable; humans are inherently social and symbolic creatures. Our capacity to live with others in complex organizations, says Brummett, depends on our ability to use symbols to create and manage those organizations. Our ability to present, represent, and order our world symbolically is fundamentally social; we use symbols in social rather than individual ways.

Another presupposition of relativism is that the social and the symbolic are primary, individuals are derivative. For Brummett, individual consciousness is always constrained by the resources available in the cultures and symbolic orders from which individuals spring. "Intersubjectivity" in this case is primary; people are born into a social context and a world of symbols. In addition, the social and the symbolic are the grounding or medium for human reality. Brummett contends that we perceive or conceive of nothing "real" which is not made that way socially and symbolically. In sharp contrast to philosophical realism, he claims that there is no "direct" apprehension of some reality apart from the social and the symbolic.

The most important implication of relativism for rhetoric concerns the fact that the social and the symbolic are malleable. Social order and symbols are by their nature changeable, and therefore arguable. This malleability is managed by what has always been the tool of social and symbolic change, rhetoric. Throughout his discussion of relativism Brummett argues that attempts to see reality as not malleable, or to see rhetoric as not relevant to changing reality, will be analyzed as politically and ideologically interested.

In the fourth chapter of this volume, C. Jack Orr posits that *critical rationalism* is the view that people become rational as they hold their conjectures open to criticism and the possibility of refutation. In its strongest form, he claims, critical rationalism is "pan critical," inviting criticism of its own premises. Orr's essay is placed strategically following discussions of realism and relativism; this is because critical rationalists believe that both naive realism and comprehensive relativism are enemies of the free society. Such a conclusion is best grasped, according to Orr, by understanding the goal of critical rationalism: to develop a critique of authoritarian ideologies without becoming authoritarian; to recognize that we see the world through frameworks of interpretation without conceding that all frameworks rest upon equally irrational commitments; and to restore the quest for truth, rather than agreement, to the center of philosophy, communication, and the enterprise of being human.

Orr makes clear that critical rationalism rests on a number of assumptions. For example, the origin of knowledge is not as important as its revision and growth. In addition, knowledge is relative; truth is absolute. Critical rationalism also presumes that rationality does not consist of the justification of beliefs, but of the continuous criticism of our conjectures and standards of criticism; thus the presuppositions of our arguments and tentatively of our conjectures should be acknowledged. Moreover, critical rationalism is premised on the claim that criticism may take multiple forms depending upon the problem being addressed; criticism is the pivotal point in the evolution of knowledge which also includes the creation of novel perspectives on life and the retention of those views that survive criticism. In his discussion Orr is quick to note that critical rationalism is more than an academic philosophy. It is an effort to create an environment in which not only negative criticism but also the positive creation of ideas are truly inspired.

According to Orr critical rationalism has much to offer our understanding of human symbol use. He suggests, for instance, that critical rationalism is fully consistent with the view that reality, as we know it, is rhetorically constructed. However, critical rationalism holds only a secondary interest in how knowledge is constructed. Its primary concern is the examination of our "rhetorical" constructions in order to eliminate error, reduce human suffering, and contribute to "the practical art of living well." Orr believes that critical rationalism is especially resourceful for helping to answer several important questions: What is the significance of rhetorical constructions of reality that point beyond themselves to an objective reality that is not rhetorically constructed? How shall we choose between competing constructions of reality without making that choice as arbitrary as a coin toss or a blind leap of faith? What are the social consequences of making agreement the aim of communication, rather than the quest for truth? What is the significance of relativism for the rhetor's sense of personal identity? What can the rhetorically rational person expect from the practice of his or her art? (What is the likely experience of courage, alienation, and resilience?) And how should the orator be educated?

At the beginning of his essay John Lyne (chap. 5) informs us that it would be misleading to assume that *idealism* can be defined from the standpoint of a universal set of propositions. More accurately, he suggests, there are several recurrent themes and concerns that assist comprehension of philosophical idealism. The essential core of this philosophy (in contrast to the philosophy of materialism) is the belief that the primary stuff of the world is mind, not matter. Even in natural science the beginning place is not the material object, but form: not matter itself, but the structure (intellectual) of matter. Because of this, says Lyne, idealism stresses the active, experiential, coherent, creative, and historical—rather than the mechanistic, ahistorical, and deterministic. For the idealist, then, concern is with the world as a field of possible and intelligible experience. Lyne makes clear that throughout history there have been a number of discrepant idealist philosophies—including subjective idealism, objective idealism, and transcendental idealism.

Lyne argues that an idealist philosophy has much to offer our understanding of rhetoric. Beginning with the observation that even those subscribing to materialist explanations of behavior must inevitably engage in persuasion, he outlines several implications of an idealist philosophy for rhetoric. Echoing Kenneth Burke, for example, Lyne posits that a rhetoric grounded in idealism will emphasize that humans act: they do not just behave. Unlike things (which move), and other animals (which behave), human behavior (action) is purposeful, meaningful, and motivated. Therefore, Burke's grammar of motives (as opposed to a grammar of mechanical causality) can be seen as the logic underpinning human behavior. And to comprehend human symbol use (e.g., language) one must be cognizant of these motives.

Similarly, Lyne contends that the power of language—the ability of words to create effects—is, in the final analysis, linked to the idealist assumption that one of the most powerful effects of symbols is the creation of a mental life. Language, and for that matter persuasion, is more than a mechanistic instrument; it is to be experienced as well as used. A rhetoric grounded in idealist philosophy, therefore, need not prove the existence of effects (in the materialist sense of the term) to appreciate the power of language. For that reason, an idealist theory of rhetoric would emphasize the mental horizons that verbal constructions make possible; it would study the influence of symbols in shaping the life of the mind.

In sharp contrast to idealism is the philosophy of *materialism*. Michael McGuire (chap. 6) contends that materialism is a position holding that all reality can be reduced to material that makes it up. He suggests that this doctrine has existed in various forms: rationalist or mechanical materialism, biological or mythical materialism, anthropological materialism, and dialectical materialism. Because of the existence of many types of materialism, McGuire introduces two categories from which to help us observe its many variations: physical materialism and social materialism. But his claim is that, regardless of type, materialists all share in common the premise that reality can be understood, mapped, and measured by reducing apparently complex superstructures to the material substructures out of which they are built. By way of illustration McGuire claims that the apparently complex phenomenon of idiocy, for example, is reducible to genetic (amino acid) material; moreover, the seemingly symbolic clash of ideological interests is actually an expression of competition for scarce resources. Materialist philosophy, therefore, affirms universal causal laws.

According to McGuire, a rhetoric grounded in materialist philosophy offers a number of important possibilities for understanding human symbol use — many of which have not yet been explored fully. The first question posed in a materialist rhetoric, says McGuire, would be: What is the material of which the phenomenon rhetoric is made? An answer to this question, he claims, must begin with language. Thus rhetoricians must ascertain not only the biological determinants of language, but must consider how language itself (including its parts) is material.

McGuire argues that investigations of this sort will necessarily lead to the question of whether there exist causal links between rhetoric and social behavior. The topics of a materialist rhetorical theory, then, will range from the biological/physical consideration of such phenomena as voice volume, pitch, gesture, and so forth to larger, critical discussions of the economic, cultural, and political variables underlying the generation and effects of messages. But regardless of which of these subjects is focused on, a materialist rhetoric will advance our understanding of why people behave as they do; for its explanatory power is rooted in the hypothesis that rhetoric is both a material phenomenon and acts as a material cause.

In his chapter (chap. 7) Michael Hyde submits that *existentialism* is most appropriately conceived as an intellectual "movement" whose principal representatives direct its course as they concern themselves with the question of what it means to exist as a human being. The movement developed against the background of the 19th century and the first part of the 20th century. And within this time period it also developed as a reaction against the epistemological prejudices of modern philosophy, the dogma of institutionalized religion, and the progressive ideology of science and technology, especially as this ideology made possible the practical conse-quences of death, destruction, and human suffering and isolation. In addressing the question of what it means to exist, says Hyde, existentialism seeks to clarify how human existence is more than what the "rational" thought of Descartes, Kant, and Hegel declared it to be, more than what the reified prescriptions of the church required it to be, and more than what the telic inclination of modern technological advances encouraged it to be.

In the first portion of his essay Hyde examines some of the central themes of existentialism that serve to define what this movement represents. Examples of some of the major existentialist premises he articulates include: reason is more than rationality; truth is not a thing but a happening, a disclosing of what is; the fact/value dichotomy is erroneous; humans are condemned to freedom, choice, and meaning; we are essentially ethical beings; and all knowledge is made possible by the workings of human emotion.

In discussing the implications of an existential philosophy for rhetoric Hyde notes that our conclusions cannot be limited to what has already been said by existentialist philosophers concerning rhetoric; for their understanding of the art is predicated upon an infrequent and pejorative use of the term. Nevertheless, declares Hyde, there is much that one can say about human symbolic influence from an existential philosophical perspective. For example, because of their insistence on "authentic communication" (a kind of rhetoric that does not persuade individuals to conform to the "untruth" of the "crowd" or "public"), existentialists would implore people to speak a rhetoric rather than only allowing themselves to be spoken by rhetoric. An existential theory of rhetoric, then, has as one of its primary goals the encouragement of an authentic performance of word. Such a rhetoric, Hyde notes, would be grounded in humankind's existential freedom, where speaking is on behalf of the "self" and its "authenticity." For existentialists, an individual's attempt to speak an authentic rhetoric involves more than history: more than what others are saying about it. By putting one's self on the line, the individual announces something about the world that has not yet been revealed in the vernacular of the community or audience being addressed. Existentialism, therefore, facilitates the construction of a rhetoric of the self and for the other (self): as Hyde indicates, it councils people in the most original performance of freedom of speech for the purpose of directing them in their appreciation of the future.

Deconstruction, says James Aune (chap. 8), is a discourse that attempts to subvert the Western philosophical tradition from within. In contrast to other philosophical perspectives on language and communication, deconstruction is distinguished by what might be called a "refusal of mastery," a refutation of the claim of philosophical discourse to provide a privileged standpoint from which stable meanings or truths can be established. According to Aune, deconstruction does not claim to be a philosophy, but the replacement of philosophy by a way of reading texts. A deconstructive reading demonstrates that any discourse (philosophical, literary, rhetorical—although such distinctions can themselves be deconstructed) is caught up in webs of signification that precede it, over which the speaker, writer, or reader has little control, and which prove to be logically contradictory upon rigorous examination.

Aune contends that deconstruction provides a useful way for reading the history of rhetoric in the West and offers a non-Hellenistic view of language, which rejects the opposition between philosophy and rhetoric, which has been constitutive of both classical and contemporary accounts of rhetoric. A deconstructionist rhetoric does not mean to reveal philosophy as merely covertly rhetorical. Aune's argument is that rhetorical practice emerged in the West as an attempt to control the world through speech; philosophical discourse emerged (at least in part) as an attempt to control the consequences of a rhetoricized politics. Hence, deconstruction does not reduce philosophy to rhetoric, but refuses a metaphysics that would define human speech and action in terms of that opposition at all. A rhetoric grounded in deconstructionist philosophy, concludes Aune, will return us to modes of interpretation characteristic of Hebraic thought; and it can be read as a fundamentally religious assault on the Greek notion of reason that has influenced both philosophy and rhetoric.

In the final chapter of this book James Mackin (chap. 9) investigates the effects of *pragmatic* philosophy on the theory and practice of rhetoric. The question of whether pragmatism can be considered a philosophical system, claims Mackin, is arguable. Certainly, in the hands of such practitioners as Richard Rorty, pragmatism is more anti-Philosophy than systematic philosophy. However, even in dismissing many of the traditional problems of the Platonic–Cartesian–Kantian tradition of Philosophy, pragmatists share with traditional philosophy a concern with the methodology of inquiry, at least a minimal cosmology, and an axiology. For the pragmatist, philosophy is subordinate to praxis. Because human thought serves the purposes of human action, pragmatism sees all of philosophy as historically embedded. Therefore, philosophy should devote itself to helping humans cope with their historical situation by analyzing methods in terms of purposes and consequences.

Mackin suggests that because of its concern with action and consequence, pragmatism (in distinction to most of the other schools of thought outlined in this book) offers a different approach to traditional philosophical problems—an approach that dismisses most of these problems on the grounds that they are irrelevant to practice. For example, the search for certainty (a major topic preoccupying Western philosophical thought) arose from the needs of the world of praxis. Moreover, declares Mackin, because of our apparently fruitless search for essences, pragmatists suspect that perhaps humans are not capable of knowing essences (even if such essences exist). Thus a pragmatic philosophy may be taken as a combination of two attitudes: a belief in a moderate skepticism about ideas, and a recognition that, skepticism notwithstanding, ideas serve humans well in practice.

Mackin posits that there is a natural fit between pragmatic philosophy (with its emphasis on the consequences of human action) and rhetoric. Rhetoric is, after all, one of the chief human methods used in coping. Considered pragmatically, rhetoric is a call for help in solving a problem. Like all human action, says Mackin, symbolic influence must be considered in terms of its purposes, means, and consequences. A pragmatic theory of rhetoric thus would be more concerned about phronesis (practical wisdom) than episteme (knowledge). A pragmatic theory of rhetoric would also analyze methods of rhetorical criticism in terms of purposes and consequences. At the most general level, the pragmatic rhetorical theorist asks, "How does rhetorical criticism help us to cope with the problems of human living?" Can rhetorical criticism come up with warranted assertions that are useful for prediction and action?

As the preceding preview of chapters suggests, the topics treated throughout this book range widely. Within these pages are raised some of the most vexing intellectual questions that have confronted and given humankind pause since the beginning of thought: questions about our existence, the makeup of reality, the nature of truth, the limits of knowledge, the character of rationality, the ethical and moral dimensions of human action, and the function of language. As is the case with any technical and meticulous account of nettlesome philosophical problems and their interrelationships, the discussion contained herein may move slowly and frequently seem taxing. But it is necessarily so; indeed it would be quite odd were our conjectures about these issues facile and simplistic. Thus, although we do not presume to render any final solution(s), our venture is offered as an exercise in philosophical and rhetorical consciousness raising. To be sure, the proof is not in the definitiveness of answers, but in the process of answering. Our hope is that readers will carefully wade through and, in the true spirit of philosophical self-risk, "try-on-for-size" the various positions (and combinations of positions); for it is only by keeping the conversation going that we will be able to discover something about the richness and complexity of symbolic influence (rhetoric), if not something about the very nature of the human condition.

REFERENCES

Brummett, B. (1976). Some implications of "process" or "intersubjectivity": Postmodern rhetoric. *Philosophy and Rhetoric, 9,* 21–51.

Bryant, D. C. (1973). *Rhetorical dimensions in criticism.* Baton Rouge, LA: Louisiana State University Press.

Carleton, W. M. (1975). Theory transformation in communication: The case of Henry Johnstone. *Quarterly Journal of Speech, 61,* 76–88.

Cherwitz, R. (1977). Viewing rhetoric as a "way of knowing": An attenuation of the epistemological claims of the "new rhetoric." *Southern Speech Communication Journal, 42,* 207–219.

Cherwitz, R., & Hikins, J. (1986). *Communication and knowledge: An investigation in rhetorical epistemology.* Columbia, SC: University of South Carolina Press.

Cooper, L. (1932). *The Rhetoric of Aristotle.* New York: Appleton-Century Crofts.

Derrida, J. (1981). *Positions* (A. Bass, Trans.). Chicago: University of Chicago Press.

Dick, H. C. (1955). *Selected writings of Francis Bacon.* New York: Modern Library.

Ehninger, D. (1972). *Contemporary rhetoric: A reader's coursebook.* Glenview, IL: Scott, Foresman.

Fisher, W. R. (1987). *Human communication as narration: Toward a philosophy of reason, value, and action.* Columbia, SC: University of South Carolina Press.

Foss, S., Foss, K., & Trapp, R. (1985). *Contemporary perspectives on rhetoric.* Prospect Heights, IL: Waveland Press.

Golden, J. L., Berquist, G. F., & Coleman, W. E. (1989). *The rhetoric of western thought.* Dubuque, IA: Kendall/Hunt.

Heidegger, M. (1973). *The end of philosophy.* (J. Stambaugh, Trans.). New York: Harper & Row.

Johannesen, R. L. (1971). *Contemporary theories of rhetoric: selected readings.* New York: Harper & Row.

Johnstone, H. W. (1969). Truth, communication and rhetoric in philosophy. *Revue Internationale de Philosophie, 23,* 405–406.

Johnstone, H. W. (1973). Rationality and rhetoric in philosophy. *Quarterly Journal of Speech, 59,* 381–389.

Lyne, J. R. (1985). Rhetorics of inquiry. *Quarterly Journal of Speech, 71,* 65–73.

McCloskey, D. N. (1985). *The rhetoric of economics.* Madison, WI: University of Wisconsin Press.

Natanson, M. (1962). Rhetoric and philosophical argumentation. *Quarterly Journal of Speech, 48,* 24–30.

Nelson, J. S., & Megill, A. (1986). Rhetoric of inquiry: Projects and prospects. *Quarterly Journal of Speech, 72,* 20–37.

Plato. (1956). *Phaedrus.* (R. Hackforth, Trans.). Cambridge, England: Cambridge University Press.

Rorty, R. (1979). *Philosophy and the mirror of nature.* Princeton, NJ: Princeton University Press.

Schrag, C. O. (1985). Rhetoric resituated at the end of philosophy. *Quarterly Journal of Speech, 71,* 164–174.

Scott, R. L. (1967). On viewing rhetoric as epistemic. *Central States Speech Journal, 18,* 9–17.

Scott, R. L. (1976). On viewing rhetoric as epistemic: Ten years later. *Central States Speech Journal, 27,* 258–266.

Simons, H. W. (1985). Chronicle and critique of a conference. *Quarterly Journal of Speech, 71,* 52–64.

Simons, H. W. (1989). *Rhetoric in the human sciences.* London, England: SAGE.

Chapter 2

Realism and Its Implications for Rhetorical Theory

James W. Hikins

It is clear to everyone that there are many things of the kind we have just indicated [animals, plants, earth, air, fire, and water], and he who would try to demonstrate the more apparent by the less apparent shows that he cannot distinguish what is and what is not evident.

—Aristotle[1]

Most people would really rather be realists, once they see their way clear.

—Thomas Russman[2]

---

[1]Quoted in Ross (1930), Book II, Section 1, p. 193a. Of particular importance is Aristotle's indictment of those who would seek to establish the "more apparent" from the "less apparent." Put briefly, Aristotle is arguing that, if we cannot trust that most of what is immediately given in experience is veridical, based on its givenness, then we can never hope to establish the veracity of immediate experience based on weaker (i.e., more remote) evidence. But, a fortiori, if we can never trust the most immediately given as an argument for the veracity of immediate experience, we can surely never trust arguments from weaker sources for *any other conclusion about anything*. The skeptic will relish this conclusion, until it is realized that "weaker sources" and "anything" refer as well to the skeptic's own argumentation and conclusions, the latter of which are, by the argument, drawn from considerably weaker premises than are conclusions about reality drawn from direct experience.

[2]Russman (1987) admits that his claim may be "only a complacent prejudice" but, based on the day-to-day conduct of even the most skeptical individuals, he may well be right (p. viii). I recall vividly a constructivist colleague who was heavily committed to the notion that humans construct all of reality linguistically. In the heat of the *philosophical* discussion he articulated the belief that one *could* walk through walls if one so chose. But he did not take up the challenge to do so, nor do I recall once seeing him try in the years since!

Myself when young did eagerly frequent
Doctor and Saint, and heard great argument
About it and about: but evermore
Came out by the same door where in I went.

—Omar Khayyam[3]

Realism describes a wide variety of philosophical theories, all sharing a common core. As J. Donald Butler described that core, "realists insist that the qualities of our experience are real independent facts of the external world. They are unchanged by entering the ken of the knower, and do not depend on any mind, finite or infinite, for their existence" (Butler, 1951, p. 276). Realism is thus both an *ontological* and an *epistemological* theory. Ontologically, it claims that much of the world does not depend on humans (or any other sentient entities) for its existence. Epistemologically, realism contends that humans are capable of knowing at least some aspects of the real world *as it is in itself.* These two properties—existence and knowledge—are inherently interconnected. For if one could not know something about the real world, one could not establish that such a world existed. And, if such a world did not exist, one could not have knowledge of it.

Most humans, of course, believe they *do* know at least some things about the world. As Joseph Margolis reminded us, "In an obvious, perhaps even trivial sense, we are all realists—no matter how strenuously we protest" (Margolis, 1986, p. xiv). We are all realists in our day-to-day lives. When not in what John Searle called "the grip of a philosophy," we exhibit no doubt that familiar pronouncements such as, "The dog is in the garage," "Jenny went to San Francisco," "Susan is in love," or "Hitler brought ruin to Germany," describe *real* places, things, emotions, and ethical dimensions of the world, each existing largely independently of humans and their communication behavior.[4] Nor do we nag and worry over "sufficiency conditions of justification," "belief," or "truth"—traditional criteria of knowledge—when advancing claims like "the world is roughly round," or "genocide is evil." We *know* these things. *Philosophical* attempts to deny them are torturous, especially when made in the context of public argument, in the world of rhetorical *praxis*. Rhetoric is a pragmatic art where

---

[3]Quoted in McGilvary (1956), p. 196.

[4]The reader should note that throughout this essay I make no fundamental ontological or epistemological distinction between what are typically labeled "physical" and "nonphysical" events, concepts, or entities. The justification for doing so is found in the theory of relationality, which holds that all existents ("physical" and "nonphysical") are the product of a fundamental ontological principle, *the relation* (discussed in this chapter). Likewise, the phrase "independent of human beliefs, attitudes, values, or communication" suggests that most events, concepts, or entities have an "ontological life" apart from humans, though (again because of relationality) they are inherently interconnected at the relational level. The source of Searle's phrase is an unpublished lecture, delivered April 27, 1984 at Tulane University.

debates among various "isms" sound otiose. After all, most consumers of rhetoric are pedestrians, not philosophers or rhetorical theorists.

Why "pedestrian realism" is pervasive is illustrated in the story of the celebrated Dr. Johnson kicking the stone to demonstrate the poverty of idealism. Realism enjoys *presumption*. Unlike dreams, hallucinations, and illusions, which more often than not appear to one experiencing them "dream-like," "hallucinatory," or "illusory," *real* experiences present, *attendant with their content,* the datum that they *are* real.[5] Frank Thilly (1914) described this presumption in Thomas Reid's (1787/1970) work: "Sensation carries with it an immediate belief in the reality of the object, and this immediate certainty supplies us with a criterion of truth" (p. 363). This is perhaps why even nonrealist philosophers agree with Immanuel Kant that it is "a scandal to philosophy and to the general human reason to be obliged to assume, as an article of mere belief, the existence of things external to ourselves (from which, yet, we derive the whole material of cognition, even for the internal sense), and not be able to oppose a satisfactory proof to anyone who may call it in question" (1787/1952 p. 12). The "givenness" of pedestrian reality also accounts for Russman's assertion in the prologue that we would all "rather be realists once we see our way clear," for there is a certain comfort and parsimony in a theory that preserves intact both the familiar furnishings of the world and our most immediate perceptions and judgments of it.

Yet for all the presumption it enjoys, realism has historically been the focus of criticism by philosophical and rhetorical theorists attempting to "whittle away at [its] credentials" (Margolis, 1986, p xiv). Why realism has been rejected by so many despite its givenness, and why this issue is significant for *both* philosophers and rhetoricians, are the principal questions addressed in this chapter. In the following pages, I explore the implications for rhetoric of philosophical realism, beginning with a historical survey of the attacks upon realism and realist replies to those attacks. This approach will generate an understanding of the complexity of realism and will lay the foundation for a contemporary realist rhetoric, developed in the second part of the chapter. In the last section I compare and contrast this realist rhetorical theory with competing views.

REALISM, RHETORIC, AND THE HISTORY OF IDEAS

An understanding of realism is of utmost importance for the rhetorical theorist. This is due to the nature of the rhetorical art itself. Because

---

[5]The point is made at length by Kelley (1986), pp. 133–139, 217–218, 236–241. The "problem of error," in all its guises, is fatal to realism only if error can be demonstrated to be a systematic and thoroughgoing feature of human perception. It is not enough to demonstrate that we occasionally err, for such a demonstration proves only that we occasionally err. To defeat realism, the skeptic must demonstrate that we err *in each and every specific case of perception.*

rhetorical practice is ensconced in the pedestrian world, and because its most direct consequences bear on issues of human conduct and welfare, any theory of rhetoric must eventually land squarely on its feet *in* the pedestrian world. However esoteric the theorist's view, it must adequately account for what we know about the natural world in which we all reside.

To reconcile these two concerns (theory and praxis) requires one to do more than make explicit the ontological and epistemological assumptions of any given rhetoric—it demands that those assumptions be explored thoroughly and systematically vis-à-vis the presumption of realism.[6] Consequently, any nonrealist theory must *necessarily* assume the burden of removing the paradoxes inherent in denying a realist view of rhetoric. Theory must be capable of accounting for the *appearance* of day-to-day "data." And it must provide the theorist an awareness of the consequences that particular tenets entail for the theory as a whole, including interrelationships with elements external to the theory. Finally, with respect to the prevailing realism of the world of rhetorical praxis, the onus is always on the antirealist to meet the question: How does one square an antirealist thesis with the presumption of pedestrian realism without incurring the burden of solipsism, skepticism, or ethical nihilism? Familiarity with realist doctrine, then, will permit nonrealists to better evaluate their own position, as a number of challenges to contemporary "constructivist," "subjectivist," and "intersubjectivist" theories in the social sciences, rhetoric, and philosophy have been made on realist grounds (Bhaskar, 1978; Cherwitz & Hikins, 1986; Grayling, 1985; Harré, 1986; Harré & Secord, 1972; Hikins & Zagacki, 1988; Keat & Urry, 1975; Kelley, 1986; Orr, 1978; Russman, 1987; Trigg, 1977, 1980; Vision, 1988; Waddell, 1988).

The Realist Tradition

Realism in rhetoric and philosophy weaves a persistent thread through the fabric of the history of ideas. For instance, Aristotle's thought is clearly realist, as is the philosophy of Thales, regarded as the first Western

---

[6]The notion of presumption I have in mind here is not a "debater's trick," but follows from an attack made by Russman (1987), among others, against the classical problem of error. Descartes' arguments (we occasionally err, so we might always err; an "evil genius" might be tricking us into believing what is false; maybe we're always dreaming) are grossly underentailed, that is, the premises cannot possibly support the conclusion. "Descartes has unconscionably gerrymandered the burden of proof to one side of the argument. The demon and the dream must be proven absolutely false or else! . . . Descartes has indeed taught us something with these arguments—he has taught us that the following slogan should be emblazoned on our minds and hearts: 'Mere possibility carries no evidentiary weight!' " (Russman, 1986, pp. 36–37). In other words, it is not the *possibility* of *systematic* error that the skeptic must establish, but the *actuality* of such systematic error.

philosopher (see Thilly, 1914, p. 225; Butler, 1951, pp. 276–279). Aristotle claims Thales posited water as the material principle of the world,

> because he saw that the nourishment of all things is moist, and that warmth itself is generated from moisture and persists in it (for that from which all things spring is the first principle of them); and getting the idea also from the fact that the germs of all beings are of a moist nature, while water is the first principle of the nature of what is moist. (Aristotle, *Metaphysics,* 983b. 18)

Although Thales accounts for the observable, changing world of phenomena in terms of the processual transformations of an elementary substance, he does not distrust his observations of the commonsense furnishings of his world. On the contrary, it is precisely the direct observation of commonsense objects, *as given in ordinary perceptual experience,* that forms the outline of Thales' physics. Unlike atomic physics — and in contrast to contemporary materialist philosophies — Thales' elementary building block is neither esoteric nor inferred; it is a familiar object of direct perception. For Thales, the furnishings of the world (ontology) and the mechanisms for coming to know them (epistemology) are thoroughly realist.

Similarly, realist Sophistic worldviews at times bear the brunt of Plato's transcendental idealist attack (Woodruff, 1983, pp. 41–44). And it is apparently realist perceptual theories that lead Gorgias to offer his carefully constructed argument against existence, knowledge and communication:

> Since things seen are the objects of sight, and things heard are the objects of hearing, and we accept as real things seen without their being heard, and vice versa; so we would have to accept things thought without their being seen or heard; but this would mean believing things like the chariot racing on the sea. Therefore reality is not the object of thought, and cannot be comprehended by it. (McInerny, 1963, p. 103)

Clearly, though no school of thought in antiquity terms itself "realist", realist philosophical positions are advanced by some and attacked by others.

In the centuries intervening between classical and contemporary times, numerous transformations of realist doctrine occurred, as replies to anti-realist attacks were formulated. Hence, perhaps the best way to understand realism is to explore the attacks and retorts comprising its evolution. In what follows, I group realist theories into several categories, treating each in the chronological order of its appearance.

Pedestrian Realism.   As previously suggested, pedestrian realism (frequently called "commonsense" or "naive" realism) is the view that reality

appears to us in perception *directly,* and predominantly *as it is in itself.*
Pedestrian realism holds that properties attendant to perception are real
properties of the things perceived. Thus the blueness of my daughter,
Dannelle's, eyes, the smoothness of my desk top, the clanking sounds of my
'69 Chevrolet are held by the pedestrian realist to be intrinsic qualities of
material objects, residing *in* the objects of perception.

Since Classical times pedestrian realism has been the background against
which to project more "sophisticated" theoretical/philosophical realisms.
However, it has also been the foundation of some Daedalian philosophical
theories, including the realism of the late contemporary philosopher, G.E.
Moore (Moore, 1903). One among his several arguments for realism is
especially noteworthy, because it seems so akin to the familiar rhetorical
principle of argument from probability.[7] Responding to arguments against
the claim that objects are given and known directly in perception, Moore
asks us to consider: What is *more* certain, that is, more likely or probably
true—that I am perceiving this pen and this hand holding the pen, or that
the tortured arguments of the idealists and skeptics are true and the pen and
hand and all other common objects are mere mental images? The denial of
common perceptual claims, Moore argues, and the contention that the
world is purely mental (idealism) or illusory (skepticism) can be sustained
only on the basis of arguments whose premises involve propositions *less
certain* than the propositions to be denied (see Hirst, 1967, pp. 77–80;
Moore, 1903 pp. 8–13; Nelson, 1967, pp. 377–378). Such grounds prompt
Moore to reject antirealism.

Moore's retort to the idealists and skeptics helps us understand why
pedestrian realism perseverates. His views appear to run parallel to
Aristotle's statement in the prologue. Hirst summarized Moore's argument:

> In no other situation [than direct perception] have we a better claim to be
> aware of something distinct, so that if sensations are not cases of awareness
> of objects, no awareness is ever awareness of anything, and we cannot be
> aware of other persons or even ourselves and our own sensations. (Hirst,
> 1967, p. 77)

---

[7]As argued for in a later section of the chapter, "probability" will be taken to mean
"probably true." As such, the notion can, and in the real world does, cover occurrences where
we are so certain of the truth of a claim that only "mere possibility," that is, *logical possibility,*
of error obtains. In the strongest cases, we may legitimately use the phrase, "virtually certain."
The payoff for conceiving probability in this way is that, although we can never be certain that
any *one* of our knowledge claims are *absolutely* certain, we *can* be assured that the vast
majority of our knowledge claims are true. Put another way, we can be absolutely certain that
most of our knowledge claims are true, though it is *logically* possible that a given claim may
be false. The burden of proof for the antirealist is not fulfilled by demonstrating that any given
knowledge claim *might be* false, but that, *in every given instance this particular knowledge
claim is, in fact, false.*

The perennial persistence of pedestrian realism, then, lies not in any informal or uninformed popularity, but in a *philosophically grounded presumption.* This presumption confers upon realism the capacity to act as a standard against which to measure the explanatory power of nonrealist philosophical approaches (that is, to address the question: Does nonrealist theory X adequately account for the *appearance as given* of a "real" world?). In addition, pedestrian realism suggests *phenomenally-given* criteria of explanation, including the requirement that any theory be able to account for the problems of illusion, hallucination, error, consciousness, mind, and so on.

Formal Realism.   In the middle ages, realism became the arch-enemy of nominalism (the view that universals are simply thoughts in the mind — mere names without referents in the extra-mental world). Frequently part and parcel of the characteristically tumescent disputation of scholastic theologians, these debates nonetheless harbor important implications for theories of language and communication. For example, in terms strikingly similar to contemporary linguistic theories (which typically view language as an arbitrary sign system) Roscelin's nominalism argues strenuously against realist theories of language. For him, universals are "mere names and words by means of which we define particular objects" (Thilly, 1914, p. 168).

Opposed as it is to the realist theory of universals, this view generated significant implications for the world of the 11th century. It is of significance to contemporary theorists because they seem obligated to address at some point the existence and use of common general terms. The challenge is to replace the realist theory of universals with some *viable alternative theory.* Yet the question of the ontological status of *universals,* still an important philosophical issue, has been virtually ignored by contemporary rhetoric and remains a pretermission of contemporary rhetorical theory (see Butchvarov, 1966, pp. ix–ixv, 3–15, 173–197; Cherwitz & Hikins, 1986, pp. 143–146). It should be readily apparent, then, that formal realism has important consequences for the theory of meaning and, by implication, for the language arts.

This importance is not restricted to the problem of universals. Richard Brinkley analyzed *meaning* in terms of *information content* generated by interrelationships of words and other categorematic sentence parts. Michael Fitzgerald (1987) summarizes Brinkley's view. As an "extensionalist," Brinkley argued that the information content of sentences refers to "extra-mental things." As Fitzgerald notes, these "designated extra-mental entities" function to "cause (in some way) the categorematic parts of a sentence to have the information-content they do have, rather than vice versa." And "this is the reason that examining the linguistic relationships between the categorematic terms in a sentence provide information about the metaphysical structure of extra-mental reality" or "extra-mental 'things'" (Fitzgerald, 1987, pp. 1-2). Brinkley's and others' (Burley, Chatton, Wycliff) analyses of the reality of universals, in combination with his view that a true sentence "indicates precisely just how [extra-mental] things exist" (Fitzgerald, 1987, p. 11) preserved, though tenuously, a version of realism that was hotly disputed by medieval logicians and ontologists. His theory of meaning as the *product of* knowable, extralinguistic, extramental entities sheds light on the realist rhetorical theory developed later.

Representative Realism.   Nominalism eventually triumphed over realism (see Thilly, 1914, pp. 226-227) and it was not until the 17th and 18th centuries, specifically in the views of Descartes and Locke, that new forms of realism were to emerge. The contribution of both these philosophers to realism is the argument that, although some form of realism is true, the old varieties of *direct* realism must be false. In Descartes, this position is established negatively, principally by way of the problems of illusion and error. As Descartes noted in the first of his *Meditations,* humans are frequently misled in the act of perception (Descartes, 1641/1960, pp. 17-18). If we perceive the objects of experience *directly* (as naive realism and formal realism suggest), such errors should not occur.

Descartes' answer to the problem of illusion was, in part, to bifurcate the world into the mental life of the individual and the realm of external things. It is only the careful, rule-governed, quasi-mathematical examination of the *representations* of experience by the mind, to the end of coming to a "clear and distinct" idea about the "real" object causing those experiences, that garners secure knowledge (Descartes, 1641/1960, pp. 73-85). Locke's more constructive contribution is a sophisticated theory of perception (Butler, 1951, p. 287-291). For Locke, the mind is a tabula rasa upon which our senses inscribe impressions. Impressions, standing at the end of a long *causal* process, begin with the external object from which minute particles, or "effluences," are given off, travel through the air (or space), and enter the sensory receptacles of the perceiver, eventually impacting on the mind. Simple sensory impressions (sensations) become simple ideas, from which we build complex ideas and stocks of knowledge through "reflection" (Locke, 1959, II.i.2.).

Another contribution of Locke that will be important in our later discussion (because thinkers such as Berkeley and Leibniz used it as a means of critiquing realism) is his distinction, anticipated by Descartes, Galileo, and Boyle, between primary and secondary qualities. The causal powers of material objects, Locke held, result in two distinct types of perception. On the one hand are features intrinsic to the external object, such as solidity, extension, figure, and mobility; these Locke termed "primary qualities." Other properties, such as color, taste, smell, and sound, are *produced in us* by the objects of perception, but are *not intrinsically part of* the object itself; these he termed "secondary qualities" (Locke, 1959, II.viii.8). Berkeley and Leibniz found this distinction untenable, arguing that if secondary qualities are "in" the perceiver as the product of one's mental life, then so might be the primary qualities. Perhaps *all* the world is mental in nature, and the external world just an illusion, the product of an active intellect. What began as an attempt to "hook up" mind with "external world" became an inherently *skeptical* theory, failing to make the promised link-up, but succeeding only too well in rendering the external world opaque to human efforts to know.

The influence of Descartes' and Locke's representationalism, and the skeptical problems it spawned, endures; many contemporary views of perception, including theories in cognitive studies, neurophysiology, and even rhetorical and communication theory are essentially representational (Patricia Churchland, 1986; Gregg, 1984, 1987). Any realist theory, if it is to be successful, must come to terms with representationalism.

The "New Realism." The critical evaluations of Berkeley and Leibniz, and the skepticism of David Hume, displaced representative realism. It was replaced by *idealism,* the view that reality is essentially mental or spiritual (a function of ideas). Berkeley's infamous dictum, *esse ist percipi,* "to be is to be perceived," was influential in philosophical circles through the 19th century and, along with Hume, is the progenitor of a number of contemporary trends in philosophy bearing directly on theories of rhetoric (including skepticism, subjectivism, and constructivism). These views seek to drive a wedge between knower and object of knowledge by pointing out that all we can have confidence in is knowledge of our immediate *ideas.* Any purported "real" world "causally related to," "standing behind," or "removed from" the knower is unknowable — this is the problem of *verisimilitude.* This legacy is passed down to both Hegel and Kant, whose views, though frequently in opposition, nonetheless concur in their denial of the knowability of, in Kant's parlance, the *"ding an sich,"* the "thing in itself."[8]

In the first two decades of the 20th century, there emerged a significant backlash against idealism and other antirealist theories. Called New Realism, this reaction culminated in Edward Gleason Spaulding's 1918 work, *The New Rationalism.* Like earlier New Realism representatives (for example, Holt, Marvin, Montague, Perry, Pitkin, & Spaulding, 1912; and

---

[8]In addition to rendering the world beyond phenomena opaque to human understanding, Kant created an additional barrier to knowledge by conceiving the mind as an active categorizer of human experiences. This led many theorists to argue not only that we do not have direct access to the real world, but that we couldn't know it even if we did, because the mind's categorizing must somehow work on or distort whatever it categorizes. As we shall see, both lines of skeptical argument are fundamentally flawed.

Nunn, 1909–1910; Perry, 1910), Spaulding's work was a trenchant critique of idealism. He was especially critical of the notion that, in the act of knowing, the object of knowledge suffers change (see, for example, Brummett, 1976). This is the "egocentric predicament" — the view that "it is impossible for me to discover anything which is, when I discover it, undiscovered by me." From this, "it is impossible to discover anything that is not thought" (Perry, 1910). Spaulding rightly judged that the "most essential realist doctrine is *the solution of the egocentric predicament*" (1918, p. 365).

Spaulding's solution to idealism and the egocentric predicament was to view reality not in terms of objects, but in terms of *relationships*. Among the relationships in the natural world, he locates the knower and the object of knowledge as "distinct" relata, claiming that "Knowing may not be existentially eliminated from the known world . . . But there is always the possibility that this knowing situation can be dealt with by an *analysis in situ*." "*The knowing* and *the known*," he argued, are "*numerically distinct*" as well as "*qualitatively different*" (1918, p. 372). If Spaulding is right, the egocentric predicament is solved; on this analysis knowledge is *independent* of its object, because the *terms* in the knower/known *relationship* are independently identifiable within the context of apprehension. Just as "being taller than your brother" indicates a relationship in which the two terms "you" and "your brother" are *essentially* unaffected by being in the size relationship, so too is the object of knowledge essentially unaffected by standing in or coming to stand in the knowledge relationship. On the New Realists' relational analysis, virtually all the objects of human cognition are objectively real, potentially knowable, and *unaffected by becoming known*.

Spaulding's optimism, like that of New Realism in general, was overwhelmed by the savagery of the First World War. In addition, the theory's contention that we perceive the external objects of reality *directly* did not seem to square with advances in perceptual psychology, which seemed to verify Locke's contention that perception and cognition are the last links in a long and complex causal chain. Physics likewise appeared to reveal a world whose reality inhered in atomic particles and forces never directly observed and frequently only imputed, inductively or deductively, in accordance with the "deductive–nominological model."[9] New skeptical arguments from error, illusion, and hallucination drove the last nails in the coffin of New Realism.

Critical Realism.   The corpse of New Realism was interred but a short while. In the 1920s and 1930s "critical realism" emerged. All critical realists

---

[9]The deductive-nominological method and its relevance to realism are discussed at length by Aronson, pp. 32–76. A discussion of the place of logic in argumentation relevant to the nominological-deductive process is provided by Corcoran (1989, pp. 18–38).

share two traits: (a) sensitivity to the problems that faced representative realists, especially the problem of verisimilitude; and (b) the urge to square their theory with recent advances in psychology. These two proclivities resulted in the construction of a complex theory of perception, at the heart of which is the doctrine that "the qualities of experience are separate and distinct from existence as such," yet "the qualities of our experience are identical with being" (Butler, 1951, pp. 183–184). The critical realists thus rejected Locke's distinction between primary and secondary qualities, arguing that perceived properties inhere *in the object*. At the same time, they, like Locke, held that the "image in the mind" and "the external object which produces the image" *are* distinct (see Butler, 1951, p. 290).

The critical realists' central project was to tie these two phenomena, mental image and external object, together to avoid the problem of verisimilitude. To do so they argued that the process of perception includes a *judgment* rendered by the perceiver about the *external referent* appearing to him/her in the *act* of perceiving. This "active external referent" is "implied by the knowledge claim" and is part of the perceiver's "intuited mental content or character complex to an external object" (Hirst, 1967, p. 82). The critical realists could then explain error and illusion as events produced by *misjudgments* on the part of the perceptual faculty regarding the image or datum generated by the external object. Yet, because "perceiving is always perception of external objects by means of the intuited data," rather than of images projected on the movie screen of the mind, the critique idealism launched against Locke was blunted (Hirst, 1967, p. 82.) During episodes of "normal perception" (when perception does not involve the occasional error in judgment and when the perceiver is not suffering pathology, drug-induced stupor, odd environmental conditions, and the like) perception is veridical.

Like its predecessors, critical realism suffers from a number of defects. For one thing, the invocation of sense data and the notion that consciousness is of the mental image of these data, still invites the problems of representation and verisimilitude. The critical realists' analysis of how the objects of perception get "hooked up" to the sense data in consciousness is unconvincing, for it lacks an explication of the physiological or neurophysiological processes involved in such linkage. Finally, the mind–body problem (how body differs from mind) is virtually ignored (see Hirst, 1967).

Appearance Realism.   As critical rationalism waned, realism was revitalized by the appearance realists. These thinkers borrow some tenets from earlier realisms and revise others. As a whole, appearance realists hold that *all* observed properties of the external world are real and apprehended directly, but that any act of perception reveals but limited facets of a more complex collection of aspects comprising the thing perceived (Broad, 1925; Hicks, 1938; McGilvary, 1933, 1956). This approach solved some vexing problems of earlier realist philosophies, such as the problem of illusion. For instance, perceptual relativists used this familiar argument: A table appearing round from overhead appears oval from an oblique angle; but the *real* table can't be round and oval at the same time, because they are incompatible properties. Therefore, we can't be seeing the real object, since incompatible properties can't inhere in the same object.

Appearance realists find no incompatibility in such examples, because the apparently incompatible properties, though present in the same object at the same time, are evident only when the table is seen from *different perspectives,* that is, the properties are not in the table *in the same way.* What *would* be strange, goes the retort, is if the table exhibited the *same* properties when seen from *different* perspectives! Conversely, the proof of the appearance realist's theory is evident in the fact that when objects are viewed from the *same* perspective, the appearances *are* the same (even when viewed by different perceivers, the round table looks round from above). Nor was the theory limited to visual perception of spatial objects. Abstract or nonphysical cognitions were similarly analyzed.

Two developments of mid-20th century science stifled the growth of appearance realism. First, physicists discovered a sub-atomic world vastly more complex than anyone had heretofore imagined. Not directly observable, the physicist's world is nonetheless held to be the seat of reality. Familiar objects as well as humans are *really* collections of atoms in the void. The world of pedestrian realism is written off as *illusory.* Second, neurophysiology had come into is own and left little doubt that perception of the putative external world comes at the end of a causal chain even longer and more labyrinthian than posited by representational realists. The problem of verisimilitude seemed inescapable.

Additional objections to specific tenets of the theory persisted. The most serious was an attack on the theory's doctrine of relations. Some versions of the doctrine relied on the notion of "internal relations," the view that everything is what it is by virtue of *all* the relationships in which it stands to everything else. For example, McGilvary claimed that *"In the world of nature any 'thing' at any time is, and is nothing but, the totality of the relational characters, experienced or not experienced, that the 'thing' has at that time in whatever relations it has at that time to other 'things'"* (McGilvary, 1956, p. 30, emphasis in original). Spaulding objected that this view rendered the "independence" of the external world problematic (1918, pp. 216–218). Reminiscent of the egocentric predicament, it was argued that the knowing relationship must systematically alter the object of knowing since, on the internal theory of relations, the knower would be a "thing" like any other, affected by and affecting in its turn everything else in the universe. In addition, the internal theory implied that every relationship, no matter how remote, was somehow *necessarily* part of the *essential* nature of everything else. My existence at the dinner table must be influencing the essential nature of Pluto as it inscribes its orbit about the sun! (see Hirst, 1967, p. 77). Such consequences appeared fatal to appearance realism.

One antirealist argument enjoying much currency since mid-century deserves separate mention. Realism asserts both the existence of human-independent reality and the ability of humans to know that reality, at least in part. Realism has thus been attacked as a conservative, even undemocratic doctrine: Those who acquire knowledge, it is claimed, assert a privileged position, with Truth on their side. And privilege can go awry, as the well-worn example of fascism in World War Two attests—an experience so burned into postmodern consciousness that the result has been a proclivity to view *any* claims to know with suspicion and hostility (see Russman, 1987, pp. 93–107). In this way realism comes under suspicion, not because of any defect in the theory, but because of the *consequences* of its occasional historical misuse. We shall examine this argument later.

In summary, realism has for centuries maintained a nagging proclivity to rise from the dead like a Phoenix. This is no less true as we enter the last decades of the 20th century, where renewed interest in realism is emerging. James Gibson (1979), Jerrold Aronson (1984), Sean Sayers (1985), Rom Harré (1986), David Kelley (1986), Joseph Margolis (1986), Thomas Russman (1987), Gerald Vision (1989), and others have offered a variety of realist theories designed to meet antirealist criticism. This chapter could not possibly describe in detail all contemporary realist theories. However, the central tenets of selected contemporary realisms are important to a realist rhetorical theory and deserve separate treatment.

Late Contemporary Realism

One version of late contemporary realism I label "social realism." Social realism accepts many of the notions common to the post-modern era, including the idea that we view reality through the "lens" of social forms (Sayers, 1985, p. 133). Unlike most postmodern social theories, however, social realism argues that social forms *promote* rather than obfuscate understanding of the *real* world. Sayers accepted Kant's argument that our minds are active and that we perceive the world in accordance with categories of our understanding. But Sayers drew conclusions far different from Kant's and far different from those drawn by other social theorists:

> Kant argues—correctly I have maintained—that knowledge essentially involves a rational element: the application of categories, concepts of interpretation to experience. *Contra* Kant, however, the vital thing to see is that our 'way of seeing things' is not an arbitrary creation; and it does not stand as a

barrier, cutting us off from things-in-themselves. On the contrary, our concepts and categories themselves reflect reality, and can embody knowledge of reality. This . . . is the realist view; and it implies, as I have argued, that species and kinds, laws and necessities, are objective features of the material world itself. (Sayers, 1985, p. 192)

For Sayers, "It is wrong to imagine that social forms merely distort our consciousness of reality and cut us off from knowledge of the objective nature of things." Instead, "it is only by social means—and especially through the use of the language—that we can gain a knowledge of objective reality, beyond the most basic and elementary level" (Sayers, 1985, pp. 132–133).

Sayers' realism makes two points: (a) the old antirealist saw of the egocentric predicament—that to come to know something is to change the essential nature of the thing—may simply be no predicament at all, that is, the assertion may be simply false; (b) whether true or false, the view is certainly *underentailed,* that is, it is asserted on grounds inadequate to generate the conclusion. That observation is filtered through social forms is not in itself sufficient to demonstrate that all observation—indeed *any given observation*—is thereby distorted. And were one to employ the paradoxical argument that we have *evidence* of distortion in various instances of perception or cognition (paradoxical because to claim something is distorted one must be able to measure it against some nondistorted exemplar), such cases could at best establish only that distortion *occasionally* occurs, not that it is systematic. As we shall see, because antirealist arguments based on social distortion (including contemporary anti-realist views like constructivism and intersubjectivism) are underentailed, they can be productively subsumed as part of a *realist* rhetoric.

Another version of late contemporary realism is "scientific realism." As described by Aronson (1984):

Scientific realism maintains a commonsensical view that there is a world that exists independently of our perception of it, and that our theories inform us about the existence and nature of this realm, even if the things of which our theories are about are not directly observed or, in some cases, directly observable. (pp. 6–7)

How do we acquire knowledge of these entities? Aronson explained:

The realist holds that the truth or success of a theory in some sense entails the existence of the theoretical entities mentioned by the theoretical terms in its language. For example, the success of atomic theory in terms of its ability to predict and explain a gigantic cluster of observable phenomena entails that atoms exist, even if we cannot see them. (p. 7)

Aronson's realism is similar to representative realism, in that the phenomenal effects of unobserved or unobservable entities are taken as proof for their existence. Mixed in is a measure of pragmatism, represented by the idea that the *success* of a theory verifies the theory's tenets.

Aronson's view attempts to avoid a straightforward phenomenalism, wherein it is claimed that we can know only the most immediate phenomena of perception. There is much riding on the phenomenalist challenge, for if scientific realism is not veridical, we lose confidence in the existence of such entities as "particles, fields, mental states, social structures, and so on" (Aronson, 1984, p. 7). On the other hand, if a scientific realism is defensible, these notions are reintroduced and much of contemporary science preserved. This result is important, because it enables one to provide a parsimonious account of the enormous success of contemporary science — success difficult to account for under wholly nonrealist assumptions.[10] Yet Aronson's view, like so many others, suffers from the problematic of representationalism. Like Locke, Aronson's scientific realism is causal chain and substance-oriented.

Another version of late contemporary realism, offered by Rom Harré (1986), is "reference realism." Harre's wide-ranging argument cannot possibly be summarized adequately in even a few pages. In general, though, Harré develops a realist view of science similar to Aronson's. However, it rejects a number of foundations upon which traditional scientific realism has been based. Foremost among these is "the principle that most theoretical statements of a scientific discourse are true or false by virtue of the way the world is" (Harré, 1986, p. 4). Harré rejected the bivalence of a true/false logical infrastructure, arguing that "a clear-eyed look at the *cognitive and material practices* of the scientific community will reveal that logic is a socially motivated addition, a rhetorical contribution to persuasive power" (p. 5).

According to Harré, the scientific enterprise is carried out by communities of scientists, "within a distinctive moral order" (p. 6). This moral order trusts in the honesty and integrity of the scientist that what is reportedly

---

[10]Rhetoric has been at odds with science — as it has been at odds with philosophy — for some time. Vico's hostility, at the turn of the 18th century, to science's claims to mathematical precision and ahistorical applicability is as good an example as any (see Bergin & Fisch, 1958). This hostility is echoed in the voice of scholars like Richard Rorty (1982), who claimed that "even in science, not to mention philosophy, we simply cast around for a vocabulary which lets us get what we want" (p. 152). It is simply difficult to reconcile this position with the scientific accomplishments of the 20th century. Did we send three humans to the moon, land them within yards of the desired spot on the moon's Sea of Tranquility, and return them to earth *just* on the basis of a spinning vocabulary? Is the design of the computer hardware that controls everything from jetliners to my word processor really *just* a product of word magic? Is science *just* a word-game? To respond "yes" to this last question seems to strain the bounds of credulity in the present century, if ever it made sense in the 18th.

observed was, in fact, observed. Harré, then, sought a realist view of science founded on the material practice (read, "praxis") of the scientific community. He called the view reference realism because at its heart is the *act* of observers referring to a real world; truth/falsity are secondary considerations.

Harré believed the most damaging attacks on realism in the past have been attacks against the notion that science is an essentially *logical* activity, governed by the true-false principles of logical bivalence, and certified by the deductive or deductive-nominological method. He contended that such a view of science is "hopeless" (Harré, 1986, p. 38). The version of realism he supported is not dependent upon traditional notions of true/false bivalence, but upon whether purported observations are in fact observations of actually occurring phenomena. Consider the following example, adapted from Harré: I am at a party and I remark to a friend, "Do you see that man, across the room, with the gin?" The friend replies, "Yes, but that's a woman and the drink I just poured her is tequila." While the person under discussion is described falsely as a man holding gin, nonetheless I have successfully *referred* to the person I wanted to point out to my friend. This example shows that the strict truth/falsity of the statement is largely irrelevant to the act of referencing. What counts is *whether I have successfully referred,* since successful reference was what was at stake. Once successful referencing occurs, we can proceed — as we do in science — to investigate in more detail the various properties of the object in question.

But there is another issue reference realism must confront, namely, the ontological "level" at which reality inheres. To this point in my summary of realism, the claim of contemporary physics that reality is subatomic or quantum in nature has not been engaged. Harré addressed this question by dividing the "referents of substantive terms in scientific discourses" into three "realms," realms demarcating possibilities of human experience. Realm 1 is the world of everyday experience, where persons encounter common objects of the world. Realm 2 contains entities that "might be available to human perception" assuming that "technical and other practical difficulties" are surmounted. Harré gives the example of the 17th century theory of microorganisms, which were then denizens of Realm 2, having been postulated but never observed. With the advent of the microscope, it became possible to experience microorganisms, which subsequently became part of Realm 1. Realm 3 contains entities at present "beyond all possible experience," such as subatomic particles. Though the inaccessibility of Realm 3 to human experience remains "problematic," the boundary between Realm 3 and Realm 2 is not incorrigible (Harré, 1986, p. 238-240). At the turn of the century, viruses were too small to be viewed through optical microscopes. Incapable of being experienced, they were properly regarded as Realm 3 entities. But the discovery of de Broglie's rules and wave–particle dualism led to the electron microscope and viruses became the subject of human experience, just as had larger microorganisms with the advent of the optical microscope decades earlier (pp. 192–93).

Two features of Harré's scheme are of immediate importance. First is the fact that we humans live our day-to-day lives in Realm 1. Although not wholly unaffected by Realms 2 and 3 it is nonetheless erroneous to award a higher epistemic status to other realms. This is especially true given that scientific progress affords opportunity for Realm 2 and Realm 3 entities to become objects of human experience. Second, occasions when Realm 2 and Realm 3 entities become Realm 1 entities through advances in science indicates that there are *interrelationships* among all three realms (as de Broglie's rules exemplify). As a result, Harré is able to preserve not only Realm 1, but Realm 2 and Realm 3 as falling within the purview of realism.

Harré, therefore, dispenses with the referential theory of *truth* while at the same time preserving an important measure of *referentialism*. The success or failure of the act of referring depends largely on whether one can avoid the problems inherent in classical representationalism, such as the problem of verisimilitude. Harré did so, he believed, by adapting a somewhat revised version of the psychological/perceptual realism of J.J. Gibson. Gibson's principal contribution to realist thought is his analysis of human perception in terms of a process that does not make sensations or ideas ontologically prior to perceptibles. Sensations, he contended, do not stand at the end of a causal chain. Instead, perception is apprehension of information immediately given (as opposed to mediately structured) to the senses in the perceiver's immediate (as opposed to mediated) relationship to the world. In the "ambient array" of energy surrounding perceiver and perceived, human sensory receptors actively seek out and pick up "infor-mation" that "specifies" the object (Gibson, 1979, p. 242). Note that Gibson and his followers are not suggesting that perception *processes* this informa-tion. Or, to put it as Harré (1986) did, the information is not used as "premises" in cognitive/deductive processing (pp. 156–157). Rather, infor-mation is itself the *conclusion* — the point of apprehension — of the object. For Harré, perception of what we might call "basic things" is *direct and unmediated*.

The tenets of perception theory frame the last category of late contem-porary realism I discuss, namely, "perceptual realism." This view has its roots in the sciences of experimental psychology, neuroscience, and other fields whose object of inquiry is the human central nervous system (CNS). Many of these sciences' attempts to explain human perception and cognition are really nothing more than sophisticated versions of the theories of vision and other perceptual faculties discussed by thinkers centuries earlier. They assume that perception and cognition can be adequately explained by careful examination of the *causal-chain apparatus* that is the CNS (Gazzaniga, 1984a, 1984b; Patricia S. Churchland, 1986).

Although they attempt to account for how we perceive the external world reliably, these attempts are still susceptible to the problem of verisimilitude and are incompatible with realism. What has changed since Descartes and Locke is not any fundamentally different explanation of how the CNS works, but the sophistication of the technology, vocabulary, and the microscopic level of explanation. No longer content to describe vision in terms of such gross features of the CNS as the retina, rods, cones, visual cortex, and like structures, now there are added a saturnalia of more microscopic descriptions. The structure of the retina alone is segmented into amacrine cells, bipolar cells, ganglion cells, horizontal cells, and pigment cells, while at even more minute levels of discrimination individual cell bodies are divided and subdivided into structural, electromagnetic, electrochemical, and functional properties (Patricia S. Churchland, 1986, pp. 112–125). Frequently added to causal chain accounts of the CNS are theories of information processing and computer science, as shown in the following brief excerpt from Churchland:

> The excitatory interneuron mediates between the input and the output of the aggregation. It makes synaptic contact with the incoming thalamic fibers, and it sends axon branches vertically along the columnar aggregation to synapse on the output pyramidal cells at various laminar levels. Given this circuitry, it is reasonable to postulate that columns are input-output modules. (p. 134)

Combined with such recent notions as "parallel processing" and "tensor network theory" (Pellionisz & Llinás, 1985) and "phase space sandwiches" (Paul M. Churchland, 1988), present-day CNS descriptions have led to all manner of *representationalist* theories, including the influential work of Jerry Fodor. Fodor (1975) set out to establish that: (a) "the only psychological models of cognitive processes that seem even remotely plausible represent such processes as computational"; and (b) "computation presupposes a medium of computation: a *representational* system" (p. 27, my emphasis). He views the mind as comprised of "modules," and calls for a rejuvenation of *faculty* psychology. The new faculty psychology sees modular CNS systems as "special purpose computational mechanisms . . . the mind is a collection of such mechanisms" (Fodor, 1983, p. 120). Contemporary CNS theories and their perceptual/cognitive corollaries have enjoyed considerable influence (Gregg, 1984, 1987; Stacks & Andersen, 1989).

Unlike much contemporary neuroscience, perceptual realism rejects the *representational* character of human cognition. Although representation and computation may be part of the story of how the CNS works, it provides, according to the perceptual realist, a very incomplete account of perception. We have already seen how Harré made use of one perceptual realist, James Gibson, in defending reference realism. Gibson's views have been expanded by, among others, psychologists Carello, Turvey, Kugler, and Shaw (1984), who attack what they call "the computational metaphor" of theorists like Fodor. They contend that the information structures stimulating the visual sense organs "is not similar to its sources, but it is specific to them, in the sense of being nomically dependent on them." Further, "it is because of the specificity of the information identified in [perception] that perception does not involve interpretive, elaborative, restorative, constructive, etc. operations" (pp. 26–27). What we see and what we hear are not copies of some purported external object—such experiences are not provisionally *similar to reality*—they are *identical to reality*. Perceptions are the "direct pick-up" of information, *not* a priori categories, syntactical computations upon representations, or ideas as the last link in a long causal chain.

Perceptual realism pays a number of dividends for epistemology and ontology. It enables us to finally link up the human perceiver with the *real* objects of the external world. It does so by eliminating all the contrivances that, since Locke, have stood as beacons for representationalism, skepticism, and eventually solipsism. For example, it removes the Lockean distinction of primary and secondary qualities. As Gibson (1967) observed:

> There is a proper meaning of the word "color" that refers to a distinctive feature of a solid substance. There is a proper meaning of the word "sound" that refers to a distinctive feature of a mechanical disturbance. The doctrine of secondary qualities comes from a misunderstanding. (p. 170)

That misunderstanding confuses the operations of the wetware of the CNS as *mechanically and computationally identical with and sufficient for* perception, instead of recognizing them as elements merely *associated*, even if *necessarily* associated, with perception.

David Kelley, also a perceptual realist, marshals a wealth of psychological evidence against representational/computational theories and recent versions of skepticism. Part of his argument derives from the child development literature, where it was for some time held that infants gradually "put together" sense data into larger and larger cognitive units. This process was, it was argued, a creative product of the child's mind, not a function of the direct perception of reality. But according to Kelley (1986):

> Even if infants were limited to sensations, this would not mean that perceptual development is a matter of automatizing computational processes. . . .

> Developmental psychologists are learning that the process of perceptual learning consists not in discovering which sensations to put together into the perception of whole objects, but in discriminating finer and finer differences among the entities which the child can pick out as wholes from the beginning. (p. 51)

Kelley also engages objections to realism. I provide as an example just part of his reply to the argument from hallucination:

> Hallucinations are apparently produced by wholly internal sources, from neuronal activity touched off by abnormal causes such as drugs, intense emotions, subconscious fears, epileptic seizures. Hallucinations, then, are not perceptions, and there is no apparent reason to think they will tell us anything about perception. (p. 133)

Kelley's analysis removed hallucinations from the realm of *philosophical* objections to realism, treating them as misinterpretations or misjudgments caused by *occasional* breakdowns of or interference with CNS wetware. Kelley claimed to have reinterpreted the psychological, representational, computational, and philosophical arguments against realism in a way that *integrates* the data upon which they are based into a realist theory of perception.

We have seen the history of realism punctuated by arguments whose variety and evolution betray a common core of concerns. A contemporary realist rhetoric will need to work out its own answers to the core of complaints traditionally lodged against realism. However, we can claim with confidence: *despite the history of attacks by antirealists, realism remains a plausible philosophical thesis.* Given realism's presumption, the question now arises, "What difference does realism make for an understanding of rhetoric?" This interrogative defies summary answer. It can be addressed only in the process of constructing a realist-based rhetorical theory. Before pursuing this task, a summary of the objections to realism is in order. The following arguments are numbered and labeled for convenient reference:

Argument 1: The problem of error. Because one sometimes makes mistakes and identifies some thing or property X as some other thing or property Y, one cannot be directly apprehending an independent object of knowledge, for if one were, error would not occur.

Argument 2: The problems of dreams, illusion, and hallucination. Dreams, illusions, and hallucinations are commonplace and we take them to be different from the actual occurrences they may be "like." Yet there is no immediate criterion with which to differentiate these "false" perceptions from veridical ones.

Argument 3: The egocentric predicament. If there are "things in themselves," they are affected and "changed" in the act of coming to know them; all observation is "theory laden."

Argument 4: The causal theory of perception. Our ideas are end products in an almost infinitely complex chain of physical, chemical, and electrical interactions; perceptions are ideas in the mind.

Argument 5: Advances in the physical sciences. Reality is to be found, if anywhere, at the micro-level of subatomic or quantum physics.

Argument 6: The ideological argument. Claims to knowledge of the real world put the knower in a privileged position and result in a coercive epistemology. This can lead to all manner of social and political abuse.

A realist rhetorical theory must respond to these challenges. Happily, such a response hinges, I believe, on the analysis of concepts more often associated with the discipline of rhetoric than philosophy. These include "persuasion," "facticity," and "probability."

RHETORIC, PERSUASION, AND REALISM

Throughout the 2½ millennia of Western rhetoric, one term stands out among all others as characteristic of both rhetorical theory and practice. That term is *persuasion*. From Aristotle's first extended treatment of the definition of rhetoric as an art whose function is "to discover the available means of persuasion in a given case" (Cooper, 1932, p. 6) to Barry Brummett's contention that rhetoric "is in the deepest and most fundamental sense the *advocacy of realities*" (1976, p. 31), the notion of seeking the adherence of an audience to the persuasive invocations of the speaker has catalyzed rhetorical thought and practice. To be sure, we have altered our models of human persuasion from the simplistic, linear, "speaker delivers message to audience" variety and now view rhetoric as more interactive. Nonetheless, the object of rhetoric remains to persuade audiences and gain their adherence. The first step in developing a realist rhetoric, then, is to understand the nature of persuasion.

Even in cultures predating the emergence of Western rhetorical consciousness, a chief aim of public discourse was to persuade. Yet in stating that persuasion is at the heart of rhetoric we have offered little clarification; one might well ask for a definition beyond the gloss that, "one who persuades seeks the adherence of an audience." In searching for a more illuminating analysis of persuasion, let us turn to the place where we find its principal features, the realm of real-world discourse. Consider one of the earliest extant examples of persuasion, a fragment from a speech by the Egyptian Pharaoh Merneptah, delivered sometime around 1200 B.C.:

> Hear ye the command of your lord; I give . . . as ye shall do, saying: I am the ruler who shepherds you; I spend my time searching out . . . you, as father, who preserves alive his children. . . . Shall the land be wasted and forsaken at the invasion of every country, while the Nine Bows plunder its borders, and rebels invade it every day? . . . They have repeatedly penetrated the fields of Egypt to the great river. They have halted, they have spent whole days and months dwelling. They have reached the hills of the oasis, and have cut off the district of Toyeh. (Breasted, 1906, pp. 243–244)

Merneptah is offering a *narrative* of recent events, in an attempt to *persuade* his followers to resist Libyan forces that invaded the Nile delta. The passage is an intricate tapestry of familiar rhetorical appeals. It includes attempts to gain the audience's interest by strong introductory remarks and reference to the Pharaoh's credibility, the use of rhetorical question, and the development of parallelism. Importantly, though, all these rhetorical devices are attendant to the infusion of what I simply call "facts." The Pharaoh claims he is the "lord," "ruler," and "shepherd" of the people; he claims he is like a "father" to the people; he claims that the tribe of the Nine Bows are plundering parts of Egypt and he summarizes the geographic extent of that plunder, and so on. The most cursory examination of any piece of real-world persuasion, from the earliest rhetorical artifacts at the dawn of history to the present day, leads to the following axiom: *Although any given example of persuasive discourse may or may not contain a particular persuasive device (figures, tropes, other stylistic devices), every instance of persuasion, without exception, will contain, implicitly or explicitly, some level of facticity; it will exhibit factual claims about the world.*[11]

This axiom suggests that the concept "facticity" is indispensable to the analysis of rhetorical praxis. Yet the history of rhetoric at times exhibits great hostility to facticity, as evidenced by the frequent treatment as "devil terms" such notions as "positivism," "objectivism," and "truth." Regardless

---

[11]The claim I am making is that "facts"—often in the form of simple perceptual judgments—that alone have no great importance or that are even describable as "trivial" when viewed in isolation, are utterly indispensable to rhetorical discourse. Questions of pedestrian facticity (basic perceptual claims) will frequently not be, in and of themselves, of central importance to a given instance of rhetorical discourse, that is, they are not sufficient to alone constitute many significant rhetorical issues. My claim is that they are, however, necessary for the larger issues of a given discourse to make sense and to be evaluated. In aggregate, they comprise the hinges of discourse upon which larger issues of, for example, rhetorical probability turn.

of one's theoretical position on epistemological and ontological issues, this paradox demands resolution. Of course, such resolution is of the utmost urgency for a realist theory of rhetoric, for if the analysis of perceptual realism described earlier can be conjoined to facticity, a realist rhetoric will comfortably emerge.

Persuasion and Facticity

To clarify the role of facticity in rhetoric, let us look more carefully at the way in which facts operate in the Pharaoh's speech. In the course of rhetorical analysis, a critic might offer commentary on stylistic dimensions of the speech, its effectiveness in gaining the adherence of the audience, its ethical quality, what the speech tells us about Egyptian culture, or even the psychological or philosophical attitude of the speaker. All these objectives are legitimate goals of rhetorical analysis. But the critic might also focus on what Walter Fisher called the "narrative fidelity" and "narrative probability" of the discourse (1984, p. 8). Is Merneptah, *in fact,* leader of the audience he addresses? Has he, *in fact,* shepherded his people like a father? Are members of the tribe of the Nine Bows, *in fact,* invading as he describes? Has the enemy, *in fact,* halted, spent whole months dwelling, reached the hills of the oasis, and cut off the district of Toyeh?

Certainly the answers to these interrogatives are crucial to the success or failure of the Pharaoh's persuasion. They might figure heavily as well in the types of criticism enumerated above. For an important element in all narrative is, as Walter Fisher reminded us, "that the 'people' judge the stories that are told for and about them." Moreover, " 'people' have a natural tendency to prefer what they perceive as the true and the just" (Fisher, 1987, p. 67). Rhetorical effectiveness of the Pharaoh's speech may depend on the success of the speaker in making the audience *believe* his facts, regardless of whether they are, *in fact,* true. But, as the history of our own century makes clear, the rhetorical contrivances of leaders, their ethos, and the leaders themselves, frequently meet an unhappy end when enterprising critics demonstrate the falsity or inconsistency of their claims.

Of course, I am extending the notion of narrative fidelity beyond the point at which Fisher is comfortable, but not farther than some of his critics urge. Robert Rowland contends that the criteria for determining the coherence of a story—which Fisher sees as the main task of narrative fidelity and probability—"must test not merely the story, but the story in relation to the world" (Rowland, 1987, p. 270). Admittedly, determining truth and falsity in a rhetor's narrative is not always easy, but neither is it impossible. Nor has it been an infrequent occurrence in recent rhetorical history. Dorothy Sayers is only partially correct in her oft-quoted folk wisdom: "She always says, my lord, that facts are like cows. If you look them in the face hard enough they generally run away" (Brummett, 1976, p. 25). As a corrective to Sayers' injunction, one might extend the metaphor, suggesting that the critic's job, in part, is to run after the herd and establish with the best evidence possible, what the facts are in any given rhetorical situation.

In assessing the Pharaoh's discourse, we can imagine all manner of commentary about the truth claims of the speech and how those claims parcel out in real-world deliberative contexts, including the advisability of engaging the Libyans in war, the need to depose a tyrannical Pharaoh, or resist his policies. Facticity will have a critical, indispensable bearing on such issues, as it does in contemporary political crisis rhetoric.

Unavoidably, facticity raises questions referencing the world of *pedestrian realism*. As such, it is bound to be greeted with hostility by those who reject the notion that facts can be appraised as states of affairs existing largely independent of human attitudes, beliefs, values, and communication. Some of this hostility may be muted if we can come to a clearer appreciation of its source in rhetorical theory. I believe that source is the persistent notion that rhetoric deals most centrally with questions of *probability*. Although public speaking texts dutifully treat such concepts of praxis as "evidence," "testimony," and "tests of evidence," and urge the aspiring rhetor not to employ "falsehoods" (thus evidencing a regard for facticity), we persist in eschewing facticity when describing the nature of rhetoric in our theoretical texts (Golden, Berquist, & Coleman, 1989, pp. 32-33, 369, 372, 389; Hauser, 1986, p. 10; Murphy, 1983, pp. 49-50). Some rhetoricians who at times seem to be arguing for facticity at other times even suggest that "the world is by its very nature probabilistic" (Rowland, 1987, p. 270). And when we do broach the issue of facticity, "fact" is frequently so devitalized as to have little affinity to common usage (that is, usage implying pedestrian realism). Thus, while conceding that there are four varieties of facts that "are themselves factual," Paul Newell Campbell suggests that in another sense of the term, "a fact is whatever the audience believes to be fact and that is also consistent with the ethical attitude of the rhetorician" (Campbell, 1972, p. 56). Because this version of what a fact is includes no criteria against which to judge factual statements, and since the ethical attitudes of rhetoricians have, historically, covered the spectrum from veracity to deception, this version of what a "fact" or "truth" is appears indistinguishable from "illusion" or "falsity." Chaim Perelman and L. Olbrechts-Tyteca (1969) correctly saw the *inherent* relationship of truth to probability: "The domain of probability is then connected with that of facts and truths, and it is in terms of these that it is characterized for each audience" (p. 70). Regrettably, their vision was not exploited in a way that would resolve the paradox mentioned above.

The doctrine that rhetoric is centrally concerned with other than factual matters, including probability, has its source in antiquity. Apparently explicit in the teachings of Corax and Tisias, its most influential exposition occurs in Aristotle's *Art of Rhetoric*. Aristotle's discussion has prompted rhetoricians to make such pronouncements as: "Rhetoric . . . deals with probable knowledge designed to promote truth and justice. It recognizes the contingent nature of propositions, and the need to speak in self-defense" (Golden, Berquist, & Coleman, 1989, p. 44). To reconcile the statement that rhetoric "deals with probable knowledge" with the statement that it also seeks to "promote truth" requires an exploration of Aristotle's use of the terms *eikos* (probability), *pistis* (probable proof), *apodeixis* (scientific proof), and *alethes* (truth). This digression is important, for it enables us to resituate facticity in its proper place in rhetoric and, by doing so, to view rhetoric qua theory *and* praxis as *inherently* and *necessarily* realistic.

Facts and Probability in Aristotle

It is erroneous to draw, as many scholars do, any clear *qualitative* demarcation between probability and truth. Those who translate *eikos* as "probability" typically neglect to make conspicuous the term's close association with "truth." It would be a more faithful rendering to translate *eikos* as "probably true" or "likely veridical," retaining a stress on truth or veridicality. This contrasts with the usual imputation of "probably occurred," "is occurring," or "will occur." I suggest that Aristotle has in mind the contrast between a probable proposition and positive fact (Liddell & Scott, 1968, pp. 484–485). Hence, we should keep in mind the question "Probably *what?*" when considering the issues rhetoric treats and understand that the answer is, "Probably *true*."[12]

Aristotle himself went to great lengths to remind his reader that rhetoric is *not* unconcerned with "facticity." Recall that the first of Aristotle's four principal reasons for finding rhetoric valuable was "because *truth* and justice are by nature more powerful than their opposites" (Cooper, 1932, p. 5, emphasis added). In addition, Aristotle found that "persuasion is effected by the arguments, when we demonstrate the truth, real or apparent, by such means as inhere in particular cases" (Cooper, 1932, p. 9).

---

[12]Shortly after completing the text of this chapter, I learned of two sources supporting my analysis of facticity in Aristotle. William M. A. Grimaldi, S.J. concludes that, in interpreting the *Rhetoric*, "we should not set up a sharp cleavage between the true and the probable as though probability had little or no relation to truth, and then conclude that rhetorical reasoning is not concerned with truth" (1980, p. 23). Similarly, Thomas M. Conley, based upon an analysis of the enthymeme and the Aristotelian topoi, contends that for Aristotle, like his mentor, Plato, "good rhetoric is based on objective truth" (1990, p. 16).

Perhaps the most influential source of the idea that rhetoric deals with probabilities is Aristotle's discussion of the enthymeme. According to Aristotle, enthymemes are "the very body and substance of persuasion" (Cooper, 1932, p. 1). Aristotle described "the materials of enthymemes" as "probabilities (*eikota*) and signs (*tekmeria*)." He continued, "A 'probability' is that which usually happens or follows, yet not *anything* that so happens, for the thing must belong to the class of things that may turn out this way or that." And signs "are of two sorts: one bears, toward the statement it is to prove, the relation of a particular statement to a universal, the other that of a universal to a particular" (Cooper, 1932, p. 13). Aristotle suggested that we look principally at the *topoi* as "the proper subjects of dialectical and rhetorical syllogisms" (Cooper, 1932, p. 15). And, of course, the topoi are such commonplaces of argument as: the greater and the lesser, time, parts to a whole, cause to effect. Although the topics point the rhetor to general resources for framing arguments — "premises from which to argue on the possible and most timely subjects he may have to discuss" — it is important to note that these resources themselves, when employed in actual discourse, are composed of facts. As Aristotle noted, the speaker . . .

> must seek his premises in the same way, by referring, not to vague generalities, but to the facts of the subject on which he is speaking, including just as many of the most pertinent ones as he can. The more facts he has at his command, the more easily will he make his point. (Cooper, 1932, p. 157)

So important are facts to the rhetorical process that Aristotle prefaced his most extended discussion of the topics with the following passage:

> Now, first of all, let this be understood: Whatever the subject on which we have to speak or reason — whether the argument concerns public affairs or anything else — we must have some knowledge, if not a complete one, of the facts. Without it, you would have no materials from which to construct an argument. (Cooper, 1932, p. 156)

In expatiating this passage, Aristotle provided precise examples of what he had in mind by "facts" for each of his three genres of speeches: deliberative, forensic, and epideictic. And for each one it is beyond doubt that he meant by facts the sorts of things that come to be known *by common observation of the pedestrian world*. In a deliberative context, for example, "How," asked Aristotle, "could we advise the Athenians whether they should go to war or not, if we did not know their forces, whether these were military or naval or both, the size of these forces, what were the public revenues, and who were the friends or foes of the State, what wars it had waged, and with what success — and so on?" In epideictic situations, "[H]ow could we eulogize them, if we knew nothing of the sea fight at Salamis, or the battle of Marathon, or all they did for the Heracleidae?" And in the courts, "prosecution and defense alike must be based upon a study of the facts" (Cooper, 1932, pp. 156–157).

If facticity is central to Aristotle's theory of persuasion, how are we to reinterpret probability? I suggest that we view probabilities chiefly as the larger issues of a rhetorical discourse, including principal themes or the general thesis of the discourse. Should the Athenians build a wall to protect themselves against invaders? Does the tyrant deserve the death penalty? Is Socrates praiseworthy? These questions are not themselves subject to immediate answer via facticity, and they may never be subject to any definitive, certain answer via simple empiricism. That is, one cannot simply "look and see" and find answers to these macroissues. But one can look and see and collect the facts to be weighed in favor of or in opposition to these larger issues of probability. One can count the strength of enemy forces; one can quantify riches squandered, rights trampled, and crimes committed by the tyrant; one can report incidents comprising the praiseworthy life of Socrates or the blameworthy life of Miltocythes. All these are facts, and as such are not likely to be problematic beyond the usual tests of veracity one applies to any simple factual judgment. *Hence, although any one item of facticity may fail to yield a certain answer to a contingent or probable question, that is, to a macroissue, the aggregate of individual facts may well offer us such certainty.* How else are we to account for Aristotle's insistence that rhetoric, properly applied, yields truth and justice?

I have confined the discussion to simple, day-to-day facticity because it is just such tellurian facticity out of which the majority of rhetorical praxis emerges. Facticity in the vast majority of rhetorical discourse is generally unproblematic. This is not to say, of course, that we cannot *make* a given instance of facticity problematic; it is only to say that the majority of factual claims in persuasion are rightly taken for granted. Once the rhetor has collected supporting materials, they are interwoven in the discourse along with other ingredients of the rhetorical art (stylistic, prosodic, taxonomic, et cetera). When the persuasive message is delivered, the rhetor may take Aristotle's advice and conclude with the closing words of the *Rhetoric:* "I have done; you all have heard; you have the facts; give your judgment" (Cooper, 1932, p. 241).

I should not leave this subject without expanding my claim, contending that if facticity was important in Aristotle's day, it is ever so much more important in contemporary rhetoric. This contention is illustrated by an incident that generated a substantial amount of real-world rhetoric – the downing on September 1, 1983, of Korean Airlines Flight 007.

Subsequent to this tragedy, the United States and the Soviet Union engaged in a series of rhetorical exchanges, trading charges and counter-charges about the *facts* surrounding the flight. A good deal of secondary rhetoric — public argument — on the part of editorialists and scholars sought to accuse or exculpate various parties to the disaster. In the most recent study of Soviet-American rhetoric surrounding the tragedy, Young and Launer (1988) argued that the discourse offered by a number of Soviet and American rhetors exemplified a genre of political discourse, namely, "conspiratist rhetoric" (pp. 217–228). At the center of the public controversy were questions of *facticity*. Some of these have been settled: Did the Soviets shoot down the plane? When? Was 007 over Soviet territory when it was intercepted? Other issues are presently answerable only with greater or lesser *probability:* Did the Soviets know 007 was a commercial airliner? Or, did they believe it was a spy plane? Was 007 off course inadvertently? Or, as the Soviets and certain American rhetors claim, was it purposely off course to enable the United States to collect intelligence regarding Soviet air defense response? Additionally, there are more purely contingent issues broached by both sides: Does the 007 incident provide reason to label the Soviet Union an "evil empire"? If the plane *was* involved in espionage, did that make the Reagan Administration callously opportunistic for jeopardizing innocent civilian lives for the purpose of cloaking a spy flight in innocence?

Some questions now in the realm of the probable may, in the future, become known with certainty: Did the United States, as some have suggested, recover the flight recorders of the jet and withhold their discovery? Does the United States, as a number of sources claim, have additional tapes of the Soviet intercept, recorded by listening posts in Alaska and Japan, that shed light on the disaster, but which have been withheld to prevent disclosure of American intelligence capability and/or culpability? As in the case of the Pharaoh's speech, these interrogatives demonstrate that facticity is a major constituent in the rhetoric surrounding the 007 incident, *as it is in all persuasion.*

Of great importance to the understanding of rhetoric, then, is the realization that answers to factual microissues permit us to draw conclusions about larger, probable macroissues. For instance, in criminal trials conducted under contemporary rules of evidence in this country, it is reasonable to assert that the vast majority of those found guilty of crimes are, *in fact,* guilty. In most such cases, factual microissues determine guilt beyond a *reasonable* doubt. Occasional errors in such judgments should not betray the fact that, *with certainty,* we can claim *most* such decisions are veridical. Likewise with other rhetorical persuasions in other domains of inquiry where conclusions are based upon facticity and wherein the facts asserted are subject to rigorous argumentative and evidentiary tests. All this suggests that issues of probability are, as our analysis of Aristotle indicates, merely one point on the continuum of facticity; they are not *qualitatively* distinct from, for example, empirical, apodictic claims.

Consider one final point about facticity: By most standards of contemporary rhetorical theory and criticism, a fact is something to be certified by an audience. Yet if we are to avoid the dizzying descent from intersubjectivity to subjectivity and, ultimately, to solipsism, we must grant that *some external criteria of facticity must be available against which to test the factual claims of any discourse.* As Young and Launer (1988) noted regarding conspiratist rhetoric, "as long as credibility is an audience-centered rather than a message-centered concept, critics of rhetoric need an external standard. . . ." (p. 254). That external standard must, at some juncture, be informed by facticity.

Facticity is a *necessary* component of rhetoric. Without facts, rhetoric is either nonexistent or devolves into mere style, adornment, and artifice — "mere rhetoric" in the pejorative sense, divorced from any connection with the natural world in which humans exist. This analysis of facticity stands at the heart of a realist theory of rhetoric.

Facticity and Realism

Recall Aristotle's admonition: Without facts, one "would have no materials from which to construct an argument." Yet facts may be challenged. "How do you know?" is one staple of criticism. But this question is not a theoretical one. It is not, as it stands, an *epistemological* query, for it emerges not out of the disputes of rhetoricians or philosophers, but is located in the pedestrian world of day-to-day rhetorical interchange. "How do you know?" is, in this sense, a call for justification from the pedestrian, not the theoretical world.

If one decides to *make* the question "How do you know?" a philosophical one by demanding *theoretical* explication of "fact", the metatheoretical questions "where shall the argument begin?" and "where will *stasis* occur?" arise. However, these questions presuppose that certain epistemological and ontological factors *already obtain*. It is taken as *given* that there *are* arguers, that there *is* argument, that persuasion *will occur* in the course of the interchange, that there *is* an immediate as well as a historical context for the debate, and that these factors are cognized *largely as what they, in reality, are.* Unless we are to believe that parties in such a theoretical dispute hold the paradoxical notion that communication and its constituents (source, message, channel, receiver, etc.) are themselves *wholly* opaque and unknowable (in which case communicative praxis could not transpire), these *minimally objective* constituents of reality *must* be viewed as *real*.

Indeed, at some fundamental level they must be held to be known veridically, *as they are in themselves*. To believe otherwise is to undermine the most basic foundations of rhetorical and communication theory and render exanimous the possibility of *all* communication (at the theoretical and metatheoretical level, *as well as at the level of praxis*).

It is in the move from praxis to theory that we confront again the presumption of pedestrian realism. The real existence of speakers, audiences, messages, channels, and contexts defines communication. Surely the mere appearance of a phenomenal world alone offers a slender reed upon which to lean the edifice of realist theory. But when coupled with the notion of human communication, wherein individuals successfully manage the phenomenal world symbolically, the force of realism's presumption is found. In other words, reality's "given in experience" is part of the presumption of realism, but communicability *about* that reality catalyzes the presumption as well.

To clarify this argument, consider the most extreme version of a popular alternative, namely, that the world is wholly constructed through symbolic interaction.[13] Without the presumption of a minimal realism, wherein there exists confidence in at least some basic furnishings of the world, coupled with at least some accurate communicable knowledge of that world, communication would cease to be a meaningful concept. Communicate what? About what? To whom? For what reasons? In what context? At what time? By what means? Communication makes sense only given a real, minimally tractable world. Clearly, communication occurs, and we get along quite well as a result, occasional misunderstanding aside. I take this to indicate that it is *the veracity of realism that drives communicative praxis, not the reverse*. Recall Thomas Reid's contention: "Sensation carries

---

[13]Protestations of my colleagues notwithstanding, I suggest that *any rhetoric unwilling to embrace a minimal realism is inexorably committed to the view that all of reality is symbolically constructed*. This is the case even of views claiming to be closely aligned with realism, for example, pragmatism. For *all* nonrealist views hold some version of the theory that humans do not have access to "antecedent reality" — that we can "never escape the process of signification in order to compare our signs with the thing signified" (Mackin, chap. 9). Nor will it do to disclaim, as the pragmatist does, that, although "portions of the world exist independent of human beliefs and actions," he/she "simply sets aside that hypothesis as one that can by definition never be supported in experience" (Mackin, chap. 9). To substantiate the first portion of this statement requires some *grounds* for belief in an independently existing world and only the realist provides these grounds. To make the latter portion of this statement is to squarely embrace skepticism, wherein reality is at best mind dependent, since ratiocination is all that remains when one removes experience (qua direct perception) as a source of veridical evidence for the existence of the external world. This is another version of the problem of versimilitude that vexes all nonrealist epistemologies. Because no nonrealist can have any grounds whatever for asserting the existence of the real world, all nonrealist theories — be they materialist, pragmatist, intersubjectivist, critical rationalist, en queue — are reducible to skepticism, subjectivism, and inevitably solipsism.

with it an immediate belief in the reality of the object, and this immediate certainty supplies us with a criterion of truth." He may be taken to mean that experience of the phenomenal world embodies its own rationale that there *is* an external world and that we can know *some* things about it (Thilly, 1914, p. 363). Communicative praxis provides a criterion of the truth of realism.

This criterion and the presumption for realism entail important consequences for the realist's burden of proof. Given the grounds of realism's presumption, both in "givenness" and in "the nature of communciation," as long as realism can be defended as a *plausible* option it is to be preferred over any alternative view. It is not sufficient for an antirealist to simply "cast doubt" on realism, for *some* evidence or argument can be brought to bear against *any* set of theoretical principles. To defeat realism's presumption, attacks against it must be "knock-down," that is, antirealist arguments must count, prima facie, against realism. Similarly, realist replies to the skeptic need merely be *plausible*. If an antirealist argument can be explained *plausibly* within a realist framework, antirealism should be rejected. The forgoing may be the rationale behind Moore's argument in favor of realism, detailed in the first section of this chapter. Making his argument explicit and viewing it against the backdrop of antirealist arguments, it contends: *In the absence of knock-down arguments against it, realism's presumption prevails. There are no knock-down arguments against realism, for plausible counterarguments against antirealism have been offered. Therefore, realism prevails.*

In the remainder of this section, I extend the analysis of realism's plausibility, showing that realism should retain its presumptive grounding for philosophical and rhetorical theory. This analysis renders implausible four of the six major antirealist arguments (summarized, pp. 25–26). I then address, in the next section, two remaining antirealist arguments and explore additional implications for rhetoric.

What formulation of realism, then, optimally meets the needs of a realist rhetoric and philosophical objections against it? I have defended elsewhere a realist-based rhetorical theory termed "rhetorical perspectivism" (Cherwitz & Hikins, 1982, 1983, 1986; Hikins & Zagacki, 1988). I do not propose to rehearse all the tenets of this theory, because they are readily available (see, in particular, Cherwitz & Hikins, 1986). Of immediate interest are those aspects of the theory interfacing rhetoric with realism: *relationality, consciousness,* and *meaning.* In explicating these concepts, recall the theory earlier termed "appearance realism." It will also be helpful at this juncture to preview briefly the importance the following discussion has for rhetorical theory. In short, the purpose is to preserve for rhetoric a *minimal objectivism,* wherein the most fundamental day-to-day furnishings of the pedestrian world are rendered *real,* that is, tractable to human perception

and cognition. This foundation established, we can explore the relevance of
minimal objectivism to rhetoric, and evaluate traditional and contemporary
issues in rhetoric, from a realist purview.

Relationality

Appearance realism argues that, in perception, we confront limited aspects
of the world. As I sit at my computer working on this manuscript, I can
easily view the keyboard and the monitor. But I am not now perceiving the
furnishings of my living room, because I am not in a position to do so. I
perceive only limited *aspects* of reality, because at any given time I stand in
a particular *perspective* to reality (the theory is often called "perspective
realism"). Even objects and events in relatively close proximity are percep-
tually unavailable. I cannot see the cables behind the monitor of my
computer, nor their electrical outlet; the table blocks my view. Perceiver,
table, and electrical equipment are *not standing in the relationships required
to permit me, at this moment, to view the electrical equipment.* Should I
move the table, these relationships would be altered and I would be able to
perceive the items in question. According to the theory, the relationships
accounting for perception in the example are but a few of the relationships
of which the world is comprised. For appearance realists, "relationality"
stands at the center of the claim that everything that is is what it is because
of its relationships to all else. It is not some elementary atomic or subatomic
particle, nor any other sort of primary *substance,* out of which entities in
the world emerge; rather, it is from *the relation* — conceived as an ontological progenitor of everything else — that all of existence acquires its
character.[14] The realist theory I defend argues that all relations are *internal*
and stresses that any given entity acquires its character from *all* relationships in which it stands to all else. On this view, even entities infinitely

---

[14]One might ask, "What, in the technical sense of the term employed in this essay, *is* a
relation — what is its character and composition?" To this question one can only reply that the
relation cannot be analyzed into notions of character or composition beyond the description
offered in the text. This is not because the relation defies other than a functional definition, but
because, in the words of McGilvary (1956), the relation is a "primitive notion." It is primitive
both ontologically (in that it is the progenitor of all that is) and epistemologically (in that it
determines what can be known about what is). Indeed, if one were able to identify
"components" or "characteristics" of relations, they would not then be the ultimate simples out
of which all else derives. That they are real components of the world, argued McGilvary, is
clear because "they are discovered by analysis of relational complexes" . . . "when we find
relations *in experience* we do not find just relations: we find relations between things; nor do
we find things alone: we find things-in-relation" (p. 226). It should be emphasized that
relationality is neither recondite nor transcendental. As McGilvary's explanation suggests,
relationality is found "in experience."

remote from one another spatially or temporally owe their nature to and can be described by their interrelationships. Even Pluto, as it exists at the precise instant of my writing these words *is* a function of its relationships, spatial and temporal, including even the nonsymmetrical cognitive relationships in which it stands to *me* as I "think about," "intend," or "observe" the planet.

This doctrine renders the most persistent antirealist arguments implausible, including the egocentric predicament and the problem of error (Arguments 1 and 3). To see how, consider the following example. Though I am not now perceiving the cables behind my computer, I do not, as an appearance realist, doubt for a moment that they are really there, carrying electricity. I am confident of this fact, because I know that *although the asymmetrical consciousness relation between myself and the equipment in question does not obtain, myriad other relationships continue to guarantee the existence through time of the electrical equipment.* For instance, the relationship of *extension* (the distance between the plugs and other points in my office) continues to exist, as does the relationship of the electrical current in the wires to certain levels of molecular and atomic excitation. These relations and numerous others make the electrical equipment what it is *and guarantee its existence over time when I am not perceiving it.*

Of course, we can imagine a short circuit suddenly occurring and the cables melting, turning into gases and ash in the process. But we know from basic science that the result is not the literal disappearance of the cables. Rather, changes are to be accounted for in terms of comprehensible, predictable *relational* notions: current, resistance, and so on. Because I have confidence in the *interrelationships* obtaining in the world, I know that as long as the image on my computer screen appears as it normally does, the power cord has not suffered a short circuit. Similarly, I can be confident that the great majority of things in the world have a stable character because they stand as complexes of relata in more or less stable relationships to all else. Where *change* or *process* is evident, it is not ad hoc or haphazard, but conforms to the constraints of relational possibility. Triangles cannot have four sides, a political act cannot be both expedient and inexpedient at the same time in the same way and under the same conditions, and a specific dimension of a moral act cannot be both good and bad at the same time and in the same sense.

Likewise, with respect to perception, relationality guarantees that the vast majority of things in the world are not radically altered when in the consciousness relation. Why? Because consciousness is but one among a vast number of relations constituting any given object of perception. To use an example from Harré (1986, p. 169), when Pasteur looked at infected tissue through the microscope he believed he saw invaders from outside the body — bacteria. When Lister looked at similar infected tissue, he believed that what he saw were human cells gone wild. But when Lister finally became convinced Pasteur was right, he didn't see anything different when he next looked at infected tissue through the microscope — the perceptual imagery was the same. Indeed there *is* a distinction between *seeing* and *seeing as*.

Relational theory thus unravels some of the mystery (and misanalysis) of common perceptual experiences. Consider the all too familiar antirealist ploy, the "gestalt switch." Examples include "seeing the duck as the rabbit," "seeing the opposing faces as a vase," and "seeing two lines that are the same length as of different lengths." As Harré and others noted, the "switch" is not itself a "perceptual achievement" — the duck doesn't *literally* disappear and become *replaced by* the rabbit, any more than Lister's "wild human cells" disappeared and were replaced by "hostile invaders" whenever Pasteur took his turn at the microscope (Harré, 1986, p. 169; Russman, 1987, pp. 66–67). Yet the gestalt switch deserves further analysis, for arguments drawn from it are easily rendered implausible and actually serve to fortify the doctrine of relationality and appearance realism. Consider first the applicability of the examples to real-world observations. As Russman (1987) noted,

> "the first thing to keep in mind here is that we are talking about line drawings. No one suggests we would have similar problems distinguishing real ducks from real rabbits. The duck–rabbit exploits the fact that a line drawing of rabbit ears can be made to look just like a line drawing of an open duck bill. To begin with, then, it would seem an inept generalization to argue from the way we handle ambiguous line drawings to problems about observation in general. (p. 67)

The epistemological and ontological puzzles generated by the gestalt switch are really pseudo-problems. As Russman noted, "[W]e know that a duck cannot at the same time be a rabbit." So "we inattentively conclude that a drawing of a duck cannot at the same time be a drawing of a rabbit." However, "drawings are not like the real thing in this respect. The duck–rabbit is at one and the same time a drawing of a duck and a drawing of a rabbit." (p. 67). In other words, there is no ontological problem, for the *drawing* can have both rabbit-like *and* duck-like properties. "Is there," asked Russman, "an epistemological problem" ensconced in this sort of example? No, for,

> Each thing we see in this world is so manifold in its properties that we can never advert to all of them at the same time. Some properties we notice almost all the time, others frequently, still others almost never. A live duck or a live rabbit may be thought of as cuddly companions or as tonight's dinner. (1987, p. 67)

Russman concluded with a statement fully compatible with and clearly illuminated by notions such as relationality and perspective: "Neither of these viewpoints is false. Ducks and rabbits both have properties that justify either way of seeing them. Both ways of seeing are as objective as you like: Objectivity is entirely compatible with selectivity of focus" (1987, p. 67).

From all this, one may conclude that the various forms and guises of the egocentric predicament signal neither an ontological quandary, nor an epistemological predicament, for they obtain far below the threshold required to "change the object of perception," just as my perception that "Tanya is taller than Dannelle" does not affect the relata involved (Tanya and Dannelle), nor the relationship by which I come to know a fact about them (their relative height). Having rejected the epistemological and ontological implications of the egocentric predicament, we see the error in extending claims like "trees make no sounds when they fall in forests devoid of people who might hear them" to the claim that "to be is to be perceived." According to our theory, *to be is to stand in some relationship to something else,* be that something else a sentient perceiver or a nonsentient "object." When the tree falls in a forest devoid of people, it still falls among the other things in the forest to which it is related. Vestiges of idealism, skepticism, constructivism, and egocentrism remain under our theory, *but they have now been rendered ontologically harmless and encompassed within the realist framework.* For instance, because, according to appearance realism, we are directly aware of only limited aspects of reality at any given time, many of our knowledge claims must be the product of *indirect* conceptualization (based on memory, extrapolation, prediction). Where direct perception is rendered difficult by "obstructions" (the desk blocks my view of the electrical outlet, alcohol impairs my vision, an ideology taints my judgment), egocentric factors may occasionally intrude.[15]

When limited direct perspectives illuminate complex issues, we should certainly be cautious about our conclusions, for humans are fallible animals. Similarly, when rhetors weave what they claim to be facts into their discourse, we should ask whether the narrative they are constructing is veridical. After all, according to Jacques Ellul, one of the hallmarks of propaganda is that it is composed not of falsity, but of truths mixed with falsehoods (Ellul, 1965, pp. 52–61). One can tell stories that report relationships that have been conjured up or misconstrue relationships, leading to but partial truth (just how this occurs is part of the discussion of meaning to follow). However, appearance realism guarantees that at the heart of our cognitions are direct perceptions of aspects of reality. This

---

[15]A popular postmodern tendency is to view virtually every artifact of human culture, discursive or otherwise, as "ideological." But such a view is merely a disguised version of the egocentric predicament. For a critique of the "all is ideological" notion see Hikins (1988).

grounding assures us that, although we occasionally err, the great majority of our judgments and perceptions are veridical. Given the success with which we communicate about and negotiate our day-to-day lives, this conclusion should not be surprising. Relationality places the egocentric predicament and related objections to antirealism in their proper context vis-à-vis reality.

This discussion of appearance realism also reveals defects in arguments against the view that all relations are internal. Rorty (1967) attacked the doctrine by claiming that, according to the theory, "the deprivation of a single property would force us to say that, in a nontrivial sense, the thing is no longer what it was" (p. 125). But we have seen that this is simply false, since the multiplicity of relational properties a given thing has at any one time guarantees that it will remain largely unchanged when only one or a few of its relationships are altered. If I suddenly decide to end my stint at the telescope and retire for the evening, Pluto is not significantly affected by the termination of the consciousness relationship between it and me! Myriad other relationships guarantee that Pluto's stable existence is insignificantly transformed by my, or anyone else's, observation.

Consciousness, then, qua egocentricity, is but one among many relational components of the world. It thus has relatively minuscule powers to "create reality." Put another way, its ontological powers are placed in their proper context and constrained by relationality. However, because consciousness *is* an essential feature of sentience (and so rhetoric as well), it requires further elaboration.

Consciousness

As with all entities, whether conceived as "physical" or "nonphysical," appearance realists analyze consciousness as a product of relationality Cherwitz & Hikins, 1986; McGilvary, 1956). Consciousness obtains when the CNS of a sentient being attains certain levels of sophistication and integration. Consciousness emerges out of this integration when a sentient being's perceptual apparatus stands in a particular relationship to an object.

Although the wetware of the CNS is, on this view, necessary for consciousness to occur, the analysis of physiological systems qua *physical* systems is incomplete, that is, insufficient to account for consciousness. If one were to rely on the physicalist explanation alone, one would immediately confront the sort of causal chain skepticism that plagued the Lockean theory of perception and its progeny. Such theories lead inevitably to the problem of verisimilitude. The appearance realist analyzes consciousness of internal states (joy, fear, pain, etc.) and external states (perception) as, like all else, a product of relationality. Relationality becomes the key to avoiding skeptical objections to causal chain accounts of human perception. Simply put, the relational theory of consciousness analyzes any act of *conscious* human perception into *two* necessary components: (a) the wetware of the central nervous system; *and* (b) the emergent relational properties of intentional consciousness. McGilvary explained:

> "See" names an occurrence analyzable, as I think, into a physiological process or act, *and* a relation of its own specific kind; and the grammatical object of the verb "see" does not name an object to which the *physiological act* physically passes over. It names a *term of this relation* whose other term is named by the grammatical subject of the verb. A relation of the same kind is found in occurrences that are named by the verbs "remember," "think," etc. In each of these cases, there is also a physiological process or act. This *act* does not "go over" to what is denoted by the grammatical object of the verb, but the *relation does* "go over" in the way in which any relation "goes over" from one term to another in relating the terms. (McGilvary, 1956, p. 46)

In other words, CNS wetware *is,* as neuroscience rightly observes, requisite to human perception. Qua physiological system, the CNS is a product of physical causality. But arising out of the causal process (itself the product of relationality) is an additional dimension, the consciousness dimension. Unlike mere physical wetware, the consciousness dimension is intentional — it is always consciousness *of* something. Hence it stands *directly,* as a term in a relation, to its object. At the level of mere bangings and shovings in the CNS, the machinations of sentience do not, as McGilvary tells us, "pass over" directly to the object of perception. But the consciousness relation *does* pass over immediately and directly to its object.

An analogy serves to clarify. When two individuals play "Tug of War" with a long rope, the rope is required to bind the two together as a causal medium out of which the contest can emerge. Likewise, axons, dendrites, and other CNS components offer a medium out of which consciousness can emerge. But in Tug of War during the act of pulling, the *relationship* of "Person X pulling Person Y with force Z" is immediate and unmediated by the rope. If we conceive the rope to be perfectly inelastic, the force of the tug doesn't move from the hand of one puller through an infinite number of points to the hand of the other puller; it happens immediately. The *relationship* "jumps back," to use a phrase employed by McGilvary, not incrementally, inch-by-inch along the rope, but instantly *across the length of the rope.* Whether the rope is 5 feet long or 500, when X pulls with a force of 50 pounds, the hands of Y feel the tug immediately (again assuming the rope is inelastic).

Compatible with recent work in realist psychology of perception (Carello, Turvey, Kugler, & Shaw, 1984; Gibson, 1979; Kelley, 1986) relationality permits one to explain how a direct intuition of the object of perception results from the complex relationships among perceiver and internal/external world. It also provides the *philosophical* explanation for how direct perception can occur, given that the CNS is a necessary component of perception.

With respect to antirealism, the relational theory of consciousness meets the argument (Argument 4) that modern neuroscience shows perception to be causal chain in nature. The realist counterargument suggests that the neurophysiological explanation (doubtlessly motivated by the urge for reductive elimination of nonmaterial aspects of consciousness) is incomplete, failing to take into account the relational nature of intentional consciousness. This analysis also renders the egocentric predicament (Argument 3) additionally implausible, for it further supports the notion that direct perception of at least some aspect of reality obtains.

The payoff for our common sense ways of understanding perception is handsome; we can reconcile such commonsense acts as "seeing the star Sirius" with the scientific fact that light from the star has taken years — "light years" — to travel to earth. If one could magnify Sirius' image enough to see the events occurring in its thermonuclear atmosphere, those events would, as I observe them now, have occurred many years ago because of the time taken (again, a relational notion) for light to reach the earth, but the events occurred, as we see them, "out there" in space. When we look up at Sirius on a clear night, the immediate given of experience is that we "see Sirius way out in space," not as some speck of light projected on the movie screen of the brain! This aspect of the perceptual experience of Sirius is accounted for by the relational theory of consciousness in the way just explained. In experience, one's perception of the star "jumps back" to the star qua external object of intentional consciousness.

Yet within the context of perception there occur what we call "errors." Perceptual errors have been used as a foil against realism (Argument 1): If we are directly aware of reality, how and why would we ever make mistakes? From all that has been said to this point, it should be clear why the problem of error is not a fatal retort to appearance realism. Unlike wholesale pedestrian realism, appearance realism denies that we are ever in contact with "all of reality all at once." Instead, we confront limited aspects of it from limited perspectives. On the basis of these limited perspectives, we garner facts with which to make extrapolated judgments (including judgments based on *rhetorical* probability). If we have ignored important aspects otherwise available to us because we are in "the grip of a philosophy," or if they are "hidden" from us because we are not in a position to see them, or if we are dreaming, suffer deficiencies or damage to our perceptual systems, or experience drug-induced hallucination, we err. But these are not grounds to abandon realism. On the contrary, in our day-to-day lives we make numerous decisions and successfully negotiate the great majority of situations on the basis of perceptual judgments and the *facticity component of our rhetoric*. Again realism's presumption should cause us to retain confidence in our most basic perceptions about the world. Dreams, error, hallucination, and illusion are occasional perturbations, not systematic distortions. As such, they can be accommodated *within the framework of appearance realism*. But the issue of consciousness and its relevance to a realist rhetoric requires more precise explication. We still must explain how objects of consciousness acquire *meaning,* and how meaning is enrooted in our language.

Meaning

The world is a great relational complex. Out of relations emerge all the properties and dimensions of existence, including what we conveniently categorize as physical and nonphysical. Brains and their associated systems are physical. Consciousness, as an intentional state of sentient beings, is nonphysical, as are ideas, values, and beliefs. Yet the physical and the nonphysical are inherently related, owing their existence to and bound by the ontological glue of relationality. As products of a fundamental onto-logical progenitor, *the relation,* all the furnishings of the world are unified. The Cartesian hobgoblin of substance dualism is avoided, and a comfort-able place for mind (as opposed to "matter") is found in our theorizing.[16]

As a consequence, conscious sentient entities are always inherently related to each and every dimension of the world, accounting for how it is that humans can *reflect* upon themselves and the world around them.[17] Because consciousness is an intentional act *of* sentient objects of reality *upon* other objects of reality and upon themselves, sentient beings may come to *understand the relationships in which they stand as terms.* Put

---

[16]The problem of dualism has vexed Western thought for centuries. Dualism's conceptual consequences (the mind/body problem and the subject/object distinction, to name two) have occasioned sulfurous debate and erected barriers between scientist and humanist, philosopher and rhetorician. The dismantling of many of these distinctions is at the heart of the efforts of a number of the authors contributing to this volume. The advantage of a relational approach to this issue is the possibility it affords to ontologically unify the world while preserving important distinctions, such as mind and body, as identifiable *aspects of the world,* as opposed to radically different *substances in the world.* The relational approach enables us to view the world as ontologically monistic while affirming that the world evidences *aspects,* the latter which account for plurality or *difference.* The issue here, of course, is the classical problem of unity in diversity or, in Platonic terms, the one/many problem.

[17]Spatial limitations preclude an explication of the notion of "reflection" in this essay. It should be clear, however, that reflection is of the greatest importance to an understanding of consciousness, human knowledge acquisition, meaning, and so too rhetoric. An exploration of reflection and its implications for rhetorical theory appears in Hikins (1989).

differently, reality has *meaning* for a sentient being because, like the terms in a mathematical relationship (such as the equation, $2 + 2 = 4$), the terms of the consciousness relationship are independent of the relationship as terms, but dependent upon the relationship as relata.

These features of relationality offer a way to explain the most microscopic components of language and meaning. All terms in a language, categorematic and syncategorematic (as well as prosodic and other non-verbal dimensions of language as symbol system), are *a product of relationality.* As sentient beings imbued with intentional consciousness, we can *associate* entities in the world (words, marks, gestures, intonation) with whatever collections of relata we choose. That is, we can limit and specify the collections of relata we will *regard* as the scope of a given symbol and associate those collections of relata *symbolically* with whatever other collections of relata we wish. A word or phrase, "Pete Rose, the Reds' manager," for example, embodies all the relationships in which we know the ballplayer to stand to us and all else. Another word or phrase, "played baseball," embodies the set of relata constituting the activity that is the national pastime. Another phrase, "in the 20th century," captures a bounded time period. By *associating* these three phrases I can embody what we all know to be a fact about the world: "Pete Rose, the Reds' manager, played baseball in the 20th century."

I emphasize that meaning is a process of limiting and associating relational complexes *by convention,* because everything is related to everything else in the larger, ontological sense. I take this notion of limiting as roughly equivalent to what I. A. Richards (1936) had in mind when he spoke of meaning as an "abridgment" of context. In the process of communication what a word "means is the missing parts of the context" (p. 34). The meaningful elements of a language thus become the missing parts of puzzles — *relational* puzzles. Linguistic terms make meaning possible by *embodying* the relationships among communicator, audience, and the world (Cherwitz & Hikins, 1986, pp. 83–88).

Naturally, there are limitations on human language use, limitations rooted in relationality. Just as humans perceive the world from limited perspectives, perspectives limit language use. As humans strive to broaden their powers of perception and cognition by manipulating the relational complex comprising the world, they occasionally misemploy language. Purposively or inadvertently, one may misidentify some aspect of reality by referencing it or its context inappropriately. One may speak of "the present king of France," and err because the relationship embodied by the locution does not obtain (there is no present king of France, though there once was and we know what it would mean to refer to him). Language can embody *relationships* successfully even when there are no *relata* currently standing *in* those relationships. We call such instances "errors," "mistakes," or "lies," depending on context (itself a relational notion). In some cases, linguistic terms may be concatenated in ways that are wholly inappropriate epistemologically and ontologically, such as when one utters the phrase, "Four-sided triangle." This locution is problematic *not* merely as a function of language, but because in the real world there can be no item of experience that is triangular and four-sided at the same time. *Relationality limits the ontological and epistemological possibilities of meaning.* Finally, there are instances of pseudo-language. As an instance of a sign system, "Da blivesta iste bevite" (unless it is a phrase in a language with which I am unfamiliar) does not embody *any* linguistic relationships (though as marks on a page it has its own relational structure, so we can make it a subject of *our* discourse).

A final implication of the relational theory of meaning concerns *universals.* Earlier I mentioned the medieval dispute focusing on whether universals are mere general terms in language (nominalism) or whether universals are actual qualities or entities to which common general terms refer (realism). Rhetorical scholars have eschewed extensive discussion of the theory of universals, except to decry the Platonic variety en passant, and even then as much on ideological grounds as on the basis of any considered theory of language (see, for example, McKerrow, 1989, pp. 91, 103–104, 105–106). This is regrettable, for one would assume that a discipline centrally concerned with language would find it requisite to provide its own treatment of the problem of universals. In the absence of such a discussion, the Platonic questions about common general terms in language will persist.

The relational theory of meaning offers a powerful account of universals that avoids some of the troubling aspects of the Platonic variety. A common general term (universal) is *a term in a sign system embodying relata or collections of relata, significant dimensions of which stand in the identity relationship to one another.* On this analysis, universals are not transcendental Platonic Forms, nor are they remote from the objects of reality they taxonomize. Instead, universal terms *mean* (embody) entities sharing *identical* relationships, that is, entities whose ontological character is shaped in whole or in part by identical relational constituencies. To be clear, "entity" here includes anything describable by common terms in a language, such as physical "things" (e.g., "dog," "cat," "house") or nonphysical "concepts" (e.g., "justice," "love," "fear"). Thus "dog" is a universal that *means* (embodies) those relationships that, together, describe any dog.

Meaning and universals are related in the following way. Humans, as conscious entities imbued with the ability to reflect upon the world, embody and associate in their language collections of identical relational qualities that do or could inhere *in the world* (collections of relata). All triangles are three-sided closed figures. These *relational* characteristics are *duplicated* in every triangle. I can understand what a triangle is just from the relational description lodged in its linguistic definition — just from the language — without ever having seen a triangle. I can understand what a chiliahedron is (a thousand-sided solid figure) even if there are no actual chiliahedrons now in existence. Consider the color red. When an object stands in relationship to a light source emitting light akin to that given off by the sun, and under mediating conditions similar to that of earth's atmosphere, and when such an object is perceived by a sentient being with the same cognitive powers as humans with normal vision, then, barring extraneous factors (such as the imposition of an opaque screen between object and observer), *the object will be red*. Likewise for universal *values*. For instance, when one's nation is the victim of aggression, the universal, "aggression," is a feature of the international *relationships* and *actions* between nations. Even though we may disagree in any given case whether a particular international incident is an act of aggression, any real act of aggression will exhibit and share *some significant measure* of the identical relational properties inhering in all aggressive acts.

The relational doctrine of universals runs counter to the familiar cliché that "meanings are in people." It is clear that, on the relational theory, an important dimension of meaning — the meaning of a universal — is located "in the thing itself." Thus although cognizance of meaning is a joint product of perceiver and perceived, meaning itself is, qua cognition, dependent upon the relational characteristics of reality. It is for this reason that we may properly say that the beauty of a striking sunset is *in the sunset*. For it is the actual observation of a sunset that occasions our ascription of beauty to it. Were it otherwise, we should be able to conjure up beautiful sunsets — or anything else — ex nihilo. That we cannot do so demonstrates that meaning is not exclusively human-dependent.

It is important to note the inherent differences between the relational theory of universals and its Platonic counterpart. For Plato, universals were perfect, immutable, timeless, ethereal, other-worldly paradigms. The individual, imperfect, mutable, instantiated, individualized furnishings of the world get whatever measure of reality they have from their imperfect participation in the Platonic universals (Forms). On the relational theory, we dispense with both the ontological duplication of a World of Forms and the nettlesome problem of transcendence which, in Plato's theory, made knowledge of reality virtually impossible to achieve for all but a few who committed their lives to philosophy. On the relational view, things in *this* world comprise the only reality there is. Universals — generated from relationships obtaining in *this* world — are as knowable as "things." I *know* what the color red is by experiencing red objects, what a dog is by experiencing dogs, what justice is by coming into contact with just acts.

But do not cultures disagree as to what properly belongs in any one category labeled by a universal? And don't some cultures make finer distinctions than others, as evidenced by the old saw of many Eskimo names for "snow"? Of course. Relational boundaries have numerous points of demarcation. Relational complexes can be taxonomized and, like diamonds, conveniently and productively cut along any number of cleavage lines. But also like diamond-cutting, not just any perspective on the world will work. Collections of relata will shatter like a miscut diamond if inappropriately taxonomized. Eskimos have numerous names for snow because such distinctions make sense in a world where understanding different types of snowfall is a matter of personal and cultural survival. In more temperate climates, differentiating numerous types of snowfall is less important. But in any case, baseballs and grapefruit are not included in the taxonomy. Eskimos taxonomize snow more discriminately than Tahitians, who don't taxonomize it at all, but Eskimos and Tahitians operate in the same relational complex as the rest of us. Thus, contrary to some uses of "perspective," there may *not* exist "contradictory truths" — and there may *not* exist contradictory realities (Brummett, 1976, pp. 28–35). Yet many alternative taxonomies — ways of looking at *the* world — *are* wholly compatible with each other, once one understands the implications of perspective as the term is used in appearance realism. On this view, genuine truths are *never* contradictory. They are only variant when taken as the product of significantly different perspectives — perspectives themselves rooted in relationality and communicated via the relational theory of language. This I take to be the source of the only theoretically respectable notion of "perspectivism," a term I believe is widely misunderstood and misapplied (compare Desilet, 1989, pp. 65–70.)

The relational theory of language affords additional insights into the issues we have discussed. Regarding the problem of error, it accounts for how errors in perception become errors in language use: because the embodiment function of language can be misused. It explains how the misuse of language can lead to human misunderstanding: because we take language use to be *at least in part* faithful narrative (a function of facticity) of *at least some* aspects of the world. This in turn provides a parsimonious explanation of why we get along so well in the pedestrian world: because facticity, though sometimes misused, normally affords us an "interface between knowledge" of at least some aspects of the real world and "rhetoric," the embodiment of that world in language (Cherwitz & Hikins, 1986, p. 71).

I have tried to show that the world and language are inherently interwoven through the doctrine of relationality. I have argued that relationality accounts for both accurate and inaccurate descriptions of the world. And I have suggested via the notion of facticity that such descriptions play an instrumental part in rhetorical discourse. It is for all these reasons that the quintessential feature of realist rhetoric inheres in "describing reality through language" (Cherwitz & Hikins, 1986, p. 62). Historically there has been competition for the "right" to garner such description among the arts and sciences. The competitors have often been avid antirealists. Not surprisingly, the lion's share of this competition issues from the world of science.

Realism in the Realms of Science, Rhetoric, and Ideology

Viewing meaning and language as the embodiment of relations, we are in a position to meet the last of the remaining arguments against realism (Arguments 5 and 6). The first suggests that the search for ultimate ontological explanations should be conducted in the realm of science, lately in the dominion of the microworld of quantum physics, not in the pedestrian macroworld. But the claim that the microworld is somehow more "real" than the macroworld is inherently flawed. For, unlike Plato's world of transcendental forms, existing quantitatively and qualitatively distinct from this world, the atomic world and the pedestrian world are part and parcel of a larger universe that harbors both. Both dimensions of reality are inherently related and we can come, indeed have come, to know both through the interrelated processes of perception, cognition, relationality, and meaning. As Russman (1987) persuasively argued in his critique of Kuhn, "there is always a neutral observation language available, lying under the biased one" (p. 2). With regard to *any* two theoretical treatments of the *real world,* there is never any ultimate incommensurability; relationality guarantees ontological continuity between the microworld and the macro-world, just as it enables humans, through the embodying function of language, to know and communicate about both.

Discoveries of contemporary physics provide no reason to abandon realism. The fact that, *molecularly,* water is a combination of two atoms of hydrogen for every atom of oxygen, and that individual molecules of water are not liquescent, does not deny the reality of liquidity when vast numbers of water molecules collect in one place (see Searle, 1983, pp. 265–266). Humans do not live *in* the microworld. Why, then, should the "reality" of the microworld be elevated to a position of preeminence vis-à-vis the macroworld? After all, the soldier crouching in a trench to avoid incoming artillery fire is likely to brook no patience with someone suggesting that Newtonian (classical) physics doesn't work in the realm of quanta. The hapless soldier cares not a whit about chasing subatomic particles in an effort to see if Heisenberg is right—what matters is the parabolic trajectory inscribed by the enemy's artillery shells. As physicist Paul Tipler noted, "Except for the interior of the atom and for motion at speeds near the speed of light, classical physics correctly and precisely describes the behavior of the physical world" (Tipler, 1976, p. 2). And as we have seen, there is even an epistemic and ontologic consistency between the microworld and the macroworld. They are bound by the same ontological (relational) glue. We are capable of coming to know both dimensions of the single universe and for this reason Harré's discussion of "varieties of realism" appropriate to the corresponding "realms" of reality is, with some qualification, attractive.

I have deferred discussing the "ideological argument" (Argument 6) until last, because its treatment will tie together the issues that have come before it, which were prerequisite for an understanding of the philosophical grounds of realist rhetoric. The ideological argument, it will be remembered, contends that realism is the enemy of tolerance — that one who claims to know will attempt to achieve rhetorical if not political hegemony over the masses. The ideological argument has as its devil-terms, "positivism," "objectivity," "truth," and "certainty" — in short, all the concepts in some way linked to *foundations* of our beliefs. We are urged to abandon entirely all claims to knowledge, replacing them with such notions as "probability," "contingency," and "belief" (Horne, 1989, p. 256; McKerrow, 1989, pp. 103–104). We should, in the words of one guru of contemporary rhetorical theorists, Richard Rorty, strive to "Keep the conversation going rather than to find objective truth" (Rorty, 1979, p. 377). Articulating a view that has become a staple of rhetorical scholarship, Robert Scott (1967) warned that "the breath of the fanatic hangs threatening to transmute the term [truth] to one of crushing certainty" (p. 12).

But is rhetoric's attack on truth-based philosophies cogent? I believe it is not. My argument relies heavily on a discussion by Richard Rorty's former student, David Russman. Russman (1987) contended that theories that deny truth-based epistemologies are subject as much, if not more, to co-optation by abusive ideologues than are truth-based ones (pp. 93–107). For example, one might contend that if truth cannot be distinguished from falsity (the skeptical view), then one can have no good reasons for persecuting anyone based on race, or political or religious beliefs. But on this view, it follows too that one can have no good reasons for *any* judgment or action, "including the opinion that persecution is wrong or should not be allowed and including any action taken to prevent it" (Russman, p. 93). Skepticism, then, favors neither oppression nor tolerance.

But the view that truth-based epistemologies foster intolerance is flawed at a much deeper level. Clearly not just *any* view held to be true or certain is pernicious; it is *specific* tenets — *specific* truths — that result in oppressive attitudes and behavior. The Nazi may hold to truths that are oppressive and intolerant. But a member of the German underground may hold to truths that not only foster tolerance, but do so by denying the tenets of Naziism. As Russman noted, the attack against intolerance can be made successfully without attacking all claims to truth (p. 95). It seems particularly obvious, for example, that an attack against truth claims asserting the desirability of toleration can only be counterproductive to the objectives of those whose goal it is to foster tolerance!

Additionally, there is not the slightest guarantee that abandoning claims to truth or certainty will guarantee a more tolerant world. To use Russman's example, one might argue, "There is no way to tell who is right in these religious or political matters; so I might as well impose my own views [beliefs?] by force, if I can" (p. 95).

Nor do appeals to history serve the cause of skepticism any better. Though thinkers like Russell and Popper tried to hang such atrocities as the Holocaust on views of truth and certainty, Russman pointed out that "the interbellum period in Germany had been characterized, not by metaphysical faith, but by skeptical despair. It was the *lack* of conviction and knowledge that made Germany an unresisting vacuum into which Hitler's vision could be poured" (p. 96). Surely convictions concerning the truth of egalitarianism, human justice based on the principle of equal rights for all, and the firm conviction in the falsity of ideologies based on intolerance offer greater protection against intolerance than does any general skepticism.

Finally, Russman spent a good deal of time attacking something that has come to stand at the heart of rhetorical analyses of human knowledge acquisition, namely, *convention*. Terms like "intersubjectivity," and the "social" or "linguistic construction of reality" are commonplace. But is a convention-based epistemology a viable alternative to more objectivist views? What if a society has, *by convention,* come to embrace intolerance? If there really are no truths, every historical instance of intolerance since the dawn of humanity has been the product of convention. This raises the following question: How does a society choose between competing candidates for a conventionally-held belief? Through a democratic process of majority agreement? Such a choice is certainly "democratic" and guarantees that those who have agreed on the belief in question have ultimate moral responsibility for its consequences. But, given the premise of no objective grounds for knowledge, such a certification process for belief is still *arbitrary* and any notion of individual moral responsibility must then be rendered vacuous. By definition, the decision was a good one because it was democratic. If democratic action becomes the sole criterion of ethical decision making, there simply is *no individual moral responsibility*.

Indeed, when convention alone — in the absence of any foundational truths whatsoever — is the arbiter of right and wrong, the phrase "tyranny of the majority" acquires a chilling maleficence. The question arises, "Where does one draw the boundaries encompassing a legitimate consensus-creating culture?" In 1939, greater Germany had clearly defined national boundaries and linguistic and cultural tradition as arguments in favor of a claim to autonomous culture. It is not unreasonable, then, to assume that the

Holocaust was the causatum of convention and consensus. Worse yet, it follows that, if the majority of Germans agreed with Hitler's "final solution," then not only was the decision "right" on the theory that cultures are the arbiter of what is right, it became more and more right as the percentage of the Aryan majority grew as more and more of its victims perished! Consensus theory must embrace the repugnant consequence that, had Hitler succeeded, his actions would have reached the epitome of moral propriety when the last non-Aryan ceased to exist. Admittedly, conviction on social issues can lead to intolerance. But, as we have seen, skepticism, even mitigated by democratic conventionalism, fares no better and likely much worse. It should be obvious that, to avoid intolerance, tolerant convictions are required, for as Russman noted, "toleration is based on conviction" (p. 105).

For rhetoric, the implications of all that has been said to this point can be summarized as follows. Humans are conscious, intention-imbued entities invested with the ability to *know* at least some aspects of the natural world in which they live. They also possess the ability to communicate that knowledge by use of symbol systems. Symbol systems have the capacity to embody both physical and nonphysical dimensions of experience, based on meaning, which is in turn grounded in the ontological properties of relations. Thus human experiences, physical, mental, ethical, and aesthetic, are as much a part of the real world as are the human communicators who populate it. Confident that reality is at least in part knowable, humans weave such knowledge, in the guise of facticity, into their efforts to persuade others, even on contingent issues where the ultimate truth is as yet unattainable. Because rhetoric is in this way anchored in reality, humans are assured at least minimally objective criteria with which to compose discourse, evaluate rhetorical praxis, and generate theory. Let us now compare realist rhetoric with the alternative theories offered in this volume.

REALIST RHETORICAL THEORY
AND ITS ALTERNATIVES

Theoretical conflicts take various guises. As philosopher Gilbert Ryle (1954) once observed, "One familiar kind of conflict is that in which two or more theorists offer rival solutions to the same problem." Yet, as he noted, "more often, naturally, the issue is a fairly confused one, in which each of the solutions proffered is in part right, in part wrong and in part just incomplete or nebulous" (p. 1). The panoply of issues treated in this book are complex, having undergone multiple transformations in the history of ideas. It would be incredible to suppose that Ryle's observations did not apply, in some respects, to *all* of them, realism included. Consequently, my commentary on the competing theories is in part conciliatory, in part critical.

One of the first questions confronting the reader is, "What difference does realism make for rhetorical theory?" A complete answer to this question can emerge only at the conclusion of the comparison that follows, but a partial answer can be articulated at the outset. I suggested in the opening pages of this chapter that one thing characterizing rhetoric is its pedestrian character. While physicists, chemists, logicians, astronomers, archaeologists, and a host of other scholars must look to remote times and/or esoteric places for the objects of their inquiry, our object of inquiry is all around us, inseparable from what those who use it call "the real world." Rhetorical discourse is found in the pubs and union halls, churches and synagogues, auditoriums, parks, courts, legislative halls, in the seats of power and the dominion of the powerless. Although, historically, we have studied the less-frequent, perhaps even less-important, forms of rhetoric, such as the "great man giving the great speech," presidential discourse, and so on, even these artifacts appear in and are about the real world.

This, I have argued, frames part of the presumption of realism, for it should be clear to us all that rhetoric is about real people and their real problems — real issues of local, national, and international consequence. It is about the need for a new sewer system, where to put the war monument, what controls to place on the economy, what beer to buy, car to drive, store to patronize. Thus, the first conclusion about the importance of realism to rhetoric and its relationship to other *philosophically-grounded* rhetorics is: Despite the lipservice paid to praxis by competing theories, *realism is the only theory that preserves intact the world of rhetorical praxis.*

A comparison of the *philosophical* positions of competing theorists vis-à-vis realism reveals the significance of this conclusion. On the realist view, a starving child in Ethiopia is not, as the idealist would have us believe, an idea in the mind of the perceiver — to treat him/her as such is to do more than to wrench the victim from the real world of pain and suffering and the material *causes* of that pain and suffering. It is to treat the victim with a callousness that must eventually breed indifference. Human actions, like other events in the natural world, are real and we have access to them. As a result, we are at times motivated, even inspired, to meliorate suffering and enhance good, knowing that our own actions affect real people in a real world. The idealist must always confront the problem of solipsism.

Or consider the thesis that our *belief* that the existence of poverty in the third world is a serious problem is true because it is pragmatically useful to believe it is true. Such a claim is illicit — if not also callous — on pragmatism's own grounds. There is, I suggest, *no* obvious pragmatic payoff, in the short run or the long term, in viewing the famine in Ethiopia — or a host of other pressing social issues — as requiring empathetic understanding and solution.

Indeed, a pragmatist might well argue persuasively—as the Social Darwinists once did—that the "useful" thing to do is let "nature take its course" and reap the benefits of scarce resources for ourselves, both now and in the future.

Perhaps that is one reason William James felt constrained to introduce the notion of God into his pragmatism (James, 1981, bk. 8)—to avoid the troubling possibility that the vision he shared with Dewey and Peirce, namely, that "true" (on the pragmatist's notion of "true") ideas are useful because they contribute to general harmony, might be co-opted (see Russman, 1987, pp. 118–125). After all, "harmony" isn't that far removed, etymologically, from "order." One need not stretch credulity to understand how Hitler's vision of harmony could subvert pragmatism in the ways envisaged previously in my discussion of tolerance. On pragmatic grounds alone, who is to say Hitler's vision of phronesis is any worse than anyone else's? Had he succeeded, the world today would likely be just as harmonious and orderly, probably much more so! And if Hitler the pragmatist is an alarming thought, Hitler the deconstructionist is horrific. Imagine Hitler in Fredrick Jameson's shoes, uttering the statement to his inner circle that what Germany and the world needs is "a sort of militant atheism, ferociously seeking to clear the ground of human interaction of all traces of a transcendental signified"? (Jameson, 1972, p. 182). Nor, in the same context, is the gentler prose of the constructivist any less reassuring, once one learns the larger project behind the urge to discover "the whole range of symbolic devices that might be used to secure cooperation and manage meaning" (Brummett, chapter 3).

What has gone wrong in these philosophical approaches to rhetoric? It is the refusal to assent to anything known independent of language. We have already seen the contribution paid to this insolvent fund by all manner of illicit skeptical arguments (error, illusion, the gestalt switch, egocentrism). Postmodernism has combined these with the notion that language, and hence conceptualization, is ontologically prior to reality—that there is no "antecedent reality" of any sort. This dogma has led to the view that "every object is constituted as an object of discourse" (Laclau & Mouffe, 1985, p. 107). But taken literally, if ever intended literally, this assertion borders on the incoherent. In the course of our lives, we are confronted innumerable times and frequently very suddenly, with objects and events we have never before experienced. Subsequent linguistic interactions may help us understand some aspects of newly confronted objects, but such interactions do not literally *constitute* them. Moreover, it is frequently the qualities, properties, and behaviors of such novel experiences—characteristics *in the object of inquiry*—that structure our discourse. The AIDS virus was not "constituted" ex nihilo by some clever sociolinguistipath [sic]; it emerged out of the natural world via natural causes and itself contributed, *in part,* to the constitution of our language—we talk about it because it kills us. My dog is very clever but I'm convinced she doesn't have a symbol system that "constitutes" her objects of perception. Yet she can open gates with her paws, chase tennis balls, and distinguish between many different people. Anyone with a clever pet is likely to bet that the animal "sees" pretty much the same object as we humans do. That we see *additional* dimensions (political, ideological, religious) is just to argue that there is a difference between *seeing* and *seeing as*. Realism is the only position in this book that does not waffle on this issue, and hence is the only position that preserves the real world of rhetorical praxis, where both *object seen* and *object seen as* influence humans and contribute to their rhetoric.

Realist rhetoric, therefore, is the only theory that permits us to see humans in the full range of their uniqueness and interactions—including rhetorical interactions—as part and parcel of the natural world they inhabit. *Not* the world of 18th century "naive realism" or the "common sense" realism of Thomas Reid (1787/1970), but the relational world of the appearance realist. In such a world, the facticity of human triumphs and sufferings—from moon landings to AIDS deaths—can be reported in the narratives that comprise our rhetoric—*in our linguistic descriptions of reality*—and in a way that makes concepts like "narrative fidelity" again the grounds for a full-bodied canon of rhetorical invention. However, because the world is conceived by the appearance realist as inherently relational in nature, facticity will not be limited to the mere pushings and shovings of the materialist metaphysic (though these will certainly be included). Denied is the contention that mental states (pains, fears, hopes, desires, thoughts, and the like) are ultimately reducible to or *identical with* brain states (see Searle, 1983, pp. 262–272; compare McGuire, chap. 6). That a thought, feeling, or idea is not *itself* a "physical stuff" is so obvious that John Searle speculated that those holding the contrary notion never "considered his own terrible pain or his deepest worry" (Searle, 1983, p. 263). On the grounds of realism, the nonmaterial dimensions of human experience bearing on ethics and aesthetics, and their attendant rhetorical praxis, are preserved without repairing to the exclusively mentalistic account of the idealist. In response to the diametrically opposed claims, "All is material" and "All is mental," the appearance realist proclaims, "All is relational." Both material and mental phenomena receive equal attention. Realism is unfettered by the traditional problem of dualism, because "mental" and "physical" are not held to demarcate ontological differences, but instead reflect differentiable *properties* emerging out of relationality.[18]

---

[18]Materialism, like the doctrine of a relational world, is grounded in its own version of an elementary ontological progenitor. As McGuire notes, " 'Materialism refers to any and all theories which explain reality and real events as composed of underlying matter and explicable

Consequently, from the standpoint of everyday human concerns, Michael Hyde's poignant recounting of Jory Graham's tragic bout with cancer can be told with as much authenticity via the realist rhetoric I have constructed as with the existential narrative he proffers (Hyde, chapter 7). Authenticity is as meaningful to and significant for the appearance realist as it is to the existentialist. In a rhetorical theory grounded in appearance realism, "authenticity" (in Hyde's sense of the term) is but one among myriad aspects of "reality" (in my sense of the term)—at the point of criticism engaged by Hyde, the terms are in one sense equivalent. In addition to permitting an escape from the sort of dominating, antiseptic, clinicalist rhetoric under whose oppression Graham suffered, realist rhetoric permits us to measure our humanity consonant with our science. It inhibits the tendency to polarize physical reality and existential reality. Most importantly, it works against such dyadic oppositions as science/humanism by underscoring that *all* human experience is experience *of* and *in* the relational world.

Rhetorical realism as I have sketched it in these pages also offers a foundation for a more useful methodology for *criticism* and *analysis* than that offered by other theories. My strongest competitors in this regard are critical rationalism, which I discuss later, and pragmatism, which deserves special treatment because of its enormous popularity in contemporary rhetorical theory.

Let us ask a question familiar to the pragmatist: "Which theory of the way the world is—realism or pragmatism—is more *useful* in explaining phenomena?" Well, in the macroworld in which rhetoric operates, realism wins hands down. Why? Consider ethics, even rhetorical ethics. The concepts of *real* time-bound, historically-located human survival, health, welfare, truthfulness, propriety, belief and so on provide all that is required to assess everything from the quality of a speech or decision to the cross-cultural features of discourse and action. Moreover, specific

---

by appeals to causation and other conditions or properties of matter" (chap. 6). But when we inquire as to what "matter" is, and at what level of the macroworld or microworld we are to look for causation, we face a quandary. The further we look for "underlying matter" as the source for causation of macroworld characteristics, the more we are obliged to look at ever *more microscopic* levels. Eventually, we find ourselves in the subatomic realm where the notion of "matter" has less and less affinity to the events of the macroworld and more and more affinity to the notion of relationality expatiated in this essay. In this realm, *relational* notions, such as "temporal and spatial coordinates as measured by different inertial observers" (Goldberg, 1984, p. 151) appear to cut more explanatory ice than do "properties of matter," whatever such a phrase might mean. Nor is it immediately obvious what notions like "space" and "time" have to do with matter, to say nothing of the intentional states of sentient beings. In short, although we are not accustomed to think in these terms, it makes more sense to suggest that matter (along with everything nonphysical) emerges out of relationality than vice versa.

instances exemplifying these concepts are clearly more immediately attainable than the remote pragmatist goals of eventual "ultimate harmony," "impulse organization," or *phronesis;* in Russman's words, the former "emphasize more intermediate notions of good" (1987, p. 131). As such, they are also likely to provide clearer explanation and more powerful prediction, for they are real events in a real world, and we are able to appeal directly to them and the world as a basis for inductive generalizations about the future.

The pragmatist, at least according to James Mackin (Chap. 9), cannot do so. Laboring under the yoke of a misguided postmodern skepticism and philosophy of language that begins with the assertion that "our notions of reality cannot be compared to reality itself," every instance of experience is, for the pragmatist, an uncertain step in a wholly darkened room. Unable to assert that we can see well enough to make *at least some minimally objective* reality claims about the room, we can never be sure someone isn't switching the furniture at every instance to render our experiences in the next moment radically different from our experiences now. But notice, replies the realist, that our experiences are *not* radically different at each moment—they are largely duplicative when it comes to the science *and* the day-to-day workings of our macroworld. And for both the realist and the pragmatist, we know this latter fact because "What we do know is what we have interacted with" and beliefs are "warranted by the interaction that constitutes discovery" (Mackin, chap. 9). It is telling that here the pragmatist falls back into objectivist language. Without it, experience becomes wholly ad hoc and no generalizations about the future, scientific or otherwise, can be generated. In short, the pragmatist's "science" *requires* a real, knowable world (not just the assumption of a real, knowable world) as much as the realist's does. But the pragmatist gags on the gnat of realism, while swallowing whole the elephant of scientific prediction!

This is the great paradox in the American pragmatist tradition: the denial of knowledge about a real world while at the same time an almost reverent invocation of modern science as a useful tool of prediction. The paradox results in some odd incoherencies, most notably the curious fact that the pragmatist is more confident in predicting the future than in assenting to the immediately given of the present!

As a result of this, it is the realist who can better answer the question that began this discussion—it is the realist who can offer the more *useful* explanations. The realist's account permits us to generate explanations and make predictions with just as much, and likely much more, confidence than the pragmatist. Moreover, realism offers a more parsimonious account for *why* our explanations work (because those explanations are rooted in the way the world *is*), and any theory that can answer the "why question" is more useful than one that cannot or will not. It is ironic that such usefulness must be argued for by the realist in the attempt to persuade other theorists; the pedestrian just yawns, for he/she knows this already!

I close with a brief commentary on critical rationalism. In my view, critical rationalism provides a large measure of the methodology for realism. It shares with realism the belief that the world is real and that much of it is not dependent on human attitudes, beliefs, values, or communication for its existence. Although confusing knowledge with *certainty* (thus erring on the side of caution, much like the pragmatist), critical rationalism offers one important caution that is wholly consonant with appearance realism. Either because humans are inherently fallible animals (a view clearly held by the critical rationalist), or because we only see a limited portion of reality at any one time (the perspectivist view of the appearance realist, as well as, implicitly, the critical rationalist), or both, we must always be cautious about elevating beliefs and opinions to the status of knowledge. And when we do elevate any claim to know, we must constantly reflect upon it, test the facticity on which it in part rests, and continually reassess it. In short, we must subject it to our best rational critique. This is the spirit in which appearance realism is offered. By recognizing that humans are only privy to limited collections of relata in the relational world, and that rhetors can and do tell false narratives (that is, offer false descriptions of reality), there always remains, for the appearance realist, the injunction to expand one's own perspective and the perspective of others. It is here that the realist rhetoric I have developed intersects most directly with all forms of rhetorical praxis. It is here that discourse, and especially *argument,* find their natural home, where claims to knowledge are inspected in the marketplace of ideas, and accepted, improved upon, or rejected.

To be intellectually honest while standing in the shadow of Ryle's commentary on the partial truth of virtually all theoretical endeavors, let me end with a challenge to those who in the future might develop rhetorical realism. The challenge concerns two issues often raised against the theory. One is the charge of "circularity," and the other is an invitation to develop further the notion of relationality. The first of these issues is a pseudo-issue. The claim is made that realists argue circularly because the givenness of reality is assumed and used in the premises of the argument. This is a pseudo-issue because, as a careful reading of the first section of this Chapter makes clear, reality is not *argued for* in the sense in which a syllogism is argued for or an axiom is *proposed* and subsequently employed as a premise in a deduction. Reality is not the conclusion of an argument or a proposal, it is a given of experience, denied only on the basis of torturous and illicit arguments.

The second issue is genuine. To consider relationality as a foundational ontological and epistemological principle is to see the world in a radically different way than most philosophers, East or West, Continental or

Analytic, have come to see it. Even building on the work of others, it will require a significant effort to construct a full-blown relational philosophy. I leave it to the reader to discover in future readings in both rhetoric and philosophy how often the terms, "relation," "relational," "relationality," and, yes, even "relationship" appear, along with kindred terms like "perspective," "aspect," and "context." In my view, a *theory of communication,* with relational analysis at its center, which enlarges upon the relational theories of ontology, epistemology, meaning, and rhetoric beckons as a task for the future.

REFERENCES

Aristotle. (1933–1935). *Metaphysics* (Vols. 1–2; H. Tredennick, Trans.). Cambridge, MA: Harvard University Press.

Aristotle. (1939). *Art of rhetoric* (J. H. Freese, Trans.). Cambridge, MA: Harvard University Press.

Aronson, J.L. (1984). *A realist philosophy of science.* London: Macmillan.

Bergin, T.J., & Fisch, M.H. (1958). *The new science of Giambattista Vico.* Ithaca, NY: Cornell University Press.

Bhaskar, R. (1978). *A realist theory of science* (2nd ed.). Brighton, England: Harvester.

Breasted, J.H. (1906). *Ancient records of Egypt, Vol. III.* Chicago: University of Chicago Press.

Broad, C.D. (1925). *The mind and its place in nature.* London: Routledge & Kegan Paul.

Brummett, B. (1976). Some implications of "process" or "intersubjectivity": Postmodern rhetoric. *Philosophy and Rhetoric, 9,* 21–51.

Butchvarov, P. (1966). *Resemblance and identity: An examination of the problem of universals.* Bloomington, IN: Indiana University Press.

Butler, J.D. (1951). *Four philosophies and their practice in education and religion.* New York: Harper & Brothers.

Campbell, P.N. (1972). *Rhetoric: A study of the communicative and aesthetic dimensions of language.* Belmont, CA: Dickenson.

Carello, C., Turvey, M.T., Kugler, P.H., & Shaw, E.E. (1984). Inadequacies of the computer metaphor. In M. Gazzaniga (Ed.), *Handbook of cognitive neuroscience* (pp. 234–236). New York: Plenum.

Cherwitz, R.A., & Hikins, J.W. (1982). Toward a rhetorical epistemology. *Southern Speech Communication Journal, 47,* 135–162.

Cherwitz, R.A., & Hikins, J.W. (1983). Rhetorical perspectivism. *Quarterly Journal of Speech, 69,* 249–266.

Cherwitz, R.A., & Hikins, J.W. (1986). *Communication and knowledge: An investigation in rhetorical epistemology.* Columbia, SC: University of South Carolina Press.

Churchland, Patricia S. (1986). *Neurophilosophy: Toward a unified science of the mind--brain.* Cambridge, MA: MIT Press.

Churchland, Paul M. (1988). Cognitive neurobiology: A computational hypothesis for laminar cortex. *Biology and Philosophy, 1,* 25–51.

Conley, T.M. (1990). *Rhetoric in the European Tradition.* White Plains, NY: Longman.

Cooper, L. (1932). *The rhetoric of Aristotle.* New York: Appleton-Century-Crofts.

Corcoran, J. (1989). Argumentations and logic. *Argumentation, 3,* 17–43.

Descartes, René. (1960). *Meditations on first philosophy.* (L.J. Lafleur, Trans.). Indianapolis, IN: Bobbs-Merrill. (Original work published 1641)

Desilet, G. (1989). Nietzsche contra Burke: The melodrama in dramatism. *Quarterly Journal of Speech, 75,* 65-83.

Ellul, J. (1965). *Propaganda: The formation of men's attitudes.* New York: Knopf.

Fisher, W.R, (1987). *Human communication as narration: Toward a philosophy of reason, value, and action.* Columbia, SC: University of South Carolina Press.

Fisher, W.R. (1984). Narration as a human communication paradigm: The case of public moral argument. *Communication Monographs, 51,* 1-22.

Fitzgerald, M.J. (1987). *Richard Brinkley's theory of sentential reference.* Leiden, Netherlands: E.J. Brill.

Fodor, J.A. (1975). *The language of thought.* New York: Thomas Y. Crowell.

Fodor, J.A. (1983). *The modularity of mind.* Cambridge, MA: MIT Press.

Gazzaniga, M.S. (1984a). Advances in cognitive neurosciences: The problem of information storage in the human brain. In G. Lynch, J.L. McGaugh, & N.M. Weinberger (Eds.), *Neurobiology of memory and learning.* (pp. 78-88). New York: Guilford.

Gazzaniga, M.S. (Ed.). (1984b). *Handbook of cognitive neuroscience.* New York: Plenum.

Gibson, J.J. (1967). New reasons for realism. *Synthese, 17,* 162-172.

Gibson, J.J. (1979). *The ecological approach to visual perception.* Boston: Houghton-Mifflin.

Goldberg, S. (1984). *Understanding relativity: Origin and impact of a scientific revolution.* Boston: Birkhäuser.

Golden, J.L., Berquist, G.F., & Coleman, W.E. (1989). *The rhetoric of western thought* (3rd ed.). Dubuque, IA: Kendall/Hunt.

Grayling, A.C. (1985). *The refutation of skepticism.* LaSalle, IL: Open Court.

Gregg, R.B. (1984). *Symbolic inducement and knowing: A study in the foundations of rhetoric.* Columbia, SC: University of South Carolina Press.

Gregg, R.B. (1987). Communication epistemology: A study in the "language" of cognition. [Review of *Communication and knowledge: An investigation in rhetorical epistemology* by Richard A. Cherwitz & James W. Hikins.] *Quarterly Journal of Speech, 73,* 232-242.

Grimaldi, W.M.A. (1980). *Aristotle, Rhetoric I: A commentary* (vol.1). New York: Fordham.

Harré, R. (1986). *Varieties of realism: A rationale for the natural sciences.* Oxford, England: Basil Blackwell.

Harré, R., & Secord, P.F. (1972). *The explanation of social behavior.* Oxford, England: Basil Blackwell.

Hauser, G. (1986). *Introduction to rhetorical theory.* Philadelphia: Harper & Row.

Hicks, G.D. (1938). *Critical realism: Studies in the philosophy of mind and nature.* London: Macmillan.

Hikins, J.W. (1988, May). *The epistemological grounds of ideological criticism.* Paper presented at the Conference on Rhetoric and Ideology: Compositions and Criticisms of Power, Rhetoric Society of America Annual Meeting, Arlington, Texas.

Hikins, J.W. (1989). Intrapersonal discourse and its relationship to human communication: Rhetorical dimensions of self-talk. In Roberts, C.V., Watson, K.W., & Barker, L.L. (Eds.), (1989). *Intrapersonal communication processes: Original essays.* New Orleans, LA and Scottsdale, AZ: SPECTRA Incorporated and Gorsuch Scarisbrick, pp. 28-62.

Hikins, J.W. and Zagacki, K.S. (1988). Rhetoric, philosophy, and objectivism: An attenuation of the claims of the rhetoric of inquiry. *Quarterly Journal of Speech, 74,* 201-228.

Hirst, R.J. (1967). Realism. In Paul Edwards (Ed.), *The encyclopedia of philosophy.* (Vol. 7., 77-83). New York: The Free Press.

Holt, E.B., Marvin, W.T., Montague, W.P., Perry, R.B., Pitkin, W.B., & Spaulding, E.G. (1912). *The new realism.* New York: Macmillan.

Horne, J. (1989). Rhetoric after Rorty. *Western Journal of Speech Communication, 54,* 247-259.

James, W. (1981). *Pragmatism*. Indianapolis: Hackett.

Jameson, F. (1972). *The prison-house of language*. Princeton, NJ: Princeton University Press.

Kant, I. (1952). Preface to the second edition, 1787. The critique of pure reason. In R.M. Hutchins (Ed.), *Great books of the western world* (pp. 5-13). Chicago: Encyclopedia Britannica. (Original work published 1787).

Keat, R., & Urry, J. (1975). *Social theory as science*. London: Routledge & Kegan Paul.

Kelley, D. (1986). *The evidence of the senses: A realist theory of perception*. Baton Rouge, LA: Louisiana State University Press.

Laclau, E., & Mouffe, C. (1985). *Hegemony and socialist strategy: Towards a radical democratic politics*. W. Moore & P. Cammack, (Trans.), London: Verso.

Liddell, H.G., & Scott, R. (compilers). (1968). *A Greek-English lexicon*. Oxford, England: Clarendon.

Locke, J. (1959). *Essay concerning human understanding*. New York: Dover.

Margolis, J. (1986). *Pragmatism without foundations: Reconciling realism and relativism*. Oxford, England: Basil Blackwell.

McGilvary, E.B. (1933). Perceptual and memory perspectives. *Journal of Philosophy, 30*, 310-330.

McGilvary, E.B. (1956). *Toward a perspective realism*. La Salle, IL: Open Court.

McInerny, R.M. (1963). *A history of western philosophy, Vol. 1*. Chicago: Henry Regnery.

McKerrow, R.E. (1989). Critical rhetoric: Theory and praxis. *Communication Monographs, 56*, 91-111.

Moore, G.E. (1903). The refutation of idealism. *Mind, 12*, 433-453.

Murphy, J.J. (1983). *A synoptic history of classical rhetoric*. Davis, CA: Hermagoras.

Nelson, J.O. (1967). Moore, George Edward. In Paul Edwards (Ed.), *The encyclopedia of philosophy. Vol. 5.*, (pp. 372-380). New York: The Free Press.

Nunn, T.P. (1909-1910). Are secondary qualities independent of perception? *Proceedings of the Aristotelian Society, 10*, 191-218.

Orr, C.J. (1978). How shall we say: "Reality is socially constructed through communication?" *Central States Speech Journal, 29*, 263-274.

Pellionisz, A., & Llinás, R. (1985). Tensor network theory of the metaorganization of functional geometries in the central nervous system. *Neuroscience, 16*, 245-273.

Perelman, Ch., & Olbrechts-Tyteca, L. (1969). *The new rhetoric: A treatise on argumentation*. Notre Dame, ID: University of Notre Dame Press.

Perry, R.B., (1910). The ego-centric predicament. *Journal of Philosophy, 7*, 393-401.

Reid, T. (1970). *An inquiry into the human mind,* ed. T. Duggan (Ed.). Chicago: University of Chicago Press. (Original work published 1787).

Richards, I.A. (1936). *The philosophy of rhetoric*. London: Oxford University Press.

Rorty, R.M. (1967). Relations, internal and external. In Paul Edwards (Ed.), *The encyclopedia of philosophy*, (Vol. 7. pp. 125-132). New York: The Free Press.

Rorty, R. (1979). *Philosophy and the mirror of nature*. Princeton, NJ: Princeton University Press.

Rorty, R. (1982). *Consequences of pragmatism (Essays: 1972-1980)*. Minneapolis: University of Minnesota Press.

Ross, W.D. (Ed. & Trans.). (1930). *The works of Aristotle*. Oxford: Clarendon Press.

Rowland, R.C. (1987). Narrative: Mode of discourse or paradigm? *Communication Monographs, 54*, 264-275.

Russman, T.A. (1987). *A prospectus for the triumph of realism*. Macon, GA: Mercer University Press.

Ryle, G. (1954). *Dilemmas*. Cambridge, England: Cambridge University Press.

Sayers, S. (1958). *Reality and reason*. New York: Basil Blackwell.

Scott, R.L. (1967). On viewing rhetoric as epistemic. *Central States Speech Journal, 18*, 9-17.

Searle, J.R. (1983). *Intentionality*. New York: Cambridge University Press.

Stacks, D.W., & Andersen, P.A. (1989). The modular mind: Implications for intrapersonal communication. *Southern Speech Communication Journal,* 273–293.

Spaulding, E.G. (1918). *The new rationalism.* New York: Henry Holt.

Thilly, F. (1914). *A history of philosophy.* New York: Henry Holt.

Tipler, P.A. (1976). *Physics.* New York: Worth.

Trigg, R. (1977). *Reason and commitment.* Cambridge, England: Cambridge University Press.

Trigg, R. (1980). *Reality at risk.* Brighton, England: Harvester.

Vision, G. (1988). *Modern anti-realism and manufactured truth.* New York: Routledge.

Waddell, C. (1988). The fusion of horizons: A dialectical response to the problem of self-exempting fallacy in contemporary constructivist arguments. *Philosophy and Rhetoric, 21,* 103–115.

Woodruff, P. (Trans.). (1983). *Plato: Two comic dialogues: Ion, Hippias Major.* Indianapolis, IN: Hackett.

Young, M.J., & Launer, M.K. (1988). *Flights of fancy, flight of doom: KAL 007 and Soviet-American rhetoric.* Lanham, MD: University Press of America.

_____ *Chapter 3*
Relativism and Rhetoric

Barry Brummett

> Several years have now elapsed since I first became aware that I had accepted,
> even from my youth, many false opinions for true, and that consequently
> what I afterwards based on such principles was highly doubtful; and from that
> time I was convinced of the necessity of undertaking once in my life to rid
> myself of all the opinions I had adopted, and of commencing anew the work
> of building from the foundation, if I desired to establish a firm and abiding
> superstructure in the sciences. (Descartes, 1641/1968, p. 26)

So, poignantly, begins Descartes' First Meditation. Descartes stands at the
fulcrum of Western philosophy, summarizing ancient concerns and framing
modern answers to what has been aptly termed the "Cartesian anxiety"
(Bernstein, 1983, pp. 16–20): What can people know for sure and how can
we know it? On what firm "foundation" can we build a method and
knowledge that will not, once youth is passed, prove "highly doubtful"?
Which principles can I embrace "once in my life" that will ground and
justify all future decisions and commitments? The Cartesian anxiety, in
short, is a yearning for *certainty.*

Certainty has also historically been an issue for rhetoric. Certainty is the
rhetorician's bane: when one *can* be certain about the solution to a given
problem, that problem is removed from the purview of rhetoric. This is
because rhetoric manages those problems and affairs that cannot be decided
through mere observation or logical necessity, and are thus arguable.
Rhetoric thus manages the realm of contingent, rather than certain issues
(Aristotle, *Rhetoric,* 1357a). For instance, there is little point in arguing
over what happens when two chemicals are combined under certain
circumstances; the way to settle such an issue is to combine the chemicals

and see. There is also little point in arguing over what two plus two equals in our system of addition; the answer is logically entailed by the system itself. But no such certain knowledge can be obtained regarding the contingent (arguable) issue, "Was Ronald Reagan a good President?" When we decide what issues we can be certain of, then we have discovered which issues must and must not be managed rhetorically.

Until fairly recently, this search for certainty has preoccupied Western philosophy and science (Matson, 1966; Rorty, 1979; Wheelis, 1971). Certainty is a potential attribute of *ideas about* reality rather than of reality itself (which is what it is, whatever that is). But what "counts" as certainty? How do we know when we have a firm foundation for knowledge about reality? Certainty in Cartesian philosophy has usually had two related components. First, that which is certain is that which *does not change* from one time to another or from one place to another if reality remains the same. If we "know" that water is made of hydrogen and oxygen in Naples, then we "know" that it must also be made of that in New York. If Maxwell's equations (which are ideas *about* electromagnetism) were true in the nineteenth century, they must be true in the twentieth (if electromagnetism remains the same, as we suppose it does).

Of course, reality itself sometimes changes; it is true that the Dodgers played in New York in the early 1950s, but now they play in Los Angeles. There did not used to be a way to prevent polio, and now there is. So even the truest knowledge may sometimes become outmoded (I am not speaking of what turns out to be "false knowledge," such as the doctrine of ether as the medium for light, or Ptolemaic astronomy). But if the best knowledge is ideally changeless, then those aspects of reality that do change are that much less worth knowing about. Western philosophy and science have therefore tended to seek and to privilege knowledge about those dimensions of reality that do not change: The Dodgers' location changes but baseballs still obey Newton's laws as they fly from the mound to the plate, the wood in bats still has the same cellular properties, and so forth. That is to say that in the West, we have privileged the knowledge that *can* be certain.

"Pure" and changeless knowledge may be valued more than "applied" and practical knowledge (Bernstein, 1983, p. 113); Einstein is more prestigious than Edison. Mathematics has, since at least Plato (e.g., *Theaitetos*), been the model and paradigm of reliable knowledge because it is composed of unchangeable propositions about an unchanging (albeit abstract) reality; then comes physical science, followed by social science, trailed by the arts and humanities which cannot make up their minds.

A second characteristic of certainty is that it is *consistent*. If it is true that it is raining here, then we want to know that it cannot also *not* be raining here. We are uncomfortable with the idea that Richard Nixon might be and not be a villain at the same time and for the same issue. We do not even like competing polls which name both Miami University *and* the University of Oklahoma the top college football team in the same year.

But when (if) *reality* is changeless and consistent, why is *knowledge* ever changeable and inconsistent? What are humans and the human condition like such that those characteristics of knowledge are even an issue? The Cartesian answer is most clearly articulated, of course, by Descartes. Early in the First Meditation, he claimed that "all that I have, up to this moment, accepted as possessed of the highest truth and certainty, I received either from or through the senses" (1641/1968, p. 27). But, alas! "I am a man" (p. 27) and my senses are liable to deceive me about the world; my human faculties of sensation and perception may fail to tell me what is out there. And so Descartes ultimately falls back on pure reason, the intuition that he is thinking, as the one sure foundation of truth.

Descartes' meditation is remarkable not for the questionable answer he gives, but for the way in which he posed the question. He posits a split between "out there" and "in here," between the world as it is and my ability to *represent* that world to myself through sensation, perception, or reason. Descartes sets up a *dualist* model counterposing knowledge and reality: Out there is a world of physical objects and processes with laws to govern them. In here we formulate ideas (knowledge) about what's out there. But the "in here" is a world of sensory equipment, neural organs with which to process sensations, an ability to reason about them, and a panoply of biases, passions, emotions, and even illnesses which prevent our organs of knowledge from working properly. Based on this split between out there and in here, between object and subject, dualism entails a *correspondence theory of truth:* Truth is a correspondence, resemblance, or isomorphism between the thoughts that I have or the statements I can make about reality on the one hand, and on the other, reality itself (Maslow, 1966, p. 110; Polanyi & Prosch, 1975, pp. 194–195). Such a theory can only obtain under a dualist split between subject and object. Such dualism, taken as "too obvious to question" (Davidson, 1989, p. 159) by many, is a mainstay of Cartesian philosophy.

Let us recall the Cartesian criteria of truth: it must be changeless and consistent. It is interesting to note that these criteria do *not* necessarily follow from dualism itself; if one postulated a changing and inconsistent reality, then a correspondence theory of truth would require a changing and inconsistent knowledge. Nor can one argue that we know that the world *must* (objectively, absolutely) be changeless and consistent, for to do so would be to presume possession of the ideal end product of Cartesian epistemology, which is perfect knowledge of the world; not even the most confirmed Cartesian will claim such a thing. The criteria of truth are rather *articles of faith* about what the world is like, a faith that is then imposed on our conceptions of what our knowledge must be like.

PHILOSOPHICAL RELATIVISM

Relativism is a philosophy based upon *rejection* of Cartesian principles at several crucial junctures. (Hikins, chap. 2 in this volume, is correct in saying that many philosophies are born by countering dualisms such as realism.) Relativism is arguably founded on Protagoras' rejection of the consistency criterion in his doctrine that there are two sides (truths) to every issue, and on Heracleitus' rejection of changelessness in his doctrine that one cannot step into the same stream twice (Jarrett, 1969). I have here taken Cartesian principles as a foil for relativism, and now turn to an explication of relativist philosophy.

Relativism is a rubric covering a number of converging positions (Goodman, 1978); the Sophists of ancient Greece were perhaps the clearest and most straightforward proponents of relativism (Barrett, 1987; Jarrett, 1969; Untersteiner, 1954;). Although relativism may be clearly understood by studying its rejections of Cartesian assumptions, not all such rejections are therefore relativist. For a working definition at this point I define relativism as *the belief that what is real and true is determined only by the social, symbolic, and historical context from which the knowing human arises* (see also Krausz, 1989, p. 1). Relativism is and has always been a marginal philosophy, an embarrassment to learned dons, a foil for good epistemologists. For that reason, it has often been in the political interests of dualist philosophers to construct and then refute weak versions of relativism. Therefore, I move in this essay toward a more specific definition of relativism which is also the most defensible of several expressions of relativism, one grounded in a rhetorical understanding.

One kind of relativism is relatively simple and uncontroversial; it might be called *de facto* relativism. Proponents of this position observe that few or no propositions held to be "true" about reality remain unchanged and consistent (Berger & Luckmann, 1966; Moser, 1968). Throughout history, even those ideas thought to be the most obvious common sense have been denied just as vehemently and sincerely by somebody else. Advocating de facto relativism entails rejecting Cartesianism by denying that the criteria of changelessness and consistency for true knowledge ever obtain.

De facto relativism is not a philosophical position; it is an anthropological argument. That is to say, it is an assertion about what people actually think, not what they should think; it describes what ethical principles are, not what they ought to be. De facto relativism is therefore often incorporated into other scholarly positions such as the Sapir–Whorf hypothesis (Hoijer, 1954; Whorf, 1956). De facto relativism can be refuted by the discovery of cultural universals (Bidney, 1959, p. 64). To argue that ideas do in fact change and are contradictory is not to show that they should or must be; de facto relativism is thus merely descriptive.

A position midway between de facto and the next sort of relativism is that knowledge, ideas, and values not only spring from cultural and historical contexts, but are justified by them. This position is much favored by scholars of intercultural communication (Condon & Yousef, 1975; Oliver, 1962; Prosser, 1973). These relativists might argue that cannibalism is justified and ethical for cannibals in their societies, that the earth was indeed flat for flat-earthists living in the Middle Ages, and so on. In contrast to de facto relativism, which is descriptive, this *intermediate* relativism is largely prescriptive about how best to interact with those of different cultures who hold radically different ideas — clearly, a major concern for scholars of intercultural communication. But this intermediate position is not quite a fully philosophical position, either, for it often fails to consider what it is about a cultural or historical context that grounds knowledge and ethics (Brummett, 1981). Because their concern is so often prescriptive, these relativists merely assert that the relativity of ideas to context *is* the grounding or justification for those ideas, without explaining why that is so.

A stronger position is what might be called *ex principio* relativism: knowledge cannot in principle be changeless and unified because of the nature of knowledge, of the knower, and of the relationship between knowers and the objects of knowledge (Barnsley, 1972; Boulding, 1956; Brummett, 1976). This position, which I call "relativism" hereafter, rejects Cartesianism most directly on the grounds of dualism, and from that attack draws subsidiary conclusions about the criteria of changelessness and consistency. This form of relativism focuses on the nature of symbolic systems and the process of acquiring knowledge, and considers what it is about context that grounds or justifies ideas.

Proponents of relativism argue that consciousness is always a process of structuring and forming. Of structuring and forming what? We must be careful in how we express this. The English language and our ability to use it are powerfully shaped by centuries of dualist assumptions, and it is therefore easy to slip into Cartesian expressions unawares. English requires us to posit a noun already in existence *to be* structured and formed, a noun existing prior to structuring and forming. And since the human being does the structuring and forming, the noun must therefore be something apart from the human, an object for the human subject to act upon: a return to the dualism of in here and out there.

It is not relativist to say that the human mind structures and forms physical sensations or raw experience coming to it, since that creates the dualist assumption of a knowing subject and independently existing objects in experience. Rather, relativists argue that people are not conscious of any cognition unless it is already being structured and formed, related to other contents of consciousness, and placed into patterns that order the stuff of awareness. We do not first have some sensation or impression and then order it; rather, we do not have a cognition at all until ordering has happened (Gregg, 1984): the verb (to know, to be aware, to perceive) comes first and it produces the noun which is consciousness. Where Descartes' *cogito* took his thinking as a sign of his existence, relativism takes the human world's existence as a sign of people's thinking. *For the human,* the world comes into consciousness as it is structured, formed, and related to other cognitions, and so forth. We are not able to say that this is a matter of the mind acting upon, perceiving, distorting, or apprehending something called physical sensations because we *cannot be conscious of anything except that of which we are conscious,* that which we are already structuring and forming. On that tautology are based many of relativism's principles. Relativists argue that the human can never step outside the position of knower to apprehend what "the world" might be like apart from our consciousness of it (Heisenberg, 1958, p. 58). Therefore, all experience and all of what we can know about experience is ordering consciousness.

Another way to describe this ordering that produces consciousness is to identify it as *meaning.* A random series of letters means very little, for instance. It means *something* if we are conscious of it; for instance, it means that someone has come along and put this odd series here. But to rearrange the letters into a word is to make them meaningful, a meaning that is the same thing as pattern and relationship (Campbell, 1982). To see any idea or cognition as meaningful is thus to be able to see what it relates to, how it fits into some kind of logic or larger pattern.

This position puts an emphasis on what facilitates or enables that structuring and forming, namely, symbol systems. Consciousness is *ordered;* one thought relates to another, is aligned or opposed to another, leads us from one cognition to another. Ordering is carried out through the symbolic systems of humans: language, mathematics, music, religion, et cetera. (Langer, 1942, 1967). These symbolic systems must be understood in two ways. First, they provide the parameters for the kinds of cognitions that can be created with them. I can have some cognitions using music that I cannot have using language, and vice versa. To think theologically enables some kinds of cognitions not enabled by thinking mathematically, and vice versa. Second, cognition is produced by the strategic manipulation of a symbolic system within its parameters: if you and I are arguing politically, using the symbolic system of ordinary English language, then within the parameters of what that system allows we urge specific, perhaps competing, cognitions upon one another. We try to shape each other's consciousness.

A symbol can be seen in at least two ways: it can represent something else, and it can order two or more entities (the symbol that is the American flag, for instance, is actually a relationship between sign and signifier that places a piece of cloth and a political unit into an order or relationship). Cartesian dualism emphasizes the representative function of symbols: symbols are useful in representing to ourselves and to each other what is out there in the real world. Relativists place the loop of representation entirely within experienced consciousness, and see the symbol "cat," for instance, as a cognition representing but another cognition, my awareness of that furry animal (see Jameson, 1981, pp. 78–82 for an example of a nonrepresentational theory of symbolism). For relativists, then, the *representative* function of symbols is irrelevant as a means of apprehending "reality" or of gaining a privileged kind of knowledge. What people take to be the representations of symbols in an everyday sense are treated as representations of other cognitions and symbolic constructions.

Alternatively, relativists emphasize more the ordering function of symbols; that consciousness is a matter of ordering cognitions, of putting them into patterns. A symbol system is seen as a logic, template, or set of rules for ordering cognitions. Consciousness is therefore an artifact of the symbolic structures being employed to make consciousness, and of the strategic uses of those structures to urge specific cognitions upon others. Furthermore, once achieved, consciousness employs symbol systems to beget more consciousness. Several important points follow from this contention. First, consciousness is always *relative* to the human, symbolic systems from which consciousness springs. The First Law of Thermodynamics, for instance, *is* the cognition generated by *this* Newtonian symbol system and held by *these* scientists, proven by evidence deemed relevant and sufficient by the same community (Crable, 1982). And because consciousness for the relativist is human experience, *is human reality,* then reality itself is relative to the human and the symbol system. At this point, relativism may seem to be open to the charge of solipsism, that traditional bogeyman of philosophers. Solipsists are for dualist philosophers what cheating welfare queens are for Republicans. Solipsism is the belief, held by practically no one, that reality is exclusively subjective and within the solitary mind of the individual. In fairness, relativists who do not go beyond this point deserve such an accusation.

But the most defensible relativism will insist, second, on examining the sources of those symbol systems from which consciousness springs. Relativism argues that these symbol systems are socially grounded; that they are in place and are sustained by social and cultural groups (just as they in turn ground and sustain cultural groups) before you or I were born. The process of changing from a newborn into a fully functioning adult is the process of becoming the kind of conscious creature that our symbol systems make us into. The most defensible relativism sees symbol systems as a *medium* from which the human and human consciousness spring (Bineham, 1986).

Some ordinary language meanings of the term "medium" are instructive in understanding this position. One kind of medium is the agar found in a

Petri dish; from this substance organisms arise. They do not grow without such a medium. They are not identical to the medium, but the medium supports, sustains, and nourishes them; it makes organisms possible. A medium is also a channel of communication, as radio is a medium. This sense of the term emphasizes not only the social nature of symbol systems but that communication through, in terms of, the medium is what constitutes the social or cultural relationship. The relativist thus holds that the individual is derivative from the social or cultural, and that the forces which shape that derivation are manifested through the symbol systems relative to cultures, systems that ultimately structure consciousness.

Relativism has sometimes mistakenly been called "subjective," or grounded in individual consciousness (Davidson, 1989; Schweder, 1989, p. 101); I doubt whether any such versions of relativism are defensible. Relativism has more fairly been called "intersubjective" (Brummett, 1976), but that must not be understood to mean that society or symbol systems are formed by pre-existent subjects coming together in a confederation (Cherwitz & Hikins, 1979, 1983; Orr, 1978). It is more clearly relativist to argue that society and its symbol systems are protosubjective, super- or suprasubjective: that subjects are derived from and generated by the symbolic resources of communities. Those resources envelope who we are and how we think, setting the parameters for acts of acceptance and rejection.

Given these assumptions, the contrast between relativism and Cartesian philosophy becomes clearer. Cartesian dualism makes no sense for a philosophy that collapses subject and object into consciousness, into experience. Nor does it make sense to locate that consciousness within a given human organism, which would still be Cartesian insofar as it is subjectivism (or even solipsism). Rather, consciousness (human reality) is located within socially and culturally held symbol systems, it is derived from the social-and-symbolic. Relativists reject a dichotomy between the in here and the out there, between subjects and objects as primary entities separate from each other (Bernstein, 1983). They posit a consciousness that is not my subjective attempt to grasp a discrete object apart from me, but is simply a consciousness, an experience. To divide experience into subject and object is a post hoc reification: we have experiences that are of a kind of unification that transcends and thus negates the distinction between subject and object.

The correspondence theory of truth is not useful in relativism (Wheelis, 1971, p. 83). There can be no question of formulating propositions or constructing ideas that are then compared to the way things really are in the world. Truth is not correspondence between ideas and world: it is agreement or endorsement of an idea by a cultural or social group (Boulding, 1956, p. 167). My idea that the earth is round or that Richard Nixon is a crook is discovered to be "true" or "false" not by examining an alleged correspondence between an idea and the way the earth or Nixon "really" are, but by comparing the idea with what others in my relevant cultural groups think. Truth is consensus, founded in "solidarity" with a community (Rorty, 1989, p. 35). In this sense, truth is not only relative to the social groups that ground me, but it is relative in the sense of being more or less. That is to say, consensus, endorsement, and agreement are rarely all or nothing affairs; they are matters of relative endorsement or agreement even within a given social grouping. So it is relatively very true that the earth is round for me, as hardly anyone in my social groups thinks otherwise; it is only somewhat relatively true that the government should increase spending on the arts, as there is less consensus on that issue. Opinion is never truly individual; my truths are always at the very least assembled from the truths available to me in my cultural groups.

It is important to note that the relativism of truth and of cognitions themselves also occurs because any one of us springs from a number of different social and cultural groundings. By the time one becomes an adult, one has been "made" by the family, the school, the church, the economy, the ethnic and racial associations from which one grew (see Althusser, 1971, and Hall, 1985, on "appellation"). These social groundings employ symbol systems in overlapping but not always consistent ways. My church employs a symbol system and urges certain thoughts upon me that are unlikely to be found in my work environment. The English language is used in both my family and school, but in slightly different ways and in the service of different values and commitments. So the individual stands at the conjunction of a number of overlapping but not identical cultural and social groundings that also ground the "truth" of what one thinks. But that truth must always be relative in the sense of more or less as it is endorsed by more or fewer of those social groundings, of greater or lesser salience.

Relativist notions of truth must also reject the criteria of changelessness and unity found in Cartesian philosophy. If the world exists apart from subjects and if it is changeless and consistent, then true statements or ideas about it must also be changeless and consistent. Yet that which is social is changing and changeable, malleable, contradictory, and often in conflict. This is true even within a single cultural grouping and its symbol systems; symbol systems contain strategic resources of ambiguity and contradiction (Burke, 1966, 1945/1969a, 1950/1969b). By "strategic" I mean a resource for use, manipulation, and advantage.

Language is inherently ambiguous and slippery; this was admitted by the analytic philosophers in sorrow (Rorty, 1967) and has been embraced by the deconstructionists with joy (Derrida, 1978; Aune, chap. 8). But if truth is grounded in language and in other symbol systems, then truth itself must be changeable, ambiguous, contradictory. What was a difficulty for Cartesian philosophers because it hampered truthful representations becomes the constitutive nature of truth for relativists because culturally based symbol systems generate cognitions.

So even within a cultural grounding, what is true will change from one moment in time or space to another. Because symbol systems are inherently ambiguous, particular commitments, values and decisions are always sites of struggle within cultures. That a culture and its symbol systems ground cognitions does not mean that particular cognitions are dictated; cognitions are always "under discussion." And for that reason alone, the truth that is consensus is not consistent or unified; it is multiple. The relativist living in the United States at this writing understands that Richard Nixon *both* is and is not a crook, because *for different groups* (political allegiances, for instance) that issue does not enjoy anything close to total agreement. The relativist does not assume that one position is "right" and the other "wrong" in some absolute sense; both "truths" exist in contradiction to each other simultaneously. Furthermore, because we are grounded in competing social groups that are often in conflict, the commitments urged upon us by those groups also create contradictory and inconsistent truths for the given individual who stands at the conjunction of such groups.

It is worth noting that in collapsing subject and object, relativism also collapses *epistemology* and *ontology,* or conceptions of *what there is to know* and *how we come to know.* Relativists argue that what there is to know is what we know, and that this "what" comes into existence for the human as the human knows it; because "know" carries with it so many connotations of Cartesian dualism, it may be preferable instead to say, "as the human thinks or experiences it."

Relativism collapses what, for the Cartesian, would be different realms of knowledge into one fundamental sort. With a distinction between knowing about the world out there and knowing about my own thoughts in here goes a distinction between knowledge and opinion. Knowledge is, for the Cartesian, true propositions about what is out there (Cherwitz & Hikins, 1986, pp. 20–30, 92, 115). Opinion is merely the subject's own voice, talking to the voices of other subjects. But with the collapse of that distinction comes a collapse of knowledge and opinion. Accompanying that collapse is a collapse of the distinction between moral and physical knowledge (although some, e.g., Meiland & Krausz, 1982, retain distinguishing terms such as ethical and cognitive relativism, respectively). For the Cartesian, knowledge about the structure of the carbon atom is of a radically different order from knowledge about proper ethical behavior. The former is certainly objective, the latter likely to be subjective. But for the relativist, these purportedly different orders of knowledge are essentially and fundamentally the same: in either case, we have only cognitions engendered by socially grounded symbol systems.

In summarizing this section, I offer a rather long and inclusive definition of "relativism." Relativism is the philosophical position which holds that: Human reality and human experience are always functions of human consciousness. We can never experience, know about, or comment conclusively upon some kind of reality apart from that of which we are conscious. But consciousness is not a mirror of reality. Consciousness is what obtains from the employment of socially and culturally grounded symbol systems. The consciousness of the past is embodied in parents who, through socialization, beget the consciousness of little children in the present whose consciousness begets its own consciousness throughout life and then perpetuates consciousness into future generations. Therefore, what is real and what is true are for the relativist always relative to the social and symbolic groundings of the person who is thinking about the real and the true.

RHETORICAL RELATIVISM

In this section, I consider the relationship between relativism and rhetoric, and the shape that a rhetoric beginning with relativist principles might take (the classic statement of that relationship is Scott, 1967). "Rhetoric" is a term that has been the subject of controversy throughout its history. For the Sophists, it was the technique of persuasion in public discourse, a means to the ends of political, economic, and social success. For Plato, it was either pandering or a highly suspect means of transmitting truth. Ramus saw rhetoric as pure stylistic technique and embellishment. More recently, debates raged over the definition and nature of rhetoric: Is it a purely discursive, verbal art form, a form of political action, can it encompass nonverbal action such as demonstrations or riots (Doolittle, 1976; Scott, 1973)? One contemporary aspect of this debate centers on the question of whether one can claim that rhetoric can be an adjunct of science or scholarly disciplines (Hikins & Zagacki, 1988).

It is tempting to dismiss these definitional squabbles as so much academic fussiness. In particular, one wonders why a simple matter such as definition cannot be finally settled by mere convention. But it is instructive to recall that the times when the definition of rhetoric has been most at issue are times of social, political, or academic unrest: the end of Athens' Golden Age, the Renaissance, the 1960s, and so on. That should alert us to the fact that to define rhetoric is not a sterile etymological exercise, it is an ideologically and politically charged act.

This is because rhetoric, as noted earlier, has always been seen as a way of managing contingent human affairs through symbols. Rhetoric is a way of manipulating meanings so as to secure cooperation. What has been at issue in defining rhetoric are the questions (a) which aspects of human experience are to be assigned to this sort of management? and (b) how does the management take place? If we say that there is a rhetoric of science, for instance (Campbell, 1975; Kelso, 1980; Overington, 1977), then we are saying that there is something about science that has fundamentally to do with the management of meaning. That position is clearly antipositivist and offends those Cartesians who see science as objective, bias-free investigation of reality. On the other hand, if we argue that riots can have a rhetorical function or purpose (Scott & Smith, 1969), we offend those essentially conservative rhetoricians who would restrict the term exclusively to verbal, discursive debates. It is in the interests of such scholars to restrict the management of meaning to those polite forums that are most likely to secure their roles as arbiters of public discourse. It is clear from these observations that to posit a *relativist rhetoric* is to admit rhetoric into epistemological and ontological matters from which it has often been banned; it is to say that what the *world* is like and how we can know it has something to do with the management of meaning.

As I already have suggested, rhetoric involves the management of meaning and the use of symbolic influence. Any rhetorical theorist will agree that rhetoric involves one person's attempt to induce certain thoughts or emotions, or to instigate actions, in another. The fact that rhetoric is inherently social is so fundamental that it may be missed: we use rhetoric (and it uses us) across our subjectivities, to influence another, to take advantage of or to establish social arrangements. Rhetoric sustains and changes communities. Rhetoric must also presuppose some sort of social grouping already in place that provides the grounds and means for it to work. That is, it must presuppose that people are in contact with one another, are disposed to attend to one another, and share a symbol system with which to communicate. Rhetoric is not something grafted onto social situations; it is inherently, fundamentally, and inescapably social.

Furthermore, rhetoric works by securing agreement, endorsement, and cooperation. This need not mean that rhetoric is always fair, honest, decorous, or that it must always serve either dominant or oppositional ideologies; but when it works, it works by influencing choice. Although rhetoric can certainly work in conjunction with coercive means of securing compliance, the rhetorical dimension of any experience of gaining the cooperation of others is that which works through *symbolic* inducement. Agreement may not always be conscious, but voluntary (as opposed to coerced or threatened) agreement and cooperation are always rhetoric's goals.

Styles and tactics of rhetoric have changed throughout history, of course, but appeals have typically tried to sway subjects who were assumed to be capable of reason, susceptible to emotion, and influenced by biases and prejudices. Aristotle's three-part division of logical, emotional, and personal proof stands as the paradigm of this range of concerns. It is also the case that, although Aristotle divided his subject into three parts, a given actual rhetorical effort will often mix appeals to reason, emotion, and the person together (see the Enlightenment rhetorics of Campbell, Whately, Blair in Golden & Corbett, 1968). Rhetoric usually operates as if the human decisions that are at issue were made in ways that required the simultaneous and integrated use of several human faculties.

Rhetoric, in sum, is fundamentally social, based on and in search of agreement, and assumes an integration of the human process(es) of cognition. These three characteristics suggest a close affinity between rhetoric and relativism. As Cartesian dualism collapses, philosophers of several different perspectives have advocated that the urge to find a certain foundation should be replaced by a "rhetorical turn" (Eagleton, 1983; Brown, 1977; Lentricchia, 1983). Typically, these philosophers argue that we should turn our attention to considering how cognitions themselves are created and managed without "worrying" about whether our cognitions correspond to a world that we can never know apart from cognitions.

A rhetorical turn is self-perpetuating. To admit rhetoric to any role in knowing is to let a particularly insistent camel put its nose into the tent of dualism. Plato of the *Gorgias* would seem to forbid rhetoric any role at all in the dissemination of knowledge. Plato of the *Phaedrus* allows it to help disseminate knowledge, but he is uneasy about it and for good reason: if rhetoric *can* lead anyone to knowledge, then is knowledge linked to or dependent on the management of meaning? Aristotle lets the rhetorical camel in a little farther in the *Rhetoric* by assigning the management of contingent, uncertain issues to rhetoric, a move parallelled by recent theorists such as Farrell (1976) who would assign to rhetoric the management of social knowledge. This then raises the problem of what counts as social, contingent knowledge, and where to draw the line. By degrees we have come to relativist philosophies that see all knowledge as the management of meaning, and thus as fundamentally rhetorical.

In other words, when a philosophy rejects Cartesian assumptions, it moves at least in the direction of relativism, and such a move is often seen at the same time as being towards rhetoric. I am trying to suggest a "natural" fit or affinity between rhetoric and relativism. This may be the "easiest" part of any chapter in this book: to show what relativism and rhetoric have to do with each other.

Rhetoric's social grounding is obviously isomorphic with relativism's grounding in particular groups and in the symbol systems used by those groups. If human experience and rhetoric are both inherently social, then rhetoric must be a primary and unavoidable dimension of our experience of reality. If truth for relativists is consensus or agreement, and if rhetoric is the way in which agreement is secured, then relative truth is the product of rhetoric. Truth, for the relativist, is something created through rhetorical struggle and not through objective observation of reality.

Finally, rhetoric has usually tried to manage meanings in nondualist ways; at the very least, it is completely compatible with such an approach. The dualist must mediate between those human faculties that allow us to apprehend an objective reality (reason, science, logic, etc.) and those human faculties that get in the way of such an apprehension, that "fool" us (bias, emotion, prejudice, etc.). Rhetoric is perfectly compatible with appeals that do not make such a distinction, but rather appeal to a human faculty that is assumed to be integrated at least with respect to dualist distinctions. To see rhetoric as appealing to logic *and* emotion *and* personal considerations may be a faculty psychology imposed after the fact on what is essentially a unitary human faculty: the faculty to consider symbolic appeals and to make decisions in response to them. So the ways in which rhetorical appeals actually work assume a kind of unity of human experience not compatible with dualism, but one right at home with relativism's view of experience and cognition.

Relativist rhetoric does not differ from other rhetorics very much in terms of the techniques it describes. Instead, it differs in terms of the relationship it describes between rhetoric and human experience. The practitioner of rhetoric would not go forth from the study of relativism arguing in a different way. But such a relativist rhetorician would have a much broader view than would one trained in more traditional schools of what "counts" as rhetoric and of which aspects of human experience can be influenced, shaped, or managed rhetorically.

The practitioner would have a broader view of what "counts" as rhetoric through seeing rhetoric as a *dimension* of human experience rather than as a discrete class of human experiences. Rhetoric is seen as that aspect of experience in which meaning is managed and agreement secured. Sometimes that dimension is central to the experience and of prime importance. Sometimes it is not. But the "rhetorical" is always present. One might say, for instance, that there is a musical dimension to all human experience, since experience involves sounds of varying pitch, harmony, dissonance, and so forth. Sometimes that musical dimension is of interest and sometimes not; but it is always a part of human experience. So it is with rhetoric. A relativist rhetoric will then attend to the rhetorical dimension of all experience and will consider whether examining that dimension will tell us something interesting about the experience.

Because relativism sees reality as fundamentally changeable and *managed* in different social/symbolic locales, the rhetorical component is a central dimension of reality for the relativist more than for any other philosopher. This does not mean that "everything is" rhetoric, or that "everything is worthwhile considering" as rhetoric. However, the embeddedness of rhetoric within all aspects of reality entails that the philosopher, the practitioner, and the critic of rhetoric are encouraged to question the *givenness* of any cognition, and to ask how such a cognition is rhetorically shaped and maintained. Relativism attacks the provincialism that refuses to question its own givens (Geertz, 1989, p. 15). It is the business of the relativist to see another way that reality could be, were the social/symbolic grounding different. As the rhetorician and relativist stand side by side, treating every given assumption not as hard fact but as a veil to be lifted so as to examine the next veil beyond, these two personae become one and the same.

For that reason, relativism and rhetoric are both profoundly *subversive,* an attribute which has been granted directly or indirectly to both through their long histories of marginality (Hariman, 1986). Both rhetoric and relativism are the barbarians at the gates of mainstream, respectable philosophies and politics. It is in the nature of established ideologies, both political and philosophical, to present their tenets and principles as given, as unarguable, as certain (Hebdige, 1979). Dominance in the polis and in the academy depends upon occluding both the relative and the rhetorical nature of basic assumptions. *If* relativism is (relatively) true and *if* rhetoric's purview, as a dimension of experience, is unrestricted, then neither philosopher nor politician may insist on the givenness or undeniable truth of any principle. That is why rhetoric and relativism are set apart from the competitions among other politics and philosophies, which argue among themselves who is right, for relativism and rhetoric will both deny that any of them can be *right* in the Cartesian, absolutist, given sense of the term. While all other politics and philosophies strive to be king of the hill, relativism and rhetoric strive to colonize more hills.

The subversive nature of rhetoric and relativism will inform the efforts of the practical practioner, who will see intentional rhetorical interventions as being allowed an almost unlimited scope in human affairs. There can be rhetorical management of the rhetorical dimension of *any* issue or problem, from ethical issues to neurosurgery. Transcending distinctions between "social" issues and "technical," relativist rhetoricians emulate their Sophistic ancestors in claiming to have application to any issue.

Similarly, the rhetorical critic who is informed by relativism is unavoidably a social critic, charged with demystifying perceptions of the given and showing what is both relative and socially, symbolically created about them. The relativist critic cannot offer single, "objective" descriptions of a rhetorical experience. Sometimes the relativist critic will be in a position to say that a particular group understood a particular rhetorical transaction in a certain way; the critic will have evidence of how the group participated in the creation of the rhetoric. But most often, the critic is not privy to how people participated in creating the realities of a rhetorical experience. In that case, the critic intervenes not only to change how the past was seen but to shape how the future may be experienced. The critic does this by showing how experience *could* be understood, how meaning *might* be created. This sort of criticism is hypothetical. Its value is political and practical rather than archival. It models for its readers an *option* in how experience might have been made, which becomes, for an attentive audience, a way in which future rhetorical experiences might be created (Brummett, 1984).

Furthermore, when compared to more traditional theorists, the relativist rhetorician has a wider range of understanding of what "counts" as rhetorical strategies. If we see rhetoric as an ongoing dimension of human affairs, then we will no longer see rhetoric as the isolated moments of speeches, essays, arguments, stylistic devices—in short, as purely verbal techniques. Instead, we will see rhetoric as the whole range of symbolic devices that might be used to secure cooperation and manage meaning. There will be a rhetorical dimension in the grammatical categories of a language, given that those categories work to predispose the language users to construct experience in a particular way. There will be a rhetorical dimension in the basic semantic categories of a symbol system, such as "male" and "female" in English, because these categories call the speaker's attention to some differences but not others. There will be a rhetorical dimension of clothing, of physical movement, of personal possessions. Relativist rhetoric, in short, is not restricted to traditional models of rhetoric, based on ancient Greek oratorical practice, that assumes that rhetoric is embodied in discrete, verbal texts.

An understanding of rhetoric as a dimension of experience also suggests a reorganization of the academy, which is in fact taking place at the moment. We tend to be organized around modes of discourse: in this department we study poetry, in that one speeches, over here the peculiar language of science, and across campus they spin their historical narratives. This will not do if there is not only a rhetoric of, and in, every kind of experience (every kind of discourse), but if other "things" that have been taken to be types or modes of discourse turn out to be dimensions of experience as well. What happens to the English and the Sociology departments, for instance, if there is a "poetic of sociology" (Brown, 1977)? What happens to the Communication and Economics departments if there is a "rhetoric of economics" (McCloskey, 1985)? This reorganization can be seen already occurring in a few strategic areas, and it is telling that *rhetoric* is presently one transcendent, interdisciplinary concern being taken up most eagerly by departments across campus (although it is a subversive virus that will infect and explode its host cells, for it is tied to no mode of discourse, as traditional departments often are). Such an academic reorganization is possible only under the influence of a relativist rhetoric that expands the arguable (and then, consequently, the poetic, the economic, etc.) beyond a discrete set of events and installs it as a dimension of all events.

In sum, I claim rhetoric and relativism for each other; that is, I argue that each is fully realized in and makes full use of the principles of the other. There is a natural affinity at work here. To see relativism as central for rhetoric is to ground rhetoric within a particular philosophical system that may very well be the "best fit" for each. To see rhetoric as central to relativism is to expand one's conception of what rhetoric is and how it functions.

STRENGTHS, WEAKNESSES, COMPARISONS

In this section I evaluate some of the strengths and weaknesses of relativism, principally through comparisons with the other philosophies explained in this book. My comparison will have three focal points: *stock objections* against relativism, *givenness* in a philosophy, and whether a philosophy is more concerned, figuratively, with *nouns or verbs*. In the first two parts of this essay, I believe that the balance of my argument depicted relativism in the service of rhetoric, showing how the former could further the standing of the latter. In this section, a central theme is to show how a relativism which is informed by rhetoric is the most acceptable sort of relativism.

Stock Objections

The objections most often made against relativism are to be found reviewed in Orr's essay (chap. 4). Because those objections *have* been made in many other writings, and because I have attempted to answer them in more detail elsewhere (Brummett, 1981), here I only briefly review the charges and show how they are best answered by employing rhetoric to help relativism.

Orr rehearses three stock objections to relativism. First, he argues that cultural frameworks are not incommensurable. Many critics of relativism have assumed that it *must* see cultures as incommensurable (Wong, 1989). Now, on the one hand, relativism *need* not argue that they *are*. Cultures are best seen as multiple and as overlapping circles in a Venn diagram. But to be commensurable does not entail being identical. The point does not, therefore, deny that differences among cultures generate differences in perceptions, values, and so on. On the other hand, this is not an objection that another philosophy can make without first endorsing the idea that cultural and symbolic systems generate reality, for the objection uses an assertion about the cultural grounding of reality (commensurability) to mistakenly tax relativism with a claim of incommensurability.

Second, Orr argues that relativists must tolerate and therefore endorse those who despise relativism. In the first place, tolerance need not entail endorsement in logic or practice. I tolerate the fine (but mistaken) scholarly work done by several contributors to this volume without endorsing it. In the second place, Orr is quite correct to say that many relativists take tolerance to be fundamental to their philosophy; this is characteristic of the "intermediate relativism" explained earlier. But I argue that such relativists are mistaken to do so. Tolerance is a psychological trait that sometimes *flows from* relativism, but it need not be foundational for relativism.

Relativism understands that a culturally validated idea (whether that is flat-earthism, antirelativism, or whatever) is true for those who are grounded in that culture, but relativism's concept of multiple and conflicting truths allows it to grant a truth in one locale while saying that, for another group (round-earthists, relativists, etc.) it is *not* true. It is at this juncture that rhetoric must rescue relativism by replacing tolerance as foundational for that philosophy. The relativist, while endorsing the reality of another's culturally grounded ideas, is free to (and may even be obliged to) *argue against* another's reality using that which *creates and manages* the reality in the first place: rhetoric. Finally, for critical rationalism in particular, the tu quoque (explained nicely by Orr) certainly does apply to this objection: let Professor Orr know that the Relativist Professor' Club has met, subjected critical rationalism to the most searching reasoned examination, and found it lacking relative to relativism. Orr must now throw over critical rationalism with us, must say that we did not use proper reasoning (in which case he exempts from criticism a certain *method*), or must insist that the Critical Rationalists' Club arrive at the same conclusion (which is either an insistence upon consensus as the standard of truth or an exempting from criticism of the dualist standard of consistency).

Orr's third stock objection is that the prescription of relativism, or of any of its tenets, must itself be a nonrelative and thus a contradictory argument. Meiland and Krausz argued that the self-contradiction charge "is usually taken to be devastating," and expressed it in this way: "Does this relativistic thesis apply to itself? [NB: the relativist must say it does] If it does, then the relativist's position itself is only 'relative' and 'subjective' and need not be taken seriously by anyone who does not already subscribe to that position" (1982, pp. 31,6). In the first place, there is nothing inconsistent about the relative truth of a relativist position; the catty (and typical) phrase, "need not be taken seriously" shifts this objection quite away from one of contradiction to one of whether relativism should be seriously entertained. That expression also tells us that objections to relativism are grounded in an unquestioned assumption that *any* worthwhile philosophy must be absolutist in proposing universal and unquestionable tenets for others to embrace. In other words, it says that a philosophy can't be a philosophy unless it is categorical and insistent. Notice also that the objection is lodged against a "subjective" relativism.

Here again, rhetoric must rescue relativism from this charge by grounding relativism in the rhetorical dimensions of the cultural and symbolic. Relativism is most reasonable when its tenets are held as arguable themselves, as propositions that seem true for these people in this locale and that ought to be accepted by others, in short, as *rhetoric*. But arguable does not mean, "not to be taken seriously." Indeed, one troubles to argue about, to urge upon others, those ideas that one takes *most* seriously. Relativism then urges and invites persuasive struggle over philosophy, even its own philosophy, but thinks of itself as relatively true (for its adherents) at the moment. Relativism's alleged self-contradiction vanishes when the relativist becomes the rhetorician, the advocate, arguing for relativism and hoping to win others over. In this way, relativism's argumentative stance differs, and should differ, from the categorical and imperative stance of most other philosophies: "To insist that the relativist should have the same purposes in argument as the nonrelativist might have is misguided" (Meiland & Krausz, 1982).

Givenness

I argued earlier that philosophies occlude their cultural and symbolic foundations by insisting on the givenness of something else. That is to say, other philosophies treat matter, or mind, or reason, and so forth as the one thing (process, entity, etc.) *exempt* from cultural and symbolic manipulation, the one firm foundation sought by Descartes. This exemption creates a sense of givenness for the exempt, that (mind matter, practice, etc.) is what we can be sure of and need probe no further, for it will not reduce to something else. It is profitable to compare philosophies on that one dimension, and to consider whether any philosophy can escape such givenness. Also, I argued earlier that relativism consistently challenges the givenness of philosophies and ideologies to show the cultural and symbolic nature of that which they would privilege. Thus, this section is a quick exercise in that sort of relativist critique.

Let us begin, perversely, with that technique (philosophy?) which would seem to delight in no foundation at all, deconstruction. I point in particular to one kind of givenness: the enterprise of deconstruction (see Aune, this volume) itself. So one *can* doubt or deconstruct; one can also confirm or stop the endless regression of possible meanings by noting where particular cultures and symbol systems fix their local, *relative* meanings. Why is deconstruction, among the many hammers given to those children at Yale, the one that is *preferred* for pounding? I will here defer to Booth's (1974) penetrating analysis of the hermeneutics of doubts and suspicion, in which he shows the cultural and political grounding of such a strategy. I only add to Booth's analysis what he himself might not care to, that deconstruction is thus a technique grounded in, sanctioned by, and thus *relative* to a certain culture and symbol system.

Other givennesses for other philosophies are more easily described. Pragmatism seems to take as a given the idea of what "works in practice," and if pressed as to what *counts* as working in practice, might respond as does Mackin in this volume by saying "all that is necessary is that our understanding of our environment be sufficient to guide practical action well enough that the species survives" (Mackin, chap. 9, p. 277). The Darwinian overtones should be enough to place this givenness of working in practice and securing survival within the cultural and symbolic systems of Western capitalism. What works in practice for a Protestant business owner may not work in practice for a Hindu ascetic, and what is claimed to be the universal givenness of survival appears not to obtain in the different cultural grounding of certain religious or political groups that encourage members to die for higher causes.

McGuire's explanation of materialism (chap. 6) calls attention to the varieties of givenness underlying the varieties of that philosophy. The givenness of this perspective insists on privileging some material as the grounding of reality, apart from what the material *means,* how it is perceived, and so on. Note that materialism can resemble relativism when it argues that different material (e.g., economic, hormonal) conditions in different locales generate different superstructural realities. Relativism would deny the givenness of each set of conditions and argue that such conditions are culturally and symbolically shaped; in other words, it would see the conditions of production under capitalism not as a given but as a rhetorically created and sustained arrangement.

The givenness underlying critical rationalism is not only that of *reason* as a method, but of a particular kind of reason based on certain models of thought and discourse. Critical rationalism is based on the rules of logic found in Western philosophy, rules of noncontradiction, causality, and so on. When this philosophy calls for *criticism,* it is actually calling for the application of culture-specific methods not fully shared, for instance, in Asian philosophies. Booth also calls our attention to critical rationalism as the highest refinement of "the principle of doubt," or hermeneutics of suspicion (1974, pp. 101–105), a principle that is grounded in and perpetuates the philosophies of Western capitalism.

Lyne's view of idealism (chap. 5) seems to hold idea itself as a given. This position seems to take idea as an irreducible with "power," grounding "a way of being," and he gives "freedom" and "justice" as two examples of such ideas. A relativist might argue that ideas must be manifested in some sort of symbol or representation, even for the solitary thinker, and that such a manifestation cannot be a neutral given but is shaped by the culture and the symbolic system from which the symbol springs. "Justice" may be manifested in very different ways from one culture to another.

Hyde's many references (chap. 7) to the "self" or the "individual" nominate that category as the most fundamental, given term in existentialism. The individual is the irreducible foundation for certainty; note Hyde's valorization of the individual's existence in his early reversal of the *cogito*. Existentialists search for an "authentic self" as if that were an absolute given waiting somewhere to be found. Hyde is sensitive to the complaint that existentialism ignores the social, but his repair of existentialism sees individuals coming together to "form authentic relationships with others." This position retains the individual as fundamental and the social as something patched together out of authentic individuals. Relativists might reply, in turn, that authentic relationships with others form individuals.

Hikins (chap. 2) is correct in identifying "the pedestrian world" or "pedestrian reality" as the given for realists. This most dualist of philosophies assumes a given and absolute reality "out there" waiting to be discovered. Realism typically enshrines commonsensical and received ways of understanding what that reality is. Relativists take vigorous exception to such a given, especially for moral reasons, noting that "pedestrian reality" has throughout history been nothing more than what the dominant ideology has said it is. The "pedestrian world" has taken as the most obvious common sense the inferiority of certain racial groups, women, children, and so on, and it is the subversive mission of relativism to expose such givens.

To point out the cultural and symbolic nature of a philosophy's given premises is to point out that those premises can be changed, managed, and altered through the rhetorical process inherent in the cultural and the symbolic. It is to ground the philosophy in something rhetorical and social, and thus, as my foregoing analysis has shown, in something relative. It is this argumentative situation that places relativism *against* all other philosophies in a peculiar way. A struggle between a materialist and an idealist, for instance, or between any other two philosophers, is a struggle over *what sort* of thing to privilege as an immutable, unalterable given underlying reality; but a struggle between a relativist and any other sort of philosopher is a contest over *whether* to privilege anything as immutable and unalterable.

Given that situation, relativism's basic principles must turn upon themselves to declare themselves as not objective, not inalterably given, not immutable. In other words, the relativist must apply relativism to itself and conclude that the cultural and symbolic cannot be absolutely identified as the foundations for shifting, relative realities.

A relativism that must stop at that point *is* emasculated, unfinished, unable to defend its own premises. Once more, rhetoric must rescue this sort of relativism. For a relativism that presents itself *as a rhetoric,* as a way of speaking grounded in certain communities but being urged upon others in other communities, has noting to fear from being turned upon itself. This sort of relativism *invites* the tu quoque. The peculiar nature of rhetorical propositions as *uncertain yet nonetheless passionately defended* (rhetorical because uncertain; defended because rhetorical) saves relativism from a vicious infinite regress; it transforms it into a benign infinite regress! For such a relativism need not insist on an inability to insist; rather, it persuades others of the essentiality of persuading (of the essentiality of persuading of the essentiality, etc.).

Nouns or Verbs

I conclude this comparison of relativism with other philosophies with a brief and whimsical discussion of which schools of thought are based on nouns and which are based on verbs. Another way to phrase this distinction is to say that philosophies are primarily concerned with, respective to nouns and verbs, either product or process, stasis or change, commodities or relationships. How obviously rhetorical my list is! And how clearly does rhetoric align itself with the right hand side of each pair. For rhetoric is that which keeps experience in process rather than reifies it once and for all into hard and changeless commodities. Rhetoric turns what is into what is becoming. I identify these two families of philosophies to show which other perspectives are relativism's first cousins, traced through a bloodline of rhetorical affinity.

Clearly, the noun philosophies are materialism and realism. McGuire (chap. 6) notes that conception of material vary widely, but that whatever it is for a given materialist, it stays still. Material is a physical or "hard" reality, be it economic conditions, glandular secretions, or climate. Actions and events are derivative, flowing from and shaped by the nature of a "noun-ish" reality. Hikins (chap. 2) quotes Thilly's contention that experience leads to a belief in "the reality of the object," a focus on *things* that is typical of the noun slant of realism. Note that an inability to see reality clearly is described as "distortion," which is an optical metaphor based on the conditions required to perceive unchanging and static objects.

The verb philosophies are relativism, of course, and also Lyne's (chap. 5) version of idealism (I think some varieties of idealism may be noun-based), existentialism, pragmatism, deconstruction, and critical rationalism. These are restless philosophies, sympathetic to the principle of change. Orr (chap. 4) notes the guarded affinity between relativism and critical rationalism in this volume. Both philosophies share a strong distrust of any given premise or pronouncement, and a preference for the ongoing negotiation of meaning found in cultures and in reasoned discussions. Mackin's (chap. 9) statement that "pragmatism bases itself in an integral relationship between action and meaning" is as explicitly verb oriented as a focus on *practice*. Pragmatism, as Mackin notes, also shares with the rhetorical Sophists a rejection of idealist certainties in favor of practical consequences (which has always been the product of rhetoric). Indeed, Rorty argued that pragmatism is what most people mistakenly call relativism (1989, p. 37). Deconstruction might almost be depicted as hyper-relativism, since relativism will stop its deconstruction of givens at real understandings fixed by communities, whereas deconstruction *moves* on to one more reading after another.

Lyne (chap. 5) notes idealism's preference for action, and argues that such realities as a person's character are not noun-ish "substances" but rather, verb-ish "achievements." Existentialists, Hyde (chap. 7) tells us, argue that "truth happens," that it is something lived rather than possessed, and is in the process of changing constantly. His focus on living in an uncertain and contingent world was particularly compatible with relativism's focus on process rather than product.

I have tried to argue that rhetoric and relativism are "made for each other," that the strongest case for either is made by incorporating the other. Historically, they have been the ugly wallflowers at philosophy's ball, and the temporary unions they have made with other suitors have been fraught with embarrassment and attempts to keep them at a circumspect distance. Defying the conventions of dualist philosophy with its attendant modes of discourse and politics, rhetoric and relativism find an attraction for each other that is as strong and natural as it is scandalous and subversive.

REFERENCES

Althusser, L. (1971). *Lenin and philosophy*. New York: Monthly Review Press.

Barnsley, J.H. (1972). *The social reality of ethics*. London: Routledge & Kegan Paul.

Barrett, H. (1987). *The sophists*. Novato, CA: Chandler & Sharp.

Berger, P. L., & Luckmann, T. (1966). *The social construction of readlity: A treatise in the sociology of knowledge*. Garden City, NY: Anchor Books.

Bernstein, R.J. (1983). *Beyond objectivism and relativism: Science, hermeneutics, and praxis*. Philadelphia: University of Pennsylvania Press.

Bidney, D. (1959). The philosophical presuppositions of cultural relativism and cultural absolutism. In L.R. Ward (Ed.), *Ethics and the social sciences* (pp. 51–76). South Bend, IN: University of Notre Dame Press.

Bineham, J.L. (1986). *Beyond dualism: The hermeneutic medium as a communication-based perspective on the Cartesian problem in epistemic rhetoric*. Unpublished Ph.D. dissertation. Purdue University, W. Lafayette, IN.

Booth, W.C. (1974). *Modern dogma and the rhetoric of assent*. Chicago: University of Chicago Press.

Boulding, K.E. (1956). *The image: Knowledge in life and society*. Ann Arbor, MI: University of Michigan Press.

Brown, R.H. (1977). *A poetic for sociology.* Cambridge: Cambridge University Press.

Brummett, B. (1976). Some implications of "process" or "intersubjectivity": Postmodern rhetoric. *Philosophy and Rhetoric, 9,* 21–51.

Brummett, B. (1981). A defense of ethical relativism as rhetorically grounded. *Western Journal of Speech Communication, 45,* 286–298.

Brummett, B. (1984). Rhetorical theory as heuristic and moral: A pedagogical justification. *Communication Education, 33,* 97–107.

Burke, K. (1966). *Language as symbolic action.* Berkeley, CA: University of California Press.

Burke, K. (1969a). *A grammar of motives.* Berkeley, CA: University of California Press. (Original work published 1945)

Burke, K. (1969b). *A rhetoric of motives.* Berkeley, CA: University of California Press. (Original work published 1950)

Campbell, J. (1982). *Grammatical man: Information, entropy, language, and life.* New York: Simon & Schuster.

Campbell, P.N. (1975). The *personae* of scientific discourse. *Quarterly Journal of Speech, 61,* 391–405.

Cherwitz, R.A., & Hikins, J.W. (1979). John Stuart Mills' *On Liberty:* Implications for the epistemology of the new rhetoric. *Quarterly Journal of Speech, 65,* 12–24.

Cherwitz, R.A., & Hikins, J.W. (1983). Rhetorical perspectivism. *Quarterly Journal of Speech, 69,* 249–266.

Cherwitz, R.A., & Hikins, J.W. (1986). *Communication and knowledge: An investigation in rhetorical epistemology.* Columbia, SC: University of South Carolina Press.

Condon, J.C., & Yousef, F. (1975). *An introduction to intercultural communication.* Indianapolis, IN: Bobbs-Merrill.

Crable, R. (1982). Knowledge-as-status: On argument and epistemology. *Communication Monographs, 49,* 249–262.

Davidson, D. (1989). The myth of the subjective: In M. Krausz (Ed.), *Relativism: Interpretation and confrontation* (pp. 159–172). South Bend, IN: University of Notre Dame Press.

Derrida, J. (1978). *Writing and difference* (A. Bass, Trans.). Chicago: University of Chicago Press.

Descartes, R. (1968). Meditations. In W. Kaufmann (Ed.), *Philosophic classics: Bacon to Kant* (2nd ed.). (pp. 22–63). Englewood Cliffs, NJ: Prentice-Hall. (Original work published 1641)

Doolittle, R.J. (1976). Riots as symbolic: A criticism and approach. *Central States Speech Journal, 27,* 310–317.

Eagleton, T. (1983). *Literary theory: An introduction.* Minneapolis, MN: University of Minnesota Press.

Farrell, T.B. (1976). Knowledge, consensus, and rhetorical theory. *Quarterly Journal of Speech, 62,* 1–14.

Geertz, C. (1989). Anti anti-relativism: In M. Krausz (Ed.), *Relativism: Interpretation and confrontation* (pp. 12–34). South Bend, IN: University of Notre Dame Press.

Golden, J.L., & Corbett, E.P.J. (Eds.). (1968). *The rhetoric of Blair, Campbell, and Whately.* New York: Holt, Rinehart, & Winston, Inc.

Goodman, N. (1978). *Ways of worldmaking.* Indianapolis, IN: Hackett Publishing.

Gregg, R.B. (1984). *Symbolic inducement and knowing: A study in the foundations of rhetoric.* Columbia, SC: University of South Carolina Press.

Hall, S. (1985). Signification, representation, ideology: Althusser and the post-structuralist debates. *Critical Studies in Mass Communication, 2,* 91–114.

Hariman, R. (1986). Status, marginality, and rhetorical theory. *Quarterly Journal of Speech, 72,* 38–54.

Hebdige, D. (1979). *Subculture: The meaning of style.* New York: Methuen.

Heisenberg, W. (1958). *Physics and philosophy: The revolution in modern science.* New York: Harper & Row.

Hikins, J.W., & Zagacki, K.S. (1988). Rhetoric, philosophy, and objectivism: An attenuation of the claims of the rhetoric of inquiry. *Quarterly Journal of Speech, 74,* 201–228.

Hoijer, H. (Ed.). (1954). *Language in culture.* Chicago: University of Chicago Press.

Jameson, F. (1981). *The political unconscious: Narrative as a socially symbolic act.* Ithaca, NY: Cornell University Press.

Jarrett, J.L. (Ed.). (1969). *Educational theories of the sophists.* New York: Teachers College Press, Columbia University.

Kelso, J.A. (1980). Science and the rhetoric of reality. *Central States Speech Journal, 31,* 17–29.

Krausz, M. (Ed.). (1989). *Relativism: Interpretation and confrontation.* South Bend, IN: University of Notre Dame Press.

Langer, S.K. (1942). *Philosophy in a new key: A study in the symbolism of reason, right, and art.* Cambridge, MA: Harvard University Press.

Langer, S.K. (1967). *Mind: An essay on human feeling.* Baltimore, MD: Johns Hopkins University Press.

Lentricchia, F. (1983). *Criticism and social change.* Chicago: University of Chicago Press.

Maslow, A.H. (1966). *The psychology of science: A reconnaissance.* Chicago: Henry Regnery.

Matson, F.W. (1966). *The broken image: Man, science and society.* Garden City, NY: Doubleday.

McCloskey, D.N. (1985). *The rhetoric of economics.* Madison, WI: University of Wisconsin Press.

Meiland, J.W., & Krausz, M. (Eds.). (1982). *Relativism: Cognitive and moral.* South Bend, IN: University of Notre Dame Press.

Moser, S. (1968). *Absolutism and relativism in ethics.* Springfield, IL: Charles C. Thomas.

Oliver, R.T. (1962). *Culture and communication.* Springfield, IL: Charles C. Thomas.

Orr, C.J. (1978). How shall we say: "Reality is socially constructed through communication?" *Central States Speech Journal, 29,* 263–274.

Overington, M. (1977). The scientific community as audience: Toward a rhetorical analysis of science. *Philosophy and Rhetoric, 10,* 143–163.

Polanyi, M., & Prosch, H. (1975). *Meaning.* Chicago: University of Chicago Press.

Prosser, M.H. (1973). *Intercommunication among nations and peoples.* New York: Harper & Row.

Rorty, R. (Ed.). (1967). *The linguistic turn: Recent essays in philosophical method.* Chicago: University of Chicago Press.

Rorty, R. (1979). *Philosophy and the mirror of nature.* Princeton, NJ: Princeton University Press.

Rorty, R. (1989). Solidarity or objectivity?: In M. Krausz (Ed.), *Relativism: Interpretation and confrontation* (pp. 35–50). South Bend, IN: University of Notre Dame Press.

Schweder, R. (1989). Post-Nietzschian anthropology: In M. Krausz (Ed.), *Relativism: Interpretation and confrontation* (pp. 99–139). South Bend, IN: University of Notre Dame Press.

Scott, R.L. (1967). On viewing rhetoric as epistemic. *Central States Speech Journal, 18,* 9–17.

Scott, R.L. (1973). On *not* defining "rhetoric." *Philosophy and Rhetoric, 6,* 81–96.

Scott, R.L., & Smith, D.K. (1969). The rhetoric of confrontation. *Quarterly Journal of Speech, 55,* 1–8.

Untersteiner, M. (1954). *The sophists.* Oxford: Basil Blackwell.

Wheelis, A. (1971). *The end of the modern age.* New York: Harper & Row.

Whorf, B.L. (1956). *Language, thought & reality.* Cambridge, MA: MIT Press.

Wong, D.B. (1989). Three kinds of incommensurability. In M. Krausz (Ed.), *Relativism: Interpretation and confrontation* (pp. 140–158). South Bend, IN: University of Notre Dame Press.

Chapter 4

Critical Rationalism: Rhetoric and the Voice of Reason

C. Jack Orr

Erik Erikson (1963) said, "in some periods of history, and in some phases of his life cycle man needs . . . a new ideological orientation as surely and as sorely as he must have food and air" (p. 22). It is a striking statement, that no doubt makes intuitive sense for anyone who has experienced an epistemological crisis and survived it. People despair of life when an inherited framework of understanding fails them and a more adequate one is not imagined (Nelson, 1987). How, then, does one adequately frame and hold a view of the world?

Cherished points of view are frequently presumed to rest upon objective standards that are knowable with certainty. When, however, a framework fails, its presumed objectivity is unmasked as a pretentious grounding. "Infallible revelations" become cultural contrivances and "proofs" are reconsidered as opinions. In times of severe disenchantment, unmasking is globally applied. Not one fallen faith, but all versions of reality are seen as human creations and "not reflections of eternal, objective truths" (Watzlawick, 1976, p. xi).

The Western world's confidence in objective certainty has been repeatedly shaken. Where do we find an "inerrant revelation", "essential premise", or "indubitable fact" that can objectively distinguish truth from error? Do not all such standards draw their authority from assumptions and commitments that cannot themselves be objectively grounded? In other words, although we may justify beliefs by standards *within* a framework of understanding, there are no independent standards that can judge *between* frameworks. Does reason, therefore, become merely parochial, a handmaiden to ideological commitments that cannot be rationally justified? Are all ideologies validated by their own terms? Must we who would avoid a dogmatically grounded worldview, ultimately choose one, or court nihilism in the vain search for an objective truth?

These issues bear upon rhetoric, especially when rhetoric is seen as the symbolic element in the social construction of reality. From this view, frameworks, paradigms, and cultural forms of life are created and sustained through a process of collective definition that is inherently rhetorical. Constructionism elevates rhetoric from discrete acts of influence within the world to the big picture, through which our worlds are viewed. What we know and the standards by which we claim to know are rhetorically constructed. There are no rhetorically untouched standards for knowledge. Erickson's search for a "new ideological orientation" is, in effect, the quest for a rhetorically compelling vision of life.

But how can we reasonably assess the rhetorical visions that compete for our loyalty? Here our earlier questions about reason and ideology return under a rhetorical guise. There are fascist and democratic views of the world, magical and biological approaches to medicine. Some societies encourage free inquiry; others kill to prevent it. Theories may be acknowledged as theories, or reified as the unquestioned truth. Although these distinctions are not as clear as we might hope, most of us take the side of democracy, biology, free inquiry, and theoretical self-consciousness.

Can we, encapsulated as we are in a rhetorically sustained vision of life, maintain these values with more rational confidence than whim, taste, custom, or a coin toss will allow? Lacking objective standards of certainty, how do we rationally distinguish between rhetorically compelling views of the world? In an age when promises of objectivity disappoint us, dogmatic and reified ideologies disgust us, and the vertigo of relativism threatens to engulf us, Can reason be our guide?

These issues invite rhetoricians to examine some of the most challenging existential and philosophical issues of our day. It is arguable, however, that this invitation should be declined. Perhaps, Erikson, despairing epistemologists, and people who write books on philosophy and rhetoric are simply "too philosophical." Why should we worry about the really *real,* or the nature of truth when philosophical answers seem to forever elude us? Can philosophical reflection grant us more than hesitancy in the face of necessary action? Is it not better to accept our culture's presuppositions, hone our rhetorical skills, manage our self-presentations, play our roles, collect our data, and never ask why?

I cannot blame someone for wishing to avoid the pathos of the examined life. It is unlikely, however, that one can live consciously and well without encountering the questions: How do I know? What should I trust? An unexpected catastrophe, a moment of wonder, or a critical decision can provoke the shaking of our epistemological foundations. Most of us will not die before we awake to the questions: What really is the case? What is worth the investment of my work?

The philosophy of critical rationalism encourages our search for truth as an "unended quest" (Popper, 1974) and holds that reason, properly regarded, can help us make progress. In this chapter, critical rationalism is explored as an important resource for understanding how we can reasonably say "rhetoric structures our world." The discussion consists of three parts. First, I review the philosophy of critical rationalism. Second, assuming a critical rational stance, I consider a variety of topics related to the question: How can we understand and practice rhetoric rationally in a world where all knowledge is fallible? Finally, critical rationalism is examined in the context of the contrasting philosophies.

CRITICAL RATIONALISM: A THEORY ABOUT THEORIES

Critical rationalism is the view that knowledge advances as we make bold conjectures, but hold them open to the possibility of refutation through criticism (Popper, 1962). In its most comprehensive form, critical rationalism is "pan critical" (Bartley, 1984), inviting criticism of its own assumptions. Taking originating cues from Karl Popper, the movement has been developed and diversified by Popper's students—especially W. W. Bartley, Joseph Agassi, and Ian Jarvie. Critical rationalism holds as its agenda the reconceptualization of Western rationality, believing that this worthy tradition is now in a state of crisis. The proposed resolution has implications for the intellectual frontiers of science, art (Gombrich, 1972), literature (Davenport, 1987), religion (Bartley, 1984), psychotherapy (Fried & Agassi, 1976), and rhetoric (Orr, 1978b).

Before I review critical rationalism let me acknowledge a personal bias. I see no reason to pursue philosophy as a way of being clever, demonstrating scholarship, or propping up the legitimacy of an academic discipline. I do not believe philosophy should be an intramural intellectual game played by specialists who speak a discipline-specific language. My attention drifts from treatises that give no indication that there is life beyond Philosophy, but is drawn to texts where philosophers reflect upon their attitudes toward life and death. Here I expect to discover the most provocative insights and, hopefully, a contribution to the "informal art of living in general" (Burke, 1973, p. 308).

Not surprisingly, therefore, I find these words from Popper (1975) to be the most revealing in the literature of critical rationalism: "Let our theories die in our stead" (p. 78). From a critical rational view, theory is the preeminent human achievement. "We approach everything in light of a preconceived theory" (Popper, 1970, p. 52). Through theory we detach ourselves from immediate experience, and construct a map of what the world is, and what our future will be. Theory is our guide into the unknown. If we are misguided, we fail or perish. Therefore, we cannot afford to follow theories blindly, but must criticize them severely to "get rid of a badly fitting theory before the adoption of that theory makes us unfit to survive" (Popper, 1975, p. 78). Refuted theories die in our stead.

We are not, however, always so fortunate. Theories do not always die in our stead. Some theories are disguised as the incontestable truth, protected from criticism, and endowed with immortality. As a result, human creativity, science, and life itself may be sacrificed to an unquestioned faith. Consequently, the only good theory is a potentially dead one; that is, one that is repeatedly exposed to the possibility of its own refutation.

The best theory is one that is severely criticized and survives. No theory, however, is finally proven. There is no guarantee that our theories, nor the standards by which they are judged, are valid. Our knowledge is always tentative and uncertain. We are fallible creatures. In Popper's (Miller, 1985) words: "Our ignorance is sobering and boundless . . . with each problem we solve, we . . . discover new and unresolved problems, . . . where we believed that we were standing on firm . . . ground, all things are in a state of flux" (p. 8).

We can never be certain that we know the truth; but we can eliminate error. When we do, knowledge does advance. How we make progress is a continuing debate, but that knowledge advances—at least in science—cannot be seriously doubted. "We know a great deal; . . . many details of . . . practical significance and what is even more important . . . a surprising understanding of the world" (Miller, 1985, p. 8).

Refutations

These deceptively simple insights reveal the spirit of critical rationalism. When fully developed, they challenge and scandalize some of the most entrenched habits of the Western mind. As a philosophy of conjectures and refutations, critical rationalism defines itself, in part, by its "friendly/hostile" critique of numerous "isms" (Popper, 1975). These isms fall into three generic brands: naive realism, justificationism, and relativism.

Naive Realism

Sylvia Plath (1971) created the image of a person living under a bell jar fogged by her own breath. Naive realists live in the bell jar but don't know it. They acknowledge no frame of reference. Truth is manifest, and self-evident to the beholder. For critical rationalists, naive realism is a benchmark of philosophical error (Agassi, 1975, p. 100; Popper, 1962, p. 8).

Critical rationalists find the most obvious examples of naive realism in religion (Jarvie, 1984; Popper, 1962). Imagine a person who claims that an infallible revelation has been received by the apostles, the church, or "the elect." However, there is no recognition that whatever God there might be, the revelation received is shaped in part by the culture, language, and assumptions of the recipient. Because no assumptions are acknowledged, none will be scrutinized. Therefore, what is at least in part a human artifact, is disguised as the objective truth and protected from criticism.

Much of modern philosophy is a self-conscious rebellion against religious claims to infallibility. Religious doctrines are repudiated because they are not derived from sound premises or established by scientific facts. But, when pressed to defend their own positions, modern philosophers often resort to self-evident premises, or facts that are manifest to "the innocent eye" (Popper, 1962, p. 15). The first approach may be called *essentialism* (Popper, 1962, p. 19); the second, *objectivism* (Orr, 1978b, p. 267). Both naively discount the influence of the knower on the known. The epistemological line between religious authoritarianism and modern philosophy is not as great as we might imagine.

From a critical rational view, any philosophy that rests its case on an essential, or self-evident truth is authoritarian at heart and has not traveled far enough from the benchmark error of naive realism. There are no "innocent eyes." No one knows the absolute truth absolutely. All knowledge is fallible, including our knowledge of the standards by which we pretend to justify our beliefs.

Justificationism

Suppose we do not anticipate a pristine disclosure of objective truth. We are not naive. We know we do not hold the absolute truth in our hip pockets (Popper, 1970, p. 56). All we knowingly possess are theories; rhetorical visions of what the truth might be. How shall we choose between our theories? We might flip a coin, take a vote, read tea leaves, or make a leap of faith. We could consult a guru, appeal to papa, or ask the bartender for advice. We might become overtly emotive, and conclude, "If it feels good, believe it." Justificationism is the view that these solutions are irrational and authoritarian. Belief dilemmas are not to be settled arbitrarily but through argument and evidence; that is, truth claims should be rationally justified.

But, what does it mean to be rational? Western thought has proposed two prominent answers to this question: intellectualism and empiricism (Bart ley, 1984, pp. 87–90). The first seeks to justify beliefs by intellectual intuition and its logical derivatives; the second upholds the standard of factual observation. Critical rationalists believe that both suggestions are inadequate, and frankly give rationalism a bad name. Neither intellectualism nor empiricism can justify its own standards by the rigors they seek to impose on other doctrines. Both are trapped in circular reasoning, or are dissipated in the hopeless search for a self-justifying criterion.

For instance, suppose I justify my beliefs to you by arguing that they are deduced from clear and distinct ideas. You wish to know why clear and distinct ideas can justify my beliefs. If I again appeal to clear and distinct ideas, my reasoning is circular and will only satisfy a person who is already committed — without justification — to this criterion. If I invoke a new standard to justify my existing one, you can ask for its justification and my dilemma repeats itself. I am left with either an arbitrary standard, or an infinite regress, normally cut short by a naive appeal to "essential premises," or "obvious facts" (Popper, 1962, p. 23).

Critical rationalists insist that justificationism has discredited rationality. It offers proof and verification, but cannot deliver the promise. Authoritarians and fideists are no more arbitrary in their views than rationalists who plead for argument and evidence. The skillful fideist knows this and taunts: "*all* standards for belief are arbitrary; therefore, I am entitled to my parochial view. You have your faith and I have mine, *tu quoque,* no further debate is possible." The *tu quoque* is a formidable defense against reason (Bartley, 1984, pp. 71–78). Neither intellectualism nor empiricism in their classic forms can defend themselves against it. As a result, the voice of reason is embarrassed into silence and a cacophony of apparent nonsense is protected from critical examination.

Critical rationalism seeks to remedy this crisis by changing rationalism's identity. Henceforth, rationality will not be the justification of beliefs, but the criticism of conjectures. But is this not also an arbitrary "standard"? Can reason ever be more than the handmaiden of a parochial perspective? Are not all schemes of rationality *relative* to an arbitrary frame of reference?

Relativism

While recognizing the relativity of all knowledge, critical rationalism excoriates the philosophy of relativism. Popper (1972) regarded relativism as the "central bulwark of irrationalism" (p. 56) in our time. The most challenging forms of relativism appear in cultural anthropology and the historiography of science. Even in these fields, relativism wears many faces. In a general way, however, the following conveys the relativism to which critical rationalism most frequently objects.

From the standpoint of relativism, all distinctions between good and bad, right and wrong, true and false are made within a framework of human construction. Frameworks may be considered as cultures, paradigms, forms of life, and so forth. There is no framework-independent criterion to judge between the frameworks. The truths of one framework cannot be translated into the understanding of another; frameworks are incommensurable. There is no universal truth; only framework-specific truths. This is a liberating conclusion, as the most hideous moments in history have occurred when one group has tried to impose its opinions, as a universal truth, on another. All distinctions between truth and error should now be seen as homebased and all frameworks respected as equals.

The intent of relativism seems unquestionably admirable. Even critical rationalists are impressed. Agassi (1963) called relativism an "intelligent error"; Gellner (1985) attributed relativism to "intellectual liberals" who champion tolerance. But, critical rationalists insist that relativism is, in fact, a hidden ally of the closed mind. It is factually, logically, and pragmatically wrong for three reasons.

First, cultural frameworks are not incommensurable. To take seriously our talk of other frameworks, we must acknowledge that we are not entirely imprisoned within them (Jarvie, 1984). If we were, we could not recognize other frameworks as "other"; the belljar would not only be fogged, but opaque. Cultural anthropology would be impossible; field notes would be merely shadows cast by our own projections. Of course, we do cast shadows. Overcoming projections is a prodigious task; but it is not logically impossible. In Popper's (1972) words: "At any moment we are prisoners caught in a framework of our theories . . . but . . . if we try, we can break out of our framework. . . . Admittedly, we shall find ourselves again in a framework; but it will be a better and roomier one; and we can . . . break out of it again" (p. 56).

Second, if all cultures are given equal respect, intolerance is made equal with tolerance. Logically, tolerant relativists must respect intolerant cultures as much as their own democratic framework. As Gellner (1982) noted: "The tolerant endorsement of human diversity becomes very tangled if one realizes that very many past and alien visions have themselves in turn been internally exclusive, intolerant and ethnocentric; so that if we, in our tolerant way, ENDORSE THEM, we thereby also endorse or encourage intolerance at second hand" (p. 182).

Third, if tolerant relativists make tolerance a universal value, a standard for evaluation across cultures, they betray their own relativism. Jarvie (1984) does not believe relativists can avoid making universal prescriptions. "Equal respect for all" is not based on the desire to honor fascists as much as democrats. In spite of disclaimers, relativists do hold universal values and, therefore, hopelessly contradict themselves.

Ultimately, the debate with relativism is not over logic alone, but pragmatics. Critical rationalists believe that the greatest possible tolerance is achieved in cultures that nurture a critical tradition (Magee, 1973, p. 76). Liberal relativists have been reared in a self-critical framework, but now take it for granted. In attempting to respect all cultures, they fail to credit the genius of their own. In other words, tolerance for other cultures rests upon a framework of self-criticism which not all cultures share. When we attempt to respect all cultures equally, that precious and precarious "meta-framework" (Bartley, 1984, p. 167) loses the voice of its own advocacy. While respecting all cultures as much as possible, critical rationalists are advocates for the critical tradition. They do not hesitate to make universal prescriptions. Not all cultural achievements are equal; those that foster a critical tradition and criticize their own tradition *are* superior (Gellner, 1985, p. 1).

Relativism is not wrong because it recognizes that knowledge is relative to a framework of understanding; knowledge *is* framework dependent. Relativism is wrong because it fails to see that some frameworks invite criticism of what is known, and subject *themselves to criticism*. These frameworks are not arbitrary, but critically revisable and therefore rationally superior.

The grand showcase of achievement for the critical tradition is science. Here critical rationalists believe they can point concretely to a tradition where human beings criticize their most cherished theories, and finding them refuted make bold new conjectures. No wonder, from this perspective, critical rationalists respond to Kuhn's historiography of science as their greatest philosophical challenge (Popper, 1972).

According to Kuhn (1962), science is relative to the paradigms in which it is practiced. There have been many "sciences" across the ages. Only revolutionary science approximates the sequence of refutations and conjectures that critical rationalists admire. Revolutionary science is rare. "Normal scientists" do not criticize the frameworks in which they serve. In fact, they probably do not understand the ultimate assumptions that guide their disciplines. They are dogmatic in spirit. They solve puzzles in the inherited perspective, so it will be patched up and sustained. Scientific rationality is framework bound, an ancillary to the dogmatic maintenance of the established tradition. Without dogmatism, science could not conduct its daily affairs.

In response to Kuhn, Popper does not deny that scientists frequently act as Kuhn says they do. However, Popper rejects "normal science" as science, in principle. With due respect for scientific tenacity, Popper looks to the Einsteinian revolution as an exemplar of what science logically can and should be. The normal scientist is, for Popper (1972), an epistemological lackey, a sad case: "The normal scientist, as Kuhn describes him, is a person one ought to feel sorry for. The normal scientist . . . has been badly taught. . . . All teaching at the university level . . . should be encouragement in critical thinking. The normal scientist . . . has been taught in a dogmatic spirit; he is a victim of indoctrination. He has learned a technique which can be applied without asking for the reason why" (pp. 52–53). Few passages more clearly reveal critical rationalism's program for science, education, and society in general.

I have examined critical rationalism's refutations of naive realism, justificationism, and relativism in the most general way. A more detailed analysis would show the extent to which critical rationalists believe that the Western world has lost its rational bearings. A brief survey will make the point. As critical rationalists see the situation: Classical rationalism has failed, since there is no way to deduce proofs from self-evident premises. Truth is not self-evident (Popper, 1962). Baconian inductivism is a fraud. Science requires an alternative interpretation. There are no uninterpreted facts from which to launch an induction, and scientific understanding is a conjecture beyond the data. Logical positivism is dead, having choked on its own disclaimed metaphysics (Popper, 1986). Relativism in one form or another seems to hold the day. Philosophers, who once sought the "logical atoms" of verifiable discourse, now analyze culture-bound language games as a sophisticated form of trivial pursuit (Popper, 1986). Kuhn (1962) relativized science using disciplines of massive confusion, such as history and sociology (Popper, 1972). Cultural anthropologists cannot decide whether witches do or do not exist without consulting "the cultural climate" (Jarvie, 1984, p. 105). Liberal religionists retreat to arbitrary commitments, and hide theological doubt from their congregations under a cloak of paternalism (Bartley, 1984). Sociologists of knowledge (Bartley, 1987a) are unable to manage the moat in their own eye, and orthodox Marxists naively assume that history can be read like a book (Popper, 1963). Meanwhile, blatant authoritarianism wins new converts, critical resolve is diminished in education, and would-be rationalists find their voices silenced by the *tu quoque* argument.

Conjectures

Reason has lost its voice! How can reason's voice be regained? Critical rationalism believes that reason needs a new identity (Bartley, 1984, pp. 161–165); a posture that promises less than proof for rational beliefs, but claims more for reason than relativism will allow. In other words, reason must find a way to solve "the great problem: How can we admit that our knowledge is a human — an all too human — affair, without at the same time implying that it is all individual whim and arbitrariness?" (Popper, 1962, p. 16). In response to this issue, the "new" rationalist will not be identified as one who says, "I am rational because I can prove or verify my beliefs." The "new rationalist" will offer instead what no authoritarian can risk: *To hold every presupposition open to criticism and the possibility of change.* The viability of reason's "new identity" depends upon the cogency of seven critical rational assumptions.

The Tu Quoque Argument is Refuted[1]

When defined as justification, reason is silenced by the *tu quoque* argument; because "standards of proof" are no less arbitrary than appeals to authority, or faith. However, critical rationalists do not demand proof from themselves or others. What reason requires is criticism and a willingness to change when criticized effectively. Critical rationalists believe that they can make this demand without slipping themselves into an arbitrary commitment. As a result, the *tu quoque* argument is refuted (Bartley, 1984, pp. 118–126). That is, by holding their own views open to criticism, critical rationalists avoid an arbitrary stance. They invite the strongest cases against their position, and state the conditions under which it could be refuted (Bartley, 1984, pp. 217–241). The fideist is asked to do the same. But the "irrationally committed" will not do this. Therefore, authoritarians and critical rationalists are not epistemological equals. Not all beliefs are arbitrary; some are criticized and some are not. Only the former merit our conviction.

Sources of Knowledge are Not Restricted

Critical rationalists believe that attempts to justify knowledge by an appeal to sources such as "facts" or "premises" will only strengthen the appeal of relativism. No claim to know is justified by its origin. All sources of knowledge *are* relative to a framework of apperception. Science is no more justified by "facts" than religion is justified by "revelation." We may claim whatever sources we will for our knowledge (Popper, 1962, pp. 3–33). Dreams, myths, or drinking black coffee can provide insights. A "religious experience" may move one to proclaim a new theory. A metaphor or myth might launch a metaphysical paradigm. No source validates or invalidates a perspective. The rationally significant issue is not, "*Where* did we discover our ideas?" but rather, "What shall we do with them once they are obtained?" Only ideas that are destined for criticism are rationally significant.

---

[1]Popper disagreed with his students on the *tu quoque* argument. Beyond *a commitment to reason itself,* he held all other assumptions open to criticism (Agassi, 1981, p. 465–476).

Critical rationalism's concern with origin is, in part, an attempt to restate the rational superiority of science. Baconian inductionism looked to facts as the source of science. But, facts are not pure, and scientific understanding always goes beyond the facts (Popper, 1986). This, however, is not an indictment of science. The glory of science does not rest with the source of its theories, but in the ability to put theory to the test.

As science is not validated by its sources, so metaphysics is not compromised by its origin. Unlike positivists, critical rationalists do not dismiss metaphysics as nonsense. "Let the metaphysicians device their theories." "Let the mythic imagination flourish." Religion, per se, is not excluded from rationality. No operational definitions are demanded before a theory can be advanced; no verification is required. In Popper's (1975) words, "We should be anxious not to suppress a new idea even if it does not appear to us to be very good" (p.85).

However, such rational hospitality has its costs. Although theories unbaptized by science are not banished into a limbo of "non-sense," neither are they elevated to a haven of supra-rationality. All conjectures are rationally significant only if *something could count against them*. This is reason's demand. If nothing is permitted to count against a theory, then it can be counted rationally "Out!" (Gellner, 1987). In Miller's (1985) words, "We are plainly entitled to exclude from serious consideration proposals that we cannot criticize and, therefore, cannot put right" (p. 9).

Criticism Takes Multiple Forms

What counts against a theory? Critical rationalism provides more than one answer to this question. Moreover, all "answers" are "checks" against a theory, rather than proofs or justifications; of course, the checks themselves are open to criticism. The following is a brief survey of critical methods used by critical rationalists.

"The check of logic: Is the theory in question consistent?" (Bartley, 1984, p.127). If people contradict themselves, they simply fail to make an arguable point. Logical consistency is a precondition for argument.

"The check of falsification: Can a theory be contradicted by statements of empirical observations?" (Bartley, 1984, p. 127). The younger Popper was impressed by the ease with which theories can be supported with evidence. The therapist Adler once assured Popper that Adlerian psychology is supported by daily clinical experience. Popper wondered what could possibly count against Adlerian psychology in Adler's eyes (Popper, 1962, pp. 34–35). Potential for falsification became for Popper, the mark of a scientific theory (Popper, 1982).

More specifically, falsification is a logical relationship between a theory and statements of empirical observation (Popper, 1972). A statement that specifies a condition to be observed in space and time is logically derived from theoretical premises. If this statement is contradicted by statements about the specified domain of observation, at least one of the theory's premises needs to be reconsidered (Bartley, 1984, pp. 186–196). While the potential for falsification makes a theory scientific in principle, actual falsification counts against the theory's validity.

However, observational statements are not infallible; facts are not self-evident. For this and other reasons (Bartley, 1984, pp. 181–185), falsification is never final. A theory that is severely tested and survives falsification is not proven, but rather corroborated.

Unlike the positivists' standard of verification, falsification does not distinguish between meaning and nonsense. Nonscientific theories, such as metaphysics, can be rationally considered. Among the ways of criticizing a metaphysical theory is the check of scientific theory: *"Is the theory— whether or not it can be falsified—in conflict with a scientific hypothesis"?* (Bartley, 1984, p. 127).

For instance, intersubjectivism, the view that reality is not independent of collective definition, contradicts realism's belief in an objective reality. Neither view is falsifiable. Each is compatible with a universe of observations. However, realism is implied by evolutionary theories, which are capable of making falsifiable hypotheses. Therefore, insofar as evolutionary theory implies an independent reality—and is corroborated—it counts against a metaphysics of subjectivism (Bartley, 1987b, pp. 36–38).

"The check of the problem: What problem is the theory intended to solve? Does it do so successfully?" (Bartley, 1984, p. 127). Popper believes that the enterprise of conjectures and refutation logically proceeds in this fashion: "Problem → the proposal of a trial solution → error elimination → and the resulting solution with A NEW PROBLEM" (Magee, 1973, pp. 60–61). To assess a theory one must understand the problem it is attempting to solve. If no solution is forthcoming, the theory fails. If a solution is found, a new problem arises.

For instance, justificationism fails to solve the problem: "How can arbitrary standards of theoretical choice be non-arbitrarily challenged?" The *tu quoque* argument counts against justificationism. Critical rationalism solves this problem, but inherits new ones: How are theories criticized? And, how are problems evaluated in terms of rational importance (Briskman, 1987)? Solutions to these problems will incorporate the gains made in solving the former problem and thereby extend those gains into new domains of resolution. However, because each solution generates a new problem, there can be no final definition of rationality. We learn to be more rational as we rationally face our problems. Rationality pulls itself up by its own bootstraps (Briskman, 1987). In Popper's words: "Our progress can be best gauged by comparing old problems with our new ones. If the progress that has been made is great, then the new problems will be of a character undreamt of before . . . The further we progress in knowledge, the more clearly we can discern the vastness of our ignorance" (p. 75).

Knowledge is Relative, Truth is Absolute

We will not discern "the vastness of our ignorance" when knowledge is presumed to be absolute, or infallible. Every claim to know the absolute truth absolutely leaves some human artifact unexamined, some cavity of ignorance unacknowledged, and some problem hidden from exploration. How do we keep before us, at all times, the penultimate nature of our most cherished intuitions? How can we unmask pretentious claims of infallibility?

Critical rationalists recommend a distinctive brand of realism. Reality is not exhausted by our perceptions or our theories. It is not contingent upon our wishes, or our will. All knowledge about reality is fallible and relative to the framework from which it is perceived. However, truth is not relative. Truth is *whatever is the case*. It is beyond human authority. Truth, as such, is absolute (Popper, 1962, p. 30). In other words, critical rationalists are realists, but not naive realists. They deny that the concept of objective reality entails objectivism. Rather, "objective reality" highlights a threefold distinction between knowledge and reality.

First, all claims to know the absolute truth absolutely are chastened by reference to an infinite reality that we cannot claim to know. "To search after truth is to start to scale a mountain of infinite height. It is no more possible that some climber will reach the top than it is that some mathematician will count all the numbers" (Bartley, 1984, p. 156). It is in the "true worship" of objective reality as our epistemological goal that "we remind ourselves that our current views of reality are partial and imperfect" (Campbell, 1987, p. 85).

Second, objective reality is the goad to continual investigation. The elusive truth calls us to an "endless," but intriguing quest. Boorstein (1983) wrote in the spirit of critical rationalism when he said, "The most promising words ever written on the maps of human knowledge are terra incognita — unknown territory" (p. xvi).

Third, the concept of objective reality points to the ultimate judge of our conjectures. The "unknown territory" holds veto power over our theories. If we conceive the world incorrectly, reality will pay us back severely. This is why we must be critically alert to clear our theories of as much error as possible.

In everyday life, we repeatedly distinguish between "the real and the apparent." We speak about "the movie" and the real world beyond the movie (Jarvie, 1987). Graduates understand the difference between "the real diploma" and the surrogate received at commencement. We distinguish between our "interpretations" and what "really is the case." Critical rationalists see no reason for placing a moratorium on such distinctions. Instead, we are encouraged to push the distinction between the apparent and the *real* to the parameters of all conceptual frameworks.

In evolutionary theory, we acknowledge a world that existed before we perceived it, and one that will endure after we perish. We compare and contrast species as they adapt to a common, independent world. A frog does not have the visual equipment to spot a nearby but stationary fly. The frog would starve, if no insects moved. We do not wish to grant subjective idealism to the frog. It sees the world in one way, we see it differently, but it *is one, objective world* (Bartley, 1987b, pp. 36–38).

Whatever we know is not properly regarded without a reminder that there is something "independent of us, that in the end decides whether our conjectures are valid" (Gellner, 1985, p. 17). The truth is absolute, but elusive. By seeking the absolute truth, while never claiming to know it absolutely, we create the possibility for endlessly revising our fallible understanding.

Knowledge is an Evolutionary Process

Critical rationalists believe that neo-Darwinian evolution gives us clues for understanding the advance of knowledge (Bartley, 1987b). That is, there is a continuity between species survival and epistemological progress. Theories and species survive as a result of *variation, retention,* and *selection.* Theories are eliminated through trial and error in a critical community, as species perish or survive through environmental *selection.* Criticism is the selective niche of epistemological evolution. *But variation and retention are also important.*

Bold and creative theoretical *variations* are required for epistemological progress. There can be no criticism if there are not conjectures. Likewise, criticism and retention are not logically estranged. While all conjectures are subject to criticism, not all conjectures can or should be criticized all the time. The fallibility of knowledge does not prohibit the retention of perspectives that have been put to the test. "Clumsily applied eradication of error may also eradicate fertility. Criticism must be optimum rather than maximum, and deftly applied" (Bartley, 1984, p. 183). In other words, critical rationalists are not epistemological masochists. Advocacy is legitimate. The voice of reason is regenerated in an environment where criticism *and* creativity are "truly inspired" (Bartley, 1984, p. 183).

Epistemology Requires an Ecology of Knowledge

Critical rationalism's view of the epistemological environment is rooted in Popper's "three worlds" of cognitive significance (Popper, 1972). World 1 is the domain of physical objects; World 2 is the self; and World 3 is our cultural heritage, with its myths, stories, problems, and theories. Knowledge is largely a property of World 3. World 2 cannot even know itself apart from World 3. That is, we determine who we are by taking definitions for the self from World 3 categories. Amassed in World 1 facilities, such as libraries and computers, World 3 knowledge transcends the self, as reality transcends knowledge.

However, the self may find within its World 3 legacy an undiscovered problem, or create a novel conjecture. The individual can be a window of creativity within a world of inherited fact. As such, the self is not determined, but socially restricted and encompassed (Popper, 1972, pp. 206–256). When an individual makes a conjecture, it becomes the property of World 3. There is an inevitable alienation of the created product (Bartley, 1987b) in every act of public advocacy. Arguments will yield insights that their authors could not have imagined. Knowledge advances through "unintended consequences." Epistemological progress takes place in the long run, as a corporate effort, in a conducive environment.

Critical Rationalism is a Social Program

Popper (1972) said that World 3 surrounds the individual, as a web encompasses the spider. But not every niche in the web is an equally good place to spin. Critical and creative rationalism require a supportive "econiche" in which to flourish. In Bartley's (1984) words, "If a rational individual is one who can tell the truth, a rational environment is one in which the truth can be told" (p. 182). Therefore, rationalists cannot support the voice of reason by merely being epistemologists. Ecological awareness and culture-building are required.

Bartley (1984) argued that critical rationalism must advance beyond epistemology to a concern with "manners and customs, and unconscious presuppositions, and behavior patterns that pollute the econiche and thereby diminish creativity, criticism, or both" (p. 183). The ecological problems of rationality will: "Force the epistemologist out of the ivory tower into which the dilemmas of justificationism have seduced him, and make of him a psychologist, a sociologist, a political scientist — even a social reformer" (p. 183). At this point, the philosophy of critical rationalism approaches traditional concerns of rhetorical theory.

CRITICAL RATIONALISM AND RHETORIC

Critical rationalism's epistemology and social program are aptly summarized in an analogy suggested by Agassi and Jarvie (Gellner, 1985, p. viii). Imagine that truth is analogous to wells that supply a city's water. The wells are beyond the city's walls, as truth is beyond human authority. No group or interested party can control the wells. The water supplies, however, are dammed within the social matrix of the city, as knowledge is relative to frameworks of understanding. The supplies *can* be controlled and tempt the city's leaders to personal and social corruption. No one can invent the wells, but institutions can be arranged to protect the supplies from corruption against the truth.

Clearly rhetoric plays a role in the social matrix that manages the supplies. Civic authorities might define a specific pool, or mirage, within the walls as *the well,* and demand unquestioned faith as the price for drawing water. The city's established intellectuals will dispute the authorities' claim and insist that all supplies, even the authorized pool, must have their "freshness" *justified* by comparison with a clear and distinct, transparent fountain that springs directly, without damming from the wells beyond the walls. The city also has its relativists who argue that there are no wells, at least no significant ones, only neighborhood pools, declared fresh by consensus, from which each community can respectfully find satisfaction.

No one in the city inspires the populace to search for better access to the wells. The blatantly irrational authorities, and the subtly authoritarian intellectuals will not seek a better discovery of the wells because for them the wells are *justifiably* known. Relativists will not inspire the search because for them there are no wells to seek. Hopefully, the city will discover a few rational rhetors who question the claim of privileged supplies, transcend communal agreement, incite a cleanup of the dams, and inspire the quest for greater access to that reality, outside the walls, upon which the city's life depends.

Beyond the limits of analogy, critical rationalism warns us not to guide rhetoric by justificationism or relativistic assumptions. Justificationism mistakenly abstracts some artifact of rhetoric *from* the social matrix, and celebrates the reified abstraction as a transparent manifestation of objective truth, a standard intuition, a premise, or fact before which all rhetorical conjectures must be justified. In terms of our analogy, a supply of water is treated as the well. As a result, criticism and creativity are diminished. The justifying standard will not become the object of rhetorical criticism, because it is not considered to be rhetoric, but a fulcrum of manifest truth upon which criticism turns. Creativity is discouraged, as rhetors seeking justification will not articulate a hunch, guess, or imaginative vision that cannot be readily justified.

Relativism puts truth totally *within* the social matrix. Truth is domesticated as custom or consensus, and the rhetor's face is turned toward agreement. Once again, criticism and creativity are endangered. It is unlikely that the pursuit of agreement can replace the terra incognita, logically or psychologically, as the inspiration for consensus-defying criticism and socially transforming visions of the world.

In other words, critical rationalism invites us to consider a rhetoric that when fully rational is bold and disciplined; one that serves as its end nothing less than objective truth, and claims for its power nothing more than a compelling, fallible, and criticizable conjecture. The key point should not be forgotten: In the name of objective truth, we must not slip into objectivism, nor fearing objectivism, disclaim an interest in what is absolutely the case. "Knowledge is relative, truth is absolute." From this assumption, we can extrapolate a summary view of a critical rational rhetoric: *Rhetoric is rationally understood and practiced when conjectures are recognized as conjectures, truth is seen as transcendent, and openness to criticism rather than justification is the rational restraint on a bold compelling vision of what the world, the self, and the human community can be.*

In the following discussion, the implications of a critical rational rhetoric are further clarified by an examination of six distinct issues: constructionism, the self, rhetorical transcendence, the rational community, the rational rhetor, and the education of the orator.

Rhetorical Constructionism

Since the 1960s, rhetorical theorists have argued that rhetoric does not merely convey, but constructs knowledge (Scott, 1976). From this view, "all our versions of reality are the results of communication and not reflections of eternal objective truths" (Watzlawick, 1976, p. xi). Knowledge is rooted within socially derived symbolic structures. Rhetoric as symbolic advocacy is a constituent element in knowledge; even a scientific version of reality depends upon rhetoric (Orr, 1978b).

Clearly, constructionism and critical rationalism have much in common. Critical rationalism's concern with theory can be equated with the constructionist's appraisal of rhetoric. From both perspectives, "We approach everything in light of a preconceived theory" (Popper, 1970, p. 52). "All observations are theory impregnated: there [are] no pure, disinterested, theory free observations" (Popper, 1975, p. 79). Regularities are not found in nature, they are theoretically imposed upon it. Science from Popper's view is "akin to explanatory storytelling, to myth making and to poetic imagination" (Popper, 1975, p. 78).

However, constructionism in one of its expressions takes a relativistic turn. From this view, not only are versions of reality rooted in rhetoric, but reality itself is a rhetorical construction. The concept of a purely objective reality is superfluous for knowledge. Truth is not correspondence with an objective world, but agreement among those who share a socially constructed frame of reference. Not only knowledge, but reality and truth are relative (Brummett, 1971).

With this view, as we have repeatedly seen, critical rationalism profoundly disagrees. Yes, knowledge is rooted in rhetorical constructions; but the source of knowledge is not decisive for the appraisal of knowledge. The key question is not "How do we gain knowledge" but, "How shall our versions of knowledge be compared, contrasted, and *qualitatively distinguished?*" Relativism cannot logically address this issue.

Relativistic constructionists do wish to make qualitative epistemological distinctions (Orr, 1978b). From their view, mechanism is defective, authoritarian reifications are in error, and rhetorically sustained false consciousness is wrong. But relativism lacks a consistent basis for making these charges. If truth is agreement, how can a mechanistic consensus be in error? If there are only versions of reality but no reality that eludes them, why is false consciousness false? On the other hand, if truth is beyond human authority, and reality is objective, then people who reify their constructs *are* mistaken.

The basic error in relativistic constructionism is its failure to distinguish logically between *objective reality* and *objectivism*. That is, relativists fear that if we acknowledge objective reality we are inevitably committed to a doctrine of self-evident truth. We are not. Objective reality as terra incognita, as absolute but elusive truth, is our ultimate safeguard against appeals to self-evidence. In making the distinction between objective reality and objectivism, critical rationalism frees constructionism of problems endemic to its "relativistic turn." This redirection has implications beyond constructionist ontology. Critical rationalism also provides a fresh focus for rhetorical anthropology.

The Self

Among the realities that we know through rhetoric is the self. How, then, shall we say the self is rhetorically constructed? We can anticipate critical rationalism's response to this question by recalling again the distinction between objective reality and objectivism. On the one hand, we must not naively assume that the self is transparently real to itself as a manifest essence that tells us what we must be. The self cannot be known apart from symbolic interaction. On the other hand, we should not conclude that the self is nothing but its socially derived identities. The discussion that follows will develop the implications of this position with regard to a salient issue in rhetorical anthropology: In what sense is the self one or many?

In 1972, Hart and Burks published their classic essay on "rhetorical sensitivity." It was a "harbinger" of the coming "situational era" in interpersonal communication (Rawlins, 1985, p. 119). Hart and Burks challenged the expressionists urge to display only the authentic, or "real self." From their view, appeals to the real self reduce the flexibility required to master a rapidly changing social world. (p.77).

To deal with expressionism, Hart and Burks chose a strategy similar to the relativistic turn in constructionism. That is, they dismissed "the real self" from rhetorical anthropology, as objective reality was precluded from constructionist ontology. The self was relativized into multiple selves. A unitary self was deemed "inappropriate" (p. 78) for explaining our many ways of being in the world. "Rather than there being a single self, a person is a set of interconnected selves" (p. 77). Therefore, "at its best, training in communication becomes a matter of helping a student (1) to widen this repertoire of selves . . . in order to deal more effectively with his interpersonal environment and (2) to discover those roles he enjoys playing" (p. 77). For similar reasons, Trenholm and Jensen (1988) wrote, "rather than worrying about the *real self,* we might better spend the time honing the various selves we need to use in the variety of situations we face daily". (p. 115).

The concept of multiple selves is indispensable for rhetorical theory and practice. But the "relativistic turn" that is used to establish the concept cannot explain the flexibility that multiple selves provide. For instances, my repertoire of selves, however wide, does not entail that *I* will be the one to select the self that in a given situation I shall become. Another may call forth one of my multiple selves. I may be alter-cast, rather than ego-cast. For this reason, Duncan (1968) concluded, "The ego must become a lord of counterpositions and not simply a go between institutional and social roles" (p. 91). The truly flexible self is not embedded in roles (Kegan, 1982), but manages them as an "agent", or an "I." When acknowledged, the elusive but continuous "I" grants us the detachment from embeddedness needed to consider, objectify, and select the selves we can be (Bartley, 1984, p. 174–176).

Hart and Burks concluded that our multiple selves are a "set of interconnected selves." But, this interconnection cannot be taken for granted. Our "subpersonalities [may be] variously at odds with one another" (Burke, 1966, p. 69). Unrelenting alterations in biography result in "a feeling of vertigo" (Berger, 1963, p. 63), "a metaphysical agoraphobia before the overlapping horizon's of one's possible existence" (p. 63). Such conflict is, according to Hofstadter (1985) "a soul ripping issue" (p. 782).

No doubt our multiple selves find integration as they are arranged in hierarchies of importance (Hart, 1988), and united through biographic narrative. According to Gergen and Gergen (1988), "one's view of self in a given moment is fundamentally nonsensical unless it can be linked in some fashion with the past. Rather than seeing one's life as one damned thing after another, the individual attempts to see life as a systematic whole" (p. 19). Thiots (1983) argued that multiple selves contribute to psychological well-being as long as one maintains "a meaningful sense of existence". A functional multiplicity of selves requires a unifying view of "who I am."

In summary, a purely relativized concept of self cannot account for the agency and integration that flexibility requires. As we shall see, insights from critical rationalism can solve the problem of expressionism without the detriments of the "relativistic turn" as it is applied to rhetorical anthropology.

First, from a critical rational view, expressionists do not fail because they invoke the concept of the real self. They fail because they are naive realists guided by justificationist guidelines. Their rationale seems to be: "I will take a social role only if I can thereby prove my real self. If the real self is not confirmed in social roles I will retreat from society, into my self where the SELF is transparently REAL."

Second, the unitary self does not need to be denied to overcome naive expressionism. We need only to insist that the unitary self *is not self-evident*. This we can do because in psychology as elsewhere objective reality does not logically entail objectivism. The unitary self, as we know it, is a *theory*. The self is constructed, not found. As Popper and Ecctes (1977), said, we know ourselves "by developing theories about ourselves" (p.109). Stripped of objectivism, the "real self" might be retained as a regulatory reminder that the self in its full potential transcends every attempt to define it.

Third, a theory of the unitary self does not inherently deny appreciation for the self's multiplicity. The sameness of our biographic identity does not preclude the acceptance of change, contradiction, and plurality within that identity. Gergen and Gergen (1988) showed that people may define themselves through "progressive narratives" that welcome change. The announcement that "I am a rhetorically sensitive person" may provide the requisite sense of unity to support contradictions. Bartley (1984) showed that it is possible to speak of the True Self as "A space in which all positionality . . . occurs" (p.174). Presumably, such an identity would cause one to expect multiplicity, while exercising the detachment that makes reflection and choice possible.

To this point, our discussion has shown that the unified self can be saved from the distortions of naive expressionism. I now argue that the effort to bring coherence to the self, or one's self-theory, can be a rhetorically generative event. That is, the resolution of an identity crisis can inspire a rhetorical effort that not only reestablishes continuity for the self, but creates vision for society. For this conclusion, I draw upon Erikson's theory of identity and Popper's concepts of World 2 and World 3.

As previously seen, Popper argued that all constructs for defining the self are drawn from cultural, or World 3, categories. Evidently, most people will acquire a *ready made* identity from socially bestowed definitions (Weigert, 1988). Some individuals, however, will struggle to recreate social categories in a novel fashion. The personal domain, World 2, can be a window of creativity within World 3. For instance, a woman who is a "mother" and a business "executive" may find a contradiction between her identities that is resolved by announcing herself to be "a nurturing entrepreneur". She has now brought new content to World 3, which her children may develop in unforeseen ways.

Erikson (1962) argued that an identity crisis is not resolved until a new identity receives social confirmation. In other words, individuals remain in crisis until some relevant World 3 niche accepts them as a "this" or "that." Imagine a seminarian who becomes intellectually disenchanted with her inherited faith. She decides she is no longer a Christian. She is a naturalist; however, a spiritual one who loves to preach. As long as there is no place for a "preaching naturalist" in her community, her identity will remain in crisis. An identity belongs as much to World 3 as World 2; it must be socially adapted.

However, a person may persist in presenting a novel identity until *the community does the adapting!* Conceivably, an individual might create a new rhetorical vision about what the world is, or the community might be, in a way that defines a home for the self's identity *and* establishes a novel social possibility. Such a person may be regarded "as crazy" and suffer a prolonged crisis or, in time, be hailed as a transformational leader. In Erikson's (1962) words: "The creative man has no choice. He must court sickness, failure, and insanity, in order to test the [new] alternative (to see) whether the established world will crush him, or whether he will disestablish a sector of this world's outworn fundaments and make a place for a new one" (p. 46). No doubt such traumatic tests are made rhetorically. A single speech, or series of speeches, may bring coherence to a conflicted self, while creating vision for the social world (Orr, 1988).

Bartley (1984) favorably quoted these words from Shaw: "the reasonable man adapts himself to the conditions which surround him. The unreasonable man persists in trying to adapt surrounding conditions to himself . . . All progress depends on the unreasonable man" (p. xiii). Putting aside differences over "reason", Bartley endorses Shaw's image of the rhetorically *creative* person.

It is a mistake to reify the self as an essence apart from society, *or* a multiplicity within society (Wrong, 1961). It is hoped that rhetorical education not only trains students in multiple role playing, but challenges them with critical problems that inspire the search for new biographical conjectures and social vision. In some cases, biography and vision may be rhetorically one.

A Rhetoric of Transcendence

Our discussions of constructionism and the self were based upon critical rationalism's view that objective reality and objectivism are logically distinct. One can speak about reality without naively presuming that the nature of reality is self-evidently known. What is logically possible can be, however, rhetorically precarious. Realists who wish to be "totally unspecific" in insisting upon "something beyond us" may in this "imperfect, dogmatism-addicted world tend to be a bit more specific" and in spite of their best efforts to do otherwise, absolutize the relative (Gellner, 1985, p. 17). How can we rhetorically construct the world, and the self, while maintaining an awareness that neither can be finally defined? Scheler (1985) stated the issue in compelling terms: "Man is not free to choose whether or not he wants to develop [an idea of the absolutely real] . . . Man, necessarily and always . . . has such an idea . . . Even without being quite aware of it, man can fill this sphere of absolute being . . . with a finite content . . . which in life he treats as absolute . . . This is fetishism and idol worship" (pp. 2–3). How do we "smash the idol" (Scheler, p. 3) without creating a new one? How can we rhetorically maintain a capacity for the rhetorical unknown?

We require, in the words of Branham and Pearce (1985), a "subversive loop" between text and context, that is, an awareness of a context for which no text is adequate. The best examples of this awareness come from Eastern mysticism; for instance Lao Tzu's saying, "the TAO that can be named is not the eternal TAO". What we need, however, for the Western voice of reason is an awareness of a transcendent context that does not transport us beyond all texts (Bartley, 1984, p. 176), but results in the critical revision of texts. In other words, critical rationalism leads us to seek a rhetoric of transcendence, that encourages a "heroic" (Becker, 1970), but always revisable investment in the social world.

From this view, individuals who self-consciously create symbols of transcendence for their communities provide especially good subjects for rhetorical study. For instance, Scott (1979) analyzed Arnold's poetic effort "to dance out" a sense of transcendence that would free the imagination from both positivism and religious orthodoxy. Rushing (1985) studied film as a rhetoric of transcendence. Most important, however, would be studies of communities that disclaim creedal limits but seek to cultivate that sense of mystery which "stands as the cradle of both art and true science" (Einstein, 1949, p 5). One thinks here of Gnostics in the ancient world (Bartley, 1984, p. 177), and Unitarians and Quakers in the contemporary setting. How do such communities, as organizations, succeed and fail?

The answer to this question holds implications beyond the advancement of rhetorical theory. As numerous observers of contemporary life have said, "wonder in the face of the mystery of being" is required to extricate ourselves from addictive materialism (Bellah, Madsen, Sullivan, Swidler, & Tipton p. 86 295), scientism (Rushing, 1985), and religious dogma.

The Rational Community

Critical rationalism's concern for transcendence is most forcefully expressed in the phrase "truth is beyond human authority." Once again, critical rationalism is strikingly at odds with relativism. Truth is not agreement. Truth is "beyond the wall;" it bears no necessary relationship to the number of people in the city who share an opinion. Even a worldwide consensus could be wrong. Therefore, unity is not the appropriate end for the rational community. "To the genuine democrat," said Watkins (1987), "there is something death-like in the ideal of unanimity" (p. 156). When agreement becomes the goal toward which a group aspires, not only rationality, but communication and community are diminished.

In *Retreat to Commitment,* Bartley (1984) gave an impressionistic account of Protestant Liberalism, an institution that has, in his view, placed cooperation before the search for truth. Based upon Barthian theology, liberal protestants unite around a minimal confession of "the authority of Christ." This commitment is self-consciously parochial and not subject to criticism. However, it may be interpreted freely. In fact, numerous interpretations are held simultaneously. Individual congregants, ministers, and theologians hold diverse theologies. These views are not only different, but contradictory. Some theologians hold positions that would be regarded as atheism if known by church members. However, the differing views are rarely expressed in *public dialogue.* In fact, ministers shield congregants from the disturbing beliefs and doubts of seminary professors. "Sophisticated theology is too much for the average congregant to bear." As a result, protestants commonly confess a creed despite having no idea what their fellow worshipers mean by the confession. Communication between congregants is more like a dance than discourse. This situation is rarely challenged, because idiosyncratic viewpoints might disturb a shared sense of unity. "Why bother to communicate if cooperation can be achieved without it?" (Bartley, 1984, p. 147).

Bartley's account of liberal protestantism may be too "impressionistic," but it reveals, by a contrasting example, what a critical rational econiche must avoid. Five propositions can be extrapolated from Bartley's discussion to construct a critical rational philosophy of communication and community.

First, *our capacity for communication is underdeveloped if we fail to engage in a cognitive dialogue that is discernible through disagreements.* Words can be merely carriers for emotions or signals that evoke a synchrony of automatic responses (Cialdini, 1988). Communication reaches its distinctively human potential with ideas, descriptions of the world, and argument.

Unfortunately, putative descriptions of the world can function as emotive exclamations, or cues to "step-in-time". "I believe in God the Father . . ." may be the functional equivalent of "ready, set, go!" Positivists believe that this is the inevitable character of religious language; critical rationalists disagree. Nevertheless, the language of any organization, religious or otherwise, can be reduced to little more than an invitation to dance.

On what grounds do we suspect that our language has reached this state of disguise? As long as agreement alone prevails, it is impossible to tell whether people are holding discussions or merely enjoying a synchrony. It is when disagreement appears that we have reason to believe that arguable ideas are at stake. Of course, even disagreement could be an odd form of dancing (Cappella, 1987). We can never prove that we are dialogically engaged. We can conclude, though, that the absence of "discernible disagreement" (Bartley, 1984, p. 142) counts against the confidence that we are communicating cognitively with each other.

Second, as with communication, *community is not fully realized in synchrony or emotional fusion* (Kerr, 1981). It is the cognitive capacity to reach autonomous conclusions that sets us apart from each other, and thereby creates the possibility for genuine mutuality. Community implies an engagement between two or more distinct persons (Jarvie, 1984). Where mere togetherness prevails over cognitive distinctions, we face each other in a state of "pseudo-mutuality" (Kerr, 1981). As the unknown is required for epistemological progress, otherness (Gurevitch, 1988) is required for community.

Third, *rhetorical efforts to preserve equanimity can destroy genuine community.* Public announcements that "we hold different views and think for ourselves," where differences are kept private, grant plausibility to the belief that mutuality exists, when it is yet to be established. Likewise, a paternalistic effort to protect the presumably unsophisticated from a truth "they cannot bear" may keep the peace, but precludes mutual respect (Jarvie, 1984).

Agreements stated at high levels of abstraction give a semblance of community, but mask disagreements and the further need for dialogue. As Bennett (1985) argued, a publicly declared consensus can become a self-fulfilling prophecy that discourages criticism. For similar reasons, Dyer (1987) concluded that "the inability to manage agreement is a major source of organizational dysfunction" (p. 96). Consensus is, of course, required for practical action, but consensus must not be confused with "the truth," or a community's ideal. Members of a rational group understand that consensus in the quest for truth can always be transcended.

Fourth, *disagreement without trust destroys community* (Watkins, 1987). Although critical dialogue cannot occur without disagreement; it will end when disagreements are stated in a way that violates trust. "If you and I vehemently disagree over a large moral issue, are we not tacitly accusing each other of an immoral outlook? And how can we trust each other if we regard each other as immoral?" (Watkins, p. 153)

As Watkins' question suggests, critical rationalists are implicitly interested in methods of rhetorical give-and-take. Jarvie and Agassi (1987) called for a philosophical "attention-shift" from epistemology to the "methodology" of "workshop rationality." Overlooked is the possibility that the logic of conjectures and regulation can be applied to interpersonal communication.

For example, in moral disagreement, I can attempt to eliminate "tacit accusations" by refusing to attribute motives to another. Instead, owning my perspective, I can delineate the facts as I see them, detail why they create a problem for me, and then ask the other to consider and possibly refute my view. Such skills are often practiced in actual workshops (Dyer, 1987, p. 99). They should not be despised because of their origin in the murky complexities of everyday life. As rhetoricians, we can evaluate and reconceptualize workshop skills from a theoretical base more adequate than the one from which they were generated. Many of our most valuable rhetorical insights arose as "unintended consequences" from theories that were false.

It is intriguing that rhetorical theorists are turning to philosophy for intellectual underpinnings at a time when a philosophy such as critical rationalism is fascinated and sometimes mystified (Jarvie, 1984, p. 122) by the rational importance of rhetorical skills. Hopefully, we are approaching the day when an estrangement between theory and practice will be rightly considered "outrageous" (Mitroff & Kilmann, 1983, p. 266).

Finally, critical rationalism appropriately emphasizes the cognitive dimension of communication, and correctly attacks an overemphasis on unity in the pursuit of truth. Socially, however, critical rationalism's greatest challenge is to itself: *A critical rational philosophy of community must be given institutional or cultural strength without precluding the possibility of self-transcendence.* How do we uniformly define a culture that resists unanimity? How is a community given structure, so that structures can be transcended? Rituals, sociability, passion, politics, socialization, and a vision of purpose create culture strength (Pacanowsky & O'Donnell-Trujillo, 1983). Even synchrony and dancing play a part! These performances are often inimical to critical rational values. No wonder Bartley (1984) lamented: There are a "thousand possible illustrations of a simple truth: it is much harder to institutionalize and to create an econiche for a program of unrelenting growth, development, and criticism than it is to create institutions and viable conditions for self-perpetuating systems of beliefs" (p. 181).

Fortunately, critical rationalists are not alone in the search for a viable self-transcending institution (Quinn & Cameron, 1988). Smith (1984) distinguished between stable and resilient cultures. Stable cultures seek a *fail-safe* world; one that is protected against failures, whether cognitive or otherwise. Resilient cultures persist by and through change. They seek a *safe-fail* world, where it is safe to fail, and learn from each mistake. No doubt resilient cultures persevere, in part, by establishing identities that are similar to "progressive narratives" in biography (Gergen & Gergen, 1988).

Weick (1980) argued that cultures persist through *eloquence,* that is, the linguistic nuance by which they repeatedly define themselves. Here then is one of the greatest challenges from critical rationalism to rhetorical theory: *What is the character of rhetorical eloquence that frames and sustains a culture of unrelenting growth, development, and criticism?"*

The Rational Rhetor

We turn now to the individual rhetor as a source of eloquence. More specifically, our concern is with the rhetor who attempts to speak rationally. Here, as with the rational community, we face a difficult challenge. How can one who acknowledges fallibility and invites criticism manage the complexities of the "open mind" in a way that results in a compelling message?

When the 41st president of the United States was inaugurated, a journalist (Gergen, 1989) wrote, "Most of today's politicians grew up after the Second World War and are afflicted by doubts and anxieties of the postmodern age. Their speeches, no matter how finely honed, rarely inspire public confidence because the men have no apparent core" (p. 26). The writer implied that complexity debilitates our psychic unity and makes a resolute voice impossible. I doubt that complexity as such immobilizes our rhetorical strength. In fact, complexity can create a resilient philosophical core (Bartunek, 1988). In many cases, it is our assumptions about knowledge that frustrate the perceived entitlement to speak with boldness.

We labor, I fear, under an implicit justificationism that tells us to restrict speech until there is proof. More than one conscientious intellectual has asked, "How can I address the world of business, or politics, with unverified conclusions? How do I know that I know? What if there is a study somewhere in the world that contradicts the point I made before my class today?" One is reminded of Luther brooding over unconscious and, therefore, unconfessed sins.

In a Yeatsian way, the vociferous dogmatist finds an ally in the would-be rationalist who will consider, reflect, moderate, and collect data but not speak boldly until the theories are verified and all the facts are gathered. From a critical rational view, the positivists' millennium will never arrive. Like Kierkegaard kneeling before Hegal's unfinished system, we wait endlessly for the fulfillment of an untenable promise. How, then, do we, as fallible but conscientious creatures, speak boldly in a complex world, where standards of proof cannot be consulted? I offer the following assumptions as a rough sketch of what the rhetorically rational person can be.

First, the rational rhetor acknowledges to herself that she sees the world from a limited viewpoint. Nothing she knows is self-evident. However, the notion that the world is seen from a limiting viewpoint does not mean that the vision is false. It may be true; one simply does not know that it is true. Under the possibility that her viewpoint is correct, the rational person ventures to speak.

Second, the rational rhetor considers the best case against his position before speaking. He searches for the most persistent and challenging attacks on his view. He wants to detect error. But the best case is not every case. Why should the conscientious person restrain speech, even though he has not heard every *possible* refutation of his view, while others will speak who neither acknowledge their frame-of-reference, nor hear any opposing voice? The world needs to hear disciplined opinions.

Third, one of rhetoric's gifts to reason is a deadline. *The rational rhetor* takes a stand. It can be a moment of high anxiety. The rational person respects ideas as "dangerous and powerful things" (Popper, 1962, p. 5). She does not want to communicate error but "there is no way known of systematically avoiding error . . . a reluctance to make mistakes typically degenerates into . . . a distaste for any kind of bold initiative . . . we must be fully prepared to correct mistakes, but if we are to correct them, we must be fully prepared to commit them first" (Miller, 1985, p. 9).

Fourth, *a speech is not justified by whether or not it is understood by the audience.* The rational person wants to have his ideas heard. However, his first concern is not audience understanding, but having something worthwhile to say. In the balance between audience commitment and message commitment, he tilts towards the message. The fear of misunderstanding can be the death of ideas. "One has always to take the risk of being mistaken, and also the important risk of being misunderstood or misjudged" (Popper, 1975, p. 86).

In a relevant study, Winter (1987) found that presidents who adapted well to their audience on inaugural day have not made the best leaders. To paraphrase Pacanowsky and O'Donnell-Trujillo's (1983) concern for organizational rhetoric, the most "influential impacts" of rational rhetoric "may occur over the long run. Consequently, at the level of the particular performance, the issue may be one less of effectiveness and more of eloquence" (p. 147). (Of course, this is an eloquence in Weick's (1980) sense of "nuances"; not an eloquence dictated by canons of style).

Fifth, the rational rhetor detaches the message from herself. There *is* an inevitable element of alienation in every act of advocacy. The rhetor "lets go" of the message. In the short run, she may invite criticism of her ideas, without yielding positions that remain cogent. (Dialogue requires not only a "thou," but a resilient "I.") Beyond dialogue, however, her message belongs to World 3. There it may be ignored, criticized, reinterpreted, misunderstood, or as a result of unintended consequences find influence across the years.

An Education For Orators

We might expect rational rhetoric to flourish in the university. Experience suggests that the performance has too often been disappointing (Bellah, Madsen, Sullivan, Swidler, & Tipton, 1986). Among the critiques of contemporary education, Kimball's historical account of the liberal arts is especially relevant to rhetoric. Kimball (1986) claimed that liberal education has traditionally served two ideals: one for *philosophers* and the other for *orators*. The philosophical ideal celebrated the search for knowledge through free inquiry. The orators prized the communication of knowledge within the university and beyond its walls. Kimball believed both ideals are currently in disrepair, but the orator's ideal is also in recession.

According to Kimball, the *philosophical ideal* has triumphed in the modern research university and resulted in fact gathering, by discrete disciplines, with little concern for values or the communication of knowledge to the larger world. Kimball blames skepticism and axiological nihilism for these conditions. Maybe so; I suspect they are attributable, in part, to an implicit but pervasive justificationist epistemology.

From a justificationist stance, the goal of knowledge is certainty through demonstrated conclusions. Such conclusions are determined by exacting standards of evidence. In order to increase certainty, one attaches (Bartley,

1984, p. 173) oneself ever more closely to precise methodologies. The realm of perceived certainty is small. One fears, above all, making a mistake. A professional lifetime may be required to master the methods that certify facts. In the process, each discipline develops its own elaborate terminology. The result is isolated disciplines, with esoteric facts, that outsiders frequently view as trivial. An interdisciplinary synthesis is nearly impossible (Toulmin, 1982, p. 237–254).

More specifically, in justificationism's econiche, "the context of discovery, which encourages 'creative imagination' is sacrificed for the context of verification which focuses on methodological sophistication and analytic rigor" (Fishman & Neigher, 1982, p. 539). As a result, education becomes intellectually uninspiring. As Featherstone (1986) argued undergraduates too often find themselves "majoring in a . . . mini-Ph.D. program run by specialized technicians." He added, "Surely this is not what Galileo suffered for, or why Socrates died. Trivial specialities abound" (p. xiii).

Kimball called upon universities to reinvest in the *orator's ideal* of creating and inspiring learning communities. From this perspective, the communication of knowledge is as important as the production of knowledge. "The heart of education is forming a community united in the disciplined effort of making meaning out of texts" (Featherstone, 1986, p. xiii). Today however, Kimball finds that the orator's ideal is largely restricted to religious colleges — where sacred texts are frequently seen as infallible. Therefore, criticism suffers. The free inquiry prized by the philosophers is undervalued by the religious orators, while the orator's concern for communication is neglected by current renditions of the philosophical ideal. Kimball's thesis prompts me to ask: *How can the educator seek and communicate knowledge in a way that inspires rational learning communities in politics, families, corporate life, and so forth?* We do not now have a comprehensive critical rational philosophy of education. But, when we do, it will surely include catalysts to push educators "out of the ivory tower" into which they have been seduced by "the dilemmas of justificationism" (Bartley, 1984, p. 209). Five propositions can be drawn from critical rationalism as a basis for educational reform.

First, *the implicit epistemologies that guide research and teaching should be made critically conscious.* Herbert Gans (1989) described with comprehensive brilliance a program for the communication of knowledge which this discussion too briefly implies. Gans argued, in part, that an "idealized version of the natural sciences" has obstructed communication between the university and the public. "The ideal is humanly unworkable; nevertheless, we cannot let go of it" (p. 11). I believe the "idealized view" stays because we do not know how to justify our work without it. Even more important, we are hampered by implicit epistemologies we cannot criticize, because they are not consciously owned. Reform begins, here as elsewhere, when theories are recognized and examined as theories.

Second, *knowledge as a product and the methods for attaining it should be de-constructed.* Popper (1983) told his students that the "scientific method does not exist"; and that he ought to know because for a time he was "the only professor of this nonexistent subject in the British Commonwealth" (p. 5). Idealized versions of science lead to reified visions of methodology that restrict learning. Therefore, Bartley (1984) argued that academic efforts should be more often marked as "first drafts," "trial balloons," or "damaged goods" (p. 208). Jarvie and Agassi (1987) called for "less definitive papers and more progress reports, less books and more book reviews and book outlines." Art work should more often be seen "in its planning" rather than in art galleries. As a result we might be willing "to alter temperamental givens" (Jarvie & Agassi, 1987, p. 442) and more readily learn from "peers . . . juniors [and] newcomers both in and beyond the university." (Jarvie and Agassi, 1987, p. 442).

Third, *learning begins with a passionate question* (Popper, 1983). The inspiring educator does not merely teach facts or skills, but arouses questions that lead to the critical construction of biographies, cosmologies, theories of rhetoric, and the resolution of practical problems.

Fourth, *the rational educator values where possible a clear and nontechnical vocabulary.* One does not go to the university, Popper (1983) argued, "to learn how to talk . . . impressively and incomprehensively . . . [or] to state the utmost trivialities in high-sounding languages" (p. 5).

Finally, *reason is the common heritage of humankind* (Popper, 1986). Rationality is not the exclusive province of academic disciplines that pursue new knowledge. People in everyday enterprise can become "reflective practitioners" (Schön, 1982). The mission of the university is not realized fully in the quest for *new* knowledge, but in educating the reflective communicator for the rational "interpretation, dissemination, and application of existing knowledge." (Lynton, 1987, p. xi).

In summary, critical rationalism provides a reworking of the *philosophers ideal* that facilitates a rational statement of the *orator's* goal. When the university values the creation of imaginative, rational learning communities as much as the production of certified knowledge, then perhaps we will see in the restoration of "a balance between ratio and oratio, the two poles of logos" (Kimball, 1986, p. 240). Reason will find its rhetorical voice, and rhetoric will become increasingly rational.

CRITICAL RATIONALISM: COMPARISONS AND CONTRASTS

Critical rationalism's capacity to renew reason's identity and voice must be assessed in a context of alternative views. In the following discussion, critical rationalism is compared with the philosophies that appear in this book. Not incidentally, our first point of comparison is *realism*. It is critical rationalism's closest kin.

According to Professor Hikins (chap. 2) realism comes in two kinds: ontological and epistemological. Critical rationalism accepts ontological realism's assumption that "much of the world does not depend on humans . . . for its existence" (p. 22). There is an objective world that transcends our will, whim, and symbolic endeavors. This world is assumed in everyday discourse; and, as Hikins illustrated, there is no "knockdown" argument against ontological realism that requires its abandonment.

Epistemological realism is a more complex issue. Critical rationalism carefully qualifies the claim that humans are capable of knowing at least some important dimensions of the real world *as it is*. As we have seen, critical rationalism rejects the doctrine of a manifest, transparent, or naked truth. Notice, however, this does not mean that we cannot know the world as it is, but that we cannot know with *certainty*. We strive to know the world, and in many cases there is no reason to doubt our knowledge. We have confidence and convictions. But we cannot claim that our knowledge is fixed, settled, guaranteed, or conclusive. We cannot close the book of knowledge. We are fallible creatures. Our ignorance is massive, and much that we know today will tomorrow be refuted.

Some brands of epistemological realism do claim *certain* knowledge. Professor Hikins, at times, also claims certainty. For instance, he argues that legal verdicts of guilt are usually settled "with certainty"; and that "questions now in the realm of the probable may, in the future, become known with certainty."

It is important to notice the context of Hikins' claims for certainty, and the realm of rhetoric it presupposes. In other words, what question are these claims trying to answer?

Hikins begins chapter 2 with examples from "pedestrian realism," such as "the dog is in the garage" and "Jenny went to San Francisco." These statements imply an objective world, knowable with certainty. Likewise, when rhetorical facticity is discussed, the typical examples are drawn from a specific episode of persuasion, where a speaker addresses an audience within a common culture. The facts at issue in these speeches are not unlike "Jenny went to San Francisco"; that is, they are day-to-day observations about the human world, wherein elements of facticity are unproblematic. Apparently, Hikins wants to know if arguments against epistemological realism can deliver a knockdown blow to the everyday confidence that we can know the facts of "simple empiricism" with certainty.

Critical rationalism's claim that knowledge is fallible, and open to criticism, does not mean that we cannot say with confidence "The dog is in the garage." Many routine observations are taken for granted, though we could if we wished make them questionable. Bartley simply does not believe it would be worth his time to debate whether or not "cats grow on trees." Issues may be closed *pro tem* (Jarvie & Agassi, 1987). Where institutions and methodologies are designed to assure criticism *in principle,* the critical epistemologist does not need to make house calls except in times of crisis. Critical rationalism is not designed to afflict the pedestrian world with comprehensive skepticism.

However, as Hikins acknowledges, the simple facts of the pedestrian world can readily be used as evidence for a larger narrative which entails an account "of the facts." Critical rationalism claims that no amount of "factual evidence" can prove, justify, or provide certainty for our larger narratives. These theories, myths, and frameworks provide the primary focus for critical rationalism's philosophical concern. Critical rationalism is a philosophy of the "big picture." As Popper (1986) indicated, "I think that the main task of philosophy is to speculate critically about the universe and about our place in the universe including our powers of knowing" (p. 211).

Bartley (1984) illustrated critical rationalism's level of analysis in his discussion of *positions, contexts,* and *meta-contexts.* A position is typically a "description, representation, or a portrayal of the environment" (p. 170). "The strawberry is so sweet" is presumably a statement of simple empiricism, where "sweet" refers to a tastable substance. However, compare the sensibility of making this statement while seated in one's office, comfortably eating in "a self-satisfied way" with "the Zen sensibility of the doomed Samurai, trapped on a collapsing bridge over a deep ravine, who savoring the moment, reaches out to pluck the strawberry growing wild on the steep bank and says, 'This strawberry is so sweet'." (Bartley, 1984, p. 171). The significance of the statement depends upon the *context,* or paradigm that directs its utterance. In addition, we develop *meta-contexts* that tell us "how and why" contexts are held. Critical rationalism seeks to answer questions about knowledge and reason at the meta-contextual level. Therefore, this chapter began with the question: "How can one adequately form and hold a view of the world?"

Professor Hikins' treatment of realism starts with a concern for "pedestrian realism," and holds that "positions" within that world can be established as facts with certainty. However, we do not function *in* the world of "simple empiricism" without an implied view *of* that world. For instance, Hikins makes this interpretive statement *about* the pedestrian world: "It is clear to us all that communication occurs, and that we get along quite well in the world as a result of communication, occasional misunderstanding and ambiguity aside." I wondered while reading these words who might object to being included in "us all." I considered some likely protests.

For instance, from the left, Marcuse once objected to the Ode to Joy chorus from Beethoven's Ninth Symphony because it "anesthetizes the anguish and terror of modern life" (Forbes, 1978, p. 11). It is a "song which is invalidated in the culture that sings it." Presumably, he would have made a similar response to the notion "that we get along quite well in the world as a result of communication." Likewise — but this time from the capitalist side — organizational theorist, Peter Vaill (1989) argues that today's manager works in a condition of permanent "white water," because business rules change just when the manager thought he knew the game. Evidently Vaill would object to the view that "misunderstanding and ambiguity" are "occasional." Family equilibrium is sustained by myths, such as "we have a happy father" (Ferreira, 1963). No doubt members who are pleased with the family system would be delighted to say, "it is clear to us all that communication occurs and we get along quite well." A family member seeking change would presumably contest the myth.

The issue here is not who is right about pedestrian felicity, but that considerations *about* the pedestrian world cannot be taken for granted as many facts might be *within* that world. Theories, ideologies, and myths tell us how to interpret the pedestrian world, and solicit its "facts" to justify a world view. Critical rationalism will not grant certainty to our theories about the world. Moreover, pedestrian "facts" cannot justify a theoretical claim.

A critical rationalist without her epistemologist's hat would scarcely blink at the everyday claim "the strawberry is sweet; the taste is immediately certain." Consider, however, this affirmation: "The world is evolving toward paradise y, and we know it with an immediate certainty [that] supplies us with a criterion of truth." Here the critical rationalist finds an archetype of irrational thought. How can theoretical claims for certainty be assessed? This is a question of epistemology, not psychophysics.

When the ideologue declares that he knows with a "criterion of truth," the critical rationalist will want to know why that criterion can grant certainty. The ideologue, seeking justification, will find himself either in an infinite regress or with an arbitrary faith. In other words, claims for certainty fall victim to critical rationalism's attack on justificationism. Therefore, while the ontological realism implied by common sense does not fall before philosophical argument, claims for certainty do.

Near the conclusion of his chapter, Hikins discusses ideology. He shows that epistemologies of objective truth are no more logically tied to intolerance than relativistic epistemologies. Relativistic constructionism *is not* an inherent friend of the open mind (Orr, 1980). I wish, however, that Hikins would more explicitly distinguish between truth and certainty.

For instance, he questions Russell and Popper's effort "to hang such atrocities as the Holocaust on views of truth *and* [italics mine] certainty" (p. 66). I doubt that Popper blamed the Holocaust on anyone's affirmation of objective truth. He may, however, have blamed fascist certainty for the atrocities. The acknowledgment of objective truth and claims for certainty about it are not conceptually equivalent. One can acknowledge objective truth in a way that beliefs remain correctable before it. But, when one's knowledge of the truth is considered certain, fixed, settled, and indubitable, then belief is placed beyond correction. The Nazis were not merely wrong; they held their views with a certainty that precluded change. Neither criticism nor experience can penetrate a mind that is closed beyond doubt against the possibility of refutation.

I have stressed the issue of certainty[2] because it bears on critical rationalism's distinctive strength and weakness. Critical rationalism is most frequently criticized because it cannot explain how reality *refutes* our theories (Gellner, 1985, p. 15). If critical rationalists held a view of naked truth, it would be easier to see how theories are laid to rest. They could be shot down by "objective bullets" (Gellner, 1985, p. 33). Critical rationalists become most equivocal in explaining how theory laden facts shoot down theories. Nevertheless, critical rationalism is distinctively ingenious in explaining how theories avoid being shot down. Theories will not be refuted, *if* they are held in a way that precludes criticism. They will not be altered if nothing is allowed to count against them.

Critical rationalism was inspired by the young Popper's disappointing experience with Marxism. As Nazi atrocities began to appear in Austria, Popper's Marxist compatriots refused to take action. Their "scientific" view of history, in this case, legitimized inaction and could not be shaken in spite of escalating violence (Magee, 1973, p. 4, 5). Nothing could count against it. A theory was sustained; people died.

The primary targets of critical rationalism's attack are theories that are maintained by what Gellner called "cognitive immorality" (1985, pp. 105-118). That is, many claims to manifest certain truth come equipped with a revelation of why people do not see the truth. Critics are "sinful," "neurotic resisters," "class enemies," and so forth. Therefore, when critics appear, their criticism is not heard as criticism, but as confirmation that there are "conspirators in the land." No argument can penetrate this armor; no experience can change the point of view. For Popper and company, such a position is rationally reprehensible. A rhetorical appreciation for critical rationalism will depend, in part, upon one's regard for "cognitive immorality" as a rhetorical problem. Rhetorical criticism can be ably guided, in this regard, by Bennett's (1985) concern that "one of the most troublesome

---

[2]Critical rationalists do not like to debate definitions; neither do I. In this discussion, I have taken "certainty" in the dictionary sense of "fixed, settled, guaranteed." As such, certainty is distinct from conviction or confidence.

problems of human communication is the tendency for schemes of social representation . . . to become closed to critical challenges" (p. 259).

An appreciation for critical rationalism is also dependent upon a constructionist view of rhetoric. *Relativism* and critical rationalism share this perspective. As we have seen, they also disagree. I will not repeat these disagreements, but, in summary, recast them.

Brummett (chap. 3) argues that "the most defensible relativism sees symbolic systems as a medium from which the human and human consciousness spring" (p. 85). Critical rationalism holds a similar view. We know ourselves through World 3, our cultural symbolic heritage. However, among the World 3 concepts that we inherit is the affirmation of an objective world that transcends our symbolic systems. There is no "knock-down argument" against this view. In fact, there are good reasons to insist upon it. In the name of objective reality we reasonably challenge reifications, and "remind ourselves that our current views of reality are partial and imperfect" (Campbell, 1987, p. 85).

We have also learned from at least a segment of our cultural symbolic heritage to ask of any proposition, no matter how popular, "Is it true?" This question implies that truth is more than agreement; we must insist that it is. For as Hikins says, when agreement or "convention alone . . . is the arbiter of right and wrong, the phrase 'tyranny of the majority' acquires a chilling maleficence" (p. 66).

Critical rationalism regards relativism as a problem, not a solution. Psychologically, however, relativism may be a temporary solution (Orr, 1978a). People who are finding freedom from dogmatic, reified ideologies see relativism as an avenue to alternative perspectives. Even on critical rationalism's terms, moving intellectually from naive realism to a relativistic view of knowledge is progress.

Relativism *is* a problem, *but* a complex and important one. Many speech texts casually state, "We see the world through a frame of reference." What would occur, I wonder, if students were asked: "Are you prepared to see the sacred truths of your religion as dependent upon a *human* frame of reference? How do you understand the research findings reported in this course, if nothing is known apart from a framework? How do you make important decisions when alternative choices seem right or wrong depending upon the frame from which they are viewed?" Students might yawn, become angry, urge a return to basic skills, or here and there take a step toward a liberal arts education (Orr, 1978a). An assignment that asks students to analyze a speech from diverse views in *Rhetoric and philosophy* appropriately invites relativistic thinking. The ability to see a phenomenon from diverse theories enhances knowledge, and an appreciation for theory. But how do we discriminate between theories and frames of reference? At this point, relativism fails us. In our age, the "great question" is intellectually unavoidable: "Can we admit that our knowledge is a human affair . . . without implying it is all . . . whim and arbitrariness?" (Popper 1962, p. 16). Critical rationalism believes this question *is* great; and that its answer is *yes*.

Idealism and *materialism* are perennial contributors to the philosophical quest. Both are metaphysical systems. Neither can be verified or falsified. They can, however, be rationally considered if held open for criticism. Critical rationalism criticizes both views. Subjective idealism is rejected because it does not recognize a world apart from the human mind. The world may be an intelligible order, but it is not subjectively dependent. Materialism is criticized because it is frequently disguised as science, and for its simplistic reductionism.

Agassi (1977) argued that reductionism can explain a domain of inquiry, without explaining it *away*. For example, we can explain aspects of psychology and linguistics through biological and chemical theories. Explaining mind in this manner, however, does not explain mind *away*. Aspects of chemistry are explained by physics, but we do not dispense with chemistry. Moreover, if a complete reduction could be achieved, we would no doubt revise our understanding of the remaining domain. That is, if mind were reduced to physics, we might seriously alter our view of physics (who knows, idealism might slip into our considerations, through the basement door). In any case, we are not today able to reduce psychology to the natural sciences. Perhaps someday we can explain away psychology; but that day is not this day. To eliminate mind from today's social sciences would make them even more trivial than too often they are.

Critical rationalism believes that both materialism and idealism are provocative. It is good for us who are "caught up" in symbols to remember we have glands and make money. On the other hand, can we deny, without affirming, the significance of mind?

Idealism comes closest to critical rationalism in terms of Popper's World 3. Although a human creation, stored in material facilities, World 3 is otherwise a quasi-platonic domain of ideation. World 3's significance for rhetoric is well expressed in Lyne's rhetoric of idealism: "The rhetorician of an idealistic cast would take seriously the mental horizons that verbal constructions make possible" (p. 163). Lyne also suggests that the short-term goal of influencing immediate conduct would be weighed alongside longer term goals, such as shaping sensibility.

It is hoped that our sensibilities will provide more than textual material for *deconstructionism*. This philosophical movement is potentially useful from a critical rational view because it highlights the human, theoretical character of knowledge. I doubt, however, that deconstructionism wishes to be considered useful. Nor does critical rationalism wish to be a host for symbiosis with deconstructionism. The parasite, however, will feed where it wishes to feed. In return, critical rationalism will want to know why the results of a deconstructionist's analysis should be considered true. What could count against such an analysis? Knowledge claims can be deconstructed but the question of truth remains. Criticism is employed to make progress, not for parasitic purposes. Deconstructionism makes implicit truth claims; it enjoys no privileged protection from many of the maladies it finds in others. Deconstructionism will be most adequately assessed when we critically examine what it inevitably constructs, in the process of deconstructing other views.

Pragmatism and critical rationalism are more compatible partners. Both hold a concern for action, problem solving, and progress. However, they part company needlessly on the issue of realism. Evolutionary pragmatism implies an unknown reality. It has neither logical nor pragmatic reasons to deny objective, but uncertain, truth.

Critical rationalists also fear that pragmatism's appeal to successful action protects beliefs against criticism (Bartley, 1984). For instance, imagine a religious confession, such as, "He descended into Hell." Theology aside, this statement implies a three-storied universe, a falsified cosmology. Modern religion has often justified such confessions on pragmatic grounds. The confession is "aesthetically pleasing, preserves a tradition, creates fellowship," or "is a symbol." Creeds have rarely been confessed with a cosmological disclaimer.

There was a time, however, when people believed in a three-storied universe. "He descended into Hell" was a cosmological claim. Ancient people tried to articulate their place in the universe, *as they knew it.* Respected cosmologies from the past deserve the decency of a candid, public refutation.

Modern religion's pragmatic defense of outworn cosmologies not only protects official beliefs from criticism, it also impedes religion's opportunity to meet a contemporary need. As Toulmin (1982) argued, "we need to understand our own position vis-à-vis the rest of nature, in ways that will permit us to recognize, and feel, that the world [*as we know it*] is our 'home' " (p. 265).

According to Toulmin, this is an ecological, ethical and practical necessity. In the evolutionary long run, the protection of knowledge against criticism is both rationally and pragmatically reckless. We may discover too late that we are pragmatically well adjusted to a false image of our situation. Our best protection against such maladjustment is the critical revision of our theories.

On the other hand, criticism is subject to pragmatic challenges (Wetter stein & Agassi, 1987). It can destroy conjectures before they are fully fashioned. Continuous criticism is both rationally and pragmatically untenable. As critical rationalism considers the pragmatic license it grants to creativity, tenacity, and dogmatism pro tem, its view of reason may be enlarged or altered.

We come now to *existentialism,* a philosophy that receives little positive attention from critical rationalism. Heidegger's philosophical style is routinely ridiculed; the religious existentialist's efforts to protect dogma from criticism by an inevitable leap of faith is assailed. Here, however, I want to stress the often overlooked similarities between existentialism and critical rationalism.

Both views recognize that the self stands out from its cultural background. The self's identity may be a property of World 3, but the self, as an undefined possibility, is not. The "I" is not known apart from a socially constructed "me," but the "I" is not reducible to the "me".

Both existentialism and critical rationalism call for the self, in Hyde's (chap. 7) words, "to speak a rhetoric rather than merely allowing themselves, as subjects of the 'herd' and the 'they,' to be spoken by a rhetoric" (p. 234). As Popper (1986) said "We cannot be intellectual cowards and seekers for truth . . . A seeker for truth must dare to be wise—he must dare to be a revolutionary in the field of thought" (p. 203).

Risk and pathos are part of the authentic and examined lives. We seek the absolute truth, but can claim no more than relative knowledge. We are always "on the way"; we do not arrive. At best, we live life on the basis of an examined guess.

Existentialism and critical rationalism warn us against denying our uncertainty. We cannot escape into "self-enclosed" systems of rationality. We find no salvation by calling an abstract theory "the absolute truth." Theories calcified into "truth" are subject to "ontological assaults" that awake us to the possibility of rebirth.

On the issue of "awakening", critical rationalism and existentialism turn to their characteristic interests. For critical rationalism, we learn from our mistakes by inviting assaults on our theories. World 3 is the objective beneficiary of our epistemological progress. Existentialism's interests remain focussed on World 2. An ontological assault on our self-protective fabrications creates the possibility of an authentic engagement in the personal question: what does it mean to exist as a human being?

Critical rationalism is not logically estranged from the existential question. In fact, Popper (1986) said that "all men are philosophers because all take up an attitude toward life and death" (p. 211). Usually, however, we do not hear critical rationalists give their personal views on life and death. Before considering a personal reflection from Popper, a short digression on religion and existential issues is needed.

Examples from religion have frequently occurred in this chapter. Three reasons account for their presence. First, for centuries religion was the Western world's promise of certainty. If we can understand why certainty failed in organized religion, we might better understand why it fails in rationalism and scientism. Second, religion has frequently been a canopy of protection against critical examination. It provides abundant examples of irrationality. Third, critical rationalists hold an inherent interest in religion. Bartley (1984, p. 181) considered how an undogmatic religion would be possible. Agassi (1981) acknowledged the religious quality in the search for an objective, but transcended truth. Jarvie (1984) assailed religious dogmatism but prized the "religious sentiment" in Russell's claim that "through the greatness of the universe . . . the mind is also rendered great, and becomes capable of union with the universe" (p. 26).

Religion is something of a test case for critical rationalism. Can religion be rendered rational by rationalism's new identity? Can rationality be found where irrationality is so readily discovered?

Joseph Margolis (1976) argued that religious questions are rational, even if religious answers are not. There are, said Margolis, "a set of peculiarly difficult problems that man faces because of the very nature of his existence" (p. 429). For instance, "no deliberate commitment that he can make, no purposeful programme of activity, can permanently postpone his death; . . . nor can he know or control the full consequences . . . that follow even from his acts . . . nor can he find a purpose behind the order of nature to certify his own purposive activity." Because these issues are inevitable, it cannot be irrational to consider them.

In critical rationalism's terms, because we have implicit theories about existential issues, it is rational to acknowledge them. Indeed, it would be irrational not to acknowledge them, for then they could not be critically examined. Religion is not only made irrational by vociferous dogmatism, but by the privatization of existential concerns. Humanity cannot hope to make progress on these issues if people who value reason ignore them.

Margolis (1976) summarized the religious question: "A man who reflects on his own strenuous enterprise—whether selfish or generously concerned with the well-being of others—*must* somehow come to terms with the fact that he and . . . others will die. What can be the point, he must ask, of any effort in the face of this inevitability" (p. 430–431).

"The point" is made all too abundantly clear by much of the world's rhetoric. In exchange for existential answers, people have fanatically devoted themselves to the most hideous causes, and some good ones, too. Whether we call Margolis' question religious, or simply existential, it will not be rhetorically ignored. It should not be rationally dismissed. Can existential issues be reasonably addressed?

At the conclusion of his essay *How I See Philosophy,* Popper wrote:

> . . . We do not know how it is that we are alive on this . . . planet—or why
> there should be something like life, to make our planet so beautiful. But here
> we are, and we have every reason to wonder at it, and to feel grateful for it.
> It comes close to being a miracle. For all that science can tell us, the universe
> is almost empty of matter, and where there is matter, the matter is almost
> everywhere in a chaotic, turbulent state, and uninhabitable. There may be
> many other planets with life on them. Yet if we pick out at random a place in
> the universe, then the probability (calculated on the basis of our dubious
> current cosmology) of finding a life-carrying body at that place will be zero,
> or almost zero. So life has at any rate the value of something rare; it is
> precious. We are inclined to forget this, and treat life cheaply, perhaps out of
> thoughtlessness; or perhaps because this beautiful earth of ours is, no doubt,
> a bit overcrowded. . . . There are those who think that life is valueless
> because it comes to an end. They fail to see that the opposite argument might
> also be proposed; that if there were no end to life, life would have no value;
> that it is, in part, the ever-present danger of losing it which helps to bring
> home to us the value of life (1986, p. 211).

Is Popper's statement religion? Is it philosophy? He called it "a bit of
decidedly nonacademic philosophy". (If so, there is some boldness here, for
it appears in an academic philosophical context). To me, the statement is
religion, philosophy, *and rhetoric.* But is it rational rhetoric?

We can assume that Popper offered his thoughts as a conjecture, not the
final truth. Objections and observations could count against his view.
Scientific hypotheses are implied in his existential deliberations. I ask the
reader, as Popper would, to criticize his perspective. How would it be seen
through the eyes of each philosophy in this book? What are the best
challenges that could be brought against it? In light of criticism, what of
merit remains? What can be credited here? What new conjectures, or
questions come to mind?

How existential and cosmological convictions are held ultimately determines their rationality. To make bold conjectures and invite criticism in a
community that encourages both is the spirit of critical rationalism. It does
not promise final answers, but progress. Rationality in cosmology or
religion advances when we replace (Adler, 1929) "big mistakes by smaller
ones" (p. 36), and by imagining what a better answer might be. Is this view
of rationality sufficiently robust to inspire and improve the rhetorical
imagination? In part, critical rationalism's sufficiency depends upon further
analysis of its assumptions. More importantly, the issue is a rhetorical
challenge: How can institutions that encourage a rational rhetoric be
rhetorically empowered?

REFERENCES

Adler, A. (1929). *The science of living.* Garden City, NY: Garden City Publishing.

Agassi, J. (1963). *Towards an historiography of science.* Beihert 2.

Agassi, J. (1975). *Science in flux.* Dordrecht: D. Reidel.

Agassi, J. (1977). *Towards a rational philosophical anthropology.* Atlantic Highlands, NJ: Humanities Press.

Agassi, J. (1981). *Science and society.* Dordrecht: D. Reidel.

Bartley, W. W. (1984). *The retreat to commitment* (2nd ed.). LaSalle, IL: Open Court.

Bartley, W. W., III. (1987a). Alienation alienated. In Gerard Radnitzkey & W. W. Bartley, III (Eds.), *Evolutionary epistemology, theory of rationality and the sociology of knowledge* (pp. 423–451). LaSalle, IL: Open Court.

Bartley, W. W., III. (1987b) Evolutionary epistemology. In Gerard Radnitzkey & W. W. Bartley, III (Eds.), *Evolutionary epistemology, theory of rationality and the sociology of knowledge* (pp. 7–46). LaSalle, IL: Open Court.

Bartunek, J.M. (1988). The dynamics of personal and organizational reframing. In R. E. Quinn & K. S. Cameron (Eds.), *Paradox and transformation.* Cambridge, MA: Ballinger.

Becker, E. (1970). *The birth and death of meaning* (2nd ed.). New York: The Free Press.

Bellah, N., Madsen, R, Sullivan, W., Swidler, A., & Tipton, S. (1986). *Habits of the heart.* New York: Harper & Row.

Bennett, W. L. (1985). Communication and social responsibility. *Quarterly Journal of Speech, 71,* 259–288.

Berger, P. (1963). *Invitation to sociology.* New York: Anchor Books.

Boorstein, D. J. (1983). *The discovers.* New York: Random House.

Branham, R. J., & Pearce, W. B. (1985). Between text and context. *Quarterly Journal of Speech, 71,* 19–36.

Briskman, L. (1987). Historicist relativisim and bootstrap rationality. In J. Agassi & I. C. Jarvie (Eds.), *Rationality: The critical view,* (pp. 317–338). Dordrecht: Martinus Nijhoff.

Brummett, B. (1971). Some implications of "process" or intersubjectivity: post modern rhetoric. *Philosophy and Rhetoric, 9,* 21–51.

Burke, K. (1968). *Language as symbolic action.* Berkeley, CA: University of California Press.

Campbell, D. (1987). Evolutionary epistemology. In G. Radnitzkey & W. W. Bartley, III (Eds.), *Evolutionary epistemology, theory of rationality and the sociology of knowledge* (pp. 47–89). LaSalle, IL: Open Court.

Cappella, J. N. (1987). Communication in the 1980s. *University of Delaware Report, 13*(8).

Cialdini, R. (1988). *Influence: science and practice* (2nd ed.). Glenview, IL: Scott, Foresman.

Davenport, D. (1987). What is literature? In J. Agassi & I. C. Jarvie (Eds.), *Rationality: The critical view* (pp. 217–226). Dordrecht: Martinus Nijhoff.

Duncan, H. (1968). *Symbols in society.* New York: Oxford University Press.

Dyer, W. (1987). *Teambuilding: issues and alternatives.* Reading, MA: Addison-Wesley.

Einstein, A. (1949). *The world as I see it.* New York: Philosophical Library.

Erikson, E. (1962). *Young man Luther.* New York: Norton.

Featherstone, J. L. (1986). Forward in B. A. Kimball, *Orators and philosophers.* New York: Teachers College Press.

Ferreira, A. J. (1963). Family myth and homeostasis. *Archives of General Psychiatry, 9,* 457–463.

Fishman, D. B., & Neigher, W. D. (1982). American psychology in the eighties. *American Psychologist, 37,* 533–546.

Forbes, E. (1978). Heroism without heroes: Beethoven. *Kairos, 11,* p. 11.

Fried, Y., & Agassi, J. (1976). *Paranoia: A study in diagnosis.* Dordrecht: D. Riedel.

Gans, H. (1989). Sociology in America: The discipline and the public, *American Sociological Review, 54,* 1-16.

Gellner, E. (1982). Relativism and universals. In M. H. & Steven Lukes (Eds.), *Rationality and relativism* (pp. 181-200). Cambridge, MA: MIT Press.

Gellner, E. (1985). *Relativism and the social sciences.* Cambridge, MA: Cambridge University Press.

Gellner, E. (1987). An ethic of cognition. In J. Agassi & I. C. Jarvie (Eds.), *Rationality: The critical view* (pp. 105-118). Dordrecht: Martinus Nijhoff.

Gergen, D. R. (1989, January 9). Ronald Reagan's most important legacy. *U. S. News and World Report,* p. 28.

Gergen, K., & Gergen, M. M. (1988). Narrative and self as relationship. In L. Berkowitz (Ed.), *Advances in Experimental Social Psychology* (pp. 17-56). San Diego: Academic Press, Inc.

Gombrich, E. H. (1972). *Art and illusion.* (2nd ed.). Princeton, NJ: Princeton University Press.

Gurevitch, Z. D. (1988). The other side of dialogue: on making the other strange and the experience of otherness. *American Journal of Sociology, 93,* 1179-99.

Hart, D. (1988). The adolescent self-concept in social context. In Daniel K. Lapsley & F. Clarke Power (Eds.), *Self, ego, and identity* (pp. 71-90). New York: Springer-Verlag.

Hart, R. P., & Burks, M. (1972). Rhetorical sensitivity and social interaction. *Speech Monographs, 39,* 75-91.

Hofstadter, D. R. (1985). *Metamagical themes.* New York: Bantam Books.

Jarvie, I. C. (1984). *Rationality and relativism.* London: Routledge & Kegan Paul.

Jarvie, I. (1987). *Philosophy of the film.* New York: Routledge & Kegan Paul.

Jarvie, I. C., & J. Agassi. (1987). The rationality of dogmatism. In J. Agassi & I. C. Jarvie (Eds.), *Rationality: The critical view* (pp. 317-338). Dordrecht: Martinus Nijhoff.

Kegan, R. (1982). *The evolving self.* Cambridge, MA: Harvard University Press.

Kerr, M. (1981). Family systems theory and therapy. In A. Gurman & D. P. Knisken (Eds.), *Handbook of family therapy* (pp. 226-266). New York: Brunner/Mazel.

Kimball, B. A. (1986). *Orators and philosophers.* New York: Teachers College Press.

Kuhn, T. (1962). *The structure of scientific revolutions.* Chicago: University of Chicago Press.

Lynton, E. A. (1987). *New priorities for the University.* San Francisco: Jossey-Bass.

Magee, B. (1973). *Karl Popper.* New York: Viking Press.

Margolis, J. (1976). Religion and reason. *Religious Studies, 12,* 429-443.

Miller, D. (1985). *Popper Selections.* Princeton, NJ: Princeton University Press.

Mitroff, I. I., & Kilmann, R. H. (1983). Intellectual resistance to useful knowledge. In R. H. Kilmann, K. W. Thomas, D. P. Slevin, R. Nath, & S. L. Jerrell (Eds.), *Producing useful knowledge for organizations.* (pp. 266-280). New York: Praeger.

Nelson, R. (1987). *The making and unmaking of an evangelical mind.* New York: Cambridge University Press.

Orr, C. J. (1978a). Communication, relativism, and student development. *Communication Education, 27,* 83-98.

Orr, C. J. (1978b). How shall we say: "reality is socially constructed through communication?" *Central States Speech Journal, 29,* 263-274.

Orr, C. J. (1980). Truth, knowledge, and a democratic respect for diversity. *Free Speech Yearbook, 19,* 16-19.

Orr, C. J. (1988, November). *A rhetorical perspective on the situated self.* Paper presented at the meeting of the Speech Communication Association Convention, New Orleans, LA.

Pacanowsky, M., & O'Donnell-Trujillo, N. (1983). Organizational communication as cultural performance. *communication Monographs, 50,* 126-147.

Plath, Sylvia. (1971). *The bell jar.* New York: Harper and Row.

Popper, K. (1962). *Conjectures and refutations.* London: Basic Books.

Popper, K. R. (1963). *The open society and its enemies.* Vol. II. Princeton, NJ: Princeton University Press.

Popper, K. (1970). Normal science and its dangers. In Imre Lakatos & A. Musgrave (Eds.), *Criticism and the growth of knowledge* (pp. 51–58). London: Cambridge University Press.

Popper, K. (1972). *Objective knowledge.* Oxford: Oxford University Press.

Popper, K. (1974). *Unended quest: an intellectual autobiography.* LaSalle, IL: Open Court.

Popper, K. (1975). The rationality of scientific revolutions. In R. Harre (Ed.), *Problems of scientific revolution* (pp. 72–101). Oxford: Clarendon Press.

Popper, K. (1983). *Realism: and the aim of science.* Totowa, NJ: Rownan & Littlefield.

Popper, K. (1986). How I see philosophy. In S.G. Shanker (Ed.), *Philosophy in Britain today* (pp. 198–212). London: Croom Helm.

Popper, K. R., & Eccles, C. (1977). *The self and its brain.* London: Springer-Verlag.

Quinn, R. E., & Cameron, K. S. (Eds.). (1988). *Paradox and transformation.* Cambridge, MA: Ballinger.

Rawlins, W. K. (1985). Stalking communication effectiveness. In T. W. Benson (Ed.), *Speech communication in the twentieth century* (pp. 109–129). Carbondale IL: Southern Illinois University Press.

Rushing, J. H. (1985). E. T. as rhetorical transcendence. *Quarterly Journal of Speech, 71,* 188–203.

Scheler, M. (1958). *Philosophical Perspectives* (O. A. Haac, Trans.). New York: Appleton.

Schön, D.A. (1983). *The reflective practitioner.* New York: Basic Books.

Scott, N. (1979). Arnold's version of transcendence—the via poetica. *Journal of Religion, 79,* 261–284.

Scott, R. (1976). On viewing rhetoric as epistemic: Ten years later. *Central States Speech Journal, 27,* 258–266.

Smith, K. K. (1984). Rabbits, lynxes, and organizational transitions. In J. R. Kimberly & R. E. Quinn (Eds.), *Managing organizational transitions.* Homewood, IL: Irwin.

Trenholm, S., & Jensen, A. (1988). *Interpersonal communication.* Belmont, CA: Wadsworth.

Thoits, P. (1983). Multiple identities and psychological well-being. *American Sociological Review, 48,* 174–87.

Toulmin, S. (1982). *The return to cosmology.* Berkeley, CA: University of California Press.

Vaill, P. B. (1989). *Managing as a performing art.* San Francisco: Jossey-Bass.

Watkins, J. W. N. (1987). Epistemology and politics. In J. Agassi & I. C. Jarvie (Eds.), *Rationality: The critical view* (pp. 151–168). Dordrecht: Martinus Nijhoff Publishers.

Watzlawick, P. (1976). *How real is real?* New York: Random House.

Weick, K. E. (1980). The management of eloquence. *Executive, 6,* 18–21.

Weigert, A. (1988). To be or not: self and authenticity, identity and ambivalence. In D. K. Lapsley & F. C. Power (Eds.), *Self, ego and identity* (pp. 263–281). New York: Springer-Verlag.

Wetterstein, J. R., & Agassi, J. (1987). "The choice of problems and the limits of reason." In J. Agassi & I. C. Jarvie (Eds.), *Rationality: The critical view* (pp. 281–296). Dordrecht: Martinus Nijhoff.

Winter, D. (1987). Leader appeal, leader performance, and the motive profiles of leaders and followers: a study of American presidents and elections. *Journal of Personality and Social Psychology, 52,* 196–202.

Wrong, D. (1961). The oversocialized conception of man in modern sociology. *American Sociological Review, 26,* 183–192.

Idealism as a
Rhetorical Stance

John Lyne

> Consciousness precedes being, and not the other way around, as the Marxists
> claim.
> — Vaclav Havel, President of Czechoslavakia,
> speech before joint session of U.S. Congress, February 21, 1990.

When Donald Bryant offered his now famous formulation that rhetoric
serves the function of "adjusting ideas to people and people to ideas," it was
meant as a practical, not a philosophical, standard (Bryant, 1953). In the
context of examining the philosophical alignments of rhetoric, it might be
worth considering just what it means to adjust to an idea. For all its implied
practicality, the adjustment Bryant wrote of is presumably something quite
different from adjusting only to circumstance, or even to psychological
dissonance. An idea, after all, is neither a tangible thing nor a condition of
the psyche, not something to decompose with the natural elements or to
blink on and off with a person's attention span. Despite their apparent
immateriality, ideas are commonly attributed with great power and influence. The stronger ones, it seems, can outlast the person, even the
civilization, of their origin.

What, then, are "ideas"? Where does one locate them? And what sort of
reality and power do they have? The *philosophy of idealism* pivots on
questions such as these, and its distinctiveness as a viewpoint lies in the way
it answers them. For the idealist, ideas are real and efficacious in the world:
they are, in fact, the measure of reality, and the most important ingredient
in that conjunction of mind and matter that we call experience. An idealist
views language, among whatever other capacities it may have, as a means of

149

embodying and transmitting ideas, of incorporating them into experience. And if this is so, it should make a difference in how one conceives of rhetorical theory and practice, or in how one conducts a rhetorical analysis.

As a quick imaginative exercise, one might consider analyzing the Declaration of Independence as rhetoric, keying in on its nature as a symbolic influence. What sort of persuasive force might one recover from this familiar cultural and political icon? Within what circumference of time and space would its impact be judged? What relationship would be assumed to exist between the document and a context? How would one think about its audience and situation? Obviously, there would be a great many ways to begin, and simply picking a "method" of analysis would beg the question as to what is worth time and attention. And any tack that one might choose would inevitably reflect fundamental assumptions about the relative influence of ideas in the world. If one held that ideas were the surface gloss on a reality determined by other forces, for instance, the Declaration might be treated as a symptom of the material relationships of its moment, or as a political act dressed up as a philosophy. The document itself might be handled as a distorted mirror of its time and place, of obscured realities to be recovered.

For an idealist, however, none of these could be the definitive task. An idealist would be struck by how the articulate power of the Declaration continues to enter and transform new contexts, shaping the quality of experience. The idealist would take an interest in the ideas to which the political culture was responding at the document's point of origin, and the apparent capacity of these ideas to inspire a sense of common cause in subsequent generations. The circumstances of the original rhetorical act and the political chemistry of that moment have long since disappeared; yet the rhetoric somehow carries forward across time and space, giving the contemporary reader some articulable and felt connection to the thought expressed by Jefferson. When his words appeared unexpectedly from the mouths of demonstrators about to be mown down in Tiananmen Square in 1989, what should we say has bridged that great chasm of time, space, and culture between colonial America and communist China? No one, presumably, thinks that these modern Chinese students were performing just the same speech acts as were performed two centuries ago in the American Declaration, or that they meant quite the same thing. A Foucauldian critic telling a story of "differences" could show the cultural and circumstantial specificity that makes theses utterances seem worlds apart. An idealist, on the other hand, is likely to contend that something more is involved – that some powerful continuity has been tapped, running deeper than the surface features of words. For the idealist it is no mere sentimentality to say that ideas live on even though their champions die; and it is only to state the obvious to say that ideas are recuperable when material circumstances are not.

According to this view, ideas, embodied in symbols, cut across time and space because they occur in minds. Their modality is not the actual and empirical, but the potential and mental. For this reason, they are the means, in memory, anticipation, and symbolization, by which we have access to the past or the future. They are, in sum, the chief implication of having a mind. Just how ideas and other things of a "mental" nature exist, and how they relate to the material world, including the brain, and how our human capacities for ideas are defined and limited, are points of broad debate and disagreement. What unites idealists is a belief in the importance of mind and idea in a world often taken to be ruled by material forces. The idealist sees the world as a context in which mind operates, and which for human beings is a field of intelligible experience.

We live in a time when "idealism" is beleaguered as an intellectual position, represented more often in parody than not. The various forms of critique that have converged in our century — positivist, economic, socio-logical, structuralist, psychological, feminist, and sociobiological — have often had as a common foil "idealist" conceptions of how the world is constituted. Idealism is portrayed by its critics as a kind of naiveté, at best, or as a source of false consciousness and fanaticism at worst. In popular usage, however, the case is somewhat more evenly weighted. To be called idealist there, to be sure, is sometimes to be cast as a dreamer, not a wideawake and serious observer of how things really are. But if America is the land "where dreams come true," it is a safe bet that the vernacular term "idealist" cuts another way as well. "Some men see things as they are and say 'Why?' " Robert Kennedy was fond of saying (after George Bernard Shaw). "I dream things that never were and say 'Why not?' " For this he is admiringly called an idealist. So there is a tension here. It is a tension between the value of having vision and of knowing what is real; and in a way, between a world of the actual and one infused with a sense of the possible.

One moves with caution between philosophical and popular uses of a term. When Henry Kissinger counsels pragmatism, one does not rush to credit Peirce. Popular appropriations of philosophical terms are almost inevitably caricatures. Even so, common usage suggests something of the generative force of a philosophical perspective, the rhetorical advantage of using one, and the difficulty of not having one. In the case of idealism, the vernacular usage seems to point to the role of vision, hope, and imagination in life. As a marker of that which is less tangible than imaginable, "idealism" perhaps plays a role in everyday life that is crudely analogous to its role in philosophy, that is, reminding us of the capacity of minds and communities of minds to confer meaning and to initiate action in reference to that meaning. This is the strand in that tangled weave called "idealism" that I want to examine, especially in its possible relationship to rhetoric as a theory and practice. My purpose is to suggest some ways of being aligned with idealism, of using its insights and strategies to fashion a general rhetorical posture—what I will call a "rhetorical policy." I am not trying to write a history. Others will find other strategies and traditions, as well as other tales to tell about idealism and rhetoric (e.g., Grassi, 1980). To be aligned with idealism, I believe, is not to choose a philosophical stance *rather than* a practical one. Rather, it is one way of being practical. Rhetoric informed by idealism is a practice of taking the long view, of venerating the coming-to-be. Like any stance, it has strengths and vulnerabilities.

IDEALIST PHILOSOPHY

Idealistic thought seeks to explain how words, thoughts, and experiences relate to each other and to the broader world, and it has taken up many of the same questions that rhetorical theory, in its own idiom, has had to address in considering the nature of symbolic influence. As a philosophical tradition, idealism collects quite a cast of characters, and there is at best a family resemblance among all their respective positions. So it would be misleading to suggest that there is a universal set of propositions to which one must subscribe in order to accept the label of "idealist." But there are some recurrent themes and concerns, and perhaps behind those, a kind of sensibility. The idealist is impressed with the apparent power of mind not only to grasp intelligible order in the world, but to live beyond physical contingency. To put it another way, the idealist is concerned with the world as a field of possible and intelligible experience. If the Cartesian dualism of mind and matter can yield to a unitary principle, the idealist thinks that it should be resolved on the side of mind, not matter.

It is important to distinguish two rather different forms of idealism, the subjective and objective, because they have very different characteristics and vulnerabilities. The *subjective idealist* stresses the dependency of things known on the mind of the individual. The world in my mind is in this view the only world I can know; all inquiry I make into the world comes to fruition only in the way it enters my mind. Pushed to a logical conclusion, this can become solipsism, the view that the self is the only thing that can be known. Such thinking enjoys considerable popularity in pop philosophy and psychology (e.g., New Age thinking), and it is a theme wrestled with in some reflective academic philosophy as well (Cavell, 1979). There is a strain of it in the work of Nietzsche, whose work is beginning to influence rhetorical theory (Danto, 1967, pp. 231–232). As one might suppose, however, subjective idealism is not a view that lends itself readily to scientific thinking or to epistemology, both generally conceived as ways of correcting the deficiencies of individual thought.

Probably the high water mark of the subjective idealism was Bishop Berkeley's in the 18th century (Berkeley, 1950). Berkeley developed with rigor the notion that things exist only as they are held in perception. Yet he could not ignore the voice of common sense realism telling him that objects did not simply vanish when no one was beholding them; and to respond to this difficulty he brought in the mind of God (no less), whose ongoing perception of the world caused it not to evaporate when we go to sleep. Few will sit still for such a solution in a scientific era, however. Indeed, with or without science, subjective idealism has always encountered "common sense" objections, which appeal to practical reality, outside of philosophical discourse. Dr. Johnson claimed to refute Berkeley merely by kicking a rock, and modern critics have added successful technologies and moon landings to the repertoire (as if the subjectivists had not noticed these things). What the rhetoric of subjective idealists seem to lack is a satisfactory account of *otherness,* of an external world only partly mastered, of other minds only partly understood.

Objective idealism seeks to accord centrality to mind without making deities of individual subjects. It finds a world that can be penetrated by intellect but does not assume that individuals grasp more than a fraction of what is knowable, or that they are anything more than partial and subject to correction. In short, there is otherness. But it is not an otherness based on the dualism of mind and matter. The orders and energies of the world are of one stuff to the objective idealist, better understood within the categories of "mind" than of mere "matter." The argument for this position must almost necessarily be understood in contrast to mechanistic materialism, or physicalism, and the deficiencies idealists see in that view.

Materialism reads the world as a complex physical interplay whereby all interaction is by physical causation, usually understood on the model of mechanical physics. As a world view, "mechanism" has historically tended to rely on accounts held together imagistically by notions such as that of the physical lever — push here, and something moves there (Pepper, 1942; Turbayne, 1970). In modern times it has looked especially to Newtonian physics as a model. Unfortunately, this kind of account does not comport well with the way human beings experience the world, that is, in terms of feelings, thoughts, shared consciousness, spontaneity, habit, and self-activation. Experience itself does not seem to be accounted for in the Newtonian universe. And as for the materialist's appeal to "matter," it does not seem to speak to our sense of comprehensible order, which seems more a question of form than of matter. For idealists, both the spontaneity *and* the orderliness of nature seem to presuppose some explanatory principle besides a "matter" that is, on most tellings, inert and insentient (Harts-horne, 1983). Objective idealism takes as its model of nature the capacities of mind and idea, which are not manifest in human beings alone, but which human beings experience as thinking, willing, feeling, communing, remembering, and anticipating. If our minds are a means of gaining the world, and of gaining power over circumstances, the reasoning goes, it must be because minds are our access to some fundamental order of the world. Rather than model understanding on the lowest common denominator, the idealist asks, the sort of causality that makes stones roll in an avalanche, why not take as a model the most exquisite and intelligible powers of which we know—the power of mind? Rather than try to account for intelligent life as some curious aberration, or "epiphenomenon," why not take intelligence as a paradigm and see what light it sheds across the whole landscape? (Chardin, 1959). The idealist is undisturbed by accusations that this is "anthropomorphic." If matter seems to lack animation, the idealist thinks, it is only because we are not looking closely enough (Cobb & Griffin, 1977). Nature is teeming with activity.

Many idealists have believed that one can make sense of the natural order only in terms of a higher intellectual content. Whatever makes the world go round, they contend, is more fully described as being like mind, that is, being active and intelligibly ordered, than by mere "matter," inert and blind. Thus conceived, idealism and realism can be compatible, as the case of Plato illustrates. Plato saw in nature a manifestation of Soul, both in the sense of intellect and in the sense of self-activation. His notion of forms was an attempt to grasp the intelligible essence of fluid experiences, the true realities. But this was no mechanical universe. The self-moved, Plato held in *The Laws* 10 (896, 897), is the source of change and motion in all things. Yet things move, for Plato, in relation to the intelligible forms, which are real, that is, ontologically distinct from merely individual occurrences. (The fate of realism hinges on the distinction, denied by nominalists, between universals and particulars—not on a commitment to forms.)

Some of this vocabulary lends itself easily to caricature—an ethereal world of forms, eternal essences, and what not. Rescued from Platonism and recuperated within a more modern idiom, however, the position commands more respect. Consider what in philosophy came to be known as the problem of universals. Given that no two things are exactly alike—that which we call a rose has thousands of varying manifestations, and no two are identical—how do we know when and how to apply the name? Must we not have some idea of what a rose must look like, and compare our observations to that? Do we have some abstract representation, above the empirical fray, to guide us? And if so, what form does such an abstraction take? There have been many approaches to answering this sort of question, and each struggles in its own way with the problem of forms, criteria, or essences. For idealists, the question becomes how to define and where to locate the forms of thought, whether they are "eternal," as Plato held, or fixed at some level closer to earth. To later idealists, the issue became how to describe mind in terms of logical or relational structures, rather than essences (Hartshorne, 1983).

Again, one need not be a philosopher to be caught up in these issues, to recognize the strategies, or to unknowingly replay a move in an ongoing historical debate. The "platonic" strategy of identifying the meaningful forms above the flow of situated contingency is firmly rooted in modern academic, not to mention popular, discourse. It lurks in the economist's models, the scientist's use of statistics, and the social scientist's theories of human behavior, as well as in the linguist's universals, the critic's genres, and the legal philosopher's quest for the nature of justice, just to name a few. In popular rhetoric, positions on finding one's true self, what it means to be a living human being, the meaning of the First Amendment, the true nature of a liberal or conservative, are often thought and spoken of in terms of stable or immutable forms. Judging from popular discourse, one might argue that idealism is quite a going philosophy. Of course such talk often reflects rhetorical purposes, and not necessarily philosophical commitments. But even if this is only a "rhetorical idealism," not philosophy in action, one would still want to account for why this perspective is so pervasive. My sense of it is that it is pervasive because it is both unavoidable and useful, and that even if it were based on a philosophical error, as Kenneth Burke (1945/1969) once said of the philosophy of "substance," it is still such a productive error that we can not afford to neglect it.

Objective idealism can support a view of history and social change in which words and thoughts are extremely influential. Hegel's view of the dialectical nature of reason, working itself out in history (Copleston, 1964), enters contemporary thinking through critics of society, such as the Frankfurt School (Jay, 1973), philosophers, such as Gadamer (1975), and even American pragmatism (Geuss, 1981). Although Hegel's vision of mind, or absolute spirit, working its way through the transformation of history probably represents too grand a metaphysics for late 20th century tastes, his notion of dialectic continues to challenge the pervasive view that "reality" can be grasped through a simple linear exposition (a view which supports a monological style of discourse). Even if Hegelian notions have often been filtered through a materalist lens, his idealistic presence remains influential (Megill, 1985).

At this point it would be reasonable to ask whether, in thinking about what the mind has access to, there is some middle ground between subjective idealism, with its extreme emphasis on individuals, and Hegelian absolutism, which posits an inevitable history. The answer, perhaps, is that there are various positions that might be described as "in between." One way is to posit universal conditions by which human beings are capable of handling ideas, that is, stable forms of thought. Are there, one might ask, stable forms of thought that do not depend on individuals? Immanual Kant provides one way of answering, because he posits conditions for understanding that are universal to human beings (Kant, 1965). Kant's *transcendental idealism* is, in various guises, very much a part of the contemporary scene, and it has various plausible formulations. Kant's categories of understanding were his analysis of the form within which humans necessarily experience the world. Categories such as space, time, and causality, he held, are not learned empirically, but are a part of every experience—the very conditions on which experience is possible for human beings, and hence transcendental. They are, so to speak, the forms of thought.

One need not assume that Kant got things exactly right in order to appreciate the notion of transcendental conditions of understanding. The notion that humans can receive experience only within a certain framework has a certain intuitive plausibility, especially in light of what we now know about perceptual filtering in animals and about computer programs. Frogs are "hard wired" to see small erratically moving objects, for instance, but not to see large, slowly moving ones. Why should we not assume that humans are also wired to see certain things, and not others (such as ultraviolet light, to give an obvious example)? It seems little more than a truism to say that human beings experience things only in terms of their own meager capabilities. Perhaps not all the world's riches can be tapped by five, and only five, senses. Kant was careful, therefore, to distinguish the things of human experience from "things in themselves," although this partition is not accepted by all idealists. Transcendental idealists believe that some kind of grounding conditions of human experience—whatever they may be—must be at work as we take the measure of the world. But how might those "transcendental" conditions be conceived? In a great many ways, it turns out, not all of which look like the stuff of mind.

There are two broad routes that can be taken, once having committed to the notion of formal conditions of thought. One can take the route of many Anglo-American philosophers in their quest for the formal, *logical* conditions of knowledge. Or one could follow the many German and French philosophers who have emphasized the *anthropological* constitution of knowledge, its specifically human shape. Both approaches have been influenced by Kantian assumptions (Rorty, 1979, p. 163). To speak of transcendental conditions in a broad sense need not involve an appeal to a mysterious "beyond." All it need involve is the common sense of our computer era, that the capability of the machine and its programs fundamentally shapes what can be done with data. If one thinks of humans in terms of the hard wiring of a machine, then one might think of something like biological limitations on knowledge and experience, or perhaps laws of cognitive or linguistic development. (Admittedly, these do not sound so much like "mental" categories, even if they might be thought of as the forms of human thinking.) Veering in the direction of anthropology, one might think of Levi-Strauss's structuralism, which is sometimes called "Kantianism without the subject," as it speaks of necessary social structures, quite apart from individual consciousness (see Kurzweil, 1980).

There are other Kantian approaches vying for our attention, including the work of Habermas in seeking a "universal pragmatics," or conditions of speech that are maximally *just* as well as effective (Habermas, 1979). Perhaps even more attention-worthy in the present intellectual climate is the Kantian flavor of the enormously influential and popular Kuhnian notion of paradigms. The paradigm is a kind of gridwork, not built into human beings, but more like a computer program. It is a composite of tradition, exemplars, norms, and practices that features some perceptions and filters others out (Kuhn, 1970). If scientific knowledge is in fact paradigm dependent, or if it simply comes by way of what Kenneth Burke (1968) called "terministic screens," then there is a Kantian point to be made about the structures that mediate experience.

There has been much debate about whether we are trapped within anything like paradigms rather than having some sort of direct access to the world (Fuller, 1988). Kant did not think we had such direct access. Our senses, he thought, give us only the "phenomenal" world, and we never can get to "things in themselves." In that sense, we are trapped within the world of our own ideas, unable to see things as they "really" are. This was a central point of challenge to Kant by Peirce (Peirce, 1958), himself a metaphysical idealist, who contended that the notion of something beyond all possible experience was empty — that the very condition of something being real was that it be an object of possible experience. Such experience might not be yours or mine, nor even of the human species. But to posit something in principle beyond experience was, to Peirce, to break with the essentially *relational* structure of the world. To be real, Peirce seemed intent on demonstrating in one context after another, is to be in relation to other things (Peirce, 1931-58).

And how do things have relations to one another? Consider the relations one might have with other human beings or with objects. The actual physical contact with either might define only the tiniest fraction of the relationship. Imagery of a lever, or of colliding billiard balls hardly appears up to the task of capturing how persons exercise influence. One interacts with other people and things in one's environment through the mediation of language and other "signs." (Peirce, interestingly enough, generalizes this across the natural world.) Peirce saw knowledge as depending on the structure of signs, rather than on innate conditions, which would mean that there are open-ended possibilities for human understanding rather than ones governed by inherent limits.

Placing philosophers such as Peirce or Plato in a "slot" can lead us away from the dynamic tensions that pervade their thinking—or ours. Labels such as "realist" and "idealist" can obscure as much as they clarify. One could call both Peirce and Plato objective idealists—as well as realists—despite enormous differences in their philosophies. Unfortunately, confusion is increased by the fact that "realism" is used in contrast to both "idealism" and to "nominalism," depending on which debate one is referring to. With reference to the realist-nominalist debate, the realist believes in universals, above and beyond the aggregate of particulars, which humans seek to discover and understand. To the realist, order is not simply something imposed by convention. The debate between nominalism and realism, raging on since medieval philosophy (Boler, 1963), is in many respects arcane and far removed from everyday worries. Yet glimpses of it pervade public disputes and even show up prominently in arguments from definition (Weaver, 1953), as when Lincoln argued that if black slaves were "men," then there are certain necessary entailments that are not a matter of arbitrary choice; or when antiabortion advocates claim that the beginning of human life is not simply a question of social convention. The question of just how malleable our forms of thought and representation are is central to much academic debate. Is practical usage constrained by a priori forms, and if so, how? Are these forms socially constructed, and if so, how? Does society lay the conditions of mind, or does mind transcend society? In a theory of meaning or a theory of rhetoric, the issue is rather crucial.

The strand I have been tracing leads from forms of thought, understood as somehow apart from the empirical flux, to a priori conditions for the human mind, to the social ordering of experience as a condition of intelligibility. How that social ordering comes to be, or how mutable it may be, opens a further set of questions. "Social," in any case, is a term that carries a special significance for an idealistic philosophy. In the work of Peirce and Royce (Royce, 1969), and even more emphatically in that of the great Anglo-American philosopher Alfred North Whitehead (1978), one finds what can only be called a metaphysic of the social, that condition by which one can share communally in the experience of others. This was an influence on George Herbert Mead, and "Chicago School" sociology (see Hartshorne, 1984). Charles Hartshorne has further developed this theory along the lines of a logic of relativity, according to which the feeling of others' feeling, and more broadly, the experiencing of others' experience, is the result of a fundamentally social dependence of experience—not just a pooling of subjectivities, but an actual interanimation of one being by another, or by many others (Hartshorne, 1970). The generative notion here, and what makes this philosophy idealistic, is the argument that terms commonly designating things "mental" — ideas, interpretations, memories, feelings, anticipations, and so on — are more philosophically fruitful than terms applied to cause and effect, inertia, and insentience. Things of mind are what can be shared and generalized.

This all seems plausible enough in analyzing human beings, but it also raises some obvious questions about the world around us. The material world, after all, does not seem to operate on the same basis as sentient beings do — why would anyone even want to make sentience the paradigm case for anything outside of the human sciences? What relevance does talk of nonmaterial categories have to the material world? These questions were addressed with some interesting results in the 17th century by Leibniz (Leibniz, 1934). As a metaphysician concerned with the nature of things and not just how we come to know them, Leibniz wrestled with the question of how freedom of action is possible. Unfortunately, most of us have our impressions of his work shaped, if we have any at all, by Voltaire's devilish caricature in *Candide,* Dr. Pangloss. Pangloss is given to repeating the Leibnizian dictum that "this is the best of possible worlds," which stated in isolation seems a fair enough target for ridicule. What Leibniz offered was not the Panglossian doctrine, however, but an account of how possibilities compete within the limits of space and time, and therefore cannot all be realized concurrently. If two people want the same plot of land, the good of each using and enjoying that plot is incompatible with its use by the other. Hence many good things, and many worthy values, are "incompossible," not possible at the same time or place. Leibniz thus saw the limits that the actual places on the possible. The world is able to manifest only those possibilities as it can at a given time; the best that is possible is rarely the best that is conceivable. Mind is thus constrained in what it can make real.

Leibniz also posed a challenge to materialism that seems even more pertinent today than when he wrote it. What we call "matter," he argued in his *Monadology* (Leibniz, 1985), is simply that which we experience in aggregate form. A rock, for instance, is not a real unity, but an aggregate of what we would now call molecules, atoms, quarks (and who knows where it all will end?). What is real, according to Leibniz, are the active unities, or "monads," such as persons, organisms, cells, and whatever lower level subjects of activity and experience there may be. This metaphysical analysis seems surprisingly prescient in light of 20th century quantum theory and nuclear physics. What to the naked eye appears as merely inert matter breaks down submicroscopically into a field of energies, or quanta, that seem anything but mechanical or inactive. Modern physics speaks of energy and animation, not of inanimate "things" (Cobb & Griffin, 1977).

So what imagery should we derive from "matter"? Indeed, what cognitive content? Is it only a broad placeholder in the materialist's vocabulary? According to Hartshorne, the concept of mere matter has throughout its history, from the ancient Greeks onward, been "a term for intellectual embarrassment" (Hartshorne, 1983 p. 48). What account of the notion of matter can the materialist give, the Leibnizian challenge goes, that does not employ terms and concepts traditionally associated with "mind," including that of self-activity? As we look closely, too closely for practical life, the thingness of things seems to disappear. The more scientifically we consider the material world, the more it looks like a bustling population of energy quanta, governed in aggregate by intelligible order—the very stuff of mind.

In the world of human society, of shared practices and sensibilities, linked by communication, the point seems even stronger. Why adopt a vocabulary that reduces active and creative beings to their physical sub-structures? In its recent manifestations, materialism tries to come to terms with the power of words and institutions rather than dismissing them as mere superstructures (e.g. Hall, 1985). But if the materialist can defeat idealism only by extending the notion of matter to cover incorporeal powers—even to make a "thing" of ideas (see McGuire, chapter 6)—then this is perhaps a Pyrrhic victory, or perhaps a case of the colonizer being transformed by the colonized. The idealist may reason thus: Let materialists pay enough attention to the influence of mass-mediated images, Wall Street panics, and everyday "ideology," and they will start to speak as though "ideas have consequences," which is what the idealist has said all along. Texts will become "sites of struggle," battlegrounds as much as they ever were for a scholastic philosopher. In short, the notion of matter will be reconstructed so as to represent whatever "matters," including words, ideas, feelings, consciousness, and meanings. On grounds such as these, the idealist might even be prepared to call a truce with those who want to say that rhetoric is "material" (McGee, 1982).

Still, it is difficult to see how the materialist can escape the language of determinism that is embedded in that story, if the story is told with thoroughness—and it really requires some thoroughness for some of the philosophical differences between materialists and idealists to emerge. So long as both stick to the everyday understandings of "material constraints," then the differences can be deferred. A common strategy of deferral is to argue that, although a complete causal account of human activity is possible in principle, we have to make do with traditional descriptions (positing "intentions" and the like) until we have such an account. Perhaps the science of the brain will one day link every firing neuron to a behavioral consequence, or maybe the social scientists will fine tune all their general-izations about causes to the point that full material determination can be seen. Then, presumably, human nature will all be "in the book" (even if it would be so massive that no one could have more than a *Cliff's Notes* understanding of it). The practical embarrassment faced by those who espouse material determinism is that they cannot conduct their own lives as if they believed the doctrine. Like the rest of us, they must muster the energy to get out of bed in the morning, agonize over tough decisions, and otherwise act as though creatures of free will. Even the determinist cannot wait around for material causes to do the work for him. Life must be "lived forward," ever advancing into the unknown and yet-to-be-determined, within contingent and unpredictable experience.

With Aristotle, the idealist will take seriously the notion of *telos*—the "final causes" that can be defined and envisioned only in terms of a thing's potential. *Telos* is the species of causality that is repressed by mechanistic science, but without which a satisfactory account of human activity is, and always will be, impossible. Mechanistic thinking precludes teleology, references to the ends, or purposes of things. In keeping with the imagery of the mechanism, accounts of causes are given in terms of what Aristotle would have called efficient cause, and by general laws governing them. Instead of saying that protesters demonstrated "in order to" bring about reforms, a mechanistic story would feature some behavioral trigger, such as discontent, which in turn would likely be attributed to economic or glandular conditions, rather than to the power of hopes and visions. The sequence of causes and effects, in this story, would line up in strict behavioral order. Because explanations by "final causes" seem to posit something in the future (e.g., an envisioned possibility) as a cause of something in the present (e.g., an action), these must be reconstructed in the language of efficient causes. The road is linear, each fork presenting only the illusion of choice. The "lure" of a destination does not enable motion.

The determinist's hope that a full causal account of human activity will render it more predictable and thus manageable is surely a false hope, however, because it rests on a paradox. The paradox is that knowing more does not reduce the unpredictability of life, but rather, it increases it, since the more one knows, the more one gains control over circumstance and therefore acts "freely." This is one sense in which knowledge is empowerment (and one explanation of "the truth shall make you free"). To assert control over one's life means not *being* controlled. To gain knowledge of causes, therefore, is to take a step toward escaping them. Determinists, be they psychological behaviorists such as B.F. Skinner (e.g., 1970) or sociobiological ones such as E. O. Wilson (1978), end up practicing the art of persuasion, encouraging us to choose their theory, which of course, we are free to reject. Their *rhetorical practice* is not in any evident way informed by principles of operant conditioning in the first case, or adaptive behavior in the other. The fact that even those who emphasize the physical causes of human behavior must, like everyone else, resort to strategies of gentle persuasion makes a good point at which to begin discussing the implications of an idealistic philosophy for a conception of rhetoric. But first a brief summary is necessary.

Idealists place the world of mind and intelligible experience at the center of their thinking. They see human beings as straddling the world of the actual and that of the possible and shaping the movement between them as creative agents. Subjective idealists stress the individual mind, whereas objective idealists stress the role of minds in engaging and constituting a world not under the subjective command of individuals. Either of these views can court extremes, although the objective idealist position seems inherently to be the more socially realistic one. Idealism may appear to be a more obvious candidate for a philosophy of human experience than of the world at large, but metaphysical idealists, after Leibniz and others, have insisted that even the material world is best accounted for as active and self-determining, rather than inert, determined, and different in kind from the world of sentient beings. If idealism has to go to this metaphysical level to counter the entrenched mechanistic world view, it has the resources to do so.

Transcendental idealism, in a sense a position between the other two varieties, looks to a priori forms of thought that span the experience of the species, or more modestly, span the thinking of an intellectual epoch or paradigm — and at this more "modest" level, the transcendental approach begins to look much less like idealism. Nevertheless, there is an important neo-Kantian aspect to even the most "materialistic" versions of this (e.g., Foucault's "epistemes"). Much contemporary thinking has turned to the notion of stable thought forms, held to govern culture (e.g., Levi-Strauss), language (e.g., Chomsky), social pragmatics (e.g., Habermas), or science (e.g., Kuhn), although these vary greatly in how stable the forms are held to be. Few of the advocates of these positions would likely welcome the label "idealist," however, and some of these approaches in fact wind up rather far from the idealistic intuitions about the primacy of mind. Idealists are generally concerned to prevent the categories of thinking, feeling, experiencing, creating, and acting from being reduced to the categories of physical causation. They credit the power of the word in the world, and will draw their battle lines wherever that power is being denied.

IDEALISM AND RHETORIC

Anyone who advises undergraduate students is forced on occasion to think philosophically. The experience can arise from something as routine as recommending an elective course in Chinese history, or physics, or Shakespeare, and confronting the question, "What can I do with that?" How does one begin to answer? The more inventive among us can tell some story in which the course in question is connected to future job performance or the attractiveness of the resume. Others will mumble something about well-roundedness, and just hope that the notion will not be probed too seriously. But being honest, these sorts of answers dodge the real issue, which is that the student's apparently pragmatic question is likely the product of a constrictively narrow conception of what is practical. The notion of "using" and "doing" are imagined in terms of physical processes, such as making and spending money. Given such an impoverished notion of "use," it is difficult to quickly produce a satisfactory answer to a seemingly reasonable question. One would have to back up to examine the presuppositions of the question, broaching the philosophical issue of what is to be valued in an education.

Idealism holds as a central value in education, as in life, the cultivation of a rich and active mental life. Furthermore—and here is the part that is difficult to sell in our materialistic culture—it should be valued for its own sake. That is to say, the life of the mind, in and of itself, can be an adventurous and rewarding reality. It does not need to be justified in terms of something else, even though it often can be. For those who think only in material terms, mental life is not quite so real—sitting around contemplating philosophical ideas is simply idling, unless it produces material changes in one's life. To the materialist there would be little to distinguish the life of the poet or philosopher who lives a quiet and modest life from that of the unreflective person of similar circumstance. Indeed, the radical materialist sometimes shares with the anti-intellectual conservative a contempt for such pursuits of the mind. Archie Bunker and Chairman Mao might have more in common than they would suspect, not the least of which would be a contempt for the "effete intellectual."

In approaching rhetoric, an idealist would take seriously the life of the mind, as something that is much more than visible behavior. The rhetorician of an idealistic cast would take quite seriously the mental horizons that verbal constructions make possible. Does the person who thinks of events in China, or who understands something of science, or who judges current events in the context of history, or makes sense of observed behavior in terms of characters in familiar literature, really inhabit the same world as the person who knows nothing of these things? The idealist thinks not. The world of mind can be expansive without necessarily showing up in visible behavior, but it is no less real for that. Conversely, mental deprivation is a restriction of one's world. Of the many forms that poverty takes, the lack of knowledge is one of the most confining. When people lack access to broadening knowledge, they are doubly imprisoned, first by the material poverty that deprived them of access, and second by being condemned to live within the limits of their immediate environment. This is, literally, violence to the spirit. Even for the affluent, restricted horizons are often permitted in the name of practicality. The destructive result is that the practical ends of material culture can either restrict or overrun the expressive order in which persons find their own value (Harré, 1979).

Thinking about rhetoric must begin with some presuppositions about the nature and function of language, and this in turn will reflect some philosophical outlook. For instance, pragmatism looks to the instrumental value of mind and language. To the idealist, the mind is an extraordinarily effective instrument, but it is more than an instrument. It is also the place where we live. Idealism respects the life of the mind as a way of *being,* and considers the unreflective life not worth the price of admission. Likewise, this affects the way in which language is appreciated. Language is often described with the metaphor of the tool box, according to which we use words to do things, as instruments for our purposes. But there is more to language than that. Like music and art, it is to be lived and felt as well as used (Langer, 1953). Language, as Heidegger put it, is the abode of being (Megill, 1985, pp. 166 ff.). It edifies us, and largely constitutes us as a consciousness in the world. One does not have to demonstrate behavioral "effects" (for instance, that books "trigger" behaviors) in order to be justified in attributing great power to language. An idealist might observe that mechanistic metaphors have so crept into social scientific thinking that some there have apparently forgotten that the shaping of a consciousness is the most important influence of public symbolization, and analysis turns to such trivia as immediate responses to stimuli.

The most powerful effects of words, the power to create a mental life, are likely to be overlooked if one uses only cause–effect notions as criteria of effectiveness, or if one credits as real only that which exists beyond the mind. Hence many a social scientist finds no apparent connection between, say, fictional dramatization of violence against women and real world enactments of such violence, because it does not exert its influence in the manner of a "stimulus." The idealist would ask, not about stimuli, but about the kind of imaginative world that has been constructed, and how by degrees the members of a culture come to participate in it. And he or she would be astonished to find that ideas, even fictional ones, lack consequences.

With Kenneth Burke, an idealist will hold that explanations of human motives must be given in a vocabulary that is recognizably a vocabulary of action, not just causation. Things move, animals behave, but persons act. Acts are *meaningful* behavior, and one simply cannot strip away the meaning and expect to retain a satisfactory account of human activity. Levers move things; but humans do not just move, they are "motivated." Burke thus set out to explore the very grammar of motives, an alternative to the grammar of mechanical causality (Burke, 1954/1969). His project is analogous to that of Kant, insofar as he too distinguishes the world of physical necessity from that of human action. Burke's categories seek to capture the very constituents of meaningful action. The "dramatistic pentad" is thus intended, not as a metaphor of the theatre, but as the very logic of human motivation.

Rhetoric often has short-term objectives, but the short-term goals of influencing immediate conduct need to be weighed alongside longer-term goals, such as shaping certain sorts of sensibility. Cultivating sensibilities, traditionally recognized as one of the functions of epideictic rhetoric, would be of considerable interest to the idealistically inclined rhetor. Filling out an imaginative landscape, populating the stage for life's dramas, and giving that stage an expansive scope, would be a contribution to the life and being of the audience. Winning hearts and minds would be something more than the propagandist's game. A cynic might say that Jefferson's claims about inherent equality, and about inalienable rights of life, liberty, and the pursuit of happiness were not only platitudes, but false descriptions of reality. Yet by treating these as "great ideas," by struggling to give them meaning, our culture is demonstrably enriched. By believing in these ideas, we move toward making them true — we fit the world to the word, as well as the reverse. They become evolving measures of what is acceptable and what is not, and hence quite literally work their way, if always imperfectly, into the structure of society. If people use these words cynically, just to manipulate others, that is possible because the words already have a weight and value. "Debunkers" of the ideological or economic motivation for the use of language should be careful not to beg the question against the possibility that language can carry the force of ideas despite any self-interested purposes of the user.

The fact that life is inevitably lived forward, toward an uncertain and contingent future, has other important implications for an understanding of symbolization, which becomes our access to the future. The future is present only in anticipation, in images and visions. We do not see the future as through a clear window, in full and determinate landscapes. Rather, we catch vague glimpses of the possibilities, outlines whose specifics can be filled in only in time. In that sense, any philosophy that thinks to the future has to be "idealistic." Sometimes the future can be vividly prefigured in acts of imagination, depending entirely on a capacity to use language and symbols suggestively. But vividly or not, the future is ours to behold only symbolically, and the power to conjure possible futures depends on our capacity to symbolize. Nothing in the future is yet concrete, only abstract, represented in word and image. Yet human beings have an inventive capacity to select from among alternative futures (not any that may be *conceivable,* but those that are *possible* for them); and this makes things unpredictable. Despite the social scientists' advertised objectives of prediction and control, mechanistic explanations of human activity are notoriously poor predictors (McCloskey, 1985).

Rhetoric trades on the insight that minds are the nexus between the actual and the possible. One holds in mind various possible arrangements of the world, in addition to apprehending the actual one. The tension between the two is what we call consciousness. The shortfall between the actual and what one would like it to be is a source of dissatisfaction and a motive for change. And if our arsenal of possibilities includes such things as "freedom" and "justice," we will have an ongoing and energizing sense of shortfall. We will know the power of a great idea to shape conduct. To know more possibilities is to have a greater consciousness and a greater repertoire of possible actions. This seems to commend aspects of idealism.

A key difference between the idealist and the mechanist might just come down to their attitude toward *the possible*. For the mechanist, to speak of various possibilities in the future is only to indicate our ignorance of what will happen, which is determined. The casual mechanisms will continue to produce just what they will. If I say it is possible that war will occur, it is only because I do not have the information enabling me to foresee what will actually happen. But the idealist thinks differently of possibilities. If I say it is possible that war will occur, it means the matter is in principle undecided. Possibilites are real options, not illusions. The capacity to envision something can enable us to bring it about or prevent it. Simply willing something is rarely a sufficient condition for success, as we live under all manner of constraints.

The causal/ideational issue is not all that is of interest to the idealist, however. Aesthetically, ethically, and epistemologically, the idealist values coherence and the integration of experience. The person is seen as striving to define an integrity, a way of being in the world, a matrix of experience that can belong to no one else, as no one else has exactly the same life history. Moreover, the personality should illuminate all with which it comes into contact. (On these points, there is a clear affinity with the existentialism characterized by Hyde in chap. 7.) The idealist will be suspicious of those uses of language that seem to constrict experience, to cut off its resonance with past and future. This viewpoint regards with suspicion attempts to "scientize" human perception by treating experimental "subjects" as though they were interchangeable parts in a framework of physics, as this excludes in principle the individual histories and memories that each brings to bear on each new experience. It also looks askance at overextended metaphors, such as that of "rational economic man," that would reduce all modes of being to a single one (Schwartz, 1986).

The discursive world appropriate to idealism is one that is expansive beyond mere circumstance, perhaps endowed with something like what

Weaver called "spaciousness" (Weaver, 1953). When this rhetoric addresses circumstance, it does not treat the circumstance as though it were a world to itself, but as a microcosm of a bigger world. In each rhetorical situation is a fragment of a larger story: the universal illuminates the particular, and the particular illuminates the universal. Working to its potential, such a rhetoric cannot be unanchored, or simply a "loose canon," firing randomly from one moment to the next. As persuasive discourse, rhetoric can pose a trajectory for the reading of experience, and the guidance of action. By reading the present moment against a broader text, it can advocate a way of assembling the pieces of perception. By configuring the "circumference" of action, rhetoric can invest settings with portents (Burke, 1945).

Rhetoricians have probably not thought sufficiently about how "a rhetoric" is able to speak beyond particular cases, to act as a forward trajectory organizing discourses past, present, and future. I would suggest, therefore, that we need to begin theorizing about the nature of *rhetorical policy,* that is, the deliberate guidance of persuasion across time, cases, and audiences. Such a rhetoric would be "gyroscopic," in the sense of being stabilized according to its own inner workings while moving dynamically across situations — keeping things on course, so to speak. It would have to be capable of bringing continuity of sense to otherwise perplexing circumstances, and of giving guidance to social construction; it would be enabling. A rhetorical policy would have to respect the social and communal ordering of experience. And it would have to be open to reality, not programmed for blindness. In that respect, a forward looking, idealistic rhetoric should be compatible with the critical rationalism sketched out in this volume by Orr (chap. 4).

An excellent model of what I am calling rhetorical policy appears in the work of legal scholar James Boyd White (1984), who has analyzed three key documents and their relationships in the formation of the American political tradition: The Declaration of Independence, the U.S. Constitution, and the Supreme Court decision in the *McCullough v. Maryland* case. Legal reasoning, White showed, can in many ways provide a paradigm for community-making through rhetorical processes. His analysis of these three documents shows just how rhetoric can form the conditions of an ongoing, self-realizing political community, which strives "to make the ideal real." In this tradition what was proposed, and largely achieved, was "nothing less than the self-conscious reconstitution of language and community to achieve new possibilities for life" (p. 231). The "truths" of the Declaration, White observed, did not attain their full political meaning at the moment of composition, but did so (and continue to do so) over time through a variety of means, such as Lincoln's use of the Declaration's statement of equality as the founding principle of the Union. The Declaration not only set forth a kind of ideal, but *envisioned a developing community of discourse that would be its ideal audience.* Its meaning would be tested, not by reference to facts, intentions, or circumstances alone, but by this question: "How would the ideal reader contemplated by this document, indeed, constituted by it, understand its bearing in the present circumstances?" (p. 271). In other words, White saw idealization as a factor in interpreting discourse and in sustaining rhetorical continuity.

The Constitution continued the discourse made possible by the Declaration, White said, setting out political roles and relationships by which the free and equal people conjured by the Declaration could come to be. *McCullough* and a variety of other court decisions acted with rhetorical continuity in aspiring to make the ideal real. Such judicial opinions "incorporate within their world both the past to which the court looks for its authority and the future (to which it speaks as an authority)." "This process," White continued, "establishes connections across time of the sort that [Edmund] Burke celebrates, but these judicial connections are not merely attitudinal but systematic and reliable. The judicial process at once acknowledges the necessity of cultural change and creates a method for effecting it" (p. 264). The tradition constituted by key legal texts unleashes a dialectical investigation in which the logic and terminology of those texts are tested and pushed to their limits, and in which one construction of language and reality is tested against another.

White saw special properties in legal texts, not parallel to other texts, not the least of which is their particular binding authority. But I argue that the parallels are what are most instructive in view of the political role of rhetoric, and especially for a rhetoric that takes the long view. The notions of the cultivation of ideals and the appeal to the ideal reader are useful beyond strictly legal contexts, for they inform broader contexts in which documents such as the Declaration and the Constitution most certainly function. Once making the decision to "keep faith" with the ideals embodied in the founding documents, as Sanford Levinson argued, then each citizen faces the choice of whether to "sign on" to those documents and actively extend their histories (Levinson, 1988). We do not come to that choice without "prejudice," nor should we expect to if our consciousness is developed in the context of a community.

A rhetoric of the sort charactered by White is directional because those who interpret it *make it so,* not because of historical "forces" or other inevitabilities. It is also self-reflexive, under constant scrutiny and gradual change. It leaves room for debate and other forms of wrangling while constituting the grounds for controversy and making connections that are "systematic and reliable". This constitutive and reconstitutive discourse is not limited to lawmakers, but inscribes all members of its community. It is possible to think of other communities in such terms, that is, bound by a common rhetorical heritage but open to ongoing inquiry. Scientific communities, for instance, might also be viewed in this way, despite their significant differences from political communities. Arguably, the continuity and character of a science is better explained, not in terms of what a science knows or what methods it uses, but in terms of the shared conception of what a good scientist does. A rhetoric of inquiry appropriate to the sciences might arguably be a self-reflectively purposive rhetoric, striving to realize its inscribed ideals by imposing constraints and then testing their limits.

An idealistic rhetoric, pursued as a policy, would be an inquiring rhetoric, but not "scientistic" to the point of denying the relevance of culture to an understanding of truth. It would hold that beliefs are justifiable or legitimated within the context of shared mentality, or culture. Consequently, it could not go along with critical rationalism in forsaking justification. In fact, it would recognize that one of the most important activities in which rhetoric is employed is the *justification* of beliefs—meeting challenges in the courtroom, in politics, in the classroom, in ethical disputes, or in these essays (see Wellman, 1971). Arguments and other rhetorical tactics are frequently marshalled in support of beliefs already held or entertained. The act of criticism, or falsification, by no means exhausts the arsenal of rationality. In holding otherwise, critical rationalism takes a very one-sided and "scientistic" view of beliefs and their origins: rational beliefs are seen as simply the survivors of falsification, not the reasonable extensions of accepted practices. This misleadingly suggests that rhetorical arguments come to us as scientific hypotheses from out of the blue, to be unprejudicially tested. Critical rationalism fails to appreciate that rhetorical discourse rests on a structure of *presumptions,* ingrained in culture and not just arbitrarily swapped for something else. Our thought and discourse are supported by a "web of belief" (Quine & Ullian, 1978), modifiable a piece at a time, depending on how a new challenge relates to existing beliefs. This web, this fabric of beliefs, discourse, and practices, is never put at risk all at once in quasi-scientific experiments.

In this discussion of "rhetorical policy" the materialist will likely pick up the scent of ideology and rhetorical distortion. Admittedly, the "gyroscopic" rhetoric I have described, with its stable strategies and strictures on intepretation, might look like nothing more than what others call ideology. That would be true however, only if one equated strategies with ideologies, or all advocacy with distortion. To the idealist there is no alternative, short of pure mindlessness, to a world in which thinking follows some regularity and preformation. But the notion that thinking can be systematically skewed or distorted also must be taken seriously by the idealist, of all people. Rhetorical theorists who adopt an idealistic framework should therefore think carefully about when, how, and in what sense rhetorical inducements may be called ideological. A general difficulty for the theory of ideology, I believe, is to identify useful criteria for distinguishing ideology, generally premised on what Marx called "false consciousness," from those ideas that are not "false." It is not clear whether anything like a formula for distinguishing the two is possible, although there are perhaps some general cautions to be offered in any quest for a rhetoric that seeks directionality without imposing a false picture.

First, any doctrine put beyond scrutiny, self-reflection, or the possibility of revision would be better characterized as dogma, not rhetorical policy of the sort considered here. To this extent the critical rationalist's spirit of openness is appropriate. Rhetorical trajectories, by contrast to mere dogma, must have some tentativeness, because they anticipate the future without actually foreseeing it. A second caution is that a system that "mechanized" interpretation could neither give a central role to human judgment nor leave any interesting place for the rhetorical. Beyond a few general observations of this kind, however, it is difficult and perhaps undesirable to prescribe idealities apart from particular contexts. *Rhetoric, let us not forget, is rooted in actual histories, traditions, and circumstances, and it assumes advocacy, not impartiality.* Rhetoricians must find ways of thinking and speaking "idealities" that inform and transform real situations by looking forward, and backward, and then pulling the relevant threads of meaning through the present. An idealistic rhetoric, in short, would take to the task of locating and shaping the life of the mind in a real world.

In sum, an idealist will have certain views that bear on a theory of rhetoric, including views toward the character and intelligibility of experience, the nature and function of language, and human freedom of action. The idealist will hold, with Richard Weaver, that "ideas have consequences," and will act accordingly (Weaver, 1948). With Kenneth Burke, the idealist will insist that persons "act"—they do not just behave (Burke, 1945/1969). And with I.A. Richards, the idealist will concur that words "interanimate" one another, literally fill each other with life (Richards, 1965). Like Plato, the idealist will be concerned with the state of the psyche, and with justice, and how language can do them good or ill. This would presumably require some attention to the long view, that is, to the cumulative and developmental results of a rhetoric that is cultivated and tested over time, such as is the case with the American constitutional tradition.

FACING THE CRITICISMS

In this section I raise and address certain criticisms that are sometimes aimed at the idealistic approach to rhetoric. Some of these criticisms, I believe, are well-founded responses to weaknesses in the way the case for idealism has been articulated.

Criticism #1:   Idealism overestimates the power of ideas. One of the contributions of the materialist perspective (McGuire, chap. 6) is that it makes us aware of the less obvious boundaries and conditions on human experience. It makes us aware that ideas are generated within full-bodied historical circumstances, within structures that enable and constrain. From this perspective we can develop a sense of accountability to history. If materialism plays a role as dialectical "other" to idealism, then it will force idealists to better account for the embeddedness of ideas within economic and historical practices. Idealists should not shrink from that task. Certainly, the notion of constraint is familiar to the idealist's way of thinking, as normative standards (e.g., the standard of the "ideal reader," or of "forms of thought") are taken as constraining what is to be made of empirical experience. It is not, after all, that the idealist discounts the empirical world, but rather, that she is interested in the *significance* of that world as it can be located in experience. In the age of mass-mediated discourse, a world of word and image no less interesting to the materialist than the idealist, the dynamics of constraint and enablement pose new challenges to both philosophies, and will no doubt prove many of their shortcomings. One positive result of this is that materialists are becoming less crude in how they think of materiality, while idealists are becoming more realistic in how they understand material constraint (Hall, 1985). If one philosophy delivered a knockout punch to the other, a productive tension (see Johnstone's Foreword, this volume) would be lost.

Still, if one is to be a *thoroughgoing* idealist or materialist, there will come a point of clash, and from that point various implications will trail out through the world view. A watershed issue is in respect to the ultimacy of physical categories. An idealist will have to part company with those who give causal relations primacy over the "inner side" of experience, or who pursue a reduction of the psychical to the physical, as McGuire appears to do in chapter 6. I will not attempt here to make the case for a broader theory of natural causality than is implied by mechanistic metaphors (e.g., colliding billiard balls, moving levers), even though quantum theory, chaos theory, and much else in contemporary theoretical physics argues for some such broadening (e.g., Crutchfield, Farmer, Packard, and Shaw et al., 1986). Rather, I rest on the claim that mechanistic explanations of human behavior are of little use to social studies, and in the case of rhetorical influence are simply not illuminating. A physics of human communication, although theoretically possible, is hardly what we need. The problems addressed by rhetoric are in the social realm, requiring social solutions. No one to my knowledge thinks that a better understanding of the physics of homelessness will move us toward a solution to that problem. Why should we expect that a turn to the physical supports of discourse will further our quest for enlightened social influence? On the contrary, a reduction of the social to the physical moves in precisely *the opposite direction* from where a rhetorician wants to go.

In the matter of physical reduction, the question is not whether it is possible to break down teleological accounts of human action into a series of efficient causes, but rather why one should wish to attack in such a manner the the very capacities that make human behavior distinctive and meaningful. One striking effect of the mechanistic approach to social meaning is that it nearly always invalidates the account that social actors would themselves give as to why they do what they do. Human beings typically account for their actions in terms of "reasons," rather than causes. People speak out "in order to" change events, or to bring about results, not "because" they were pushed along helplessly by the forces that be. Human beings are purposeful systems — *teleonomic,* in the argot of systems theory. Again, this is not to suppose that it is impossible to reduce human behavior to a story of physical causation, but I follow Burke in calling such attempts at mechanization a reduction to the "scenic" component of motivation. It amounts to telling the story "from the point of view" of the physical environment, and that has a partial utility.

Not all such exercises in perspective taking are harmless, however. A problem in this instance is that the high ethos of science in our culture can lead people to believe that any scenic story that science might tell, be it in terms of brain chemistry or social laws, is the full story. Burke's point is that it would be a very one-sided version of what should be a five-sided story. Suppose for a moment that science did one day give us a full account of what makes the brain tick, and further, that this were linked systemically to the complex social situations in which various behaviors might be produced. Let us suppose, that "the book of human behavior", referred to above, does get written. Would it follow that accounts strictly in terms of physical causes would suffice for all practical or theoretical purposes?

It is difficult to see how this could be the case. The qualities of experience would still be experienced as qualities, and in terms of personally and socially meaningful categories. A piece of music might be causally delineated as sound waves oscillating against my ear drum and stimulating certain centers of the brain — but it would still be music to me. My interest in justice might be translated into some psychological story of personal inadequacy — but the question of justice at the social level would still remain. Scientific explanations cannot resolve the "ought" questions for us: What kind of society do we want? Where will we devote our resources? To what ends will we use knowledge? If we knew everything there is to know, that would still be just a starting point for answering questions about what we will *do* with that knowledge. This is why accounting for human activity is not the same sort of problem as accounting for planetary motion. The notion that a reduction to causal origins supercedes all other levels of meaning and experience seems an odd doctrine to apply to human beings.

Criticism #2:   Taking words at face value, idealism fails to acknowledge the material interests that motivate discourse, and the way discourse may serve to mask those interests. Every word ever uttered comes from some historically situated person, whose personal interests, motives, and perspectives are behind the words uttered. Some critics take this as reason for systematic suspicion of all rhetoric, which is seen as designed to mask self-interest, often unconsciously. But materialists (e.g., behaviorists, sociobiologists, Marxists) are also under the particularly heavy theoretical burden of having to account for any apparent purposefulness strictly in terms of origins. This means, among other things, that the "forward attraction" of an idea, or vision, has to be reread as a "merely" phenomenological occurrence, which in principle can be broken down into an account by causal origins. Persons might think they are acting in order to bring about justice, or some such fine result, but they are simply responding to their circumstance and conditioning. Noble motives are only the stories with which we delude ourselves—or fool others. In other words, truth, justice, beauty, goodness, freedom, and such are not powerful ideas, standards against which actual experience can be measured, but simply a way we have learned to talk, devices with a rhetorical use in elections, and so forth. In much Western economic thought, as in so-called vulgar Marxism, the task amounts to translating every motive into economic interest; in more fashionable literary Marxism, the unmasking is more subtle, and interests are conceived more variably.

The critic who unmasks hidden motives may perform a valuable service; but to assume systematically that all idealistic talk promotes special interests at the expense of others, or that the value of discourse is to be measured solely by its origins, is unwarranted. Tzvetan Todorov (1989) put the matter well:

> The distinctive trait of human beings is not only to have specific motives, but to be capable of surmounting them. Everyone (except Callicles) knows the difference between what is advantageous and what is just. The fact that algebra was discovered by the Arabs does not make it any less true in China. The fact that declarations of human rights were drawn up in Europe does not mean these rights need not be respected in South Africa. And the possibility of consensus, the aspiration to universality, is obviously much closer to the democratic ideal than are the philosophies that present the world as given over to irreducible interests, to a war among races, nations, classes, or sexes. (p. 29)

This does not mean that any statement of reasons or motives must be taken at face value, of course. People distort and misrepresent their motives for any number of reasons, consciously or not, sometimes going so far as lying. But unmasking such hypocrisies does not necessarily strike a blow for materialism. In fact, idealism has much better grounds than materialism for criticizing hypocrisy and dishonesty, as these are offenses against the integrity of thought that idealists, of all people, should take seriously.

I argued previously that the materialist cannot really act in such a way as to support the thesis of determinism. Likewise, I would turn criticism #2 back on the materialist, who surely does not want his or her own words to be discounted as mere self-interested posturing. Behind the often cynical face of the materialist critic lurks an alternative vision of how things should be, against which the status quo falls short. Such critics are often little more than wounded idealists, who are moved especially by the sense of injustice. They draw their sustaining breath from their ideals, not from their technical capacity to debunk. This is perfectly understandable. I am arguing that it is not a mistake to take ideals seriously, and that the view that words are mere masks is not systematically sustainable from any standpoint.

Criticism #3: Idealism ignores historical differences, mistakenly treating words from different contexts as part of a common discourse. The work of Michel Foucault (esp. 1970, 1975) has been especially powerful in showing the discontinuities in history and historical understanding, and the corresponding problem in assuming that language can be moved from one time and place to another and retain its meaning. Language, Foucault showed, does not just float freely from one framework to another. Rather, it is bound up with all the social practices of its time and place and is not easily separated. In a rather different way, Wittgenstein (esp. 1958a, and 1958b) developed a similar point about the dependence of language on the context of other related practices.

An example from popular culture helps to bring the problems into focus. For years television celebrity Steve Allen hosted a program called "Meeting of the Minds," which brought together well known historical personages from widely disparate times and places to discuss issues. The fiction of the program was that when Plato, Thomas Jefferson, and Madame Curie chatted across the table, they were participating in the same discourse. In a way, this represents the idealistic perspective, taken to an extreme, where the problems can be easily spotted. The communication problems, one might conclude after some reflection, would be considerable. After all, how *could* Jefferson and Plato have had a common discourse (assuming perfect translation), given their different historical experience and the greatly differing contexts in which their words had meaning? Different cultures at different times read different things into their words, and these investments of meaning are always in flux. What right has anyone to assume that the meaning of words is fixed over time and across culture—that they have a fixed "essence"?

This line of questioning, I believe, poses a major challenge to idealism, perhaps to the point of requiring significant rethinking on the part of idealists about such things as meaning and language. The key to a successful response, I believe, requires distinguishing idealism from essentialism. Essentialism, the view that things are defined by their essences and hence subject to fixed and invariable reference, is characteristic of the Platonic view of the world and is also an unexamined assumption behind many "common sense" theories of meaning. Whether "justice" has an essence is a question beyond the scope of this paper, and so Plato need not be taken head-on here. Viewed linguistically, however, one can make the case against essences by appeal to actual usage. When one examines the actual history and sociology of words, it becomes quite difficult to maintain that there are any inviolable core meanings across time and culture. Hence the problem of Steve Allen's mythical conversation: people from different discourse communities cannot be assumed to share fully in each other's meanings.

Pushed to a logical extreme, this discontinuity theme can complicate the analysis of any act of communication. For, arguably, no two people use their words in exactly the same way. Taking the problem to this logical extreme can also suggest a solution, however. If communication depended upon perfect synchrony in the way people used language, then it might occur only rarely. But we know that satisfactory communication occurs quite regularly. Communication, or participation in a common discourse, requires only a continuity in meaning sufficient for the purposes at hand. Idealism thus does not require fixed essences, but only continuities in meaning. There must be some discernible trajectory along which words such as "liberty" and "justice" move if we are to be in any sense heirs to what the Constitutional Framers or others even more remote in history have had to say on these subjects. One can readily see that the 18th century American conception of justice did not place Black people on an equal footing with Whites; but one might also see a logic of the term's development whereby the definition did "ideally" come to include both Blacks and Whites. Provided there is some continuity, which will always be only a relative continuity, communication is possible. The role of community again becomes manifest here, as communities help to supply continuity of meaning.

In a way, some dose of idealism seems required in order to make sense of the notion that the writers of the Declaration and the Constitution still speak to us in the 20th century and that we are in some sense part of a common discourse community. A materialist will have little difficulty demonstrating the differences of time, place, and social understandings that separate us from those authors. The question for the idealist, after all those differences have been understood, is: What carries forth across all those material differences? Which elements of meaning transcend the circumstance of utterance and continue to animate thought? What has been "interiorized" across a range of human experience? The idealist rejects the notion that the connection a 20th century person might feel to thinking in another century *must be* based entirely on an illusion created by the use of the same terms. Words, from this perspective, are not just behavioral triggers but a genuine repository of consciousness.

Criticism #4:   Idealism is overly subjective and relies on immediate experience. This criticism applies best to subjective idealism but loses its grip on the objective idealist position, which assumes the communing of minds. The latter variety of idealism does not depend on an unmediated presence of knowledge within a *cogito.* In Peirce's work, for instance, mediation by signs is a central motif precisely because of his belief that the world had to be intelligible to mind: there is, so to speak, no "bottom line" for knowledge, no point at which one simply grasps something uninterpreted and stops the active intellect (Peirce, 1958). Rather, it is the nature of minds to go on intepreting, and this process, called "semiosis," is in principle endless (Eco, 1976). Some find this way of thinking threatening, "idealistic" in a pejorative sense, as though it would pull the solid floor out from under us, or reduce everything to a subjective construction. But knowledge is not a floor, and one does not need immutable standpoints in order to be engaged with the world.

Perhaps the fear of semiosis (shall we call it "semiophobia") grows from impoverished notions of signifying and interpreting as something highly subjective or ephemeral, something apart from real world practices. Some contemporary "textualists" have, almost perversely at times, encouraged this perception. It is important to note, however, that the notions of interpretation that arise in American idealistic philosophy are very much tied to notions of community. Peirce stressed the ongoing processes of empirical, but socially mediated, inquiry. His project was truly a "rhetoric of inquiry," concerned with how a complex weave of interpretative practice, scientific, aesthetic, or practical, develops and stabilizes within cumulative intellectual investigation; that is, how it settles into belief (Lyne, 1980, 1982). His contemporary, Josiah Royce, well known for his idealism, shared Peirce's interest in the role played by communities in structuring interpretation, and he envisioned broader and more inclusive communities. Royce posited an all-inclusive community, not a realm of discontinuous paradigms, as a regulative ideal for inquiry (Royce, 1969), a notion in some ways comparable to Peirce's notion of the idealized "final opinion" as the measure of reality.

Thus, one might say, Peirce and Royce sought the conditions of knowledge in communities of inquiry, which themselves must be constructed. To the extent that it aligns with critical inquiry, a forward looking, idealistic rhetoric should be compatible with the critical rationalism sketched out by Orr in chapter 4. In a sense, however, it would be a more socially mediated rhetoric than that aligned with critical rationalism, because it makes the community of minds the support and matrix of inquiry, not merely an accidental circumstance. Popper's critical rationalism seems to leave insight and conjecture wholly fortuitous and unrooted in history. A rhetorical theory based in objective idealism, by contrast, would expect to find its direction and heuristics in the community of inquiry. It would find in discourse rather than in cups of black coffee the sources of invention and discovery.

Criticism #5:   Idealism risks balkanizing rationality by locating it in a plurality of paradigms or other humanly dependent unities. The transcendental variety of idealism locates the forms of thought and, by implication, the framework of rationality, at some general level beyond that which is merely local. At its most general, it sets the grounds for a human rationality. In the case of paradigm-dependent rationalities, this criticism has some bite. The general *zeitgeist* toward relativism in the field of rhetoric is in many respects influenced by talk of local knowledge, context-specific rationality, and paradigm dependent explanation (Nelson, Megill, & McCloskey, 1987). In many ways, this is an important corrective to overly broad and abstract conceptions of knowledge and rationality, and is to that extent to be welcomed. The risk it incurs is just the type of balkanization suggested above. That is, the reaction to the universalizing impulse of modernism might lead to another extremity, that of myopic and ad hoc notions of rationality, tailor made to fit existing practices, but incapable of playing the more expansive role that rationality has traditionally been expected to play. If rationality becomes *too much* a local affair, then it will be unhelpful in adjudicating among the rival practices that inevitably confront one another. The risk this approach brings is in setting arbitrary and nonnegotiable limits on thinking, and closing off growth, inquiry, and exchange among different discursive realms.

In his recent appeal for a tradition-dependent notion of rationality, Alasdair MacIntyre (1988) courted this very dilemma without much success in resolving it. Working locally within traditions will serve reasonably well provided one is living in an isolated community; but in a pluralistic society, one is bombarded with a variety of traditions and other intellectual and social possibilities. A rhetorical theory needs to be able to account for how one might engage in reasonable and persuasive discourse across the bounds of traditions and discursive formations. If I can only articulate my case in the self-enclosed logic of my own community, "paradigm," or whatever, then I am sealed off from a larger rationality and barred from participation in a larger community. This is surely not a rhetoric that encourages growth and exploration—not truly a rhetoric of inquiry (Lyne, 1985). The pluralism it would foster would be a dogmatic pluralism, a condition in which one would somehow find oneself with a discourse community, presumably by birth or other biographical accident, and have no rational way out.

This is not the better pluralism of our tradition. At this stage in history, perhaps more has to be offered than John Stuart Mill's "marketplace of ideas" metaphor to explain how the movement from one intellectual condition to another is possible; but all in all, even with its capitalistic flavor, it is probably a preferable metaphor to those that make discourses so local that no "commerce" among them is provided for. Somehow, a rhetorical theory must keep open ways of discussing not only local discourse, with its particular logics, topics, and folkways, but also ways of productively configuring the economy of commerce among discourses, and the politics of joint undertakings and compromise. These broader enterprises presuppose a "common coin" in the language spoken and a common access to the rationality employed. An idealistic rhetoric presumes that such a common coin either exists or can exist. And it would search for ways of expanding the universe of discourse and the intellectual community itself through persuasion, not by an imposed hegemony or a universalized method.

Criticism #6:   Idealism wrongly points to ideas as self-contained essences rather than to a world that is increasingly understood as structural. Properly framed, this may be the most challenging criticism that idealism faces. In 20th century thought, one province of knowledge after another, from physics to literary analysis, has fallen to a more structural analysis, where fields and webs of meaning rather than autonomous objects or ideas are seen to make up the fabric of knowledge (Hayles, 1984). Not only that, but we are now absorbing the lessons of an evolutionary perspective on the world, which wipes away fixed and eternal boundaries (Toulmin, 1972). If idealism points to a world of Platonic forms, then it will be increasingly difficult to defend against these two great shifts in human consciousness. As in criticism #3, however, I suspect that a successful response depends on distancing idealism from essentialism. In fact, the major proponents of idealistic metaphysics in this century have aligned with the logic of relativity (Hartshorne, 1970), so the intellectual groundwork has already been laid for their separation. As defined in this essay, idealism is not a philosophy that depends on fixed ideas, but rather a position on the intelligible structure of the world, and the centrality of mind to that world. In this relational idealism, there is nothing isolated or immutable about minds. Rather, they experience one another within a social structure. Indeed, sociality is conceived as shared experience, not just shared "subjectivity".

The tradition of Marxist critique has shown the profound embeddedness of intellectual activity within socioeconomic frameworks. It is no longer possible to revert to an intellectual practice completely innocent of this understanding. Ideas occur within historical contexts, within positioned, interested, and motivated parties. Rhetorical theory and criticism, traditionally sensitive to situations, must continue learning to provide better accounts of this deeper embeddness in historical relationships and relationships of power (McGee & Lyne, 1987). Idealism earns its reputation as naive if it treats ideas as occurring in a pure intellectual space. Again, however, lessons are to be drawn from the extremes. If there is a danger in treating ideas as a separate and disembodied world, not contingent on human experience, the danger at the other end is to make them only "epiphenomena" hovering like a wisp of smoke above the "real" world. The latter danger entails a loss of vision, because it locates reality only in what is. Ideas are the eyes of experience, scanning the horizon for unmet possibilities. The mental life is what prevents us from being prisoners of mere circumstance; through it we simultaneously inhabit the world of the actual and the world of the possible.

If certain versions of idealism inhabit only the possible, thereby becoming fantasy-like and unaccountable to historical existence, then the corresponding extremity for materialism is to inhabit only the actual. The genius of idealism, and its indebtedness to Aristotle among others, is in refusing to equate reality with the merely actual. Reality, for the idealist, is *the actual plus the possible.* That is why is it so perfectly suited to the rhetorical enterprise, positioned as it is between actual and possible, working to move from one to the other, or to keep the gate between them. A rhetoric that could work only within the category of what "is" would be disabled.

An idealistically based rhetorical theory brings strong caveats to those forms of criticism that purport to debunk the "centering" of consciousness. If subjects are indeed fragmented and disunited in the way deconstruction and other recent trends in literary criticism contend, then this would pose the challenge of finding acceptable ways of reunifiying subjectivities and restoring to individuals the capacity to think and act with integrity; for the character of a person, to the idealist, is not simply a substance to be posited or debunked, but a kind of achievement in the face of experience, a working out of the personal intuitions within diverse materials and circumstances (making the abstract concrete, as Hegel would say). Deconstruction would be a healthy exercise, provided it is followed by the work of *reconstruction,* or at least the attempt. Showing how the psyche has been constituted from various, often competing, forces is of value only if it leads to reintegration or a higher order of understanding. And sometimes that reintegration will require painful and disruptive change—integrating the complexities of experience should not be confused with resort to soothing rationalizations. In short, critical insight, as with any new knowledge, will be valued in proportion to how well it can be integrated into experience. Thus, fractured subjectivity would be approached in much the same way as fractured scientific knowledge, that is, with a mandate to find a higher order of integration.

Now it seems clear that such integration cannot occur in the minds of individuals alone. A well integrated human being is a socially integrated being, whose knowledge and experience is little more than a fine tuning or variation upon broader social understandings. One does not start from scratch in acquiring knowledge: most of what anyone knows is a social legacy. Likewise for those modes of being and appreciating that we call culture. So the idealist cannot be a hermit, who retreats to an isolated self. Rather, she seeks shared mentality in the social, in a community of coherent experience. Separation from "the social" is in fact no more possible than separation from oneself, however much one might want to from time to time. The self has to find itself in relation to the social, locate some pattern in the broader weave. Its quest is coherence, not homogeneity; the aesthetic ideal of "harmony in contrariety." Its telos is a community of minds, and from this it takes aesthetic as well as ethical guidance. It is not just "ideas," and the articulate level of experience that are shared, however; less articulable symbolic experiences, shared social content such as art and architecture, also bind us together in shared cognition and affect (Cassirer, 1944).

Criticism #7:   Idealism leads to the dangers of ideology. The awareness of ideology is another legacy of the Marxist critique by no means limited to Marxists. The dangers of ideology became apparent to the generations who saw the insanity of World Wars I and II, and so some, such as the Vienna positivists and some American sociologists, set out to start anew by trying to getting beyond ideology. Generally speaking, ideology is something that one notices in one's opponents rather than in oneself, although some forms of ideological criticism encourage awareness of the critic's own ideology (McKerrow, 1989). The danger we want to avoid, even when operating self-consciously from an ideological position, is to be *trapped* in an ideology, so that reality becomes systematically distorted in an unhealthy direction. Ideological discourse can be used as a club to beat people into conformity against their own better judgment, and this is something that can occur from virtually any philosophical position. As Hikins notes in chapter 2, realism is sometimes accused of providing just such an ideological club. He rightly turns the criticism around to show that ideology can take wing in departures from realism. (But realism, let us not forget, is also an "ism.")

If there is nothing "outside of discourse" to anchor understanding, the general criticism goes, then surely the potential for abuse of language and flights of madness is great. The realist's intuition seems right about that.

Discourse must be accountable to something beyond itself. But what is the nature of that accountability? A simple correspondence check? For our sake, it is fortunate that Jefferson did not first undertake to verify that "all men are created equal" before announcing this guiding ideal. The problem for the realist rhetorician, as for everyone else, is that discourse can never be held in check by externalities alone; it can never be just a mirror of nature. Modeling rhetoric after idealized science seems at the outset a cruel amputation of the varied social uses of language, even if it could work. As the existentialists have labored to show us, we are only part-time scientists, as that kind of knowing occupies only a fraction of human existence. Ways of talking are inherently bent toward values, attitudes, and purposes; moreover, ways of talking are also ways of being. This is why every program to create a "neutral" information-only language has inevitably failed in anything beyond narrow technical tasks.

Discursive accountability is not a mere technical task, and its ways are many. Discourses are, for one thing, accountable to the other discourses in which they are embedded, or by which they are surrounded. We sometimes fall easily into the misleading picture of an "inside" and "outside" of discourse, as though Discourse were just one place to be. But as social beings, we move in and out of discourses all the time: we leave one frame and enter another, check one standpoint against another, declare one claim false from the perspective of another, escape a misleading form of talk by going to another, pit two arguments against one another, renounce prevailing wisdom for something better, put our words to new empirical tests, array evidence, construct new conditions of falsification, talk ourselves out of a present condition and into a new one. We make rhetoric accountable in many ways, most of which involve more rhetoric.

There are a thousand tried and true ways of testing out verbal claims put before us, and few if any of them require a clean exit from language. (Dr. Johnson's famous kick was, after all, another signifying gesture.) Discourse is not a single hot air balloon, waiting to be pricked by some honest realist. The image of a pure touchstone by which our words will be authenticated is the stubbornly dysfunctional part of realism's legacy. It is equally dysfunctional when its opponents, in renouncing truth and reality, let the external touchstone imagery stand in for the broader issue of accountability in discourse. One should always be on guard against being badly handled by rhetoric. But there is no protective shield that will save us from bad judgment or bad ideology, except the ones we ourselves construct in words and practice. Idealism should be no more prone to ideological zealotry than any other "ism."

Criticism #8: *Idealism is at odds with the common sense world in which rhetorical practice occurs.* Rhetoricians respond of necessity to the practical world often neglected by philosophy, and when we wax philosophical, we understandably want the best of both worlds. Thus Hikins, in chap. 2, makes an appeal to "pedestrian realism" in order to link realist philosophy to rhetorical practice. In everyday life, it seems only reasonable to acknowledge, we take the world of our experience to be real, and this serves perfectly well for most of our purposes. But this begs the question as to how "reality" is to be analyzed philosophically. Thales, as Hikins points out, was a realist who happened to believe that everything was made of water. This example, its "realism" not withstanding, does not seem to score a point for common sense (nor for that matter does it make a very tempting philosophical position). The fact is that much of what is now called realism in philosophical discourse depends precisely on the claim that the world of familiar objects is *not* the real world! As the realist philosopher Hilary Putnam put it: "Realism with a capital 'R' is, sad to say, the foe, not the defender, of realism with a small 'r'. " (Putnam, 1987, p. 17). Contemporary Realism tends to look to high-powered scientific theories, and science yet-to-be, for its sense of what is real, and *away from* the common sense world of pedestrian realism. Common perception gives way to high rationalism. But this discrepancy is concealed by the use of the *term* "realism," in which its users find a great deal of rhetorical capital. (Putnam characterized it as a seducer of the innocent.) Rhetorically speaking, being against that which is "real" is on a par with being against that which is "good." The use of such terms can easily paper over manifest differences of position. The ambiguity of the term "realism" calls into question just what is to be presumed if, as Hikins suggests, presumption is to be given to realism.

Let me suggest another route to salvation for those who want to preserve common sense realism against the ravages of skepticism on one side and of abstract rationalism on the other. Contemporary realism has become so far abstracted from the world of everyday perception that some form of idealism may be required to bring it back down to earth. Idealism, after all, credits human experience as being real, without necessarily giving it final authority. The scale of human thought and perception are its natural home, its base of operations for wider ventures. To the common sense realist concerned with preserving the familiar world, I extend an invitation to embrace philosophical idealism, thus helping to save that world against erosion by the wildly abstractive and rationalistic tendencies incident among Realists. Furthermore, if the pedestrian realist wishes to hold skepticism at bay, then the idealist will again welcome him as an ally, as skepticism is a by-product of *the unrealistically high standards Realists set for knowledge.* It is they, among others, who have told us that the true realities are the ones on which only science and epistemology have a purchase, and even these are commonly described as inadequate to the task. Idealism does not so lightly dismiss the content of our own thoughts and experiences.

SUMMARY

Idealism, I have tried to show, is less a unified doctrine than an intellectual tendency or attitude that is articulated in a variety of ways in Western philosophy. The elements of this tradition are not all consistent with one another, and they are not incompatible with all the elements of other philosophies. The idealistic intuition comes to focus most readily in response to doctrines that seem to diminish the capacities of mind and spirit or to discount the validity of the felt experience. This intuition reasserts the role of hope and vision and makes human beings pivot points rather than pawns in the events of history. As a metaphysical position and as a philosophy of life it has much to commend it. As a dialectical counter to materialism, it keeps open a productive debate. But one does not have to be committed to philosophical idealism in order to find in it a point of entry for rhetorical theory, criticism, or practice.

The title of this essay speaks of idealism as a "rhetorical stance." This is to emphasize that rhetorical practice requires us to position ourselves, to take a stance, or to find a voice, in respect to a great many matters that come before us. Rhetoric is used in too many ways and for too many purposes to be governed entirely by a philosophy. "Idealists," certainly, can find themselves on opposites sides of many debates without forfeiting their idealistic outlook. Moreover, no general philosophy could possibly guarantee consistent application through concrete circumstances. In that sense, I believe, rhetorical practice is inherently resistant to the "totalizing" schemes that Aune warns of in Chap. 8. Yet an idealistic stance can provide a stable set of strategies for approaching certain recurrent pressures on discourse, and it can offer topics and lines of argument that hold open a "space" for ideals in a world of practical contingencies. As a theoretical stance, it needs to strengthen those strategies as it faces the challenge of sophisticated behavioral and materialistic theories from the social sciences and humanities. As a stance in rhetorical criticism, it will support interpretations that show the continuity of thought, experience, and tradition, and that find the sameness amidst the manifest differences. It will celebrate that discourse which succeeds in transcending difference and constructing what Kenneth Burke called "consubstantiality." As a practice, it cannot reject a sensible pragmatism, provided it is a pragmatism of the long view. *Idealistic rhetoric is one which meets practical contingencies not just to resolve them, but as a ladder to get beyond them.*

I suspect that an idealistic bias may come naturally for those who labor in the world of words, because creating and manipulating symbols seems to be the way minds are accessed. If the past is recuperable only in memory, and the future is with us only in anticipation, and both processes are symbolic, then we have a double dependency on symbolization. That complex state of dependency involves incipient valuing and action, as the pragmatists insist. And so, the dependency is also an enablement. For the idealist, a considered placement in the world beyond the moment is also required. In navigating through experience, being "realistic" is not enough: life requires a broader sense of direction. This is found only as the material world is transformed into a *significant* world, charged with a dual sense of what is given and what is yet to be realized. When we must look to the past or to the future searching for direction, a place in a trajectory, this is when idealism most commends itself as a rhetorical stance.

REFERENCES

Berkeley, G. (1950). *The works of George Berkeley, Bishop of Cloyne* (Vols. 1–9) (A.A. Luce & T.E. Jessop, Eds.). New York: Thomas Nelson and Sons.

Boler, J. (1963). *Charles Peirce and scholastic realism.* Seattle: University of Washington Press.

Bryant, D.C. (1953). Rhetoric: its functions and its scope. *Quarterly Journal of Speech, 39,* 401–424.

Burke, K. (1969). *A grammar of motives.* Berkeley: University of California. (Original work published 1969)

Burke, K. (1968). *Language as symbolic action.* Berkeley: University of California Press.

Cassirer, E. (1944). *An essay on man.* New Haven: Yale University Press.

Cavell, S. (1979). *The claim of reason.* New York: Oxford University Press.

Chardin, T. de (1959). *The phenomenon of man.* New York: Harper & Row.

Cobb, J.B., & Griffin, D.R. (Eds.). (1977). *Mind in nature.* Washington: University Press of America.

Copleston, F. (1964). *A history of philosophy* (Vol VII. Part I). New York: Image Books.

Crutchfield, J.P., Farmer, D., Packard, N.H., & Shaw, R.S. (1986, December). Chaos. *Scientific American,* pp. 46–57.

Danto, A. (1967). *Neitzsche as philosopher.* New York: Macmillan.

Eco, U. (1976). *A theory of semiotics.* Bloomington: Indiana University Press.

Foucault, M. (1970). *The order of things.* New York: Random House.

Foucault, M. (1975). *The archeology of knowledge.* New York: Harper & Row.

Fuller, S. (1988). *Social epistemology.* Bloomington & Indianapolis: University of Indiana Press.

Gadamer, H.-G. (1975). *Truth and method.* New York: Seabury Press.

Geuss, R. (1981). *The idea of a critical theory.* New York: Cambridge University Press.

Grassi, E. (1980). *Rhetoric as philosophy: the humanist tradition.* University Park, PA: Pennsylvania State University Press.

Habermas, J. (1979). *Communication and the evolution of society.* (T. McCarthy, Trans.). Boston: Beacon Press.

Hall, S. (1985). Signification, representation, ideology: Althusser and the post-structuralist debates. *Critical Studies in Mass Communication, 2,* 91–114.

Harré, R. (1979). *Social being.* Totowa, NJ: Littlefield, Adams.

Hartshorne, C. (1970). *Creative synthesis and philosophic method.* LaSalle, IL: Open Court.

Hartshorne, C. (1983). *Insights and oversights of great thinkers.* Albany, NY: State University of New York Press.

Hartshorne, C. (1984). *Creativity in American philosophy.* New York: Paragon House.

Hayles, N.K. (1984). *The cosmic web.* Ithaca, NY: Cornell University Press.

Jay, M. (1973). *The dialectical imagination.* Boston: Little, Brown.

Kant, I. (1965). *Immanuel Kant's Critique of Pure Reason* (N.K. Smith, Trans.). New York: St. Martin's Press.

Kurzweil, E. (1980). *The age of structuralism.* New York: Columbia University Press.

Kuhn, T. (1970). *The structure of scientific revolutions* (2nd Ed.) Chicago: University of Chicago Press.

Langer, S.K. (1953). *Feeling and form.* New York: Charles Scribner's Sons.

Leibniz, G.W. (1934). *Leibniz's Philosophical Writings* (M. Morris, Trans.). London: J.M. Dent & sons, Ltd.

Leibniz, C.W. (1985). *G.W. Leibniz: The Monadology and other Philosophical writings* (R.C. Sleigh, Ed.). New York: Garland.

Levinson, S. (1988). *Constitutional faith.* Princeton, NJ: Princeton University Press.

Lyne, J. (1980). Rhetoric and semiotic in C.S. Peirce. *Quarterly Journal of Speech, 66,* 155–168.

Lyne, J. (1982). C.S. Peirce's philosophy of rhetoric. In B. Vickers (Ed.), *Rhetoric re-valued* (pp. 267–276). Binghamton, NY: Center for Medieval and Early Renaissance Studies.

Lyne, J. (1985). Rhetorics of inquiry. *The Quarterly Journal of Speech, 71,* 65–73.

MacIntyre, A. (1988). *Whose justice? Which rationality?* Notre Dame, IN: Notre Dame University Press.

McCloskey, D.N. (1985). *The rhetoric of economics.* Madison, WI: University of Wisconsin Press.

McGee, M.C. (1982). A materialist's conception of rhetoric. In R.E. McKerrow (Ed.), *Explorations in rhetoric: Studies in honor of Douglas Ehninger* (pp. 23–48). Glenview, IL: Scott, Foresman.

McGee, M.C., & Lyne, J. (1987). What are nice folks like you doing in a place like this? some entailments of treating knowledge claims rhetorically. In J. Nelson, A. Megill, & D. McCloskey (Eds.), *The rhetoric of the human sciences* (pp. 381–406). Madison, WI: University of Wisconsin Press.

McKerrow, R.E. (1989). Critical rhetoric: Theory and praxis. *Communication Monographs, 56,* 91–111.

Megill, A. (1985). *Prophets of extremity.* Berkeley, CA: University of California Press.

Nelson, J., Megill, A., & McCloskey, D. (Eds.). (1987). *The rhetoric of the human sciences.* Madison, WI: University of Wisconsin Press.

Peirce, C.S. (1931-58). *Collected papers* (Vols. 1-6. C. Hartshorne & P. Weiss, Eds.); Vols. 7-8. A. Burks, Ed.). Cambridge, MA: Harvard University Press.

Peirce, C.S. (1958). *Peirce: Selected Writings (values in a universe of chance)* (P. Wiener, Ed.). New York: Dover.

Pepper, S. (1942). *World hypotheses.* Berkeley, CA: University of California Press.

Putnam, H. (1987). *The many faces of realism.* LaSalle, IL: Open Court.

Quine, W.V., & Ullian, J.S. (1978). *The web of belief* (2nd ed.). New York: Random House.

Richards, I.A. (1965). *The philosophy of rhetoric.* New York: Oxford University Press.

Rorty, R. (1979) *Philosophy and the mirror of nature.* Princeton, NJ: Princeton University Press.

Royce, J. (1969). *The basic writings of Josiah Royce* (Vols. 1–2) (J.J. McDermott, Ed.) Chicago: University of Chicago Press. Plato (1963), *LAWS* (A.E. Taylor, Trans.; E. Hamilton & H. Cairns, Eds.). Princeton NJ: Princeton University Press.

Schwartz, B. (1986). *The battle for human nature.* New York: W.W. Norton.

Skinner, B.F. (1970). *Beyond freedom and dignity.* New York: Alfred Knopf.

Todorov, T. (1989, July 3). Crimes against humanities. *New Republic,* pp. 26–30.

Toulmin, S. (1972). *Human understanding.* Princeton, NJ: Princeton University Press.

Turbayne, C. (1970). *The myth of metaphor* (1st rev. ed.). Columbia, SC: University of South Carolina Press.

Weaver, R. (1948). *Ideas have consequences.* Chicago: University of Chicago Press.

Weaver, R. (1953). *The ethics of rhetoric.* Chicago: Henry Regnery.

Wellman, C. (1971). *Challenge and response: justification in ethics.* Carbondale, IL.: Southern Illinois University Press.

White, J.B. (1984). *When words lose their meaning.* Chicago: University of Chicago Press.

Whitehead, A.N. (1978). *Process and reality* (Corrected ed.). (D.R. Griffin & D.W. Sherburne, Eds.). New York: The Free Press.

Wilson, E.O. (1978). *On human nature.* New York: Bantam Books.

Wittgenstein, L. (1958a). *The blue and brown books.* New York: Harper & Row.

Wittgenstein, L. (1958b). *Philosophical investigations* (3rd ed.). New York: Macmillan.

Chapter 6

Materialism: Reductionist Dogma or Critical Rhetoric?

Michael McGuire

If a theory of rhetoric is to be developed in our century in such a way as to achieve consistency with or receive support from scientific knowledge, methodology, and philosophy, it may need to begin with materialism. Just as science seeks explanations for phenomena in terms of physical causation, social sciences began in this century to seek causal statements about human behavior rooted in physical facts—in material. To beg off as a humanist and ignore this body of knowledge and way of thinking is to strike an ostrich's pose and to do a disservice both to rhetoric and to humans. The very question raised by materialists is whether or not we can understand, thus perhaps improve upon and control, both natural and social phenomena. Their answer is that we can, if we look for material causes.

Rhetorical theorists need to consider the material of rhetoric in several ways. If language is the basic material of which rhetoric is made, what are the properties of that material? Is language, like hair style, merely an accidental feature of human life, or is it, like the opposable thumb, biologically determined for our species? Quite differently may we ask whether rhetorical activity constitutes a response to the material of the human environment, and whether the environment is changed materially by rhetoric. These are not all new questions for rhetoric; some are very familiar. The answers to be hinted here are new.

Materialist philosophies are neither well-understood nor "natural" to Anglo-Americans; they require rethinking and even rejecting many assumptions that seem to be only common sense and sound metaphysics. Because materialist philosophies are diverse, with roots reaching at least as far back as the 7th century B.C. (Reese, 1980) with a strong tradition in Western thought from the 6th century Ionian and 5th century Eleatic philosophers, followers in turn of Thales and Parmenides (Campbell, 1967), readers need to observe some disclaimers at the outset. In the first part of the discussion that follows I explain and illustrate the materialist perspectives that have currency in our century—not long-discarded notions, such as that the entire world is made up of water or air. Because of the large number and encyclopedic range of types or schools of materialism, I bifurcated the later discussion into broad sections on *physical materialism* and *social materialism* (both labels my own invention), which follow my definition of materialism generally. Finally, I tried throughout to avoid both a literature review approach and the tediousness of overreferencing by providing for the first section of the essay generally available and competent review articles in lieu of advocacy by proponents of the views I am exploring.

MATERIALISM DEFINED

"Materialism" refers to any and all theories that explain reality and real events as composed of underlying matter and explicable by appeals to causation and other conditions or properties of matter (Brugger, 1972). Lacey (1976, p. 133) defined materialism as "the view that everything . . . is made of matter: only matter exists, and mind, spirit, etc. are either illusory or can somehow be reduced to matter." Materialists are traditionally the philosophical enemies of and contradiction to idealism and related dualist philosophies, like those of Descartes (though even he was a pure materialist in his explanations of nonhuman animal behavior; Smart, 1986). Materialists do not necessarily agree to an exact definition of "matter," but subscribe to an open-ended list of physical properties such as temporal and spatial location, mass, shape, motion, and so on. In reply to phenomenology, some materialists allow that sensations and thoughts exist in addition to material, but that they are wholly dependent on it, and have no real causative force of their own. This matter that forms the basis of reality is knowable and measurable, even though it is not immediately perceptible in most cases.

The idea that we do not always "see" the matter at work structuring reality leads to the need to separate the apparent from the real, but not in the manner that idealists like Plato did (nor for that matter in the manner of Kant or Hegel; see Lyne chapter 5). All materialists eventually make an argument of the form: *all apparently complex and spiritual phenomena are reducible to material events; therefore, complex superstructures can be understood in terms of underlying, material substructures.* (The full range and appeal of this "Ockham's razor" argument will become clear later in this chapter.) This principle does not clarify *how far* beneath the surface we must dig to arrive at material truth, and we will consider the point in detail later. Nonetheless, part of the appeal of materialism's advice to dig at all is to be found in the widespread knowledge that technical tools—despite the ringing critiques against them by other philosophies represented in this volume—have taught us infinitely more about our world and ourselves than we could have gleaned without their intervention: as a short list I offer microscopy, telescopy, X-ray, and monoclonal antibody research as examples few would dispute of technical tools augmenting our native abilities to learn about material reality, and improving our knowledge of reality—reality *otherwise* unknowable.

Materialism is defined best, then, as the school of philosophy that holds as its first principle that all reality is composed of material, even if the nature of combinations of material and of human perception of material sometimes hide that fact from us. *There are no nonmaterial phenomena; there are only nonmaterial interpretations of phenomena.* The classic concept, or paradigm case, usually called "Mechanical Materialism," (Smart, 1986) is of a world made of matter and its related concepts—space, time, void, energy—all of which obey certain universal, physical laws. The consequences of accepting this principle are not uniform, however, and may be pursued usefully in the two very different fields of physical and social materialism.

Physical Materialism

I have chosen for the sake of economy to group together things that are, nonetheless, very dissimilar. It would be both refreshing and important to have a discussion at last of the physics/physiology/psychology of communication. What follows is an overview of materialist conceptions in the sciences. What makes up this section may be taken as polemic; if so, those who would make of science mere rhetoric are urged to reconsider their interpretations.

For a brief time in this century, it appeared that a rigid distinction might be maintained between the physical and the life sciences—between inorganic chemistry and physics on one hand, and biochemistry, genetics and physiology on another. Such distinctions may not be tenable in light of current research and theory. What has happened constitutes an immense theoretical revolution seeking grand unified sciences, all of which share the materialist foundation both methodologically and philosophically (Smart, 1986). In fact, as Campbell (1967, p. 179) observed, "The enduring appeal of materialism arises from its alliance with those sciences which have contributed most to our understanding of the world we live in." The borders between physical and life sciences vanish as more is learned about living systems (organisms).

How is life to be explained? Let us consider one common problem of basic, current research. Most of us understand that a human's life originates as a single cell (fertilized ovum) which becomes a human being in a matter of weeks. Why? The cell does not replicate, or we would be large blobs of a single cell's offspring. What is it that tells specific cells in the evolving embryo to become neural cells, or bone cells, or heart muscle cells? It is a material (rather, several materials) commonly called protein, apparently different in each case, whose presence or absence correlates with different cell specializations (i.e., the proteins in neural cell development differ from those in muscle or bone development). No appeal to spirit, whether mind, soul, or God is necessary to account for cell specialization as long as the proteins governing various specializations can be isolated. In sum, solid material can explain embryonic development, and such parsimonious explanation is self-recommending to any theorist either in science or philosophy. Of course, years will pass before the specific molecular weights of different proteins involved in this process all are disclosed, and the technology and procedures are complex. But those solvable problems of research are not objections to the theory.

The remaining question to challenge this view of development can be framed openly: "What causes a specific protein to appear and do its work (or not to appear)?" Nonmaterialists presumably "account for" the presence or absence by appeals to spirit, mind, soul, or God. Materialists instead seek to isolate the material, presumably in gene sequences, to explain this phenomenon by recourse to cause instead of miracle or mystery. Cell biology is the cutting edge of the life sciences, and the organization of materials within cells proves to be exceedingly complicated, but powerful for both explanation and prediction.

There is also work being done in what we might call "brain physics." The brain is being studied from many material points of view: electro-chemical activity, hemispheric dominance and traits, chemical alleviation of specific and general neural or psychological disorders, physical reconfiguration of brain-damaged persons' neural activity, and more. Materialists hold that there is no such "thing" as a mind—that a mind is a label for the activity of a brain. Accordingly, the depressed "mind" is sometimes cured by providing the chemical dopamine in adequate quantities. The radical materialist position would be this: All thought is caused and controlled, not consciously by will, but by the actions of chemical materials on one another. What triggers the actions, the hidden mechanism of control or direction, is not entirely clear, but material explanations account for all extreme cases with clarity and will eventually account for normal cases as well. That is, chemical explanations of chemically induced hallucinatory states and psychoses already have to be accepted as true. Only a naive idealist could ever claim to see God in a dose of LSD; a materialist sees a hallucinogenic chemical with predictable effects on human brain chemistry. And for years, everyone has known that the chemicals used for general anesthesia do in fact knock everyone out; that severing the frontal lobe precludes certain behaviors; sleeping pills work; there are chemicals to prevent sleep; and so forth. The brain is a physical mass regulated by physical laws. The mind is merely added as an afterthought.

Now, this should not be taken as evidence that all materialists argue *only* chemical or physiological causation in human action. Although the foregoing may seem to raise issues distinct from those addressed throughout this volume, there is a strong connection between materialism and the analytic tradition of philosophy as seen through the dualists G. E. Moore and Bertrand Russell, through Gilbert Ryle, and through the positivists Carnap, Ayer, Stevenson, and Hempel (Weitz, 1966). Especially clear is the connection between analytic behaviorism (i.e., Gilbert Ryle) and materialism. I argue that a need exists to explore the materialism inherent in any "stimulus–response" model of human behavior. Although one might think behaviorism is a social materialism, because it is a psychological enterprise, it is not social, and must be treated as a physical materialism.

Behaviorists have causal explanations for behavior that appeal to environmental conditions as their material bases. (Some also acknowledge the intervention of physiological factors.) It seems, on their account, that for every psychotic who wears a straitjacket because his genes make him too dangerous for us to tolerate in our society, there is one who wears it because her environment, filled perhaps with double-binds or unbearable events, made her crazy. Most of the "material" behaviorists rely on to explain human behavior is observable, perceptible material. For example, Pavlov's dog hears the bell; Skinner's pigeon sees a light; I catch the smell of familiar cologne. The dog drools, the pigeon pecks, I smile broadly. The behaviorist, however, nowhere surrenders causation by these material realities to some phantom-like free will, intention, soul, or even cognitive processes.

That behaviorists have tried to share the research methodological assumptions of materialists is generally known. That fact, however, is less important than the shared philosophical assumption that *actions can be explained by material causes which precede them.* Moreover, there is no inconsistency inherent in biological and behavioral materialism (although individuals can make one). That is, there is no reason not to imagine that physiological material conditions different organisms to respond to stimuli differently, or the same organism to respond differently at separate times. And it is equally clear that environmental conditions bring forth physiological responses, as when sets of circumstances usually called "terrifying" do produce adrenal activity at abnormal levels. In short, these two different materialist views can be consonant, and may even seem jointly necessary to full explanation of many of the phenomena of human behavior.

In shifting our attention away from materialism's most universal claims to its claims in connection with human behavior, we have come to one final point that needs consideration. One attack on materialism as a reductionist theory—and I find it interesting that the *attack* is reductionist—is that it deals inadequately with the issue of "higher organization". The attack runs this way: materialists say that simple matter explains everything, but it can't explain why specific quantities of plastic, glass, copper, and more function as a TV set when and only when assembled in one unique pattern. In sum, it is not matter but organization of matter that explains the TV. The analogous argument for humans is similar: the chemicals of which we are made do not "act" as we do unless arranged as we are. Accordingly, the argument concludes, materialism is inadequate because it is reductionist and misses the issue of organization of matter. There are two forms of this objection.

If there were a social behaviorism—and there is—its proponents would argue that behavior is learned from and conditioned by the behavior of other complex organizations of matter (people). Physical materialism is not the first recourse even to explain such obviously material differences as sex-related behavior. Sex roles, it is argued, are learned behavior. If so, these behaviors would be products of cognition and will, not material cause. Those making such an argument could be instructed usefully by the research of Margaret Mead, Anke Erhardt, Patricia Goldman, Sarah Blaffer Hrdy, Annelise Korner, Eleanor Emmons Maccoby, and a number of other women scientists who have devoted their careers to studying brain, hormones, and behavior, both human and animal. All have concluded, not, no doubt, without some anguish, that even if all the social training in the world became uniform, and if sexism vanished, there would be something different between men and women, and that that difference is unavoidable because it is biologically caused (Konner, 1983). One need not deny the role of learning to retain a materialist posture in explaining behavior: Why can't both occur? Why can't learning itself also be, ultimately, a materially explicable process? There is no reason.

The second attack on materialism is made by phenomenologists and the spiritualists. Every person is unique; reality exists in the mind (not brain); things-in-themselves cannot be known. Materialists remind us that the mind depends on the brain—that is, any mind a person has is susceptible to alteration by chemical (drugs) or mechanical (trauma damage or surgery), admittedly material agents. The position against the possibility of knowledge of things is especially unpersuasive when uttered as epistemological dogma. The very discussion of things we can't know does seem to concede their existence—their reality. The incompleteness of knowledge and explanation shows the difficulty, not the impossibility, of achieving them to everyone's satisfaction. To scientists, to all physical materialists, the pursuit of a paradigm is now a matter of elaboration, with new discoveries already expected and predicted, and better understanding of the nature of matter and the workings of physical laws.

Physical materialism is often seen as reductionist dogma. It is as if people accepted Kurt Vonnegut's description in *Breakfast of Champions* of Dwayne Hoover's bad chemicals as a summary and sophisticated statement of a physical materialist viewpoint on human behavior. Physical materialism, however, when worked out fully, may involve both physiological–chemical and environmental–observational explanations in an intricate web of causation and explanation of behavior—including rhetorical or communicative behavior.

Social Materialism

Theories fitting under this label are somewhat better known to most Americans than those discussed above. Still, this approach is outside the general Anglo-American philosophical tradition of our century to this date, even if the situation is changing rapidly in the arts and humanities, and a bit more slowly in the social sciences.

The origins of social materialism appear in the works of Karl Marx, although contemporary social materialism would not entirely appeal to him. Because of the potential confusion that results whenever his name is brought up, I want to make a distinction here to keep us on track. Between Marx the advocate of political Marxism, and the writer of provocative Marxian social-historical theory, may be found more gulfs than one. I am not interested here in political marxism; I think we cannot ignore marxian social theory, which is based on the concept of dialectical materialism.

Marx can be rejected for some of his history, roundly critiqued for much more, yet admired even by detractors for contributing a better method to the writing of history (Hook, 1955). Marx believed that to understand history we would have to look not to ideas, but to material interests—or, economic causes. That is, Marx believed sincerely that history came about as it did because of discernible, predictable changes in the relations of production and consumption. He did, however, leave this role open for ideas: some ideas form *ideologies,* linked to specific economic or class interests, and once adopted and advocated, can serve as motivators for or masks of conflict. Marx was emphatic that these ideologies are forms of "false consciousness," that is, consciousness alienated from its real–material conditions, and conditioned instead by a shrouding group of false ideas. Ideology usually reflects what the ruling class wants its victims to believe; hence it is tied to material interests, not necessarily material facts (Hook, 1955). The ruling class puts on the emperor's new suit of ideology and proudly shows it around town, offering it as a sort of marvel. Until someone says that the emperor is naked, the parade continues apace. Usually it continues anyway; those who have been saying the emperor looked splendid have too much dissonance.

Marx's interest in ideologies led to a methodology for social materialism: treat ideas as surface phenomena, and look beneath them for material causes. Even though some materialists, like Smart (1986), reject the connection of dialectical materialism to materialism on the grounds that the links are vague, the perspective of looking beneath the surface forms a methodological analogy that has been noticed widely. The connection to materialism strikes me as sound. That is, there have been others looking beneath the surface, not for material causes, but for psychological ones — Freud, Nietzsche, and Jung (Kaufmann, 1968). As insightful as I find Nietzsche's depth psychology, treating things as symptoms of deep, underlying psychological causes, it is immaterial; so, too, are Freud's interpretations of dreams and psychopathology. However, there are social materialists' positions that merit our attention.

Structuralism

Claude Levi-Strauss is the leading figure in structural anthropology, and in the broader movement called "structuralism." Following both a Marxian tendency to look beneath the surface and the important teachings of the Swiss linguist Saussure regarding the structure of linguistic meaning, Levi-Strauss (1963) proposed and conducted a scientific cultural anthropology that made him world famous, earning him both disciples and detractors. Structuralism is committed to the principle that beneath every social structure is a deeper structure that caused it to be exactly as it is. All human, social phenomena are thus said to be "language-like," and analyzable in terms of law-governed, structural relations between their sub- and superstructures. Although not all structuralists connect their underlying universals to genetic causes, stopping short at cognitive or psychological structures which are homologous to one another, such a connection can be argued. And such an argument for connection has been made for language.

Structuralists are interested in both real material (linguistic or otherwise) and any abstractions or structures related to it. In linguistics, for example, the abstract structure of a language (words and syntax) is inferred from analysis of the material (utterances) at hand. Such a method isolates both the differences between languages and the universals of language. The same thing, Levi-Strauss (1963) showed, can be done for other social phenomena, from myths to kinship systems to precious metals as standards of value. Structuralism, however, differs from physical materialism in that its interest is not primarily on the raw material of social relations, but on the abstract models built from that material — the social structure.

It is a testament to American academics that we already have post-structuralism, although little was done in this country fully to work out structuralism itself in several fields, rhetoric included. Perhaps the scientistic demands from a method committed to finding the truth and scientific laws was too much for some to tolerate; perhaps, too, structuralism seemed to demean humans' abilities by implying that things like language are genetically caused species traits, not mysteries or achievements. And some of Levi-Strauss' own findings in connection with kinship structures were insufficiently sensitive to women's feelings and had to be rewritten. Never mind their accuracy in describing the distribution of females among males in some societies; an ideological impulse stronger than science is at work here.

Post-structuralism (& Deconstruction)

Richard Harland (1987, p. 3) summed up the shift away from structuralism to post-structuralism: "Post-structuralists bend the philosophical implications of the Superstructuralist way of thinking about superstructures back round against the traditional stance of Objectivity and the traditional goal of Truth. And, with the destruction of Objectivity and Truth, scientific knowledge becomes less valuable than literary or political activity; and detailed observational analyses and extended explicatory grids are discarded in favor of instantaneous lightning-flashes of paradoxical illumination." If the Anglo-American tradition of literary criticism and linguistics viewed language as referential, and literature as a potential special case exception, then post-structuralism is its antithesis, viewing all language as nonreferential. This principle must be explained further.

If there is a single tenet common to all post-structuralism, it is the claim that texts are immanent (see Aune, chap. 8). On such a view, the real material of the human sciences is not the human, but is pieces of discourse without an uttering subject at all (Hacking, 1986). This approach to and redefinition of social science, associated with Michel Foucault's early work, also is found in the post-1968 European intellectual trends reflected in the work of Foucault's famous student Derrida, and in various of the writings of both H.-G. Gadamer and his rebellious student Juergen Habermas (Hoy, 1978). This movement I think is foredoomed to fail. Foucault himself had to turn away from the study of pure discourse, and in so doing he valuably grew to return attention to the material conditions surrounding the production and use of discourse — to interests, to power, to knowledge. Discourse then ceased to be the material object of the human sciences in the sense that it was a superstructure linked, not as in the past to an individual writer or speaker, but to some material interest of a class using the discourse to define and constitute the very subjects over which power ruled. The point, as

Foucault has shown, is not merely to consider purposive and deliberate applications of power, but to come to understand how a power implicit in formations of discourse shapes everyone's reality (Foucault, 1980).

With this turn in post-structuralism we return to the Marxian point that material interests underlying discursive formations must be disclosed. But we no longer can afford to take the view that a ruling class inflicts its will upon others with a clever, disingenuous ideology. Foucault has suggested that often we cannot locate the origin of power or its related knowledge; other times the finding is difficult; and rulers and servants alike are obedient to a system created prior to their arrival. This leads us to reconsider as a materialism of sorts, the sociology of knowledge.

Sociology of Knowledge

One of the most interesting developments of the past half century has been the project to adopt a material perspective on ideas. The work of Peter Berger and Thomas Luckmann (1966) is the classic in this area. Rather than offer a philosophical, epistemological consideration of the ideas and beliefs people have, Berger and Luckmann open the door to consider the material consequences of these ideas, and to analyze the social networks transmitting them to some—but never all—people in a society. The impact of their perspective on rhetoric will be discussed later, but needs mention here, too. Their important insight is to distinguish between the socially constructed aspects of reality and the naturally given aspects, and to help us see the largeness of the former category, frequently ignored in the past.

Not everyone is either clear or sanguine about the possibilities of separating the socially from the empirically real. Yet exactly such a distinction can be crucial to a discussion of materialism, and is necessary for a thorough discussion about the role rhetoric plays in constructing or constituting reality. The distinction is problematic because social reality is both part of, yet abstracted from and explanatory of, empirical reality (McGuire, 1982a). In fact what we need is a grasp of concrete abstractions. Concrete abstractions must be relations such as hot and cold, up and down, uncle and niece. Even if one seeks to argue the inherent subjectivity of these perceptions one is compelled to accept their facticity as well. In short, relations between material objects, although not themselves material in a hard sense, are essential and inherent parts of an empirical, material reality, even if they seem subjective, human constructions.

We need not be subjectivists nor idealists to grant legitimacy to claims like, "The coffee is hot"; "My martini is cold"; "Tahoe is my daughter." In fact, such claims might be treated as materially verifiable and fasifiable whether they are viewed as self-reports or reports of external events and states of affairs.

Summary

Materialist philosophies rely upon explanation of the world (both social and physical) as a regular, predictable—because law-governed—place. Materialism seeks explanations by looking beneath the obvious surface of phenomena. There is not uniform agreement upon what material should be looked at to explain what phenomena. Accordingly, we can find one materialist accounting for sex differences as learned behavior, and another accounting for them as biological consequences, for example, of hormones. A general caveat does have appeal: The simpler the explanation, the more basic and the better it is. Accordingly we must expect a future in which some apparently reductionist explanations gain currency and hold their value. Materialists exorcise us of many a formerly possessing spirit, soul, demon, or mind, and unlike the shaman, they replicate these exorcisms universally.

MATERIAL RHETORIC

We now begin to confront a question some will find disquieting: "What would a genuinely materialist theory of rhetoric look like?" These waters have been little muddied, despite a few recent essays raising the question (Charland, 1987; McGee, 1982; McGuire, 1982c; Railsback, 1983). Because it is not my intention here merely to review those essays, I will pursue the question posed in what I take to be a novel manner. First, however, we may consider generally how rhetorical theory would be altered by accepting the claims of materialism outlined above.

The first question a material rhetoric would have to address is, "What is the material of which the phenomenon rhetoric is made; what will a theory explain?" The most obvious answer is that rhetorical artifacts are made of language. Accordingly, whatever parts of language rhetoric claims to explain would have to be treated materially—which means, we will see, rhetoric must consider to what extent biological determinants of language are relevant to the practice of rhetoric, as well as consider the pieces of language themselves as material. A second consideration becomes whether any causal links will be claimed for rhetoric (language as used) on social behavior—also materially real. If so, the causal elements must be discovered and explained. It is clear, I hope, from the foregoing discussion of different types of materialism that more than one line of inquiry is possible here, even if we pursue the methods for which materialism is known. Accordingly, we will follow materialism's assumptions, conclusions and methods in what follows to explore some paths open to a materialist rhetoric.

Materialists build theory, not only by looking at necessary material, but also by incorporating knowledge from other materialists and reasoning analogically. Eric Lenneberg (1960) once showed the usefulness of analogical reasoning about social phenomena in a marvelous monograph about language. Processes that are too gradual to be experimented on, like biological evolution, still have known characteristics that may be compared to other slow processes, like linguistic evolution. Lenneberg compared the evidence about and the history and qualities of bipedal gait with those of writing to show that the criterial aspects of a hereditary trait (gait) are not the same as those for writing. He went on to show, however, that language does share three of the four criteria for inheritance with gait, and that the fourth criterion is indeterminate. Such argument serves more to open minds than settle questions.

To the extent that rhetoric continues to treat language as a central component of the act, questions about the biological basis of language may haunt it. But on a different tack, taking Lenneberg's heuristic lesson, what would happen if a quantum mechanical model were compared with rhetorical theory? Quantum mechanics (which sometimes oppose the central state or physical materialists) revolutionized physics. What if rhetorical studies took a hard look at quantity and reasoned analogically? Vague reports from the news media suggest to us that the candidates who spend the most money on campaigns win most often. The implication of such a fact is that quantity alone — not quality, not reason, not style — *determines* persuasion. It seems at least worth considering, and offers a path for future theory not elsewhere recommended: to reason by analogy to firm, scientific knowledge.

Symbol-Using Animals

It became commonplace some decades ago to refer to the naked ape as the symbol-using animal. Nietzsche, of course, had put the matter more bluntly, calling us the animal that must lie, that must knowingly, willingly lie. Such romantic descriptions might better be replaced by the science of Eric Lenneberg, who once observed that "clarity on the problem of the biological foundation of language is of utmost importance in formulating both questions and hypotheses regarding the function, mechanism, and history of language" (1960, p. 869). In 20th century parlance, we are not concerned either with some "human nature" or the individual's discovery that talk helps or a divine insistence on a tongue; the different aspects of language that are genetically governed (e.g. phonemics, acquisition stages) can be known, and those that are purely learned (semantic systems) can be known, and there may remain some of which we are unsure. Accordingly, *the first demand a materialist would make of rhetoric is to inquire into its scope to determine whether it claims as its realm* ALL *symbolization or only some*—for example, only learned aspects.

This question is a far cry from the classical era ponderings over natural talent, practice, and theory. If one gives the embracing answer here, and assigns, as did McGee (1982), to rhetoric the status of "a natural social phenomenon in the context of which symbolic claims are made . . .", one is obliged to deal with the genetically determined aspects of this "natural" social phenomenon fully. A rhetorical theory that broadly defined must account for (a) the acquisition of language in terms now current in linguistics; (b) the presence of language or speech defects in terms now medically and therapeutically current; and (c) what is understood by neurophysiologists about brain activities involving the storing and invoking of symbols. Small wonder no one has sincerely presumed to be competent at such a task. But one must ask why anyone defining rhetoric as any use of symbols can turn away from the accumulated evidence alluded to above, and why anyone thus defining rhetoric would not follow appropriately rigorous methods of natural science to observe and experiment when possible.

It is, I believe I have suggested, a yearning for the pastoral or romantic to tolerate discussions of the symbol using animal as if they afforded genuine explanation. To such bucolic bleating one cynical answer coming from deconstruction is that we are the animals *used by* symbols! To satisfy a physical materialist, a theory of rhetoric claiming to account for all symbol using—especially one using a vocabulary suggesting that symbol use is "natural" or "animal" in us—would *have* to deal in physiological and genetic facts.

Is there, then, some more limited definition of rhetoric to permit responsible theory-building within a reasonable sphere? No. The question is badly put, even though it seems natural. The point must be that research on limited problems can proceed apace, and should, even though we lack a satisfactory general theory of rhetoric. However, a materialist would place demands on the questions asked and methods used to answer them. It seems to me that, for now, physical materialists are justified in observing that rhetorical theory has not tried to answer questions about many potentially important variables. Why do some people seem to have much greater facility with language than others? Why, during maturation, is there a stage where females routinely outperform males? Are there biologically caused images or symbols (perhaps even along the lines Jung believed) in rhetoric? What experiments can be performed (or historical observations made) to establish with certainty which aspects of rhetoric are learned, and which genetically caused?

The other question-begging aspect of material definitions has not yet been mentioned. It is this: Unless one first has a fairly clear idea of what material or phenomena to collect and study, one cannot proceed with criticism or theory. That is, a demand to build theory out of material without any preconceptions does not make sense. Accordingly, even a definition like "use of symbols" is simultaneously limiting and prejudiced, yet too broad. If it were my place here to stipulate a definition of rhetoric that would be agreeable yet might be forced into consistency with materialism, I would define it as the strategic use of language in and for the public.

In brief defense I would observe only that verbal strategies must surely hinge on cultural values, and so are learned, not innate. Second, language includes all of its accompanying paralanguage (often mistakenly called nonverbal), and can occur in oral face-to-face, written, and electrically amplified or recorded modes. Hence, writing is not nonverbal, any more than vocal tone and inflection or printed punctuation or gestures. These things do exist materially and can be measured precisely. Any abstractions made from the material may yet prove justified even by material criteria—for example, why a certain speaker makes someone respond favorably, why a song makes someone feel a certain way, et cetera. In the end such ethereal reactions may prove materially explicable; for the time being, while they aren't, I may admit them to the darkness on the edge of town as problems awaiting a solution.

Dialectical Materialist Rhetoric

It will not be comforting to acknowledge that rhetoric from this perspective is ideological dupery. A new history of rhetorical theory could be written emphasizing the linkage of rhetoric-as-taught with economic interests and power groups. Aristotle had no genre for slaves to throw off their chains in social triumph and advance to the broad, sunlit paths of citizenship. Cicero, one of the most conspiring, bluffing Romans surely never gave a Spartacus a thought; medieval rhetoric slumbered in the church aisles; Bishop Whately's purposes, even when forced to seem intellectual, hardly can be divorced from his bishopric. An all-out Marxian critical history of rhetorical theory would be a refreshing addition to the topic area.

I would let it stand as no objection that Marx himself used rhetoric to advance his own political goals. That is, I maintain no position of privilege for him against his own critical method. Indeed, the second connection between Marxian materialism and studies in rhetoric would be the application of Marxian principles to the criticism of actual discourses. It is evident that all such criticism would entail finding the substructures of such discourses, individually or collectively, and that economic interests would have to be shown to speak through them. There are more and other possibilities (Grossberg, 1979); I have sketched only a few. To critique mass communication fully, for example, it may well be necessary to assess the economic motivations in that industry.

Structuralism and Deconstruction

Here I am grouping for economy, and will show also a connection that justifies this pairing. Structuralism takes the nature of language to be the model or homology for all social phenomena. Language consists of its material component—what got said—and an immaterial, but necessary component—the whole language with all its possible sentences, without which the speech wouldn't be reliably meaningful. Accordingly, all social structure consists of both material things, like institutions, and intangible structural laws that bind them together. From these observations two potentially useful directions for rhetorical studies emerge. The more obvious, even if it has had detractors (Warnick, 1979), is to apply structural method to particular pieces of rhetorical discourse to show in them things that were not immediately apparent before they were de- and reconstructed (McGuire, 1977; 1984). Similarly one can analyze the workings of a specific kind or form of language, like narrative (McGuire, 1982c; 1987a; 1987b), treating it as analyzable material. By its very nature, language has an underlying structure or "material" which is its meaning, as well as a material overlay of words.

What is less obvious is that structuralism also has metatheoretical potential. Rhetorical theories of the past define social institutions in which they are applicable; accordingly, they reveal for us both the kinds of language and kinds of settings where what was called rhetoric was appropriate (McGuire, 1982b). Different rhetorics from different cultures or times can be compared for shifts in both social setting (say, the addition of preaching) and recommended linguistic material (forms of argument, evidence, style). In other words, a structural study of rhetorical theory can disclose the gradual evolution of rhetorical material—both linguistic material (as enthymemes give way to epicheiremes) and social material (as rhetoric addresses new social forms like consciousness-raising group discussions, marches, or songs).

Deconstruction (perhaps all post-structuralism) takes a different tactic by treating the existing material piece of language as autonomous—sui generis. Authors are absent, in some versions of this approach, notably those of Derrida and Ricoeur, so that texts create their own contexts and authors begin to disappear (Hoy, 1978), presumably merely the spokespeople of power–knowledge blocks working through them unconsciously. However, the reader emerges as ever important, because the meanings of texts are not transcendent of history, but always turn back or advance further into it.

Hence, not only material language is important here; readings or interpretations assigned to works — which for Gadamer form the work's history and effect (Hoy, 1978) — are important pieces of social history awaiting our study. And those interpretations are materially real. Surely it is an ultimate form of criticism; it finally elevates the critic over the author completely, declaring the latter's role in writing trivial, and making the former's role as guardian and explainer everything (we may hear an interest speaking to us there). By this view, it is not Shakespeare's *Hamlet* that is of interest, but all the Hamlets recreated, interpreted, by all the critics, audiences and teachers who alone can make the text have meaning. (Also see Aune, chapter 8, for intertextual meaning and a different view of deconstruction.)

Constitutive Rhetoric

A different path for rhetorical theory not entirely inconsistent with materialist philosophy might be found as a derivative of the sociology of knowledge. Here the theorist merely assumes rhetoric, and then traces out its real–material, social consequences. This is not the same as deconstruction's end point, however. As I understand it, this idea, heavily influenced by Michael McGee (1980), has rhetoric create social reality. The ideas of rhetorical discourse are transformed into material consequences by the behavior of people. Here what is material is neither the antecedent conditions for rhetoric nor the discourse itself; it is the effect of discourse that is materially real. A debate is held, and a new bomber funded; Willie Horton becomes a household name, and George Bush gets elected. Although there may be some serious questions about causation in any such case, a slight adjustment in the assertions about materiality may appear as a remedy. If the real consequences of discourse cease to be material in the classic sense, the model is untestable: that is, if one argues that people's self-concepts are changed or created, those somewhat immaterial effects are impossible to submit to verification/falsification — even when the critics claim that a "people" is created (Charland, 1987; McGee, 1975; McGuire, 1976). The very concept of a "people" is an untestable, metaphysical blend of the concrete (group behavior) and the abstract (self-identity).

However, from the point of view of social materialism, such a view may have much to recommend it. Here is the possibility by extension to deal with concrete abstractions by treating ideas as things, John Lyne's (chap. 5) objections notwithstanding. And although I do not have in mind a history of ideas, it seems to me that the ideas governing social reality evolve through rhetorical exchanges. One of the most interesting topics for such a study would be the idea of "rights" that people (or lab rats) have.

From whence rights stem is unclear. Most seem *ad hoc* representatives of some group's interests, because any matrix of agreement between them is indeed obscure. Why would the same society have abortion legal and euthanasia assistance not — is there less love on the part of a child helping a begging parent get means for suicide than in the heart of a woman choosing to abort a fetus? What convoluted chain of reasoning has created animal rights groups in a society that has to put to death thousands of excess animals every year? How did the right to vote get extended as far it has? Why is the access to medical care related to wealth, whereas anyone who desires and cannot afford it gets a lawyer free? These rights may be only appellate courts' reinterpretations of laws to the advantage of a noisy nuisance of which they want to be rid. Whatever the case, topics such as that can be studied materially and usefully.

I believe that rhetorical material can teach us what people have thought or still do. That is, one legitimate reason for viewing rhetoric as epistemic is that studying the discourse of the past informs us about the ideas people had about real social problems — or we find through debunking the illusions to which they clung. In either case we treat concrete abstractions by analysis of discourse. Constitutive rhetoric seeks a critical, social theory in the post-Marxian tradition of sociology of knowledge.

Summary

Different conceptions of "material" are possible, and each suggests different possibilities and constraints for the development of rhetorical theory. Traditional, central-state materialism, which I have covered here as "physical materialism," would require both biological components and other physical considerations (even voice volume, pitch, gesture, raw physical size, style of type, size of page, number of repetitions, etc.). In short, a communication science could generate by experimentation and survey hypotheses for a theory of rhetoric — a theory of the real–social world. Social materialism seems to point in the direction of critical studies of messages designed to disclose their economic or power interests, cultural values or meanings being manipulated, and possibly the effects of messages on human actors.

From a materialist point of view, rhetoric can make meaningful contributions to our knowledge of why people do what they do if messages can be shown to be significant, material causes. Second, even at its simplest theoretical level, rhetoric can describe the material possibilities of language and its physical accompaniments: metaphor, rhythm, enthymeme, rhyme, narrative, asyndeton, pitch, volume, gesture, and more.

CRITIQUES AND DEFENSES OF MATERIALISM

This volume shows both allies and enemies of a materialist philosophy. Materialists can be perfectly comfortable with many of the claims of realism, pragmatism, and some approaches to critical rationalism and deconstruction. Materialists have more trouble with the contentions of idealists, symbolic constructivists, and most existentialists. Yet nearly all of the attacks on materialism, emanating from any and all of the other philosophies represented here (and the many that aren't), follow a single line of paired objections. The critique is sufficiently common and important to require both exposition and response here.

Materialism is accused of being both dogmatic and reductionist. Indeed, some scientists call the school of thought by the name "reductionism." The attack on materialism as dogmatic constitutes a reaction against materialism's insistence on material cause–effect relationships. These relationships are presuppositions and cannot be proved to prevail in life—especially human life, goes the argument. The argument is old-fashioned sounding because it is old-fashioned, and its linchpin is free will. The most modern version of this attack is the mild-mannered distinction between motion—the rock rolls down the hill and materialism is true—and action—the human being rolls down the hill (by choice) and materialism is false.

The best answer a materialist can give for now *may be* that we cannot at present know or prove conclusively all the causation in human life, but our ignorance is not a refutation of the possibility. Our materialist can go on to point out that, in contrast to the inability to explain rolling down the hill, materialism can and does explain some more important life events: one's sex, genetic diseases, certain paramaters and limits of intelligence, causes of cancer, cures for polio, treatment of speech disorders, chemical cures for chronic depression, hormonal determinants of behaviors, and more. This is an appealing defense which nevertheless begs the question by ignoring the root issue of free will. (It does, however, reveal the extent to which matertialism has made inroads into our lives which even its most fervent antagonists have no choice but to concede.) So the second best response a materialist can make when accused of dogmatism is the *et tu* reply that asserting that humans have free will is itself a dogmatic move since proof of this is lacking and, indeed, impossible. And here emerges a crucial difference between materialism and some of its rivals: materialism admits and explains the grounds of its own refutation. It does not wallow about in a swamp of agreement; it proves this and refutes that. It also admits its own areas of uncertainty, asking only for the needed time and study to move toward the level of certainty it seeks.

But there lingers the charge—why it is perceived as a defect is unclear—that materialism is reductionist. Presumably that complaint is intended to assert that materialism oversimplifies phenomena. But it is far from simplifying to inquire into the processes of genetic causation; indeed, few persons launching the attack on materialism could ever keep track of the "oversimplification" known as molecular biology. The materialist finds, on the contrary, that explanations of brain synapses are much more complex and theoretically elegant than assertions of "mind" and "will"—indeed, *those* seem reductionist dogma to a committed materialist: unprovable, irrefutable concepts offered as explanations, when they are instead only shorthand names for what the uneducated want to believe and feel must be true.

Not only physical materialism is accused of dogmatic reductionism. Marxian materialism is always susceptible to the attack that it sees everywhere only economic causes and explanations, and that those do not account for all human activity. Behaviorism cannot account adequately for language, a central component of any rhetorical theory and artifact for critical acts. And it is exactly where their conjunctions with materialism are possible that deconstruction and symbolic constructivism are most doubted and debated by their own advocates and practitioners (See Aune and Brummett, chaps. 8 and 3, respectively).

In responding to all these accusations materialism has become flexible. John Lyne (chap. 5) wants very badly to deny materialism the flexibility that he thinks is materialism's own contradiction and to deny that any material connected with rhetoric is governed by Newtonian or Darwinian laws. It is, of course, possible that the science of acoustics is Newtonian, so that sound cannot be part of rhetoric any longer nor can motion; and if optics are explicable, then we must rule out also whatever is seen. Darwin, of course, knew little about how genetics works, because his focus was on species' adaptations to material environments, not on mutation (the only operative force in evolution in our species today). But biological determinists include linguists like Eric Lenneberg, and if we must dismiss the biologically determined trait of language from rhetoric, what is left is exactly what idealism is all about: thoughts within a single mind, not to be studied as electro-chemical processes or reactions to external stimuli, but ideas springing ex nihilo—from a free will. Like that most typical idealist Descartes, Lyne wants to claim that ideas are proof of his own ego and free will, and hem materialism into a shirt several sizes too small by asserting that language is immaterial, because incorporeal. In so doing, he splendidly refutes the concept of material dominant in the 6th century B.C., but he is quieter about the research and theory in genetics and molecular biology done in our own lifetimes. What if "free will" is a genetic characteristic of our (and perhaps some others) life form—that we "feel" this as a symptom of our genes? What if our environment requires us to believe in it—it is taught to us as a guilt-control mechanism? If those impertinent, Nietzschean questions are bothersome let me ask instead, "What percentage of human behavior is chosen by free will as opposed to 'determined' by organic or external, material causes?" By Lyne's version, the materialist cannot allow for any choices at all to be made by people; then it would be fair to insist that he maintain that all behavior results from free will, including sneezing, urinating, waking up and getting up, having sex, and speaking a language. The attack that materialism is reductionistic is itself a reductio ad absurdum, which I have reversed for fun.

A concept of constrained will, of limited choice, need not be inconsistent with all materialist philosophies. If learning, a materially explicable process, informs choice, then some role for materialism must be maintained in accounting for human behavior even if one wants to maintain that the behavior was "freely" chosen from a (one must note, *limited*) range of alternatives. That there are both biological and environmental constraints or determinants of learning is not only not an argument against materialism, but a reason to avoid oversimplifying materialism by observing that genetic material is acted upon by and acts upon environmental material.

One seeming problem for a materialist rhetoric is the problem of meaning. Here we confront the sharpest incorporeal edge of language, the central phenomenon and material of rhetoric. On one hand, the idea that meaning is indeterminate—is not in language itself, but is attributed variously by different people—seems to overturn any possibility of a material, causal theory of meaning. Yet seen differently, this shows us that the material causes for linguistic meaning are to be found inside the brain as well as outside in linguistic material.

For example, one learns a language because of environmental material—the sounds and words of English, or German, or Chinese; and because of genetic material, which gives humans the capacity so rapidly and uniformly to learn language at all. This suggests that both biological and environmental material determine whether or not one can assign any meaning at all to an utterance, much less whether two people assign the same meanings. For example, allusions have no meaning to listeners unfamiliar with the piece of literature or history alluded to; exposure to some other linguistic material is necessary, just as it is to speak a language at all. Materialist explanations of meaning may yet become standard.

But verbal meaning is only part of the issue where rhetoric is concerned. Whatever position critics take on the value of genre criticism, a genre only can be detected as a collection of materially similar pieces of language, usually occurring in materially similar social settings, for example, in graveyards, at graduations. And the quintessential evidence for argument in criticism is text citation to show real passages of language that reveal the characteristics the critic attributes to the discourse. No matter one's ultimate direction or beginning—concern about effects or questions of invention—

linguistic material is the rhetorical artifact, the sine qua non of both theory and criticism. That suggests a materialist position previously not advanced, and that position will conclude this discussion.

Rhetorical Material

If we take issue with McGee's (1982) position on rhetorical theory as being all idealist in contrast with his approach, we may do so by noting that some of the idealists he consigns to the fire were doing a superior job of describing the materials of which rhetoric is made. I will use here Cicero's idealist theory on grounds of its familiarity to rhetorical theorists, and its remote location from some of the issues that most bother our own era. If we take (stipulatively) Cicero's canons as our starting point, what genuinely material theory could be elaborated? I will try to sketch it here.

Invention

Ideas, said Lyne (chapter 5), are not material. I do not differ with that claim, but I think our definitions of "idea" may differ. The *loci* for invention are structures describing material relations (McGuire, 1982a) or material itself. The end product of rhetorical invention is an argument, which is a linguistic object (materially real) recognizable by its own specific, material structure. A syllogism, for example, is materially different from a sonnet. By the same token, arguments invented from different loci are materially different, because even if some of their linguistic material is the same, the *organization* of that material makes two different things. (To refer to an earlier example of the principle and problem of organization, one organization is a TV set, and another is just copper, glass, plastic, etc.)

Other than loci of invention, we are familiar with the less systematically explained argument by example. This is an "argument" made by telling a story (true or fictive) that parallels the present case. Some of the material for these is Aesop's fables some is history some is made up on the spot. The point is that rhetorical material is described in fairly elegant detail in the classical rhetorical theories which have been mainstays of our profession for over 2000 years. To dismiss these as idealist (McGee, 1982) is to miss the point; the structures of linguistic material are found in language-in-use, not dreamed up out of nowhere. (Though one might observe that Aristotle dreaming up the syllogism was no mean accomplishment.)

Arrangement

If rhetorical theory is to continue to describe (and prescribe) discourse, it needs a vocabulary for the arrangement of pieces of discourse. In the classical era, this posed only minor problems — to describe a well-organized oration. As the scope of rhetoric broadens, competent description and explanation of other organizations is necessary. What material is used, for example, in contemporary soft drink advertisements? Lots of pictures of attractive young people cavorting outdoors in various states of relative undress. (Except the Christmas season.) And how is any verbal message intertwined with the pictures? That is an issue of arrangement.

When even the simplest pattern of organization is explained, it describes the material contents of each part. For example, introductions name the topic to follow, contain descriptions of author's *ethos* — in short, the linguistic material is prescribed and/or described. A summary is not an idea; it is material repetition of one's main points without elaboration. Of course, this includes using the topics of invention; for example, to praise might entail (in a given culture) identifying ancestors, recounting the person's economic status, or discussing offspring. In any case, the purpose of describing organization is to delineate the arrangements of pieces of language which are recognizably, materially (substantially) different from one another. One presumes that a theory of organization or arrangement ultimately describes how a whole speech (or other artifact) is assembled or constructed from smaller pieces of linguistic material.

Style

Most treatments of style deal with "microscopic" units of linguistic material, at least in comparison with the units or arrangement. Although style can be characterized by descriptive generalizations like "plain," most thorough treatments of style elaborate possible pieces and arrangements of language below the level of a sentence, and some that cut across sentences. Rhyme is based upon the material coincidence of sound, as is alliteration, but the difference between them, audible, is materially real — sound waves. Past discussions of style have treated such specific material details as omission of articles, repetition of a word or phrase beginning successive clauses, and a balanced number of syllables in all clauses of a sentence. Besides those devices are such figures as metaphor, oxymoron, and personification.

If subjectivists were right and meaning were purely personal, and irrelevant to linguistic material, we could not even detect metaphor and oxymoron. I take it as self-evident that my other examples concern the material of which language is made — mainly sound, and units of sound recognized as specific words, and ways to make patterns out of sounds and words. This canon of rhetoric clearly deals with manipulating material. Any claims about aesthetic or persuasive effects these manipulations have seem tenuous. Black (1970), however, suggested that identifying the dominant metaphorical material in a discourse may help us to construct the likely or solicited audiences, and it is possible to argue that individual writers and speakers exhibit quantifiable preferences for metaphors of a certain type as well. Whether these can be proved to reveal a world view (which caused them to be chosen) or not remains uncertain, but the possibility to connect rhetorical material with mental causation is both suggestive and reasonable.

Memory

Memory resides, not in the mind, but in the physical brain. Long- and short-term memory appear to function differently and be lodged in different regions of the human brain. Trauma damage cases have begun revealing to neurophysiologists where some of the centers are. Evidently biological determinants can govern memory, as well as other mental capacities. This is not the place, and I am not the person, to review fully the medical evidence on this topic.

But memory's relevance to rhetoric is manifold. A simple connection is that to avoid having to orient much of an oral presentation to one's manuscript or notes, a memory capable of holding and recalling the information is invaluable. Thus, freedom to achieve a spontaneous-seeming relationship with an audience is secured by adequate memory. Second, no mechanical system of invention, like lines of argument, works unless one can first learn and remember the lines. Third, for the invention of narrative example arguments based on history or literature, one must retain in memory the stories to be used. Another obvious issue of memory concerns style, where remembering the figures can augment creating them, and remembering passages of other prose provides quotations for use as embellishment, evidence, or both.

Delivery

Little is more clearly materially real in oral rhetoric than the delivery: a voice with measurable volume, rate and pitch; a physical body in motion in space and time. The "normal" vocal and physical patterns accompanying speech are acquired in the same way and at the same time as the language itself. Americans learn to raise vocal pitch at the end of an interrogative sentence; Italians learn to gesture in particular ways in conversation. Even if, like some elocutionists, one decides that voice, face expression, gesture, and motion should be taught as a set of mechanical moves, the elements are material. I will not comment on claims that delivery (or nonverbal communication) is the most effective aspect of every communicative act. As far as I know, no one can produce reliable data in support of such a claim. But there can be no doubt that what people see and hear is part of any oral rhetorical experience, and it should be presumed to have some effects on observers. It is possible that someone will one day contrive a way to measure those effects discretely, hard as they will be to isolate from the larger web of the whole event.

What would be the role of theory in the meantime? As always, theory can and must describe with clarity. It ought to seek information to help explain and predict, and to get beyond the anecdotal and obvious: It is a meager harvest if all we can offer people is such generalization as "don't show up to deliver a eulogy for a U.S. President dressed in a Hawaiian shirt with gym shorts and one red tennis shoe." Yet there we can discern already that some effects of aspects of delivery can be predicted with reasonable accuracy, and a materialist rhetoric would have to get about refining those predictions and explanations to get beyond ridiculous extremes and achieve serious usefulness.

Those, then, are some thoughts about pursuing very familiar rhetorical topics materially. To do so has not been popular in the past, nor is it yet. To do so in the future will be more difficult than some other paths, but may yield some greater rewards. But another possibility exists which must be addressed: what rhetorical criticism might look like if materialism were its philosophical first principle.

Critical Studies

One of the ways theory can be and, at least since Aristotle, has been built is by observation and reporting of actual occurrences and possibilities. Critics armed with the premises and analytical methods of "social materialism" have much to teach us about rhetoric. I do not see a role at present for a physical materialist approach to criticism; but who knows — Einstein gave his brain to science for study.

However, materially informed criticism can and does follow structuralist (McGuire, 1977; 1982b; 1984; 1987a), Marxian (Grossberg, 1979), and deconstructionist (Aune, chap. 8; Hoy, 1986) methods and models. If I may offer a constructive suggestion at this juncture, it is that, too often, critics talk about methods, rather than actually applying them (Francesconi, 1986; Grossberg, 1979; Warnick, 1979). (I say that fully aware that the specific purpose of this volume is similar.) But I think I need produce no evidence to make the claim that materially informed criticisms (Marxian, structuralist, deconstructionist) are far outnumbered by neo-Aristotelian, Burkean, and even fantasy theme essays. Why might this be?

Materialism as a philosophy is methodologically demanding and sophisticated. To master the methodology of any of its offshoots requires significant effort. And the term "methodology" can be applied unembarrassedly to materially informed analyses, whereas it seems to me quite inaccurate and inappropriate to apply that term to Burkean or fantasy theme analyses. In the current climate of philosophical suspicion against methodology, contributed to by Gadamer (1960) as well as Polanyi (Watson, 1982), my remarks may fall on unsympathetic ears. But the methodologist needs as much intuition as the Burkean to choose carefully the artifacts to be dissected rigorously. And besides the mastery of his craft — criticism — he will find he needs the art of writing. His explanation must not just make sense; it must have some appeal. Although every reader should react to such criticism with "of course, that's right, now I see it!", it is also important that these replicable criticisms report their disclosures in interesting ways. Verifiability is not the sole criterion in methodological research. But it is not a criterion at all in most rhetorical criticism, and a materialist would argue that it should be.

In sum, the other relationship of materialism to critical studies is that materialist theories can direct critical inquiry with their perspective and methods. On this two way street, theory is built up (or verified or falsified) by analysis of materially real artifacts, and the study of artifacts is guided by theoretical assumptions and demands, as well as by the overarching perspective of materialism.

REFERENCES

Berger, P. & Luckmann, T. (1966). *The social construction of reality.* Garden City, NY: Doubleday.

Black, E. (1970). The second persona. *Quarterly Journal of Speech, 56,* 109–119.

Brugger, W. (1972). Materialism. In K. Baker (Ed. & Trans.), *Philosophical dictionary* (pp. 242–243). Spokane, WA: Gonzaga University Press.

Campbell, K. (1967). Materialism. In P. Edwards (Ed.), *The encyclopedia of philosophy* (*Vol. 5,* pp. 179–188). New York: Macmillan.

Charland, M. R. (1987). Constitutive rhetoric: The case of the *Peuple Quebecois. Quarterly Journal of Speech, 73,* 133–150.

Foucault, M. (1980). *Power/Knowledge.* New York: Pantheon.

Francesconi, R. (1986). The implications of Habermas's theory of legitimation for rhetorical criticism. *Communication Monographs, 53,* 16–35.

Gadamer, H.-G. (1960). *Wahrheit und Methode: Grundzuege einer philosophischen Hermeneutik.* Tuebingen: Mohr.

Gadamer, H.-G. (1976). *Philosophical Hermeneutics* (D. Linge, Ed. & Trans.). Berkeley: University of California Press.

Grossberg, L. (1979). Marxist dialectics and rhetorical criticism. *Quarterly Journal of Speech, 65,* 235–249.

Hacking, I. (1986) The archaeology of Foucault. In D. C. Hoy (Ed.), *Foucault: A critical reader* (pp. 26–40). Oxford: Blackwell.

Harland, R. (1987). *Superstructuralism: The philosophy of structuralism and post-structuralism.* London and New York: Methuen.

Hook, S. (1955). *Marx and the marxists.* Princeton, NJ: Van Nostrand/Anvil.

Hoy, D. C. (1978). *The critical circle: Literature, history and philosophical hermeneutics.* Berkeley, CA: University of California Press.

Hoy, D. C. (1986). *Foucault: A critical reader.* Oxford & New York: Basil Blackwell.

Kaufmann, W. (1968). *Nietzsche: Philosopher, psychologist, antichrist* (3rd ed.). New York: Vintage Books.

Konner, M. (1983). *The tangled wing: Biological constraints on the human spirit.* New York: Harper/Colophon.

Lacey, A. R. (1976). *A dictionary of philosophy* (2nd ed.). London: Routledge & Kegan Paul.

Lenneberg, E. (1960). Language, evolution and purposive behavior. In S. Diamond (Ed.), *Culture in history: Essays in honor of Paul Radin* (pp. 869–893). New York: Columbia University Press.

Levi-Strauss, C. (1963). *Structural Anthropology* (C. Jacobson & B. Schoepf, Trans.). New York: Basic Books.

McGee, M. (1975). In search of "the people": A rhetorical alternative. *Quarterly Journal of Speech, 61,* 235–249.

McGee, M. C. (1980) The "ideograph": A link between rhetoric and ideology. *Quarterly Journal of Speech, 66,* 1–16.

McGee, M. C. (1982). A materialist's conception of rhetoric. In R. E. McKerrow (Ed.), *Explorations in rhetoric: Studies in honor of Douglas Ehninger* (pp. 23–48) Glenview, IL: Scott, Foresman.

McGuire, M. (1976). Rhetoric, philosophy and the Volk: Johann Gottlieb Fichte's "Addresses to the German Nation". *Quarterly Journal of Speech, 62,* 135–144.

McGuire, M. (1977). Mythic rhetoric in *Mein Kampf:* A structuralist critique. *Quarterly Journal of Speech, 63,* 1–13.

McGuire, M. (1982a). Some problems with rhetorical example. *Pre/Text, 3,* 121–136.

McGuire, M. (1982b). The structural study of speech. In R. E. McKerrow (Ed.), *Explorations in rhetoric: Studies in honor of Douglas Ehninger* (pp. 1–22). Glenview, IL: Scott, Foresman.

McGuire, M. (1982c). The structure of rhetoric. *Philosophy and Rhetoric, 15,* 149–169.

McGuire, M. (1984). "Darkness on the edge of town": Bruce Springsteen's rhetoric of optimism and despair. In M. Medhurst & T. Benson (Eds.), *Rhetorical dimensions of Media: A critical casebook* (pp. 233–250). Dubuque: Kendall-Hunt.

McGuire, M. (1987a). Ideology and myth as structurally different bases for political argument. *Journal of the American Forensic Association, 24,* 16–26.

McGuire, M. (1987b). Narrative persuasion in rhetorical theory. In H. Geissner (Ed.), *On narratives: Proceedings of the 10th International Colloquium on Speech Communication* (pp. 163–178). Frankfurt/M.: Scriptor.

Railsback, C. C. (1983). Beyond rhetorical relativism: A structural–material model of truth and objective reality. *Quarterly Journal of Speech, 69,* 351–363.

Reese, W. L. (1980). *Dictionary of philosophy and religion: Eastern & Western thought.* Sussex: Harvester.

Smart, J.J.C. (1986). Materialism. In *The New Encyclopedia Britannica.* Chicago: Encyclopedia Britannica, Inc.

Taylor, R. (1963). *Metaphysics.* Englewood Cliffs. Prentice-Hall.

Warnick, B. (1979). Structuralism vs. phenomenology: Implications for rhetorical criticism. *Quarterly Journal of Speech, 65,* 250–261.

Watson, S. (1982). Polanyi's epistemology of good reasons. In R. E. McKerrow (Ed.) *Explorations in Rhetoric: Studies in honor of Douglas Ehninger* (pp. 49–68). Glenview, IL: Scott, Foresman.

Weitz, M. (Ed.). (1966). *Twentieth-Century philosophy: The analytic tradition.* New York: The Free Press.

Chapter 7

Existentialism as a Basis for the Theory and Practice of Rhetoric

Michael J. Hyde

Existence constitutes the highest interest of the existing individual, and his interest in his existence constitutes his reality.

Søren Kierkegaard (1846/1971, p. 279)

The philosophical movement of existentialism was developed by its representatives as they concerned themselves with the question of *what it means to exist as a human being.* Existence, the existentialists forever remind us, is its own demonstration: The constantly occurring lived experience of human being requires no manner of abstract thought to prove its presence. *Cogito ergo sum?* No, the "I am" must always come first! Thought presupposes existence; it is but a way of existing. Hence, if the question of what it means to exist is to be answered in an experientially adequate and authentic fashion, then, according to the existentialists, one must return to his or her own concrete existence as it is actually being lived and experienced so to witness and describe the demonstration at hand. This endeavor calls for a phenomenological appreciation of human existence rather than a "scientific" one. Science is necessarily constrained by its already-thought-out methodologies to give only a "rationale" or "explanation" about existence. A phenomenology of existence, however, takes us beyond the epistemic domain of the "symbols of science"; for "existential phenomenology" begins "by reawakening the basic experience of the world of which science is the second order expression" (Merleau-Ponty, 1945/1974, p. viii).[1]

---

[1]A detailed discussion of existentialism's historical and methodological relationship with phenomenology is beyond the scope of this essay. A very lucid treatment of this matter is contained in Schrag (1961, pp. 3–25).

213

In addressing the question of existence, existentialists seek to clarify, among other things, how human existence is more than what the "rational" thought of those like Descartes, Kant, and Hegel declared it to be, more than what the reified prescriptions of the church demanded it to be, and more than what the telic inclination of modern technological advances encouraged it to be. Some of the more influential descriptions of this "more" of existence are found in the writings of such existential thinkers as Søren Kierkegaard, Friedrich Nietzsche, Karl Jaspers, Martin Heidegger, Jean-Paul Sartre, Gabriel Marcel, and Maurice Merleau-Ponty. These thinkers, to be sure, hardly constitute a chorus that is constantly in tune; their contributions to the movement of existentialism admit significant philosophical, religious, and political differences. Yet they still laid claim to the importance of inquiring about a specific question; and in their respective inquiries are found a number of common themes that bring definition to the movement that these intellectuals helped to inspire.

In this essay I explore how existentialism can contribute to the theory and practice of rhetoric. As I hope to show, this contribution takes form in the ways in which the themes of existentialism speak to us about the "total contingency of human existence" (Barrett, 1958/1962, p. 65) or, if you will, about that which enables rhetoric to make its living. The business of rhetoric is to "deal with what is in the main contingent" (Aristotle, *Rhetoric,* 1357a15). By informing us about the nature of our certainly uncertain existence, existentialists hope to call us to responsible action in dealing with this total contingency. The importance of rhetorical theory and practice is affirmed when this call is made and understood.

Rhetorical scholars have been discussing their understanding of the teachings of existentialism for nearly thirty years now.[2] My intention here is not to put a cap on these discussions by offering a definitive reply to the question directing this chapter. Rather, I conceive my task as an "existential" attempt "to keep the conversation going" (Rorty, 1979, pp. 357–394) about a philosophical movement that still has something to say to rhetorical scholars. In performing this task I undoubtedly will be repeating at times what some have already said about the topic. I hope, however, that such "repetition" is understood in its most positive, existentialist sense: that is, a recalling of past possibilities that are deemed appropriate for guiding present and future thought and action (Kierkegaard, 1843/1941).

Part one of this chapter contains an examination of some of the central themes of existentialism that serve to define what this movement represents.

---

[2]For example, see Wieman (1961); Baird (1962); Anderson (1963); Christopherson (1963); Scott (1964); Lanigan (1969, 1974); Campbell (1970, 1971); Smith (1972, 1985); Rosenfield (1974); Consigny (1977); Poulakos (1974); Hyde & Smith (1979); McGuire (1980); Hyde (1980, 1983a, 1984); Stewart (1986).

Part two provides a discussion of how these themes are suggestive for understanding what rhetoric is and how it operates. Part three offers a critical assessment of the philosophy of rhetoric that emerges in the first two parts.

SOME CENTRAL THEMES OF EXISTENTIALISM

Reason, Emotion, and Truth

Dostoevsky's *Notes from Underground* (1864/1960) occupies a prominent position in the *literary* canon of existentialism because of what its "narrator," that "hyperconscious" soul, says about such things as how "man is a frivolous and incongruous creature"; how he has "a passionate love for destruction and chaos"; how he will use this "fatal fantastic element" to guard against being "calculated and tabulated" by the "positive rationality" of science, thereby "proving to himself continually that he is a man and not an organ stop"; how the "conclusions of reason and arithmetic" (e.g., "two times two makes four") are not "always advantageous for man"; and how "two times two makes four is no longer life . . . but is the beginning of death," the beginning of the end of man's "free will" and "creative" spirit (pp. 9–30).

The picture being constructed here is one where the oppositions of reason *versus* emotion and rationality *versus* irrationality are at work, and where truth is up for grabs. It is a picture of humankind's "modern" predicament in the positivist age of the 20th century, an age when the "truth" of Christianity was losing ground to the "truth" of scientific and technological progress, and when it could be said in a spirit of "joyful wisdom" that "God is dead" and that *"We have killed him"* (Nietzsche, 1882/1971, pp. 167–168). Diagnosing the predicament's twentieth century development, such acclaimed existentialist artists and philosophers as Kafka (e.g., 1925/1968), Sartre (e.g., 1938/1949), and Camus (e.g., 1942/1955) would further tell us how the human condition is one of "contingency," "alienation," "suffering," "meaninglessness," "anxiety," and "guilt"; in short, humankind's evolving modern predicament is a clear indication that existence, life itself, is "absurd." Or, as Dostoevsky's narrator would have it: ". . . one may say anything about the history of the world — anything that might enter the most disordered imagination. The only thing one cannot say [,however,] is that it is rational. The very word sticks in one's throat" (Dostoevsky, 1864/1960, p. 27).

Rorty (1979) defines and defends "Existentialism" as "an *intrinsically reactive* movement of thought, one which has point only in opposition to the tradition" (p. 366). Indeed, much of what existentialists say about the question of existence is rooted in their reactive stance against the tradition of classical rationalism and its equating of man's essence with his being an *animal rationale*—something living that has reason and that must overcome its emotional tendencies if it is to know and speak the truth. The above assessments of human existence certainly reflect this reaction, thereby adding grist to the mill for those who would interpret existentialism as being but a philosophy advocating irrationalism. Does not Sartre (1943/1973), for example, tell us that "all human existence is a passion," an emotionally driven and forever failing struggle on the part of "man" to be one with himself, to be perfect, to be "God" (pp. 784–796)?

But one must be careful here. When existentialists ask us to consider how emotion plays a role in human existence, they are not attempting to throw reason and rationality to the wind, nor are they attempting to deny that emotions can be the source of "stupid" behavior. Nietzsche's contributions to the movement of existentialism, for example, make such a denial an impossibility. Rather, an existentialist appreciation of emotion is one that places it in the company of reason and rationality and credits it with having an active and truthful purpose.

Emotions, existentialists tell us, function as vehicles for the active sensibility of human beings; that is, they provide the "perspectives" (Nietzsche, 1887/1969, p. 119) for seeing the world as interesting, as something that matters and that warrants interpretation (Heidegger, 1927/1962, pp. 172–182). Emotions are not primarily "psychical" phenomena originating purely from one's "inner condition"; rather, they emerge in the interaction between a person and the world as the world is perceived by the person through an act of consciousness. An emotion operates as an act of consciousness; it serves to orient a person toward the world in a certain way (Sartre, 1939/1948).

When any given mode of emotional consciousness (e.g., joy) is prolonged through time such that it continually influences how a person perceives and thinks about the world, a person's emotion becomes mood-like in nature (Hyde, 1984, pp. 128–129). Moods are generalized emotions permeating the temporality of a person's existence (Solomon, 1976, p. 133). Even one's passive indifference to the world wherein thought appears to vanish into the "pallid, evenly balanced lack of mood," still warrants recognition as being an emotional orientation between a person and the world; it is still a mood. Moods are therefore an ever present quality of human existence. "The fact that moods can deteriorate . . . and change over means simply that in every case . . . [a human being] always has some mood," some mode of emotional consciousness that enables him or her to "disclose" and understand the world in a specific way (Heidegger, 1927/1962, p. 173).

In performing this interpretive or hermeneutical function, emotions can serve a truthful purpose. From an existential–phenomenological perspective, truth *happens* as a disclosure of the world, as a revealing or uncovering of something that is perceived to be (Heidegger, 1927/1962, pp. 256–273; 1975/1982, pp. 213–224). (Importantly, any talk about epistemological theories of truth — such as "correspondence" and "coherence" — presupposes the conception of "truth as disclosure" being noted here.) It may thus be said, for example, that the emotionally intense visions of suffering that Picasso was able to disclose in his 1937 paintings, *Guernica* and *Head of a Horse,* are displays of truth, displays that, in their own way, are as reasonable and rational as the assertion "Two times two makes four." Unlike this later "objective" assertion, which need only function on an intellectual level for its content to be apprehended, Picasso's displays are "subjective" and function first and foremost on an "existential" level. His paintings project a protest against the brutality of fascism in particular and modern war in general; at the same time, they project the *real* suffering that he was experiencing and living as he visualized the pain of creatures under attack and being destroyed (Berger, 1965, pp. 30–31, 164–170). The paintings are not what Picasso thinks but what he *is,* passionately; they express a subjectivity, an existential truth. Kierkegaard's (1846/1971) claim that "truth is subjectivity" (pp. 169–224) captures what is going on here. Schrag's (1961) clarification of what this claim means is noteworthy, especially in light of the Picasso example: "Existential truth is a mode of existence and a way of life. It is something which one *is* rather than *has,* something which one *lives* rather than *possesses*" (p. 7).

Picasso's existential truth cries out for others to appropriate it and thus make it their own. Without this act of appropriation, Picasso's truth can go no further than Picasso. Others must realize it and integrate it into their modes of existence as a directive for *what must not be done* to human beings. If a truth is to live on as something more than an intellectual topic, it must become subjective; it must be forever vitalized by the "passion" of existence (Kierkegaard, 1846/1971). Without this passion, truth is, at best, sterile; at worst, it is dead.

In developing their view of human emotion, existentialists encourage us to understand that any form of cognitive determining owes at least something to the disclosive capabilities of emotion. "Reason" itself poses no exception here: Even when reason is couched in the most positivistic language (such that it can be "objective" in its registration of "facts") its announcements will always be rooted in what emotion makes possible — that is, an interpretation of some matter of interest. Hence, the so-called "dispassionate" claims of reason — as made by science, for example — can never escape the emotion that begets their existence. By adhering (passionately?) to the belief that "man *is* a rational animal," Western philosophy devotes much of its over 2000-year history to teaching us that this escape is not only possible but necessary if the thing called "truth" is to be discovered. Existentialists teach otherwise.

But again, this is not to say that existentialists are opposed to reason and rationality. They recognize that we exist as *animalia metaphysica* (Merleau-Ponty, 1948/1971, pp. 83–98), that we therefore "have a nostalgia for something final and absolute" (Earle, 1976, p. 157), and that reason and rationality should always be on hand to offer us important directives for coming to terms with this passionate longing for completeness (Jaspers, 1935/1973; 1938/1984). We are this longing, say the existentialists; our history makes that certain. But our future—which this history once was and, one hopes, will be time and again—also makes clear that uncertainty is also and always a part of the project. "Because of the uncertainty of temporal existence life is always an experiment" (Jaspers, 1951/1970a, p. 125), or an "objective uncertainty" (Kierkegaard, 1846/1971, p. 182). With Kierkegaard and other Christian existentialists, we may interpret this "paradox" in an onto-theological way and see its "mystery" (Marcel, 1950) as a sign of God's infinite presence here on earth (Bultmann, 1957; Tillich, 1951/1957). With Nietzsche (1901/1968, pp. 549–550), we may be equally metaphysical but interpret it as having nothing at all to do with God and having everything to do with both the world's and humankind's "will to power." Existentialists, you see, can also be nostalgic. Yet they always temper their nostalgia with a good dose of existence, of objective uncertainty, of temporality, and are therefore ever ready to speak passionately against any form of over-confident reason that would put an end to our nostalgia by finalizing its temporality in a self-enclosed rationality, a "system" of abstract thought calling itself "the Truth." The "ambiguity" (de Beauvoir, 1948/1972) of existence always outstrips and transcends any attempt to build such an "existential system." Those who think that such a system is possible are forgetting what it means to exist (Kierkegaard, 1846/1971, pp. 107–113); they are forgetting that "The goal of a philosophical life cannot be formulated as a state of being, which is attainable and once attained, perfect. Our states of being are only manifestations of existential striving or failure. It lies in our very nature to be on-the-way" (Jaspers, 1951/1970a, pp. 129–130). This reminder leads to the next set of related themes characterizing existentialism.

The Self, Temporality, and Freedom

Existentialists see human existence as being composed of three interrelated and interdependent experiential realms: the *Umwelt* (the environmental/biological world), the *Mitwelt* (the communal world), and the *Eigenwelt* (the world of the self). When, however, existentialists speak to us about the importance of remembering that it "lies in our very nature to be on-the-way," it is the *Eigenwelt* that commands their attention.

An existentialist understanding of the world of the self centers on its temporal nature, its continual way of being "in process of becoming" that which it is (Kierkegaard, 1846/1971, p. 79; 1849/1973a, p. 163). Brock-elman (1985), for example, notes that "Selves are not things 'in' time, but temporal *processes* or *dynamic activities.* Selves are tensed" (p. 12). In constructing his dialectical system of logic to suggest how the reality of existence could be captured in a final "moment" of speculative conscious-ness, Hegel (1807/1967; 1816/1951) confounded this nature of the existing individual or self by reducing it to the timeless and logical "becoming" of pure, abstract thought. For the concrete, existing self, however, *time is of the essence:* To be a self is to become a self, and to become a self is to be forever caught up in the temporal and historical process of acting out one's own existence for as long as one lives. With both Hegel and this last point in mind, Kierkegaard (1846/1971) writes: "To be finished with life before life has finished with one, is precisely not to have finished the task" (p. 147). Immersed in his system of logic, Hegel *thought* he finished the task; his own existence, which is to say his "self," proved otherwise.

The existence of the self, be it yours or mine (or Hegel's for that matter), unfolds in and through its temporality. In stressing and developing this point, existentialists are moving us toward an ontological conception of the self, a conception that equates the self not first and foremost with what it means to exist as a teacher, a wife, a Christian, or whatever, but rather with what it means to exist as a human being. The self of a human being, or what Heidegger (1927/1962) terms *Dasein,* is its existence, its temporality, its "potentiality-for-Being" its possibilities. A human being's "own Self" finds its existential origins in this ontological "ability to be" that makes possible one's becoming a teacher, a wife, a Christian, or whatever. For any human being, this "ability" is uniquely his or her own (*eigen*); it defines the "authenticity" (*eigenlichkeit*), the most primordial "truth," of a human being. Hence, in the truest and most authentic sense of the term, this *self*-activity can be claimed by any person to be personally and properly "mine" (pp. 67–68, 163–168, 263; also Heidegger, 1975/1982, pp. 160–161, 170–173, 276–279, 286f).

We hear this claim being made, for example, whenever patients assert their freedom and demand that they be treated as "persons," as unique individuals, and not only as diseased bodies whose treatment "only by the numbers" reduces their existence to the statistics of mortality and morbidity tables (Hyde, 1986; 1990). Speaking more generally, we hear the claim whenever oppressed people and their supporters decide to be true to their selves and thereby take on the task of calling for a more authentic use of power — one devoted to promoting humankind's freedom of choice and thus what Nietzsche (1908/1969) describes as its "lofty *right* to its future" (p. 218). For Nietzsche, and existentialists generally, there is nothing more important that an individual can recognize and say "yes" to than what he or she is as a self who is always in the historical process of becoming itself. With this recognition and affirmation comes the courage for self-determination, the courage to question the nihilistic tendencies of the "herd morality" that seek to "unself man," to "corrupt" his *"innocence of becoming"* and his "instinct for freedom" by conditioning him to think, preach, and practice only those "truths" sanctioned by the herd (Nietzsche, 1887/1969, p. 87; 1901/1968, p. 299; 1908/1969, p. 292).

To say yes to the self is to say yes to freedom; existentialists would have us realize this fact: The self *is* freedom. In accordance with Kierkegaard's (1849/1973a, pp. 162–175; also 1846/1971, pp. 70–78) original observations, existentialists discover freedom to be "the dialectical element" of "possibility and necessity" structuring the self's temporality, its historical process of becoming itself. The possibility of the self defines its "infinitude," what it has "not yet" become in its existence, in its ability to be. The necessity of the self defines its "finitude," what it has been so far during its lifetime and is now. Freedom is the self's way of living this polar structure of its temporality: it is the constant interplay or "repetition" (Kierkegaard, 1843/1941; Heidegger, 1927/1962, pp. 436–438) between the possibility and the necessity of the self that takes form as the self engages in the acts of deciding and making choices about its future. Importantly, this interplay is not a matter of choice. The self *is* freedom. In any given situation, the decision not to assume the responsibility of making choices is still to have chosen not to choose. For Sartre (1943/1973), for example, it must thus be said that we are "condemned to be free"; we are "absolutely free and absolutely responsible" for any "situation" in which we exist (p. 653).

But with Sartre one must be careful. The "Sartrian Man" (Marcel, 1956/1968, pp. 47–90) is one whose freedom is "total and infinite" (Schrag, 1961, p. 196). Like Marcel and Schrag, however, most existential philosophers take exception to this "ultimate" (Guignon, 1986) view of freedom. This exception may be phrased as a question: If, as Sartre admits, freedom only and always takes place "in situation," then how can it be infinite, how can it avoid not being conditioned by the self's concreteness, by the necessity of the self's finitude, by what the self of a person was and is now?

The self's freedom is situated; its infinitude, its ability to be, its potentiality-for-Being its possibilities is always anchored to and constrained by past decisions, present involvements, the self's biological condition, and existing environmental factors — all of which pose the threat of fatalism and determinism. In reality, then, the self's actual freedom is not absolute but *finite* (Merleau-Ponty, 1945/1974, pp. 454–455). As its ability to be unfolds in and through time, freedom is never without that which can and does make its life a task, a struggle, a continual effort in survival. Jaspers' (1932/1970b) way of stating the matter is noteworthy: "A decision has been made; its outcome controls me, and at the same time it is still up to me as long as I live. The decision that has been made makes me feel inevitably determined; the chance to make my own decision makes me feel originally free" (p. 109). The feelings of being determined and being free go together. They form an existential dialectic: necessity *and* possibility; infinitude *and* finitude. Selves are tensed. The tension is historical, temporal. The tension is freedom.

Because we are those beings who have the emotional capacity to take an interest in and be concerned about our existence, about who we are as selves, we can have the experience of "selfhood" (Kierkegaard, 1849/1973a, pp. 146–147; Jaspers, 1932/1970b, pp. 34–42). The experience is one where, through an act of reflexivity, the self becomes related to itself and can now ask the question: Who am I? As the question is answered I not only disclose to myself something about my personal identity but I also come face to face with the question of my freedom: What, if anything, am I to do about who I am? Of course, my freedom is always there: I am in the habit of living it everyday. But if I am to know something about this freedom such that I can take control of it and have a personal say in how it should be practiced, I must add to the habit of living it the habit of thinking it. Am I a good husband? A good son? A good teacher? A good friend? Existentialists ask us to consider such questions in light of another one: What does it mean to exist as a human being? This question asks about that which makes it possible to ask the other questions and live their answers.

In turning now to a discussion of the next set of existentialist themes, we will see what it is about the modern world that encourages an avoiding of the question, why the question cannot be avoided, and how the question, when it is taken seriously, calls for an authentic response.

The Modern World, Ultimate Situations, and Authenticity

In his 1933 essay, "On the Ontological Mystery," Gabriel Marcel (1956/1968) offers an assessment of the plight of "modern man." The assessment is somewhat reminiscent of what Dostoevsky's narrator had to say about the topic; but it is also an important update. By 1933 "progress" in the modern world was readily associated with the development and maintenance of scientific and technological expertise. Such expertise brought with it "the emergence of a kind of vital schedule," a "time table" existence that conditioned individuals to see themselves "more and more as a mere assemblance of functions" (Marcel, 1956/1968, p. 10). As the guidebook for the 1933 Chicago World's Fair approvingly put it: "Science finds — Industry applies — Man conforms" (Pacey, 1983, p. 15). For Marcel, the situation was an indication that "modern man" had lost the awareness of "the sense of the ontological," the sense of what it means to exist as a human being: "if ontological demands worry him at all, it is only dully, as an obscure impulse" (1956/1968, pp. 9–10). And, as Gadamer (1976/1983) notes, this impulse must remain obscure in a "technological civilization" if the individual is "to maintain himself as *what he is:* one inserted for the sake of the smooth functioning of the apparatus" (p. 74, italics added).

With the existentialists, we have seen that for "the self" *time is of the essence.* In the modern world, with its technological imperative, the ontological significance of this phrase is given a *new* and more *functional* meaning — one that is better suited for the times and that thereby notifies us that "there is so much to do and so little time to do it, that he or she who hesitates is lost." Existentialists, to be sure, take exception to this transformation and to the "rational" habit of living that it breeds. The exception is registered throughout the movement of existentialism (e.g., Marcel, 1947/1978; Ortega y Gasset, 1930/1957; Jaspers, 1931/1959; Heinemann, 1953/1958; Barrett, 1958/1962; Wild, 1955). Importantly, this exception is not intended to create a community of Luddites. Rather, it seeks to have us remember *who we are* and *what we have become* in the modern world; it is an attempt to get us to realize that by allowing our sense of the ontological to atrophy in the face of a world driven by "technique," we are developing a "self-forgetfulness" (Jaspers, 1951/1970a, p. 121), a trained incapacity to understand that we are always more than the functions (roles) we perform and identify with in the sociopolitical apparatus of modern technological society. This "more" shows itself in our existence, our freedom, in our nature of being on the way, in the fact that, as selves, we are always in the emotional, historical, and temporal process of becoming who we are. For existentialists, only by remembering and respecting this fact can we prepare ourselves for dealing authentically with another fact of life — one whose various facets, what Jaspers (1951/1970a, pp. 19–23) describes as life's "ultimate situations," inevitably undermine the security promised to us by the ways and means of our technologically motivated lifestyles.

To exist is to live forever in the midst of ultimate situations; and this means that "I must die, I must suffer, I must struggle, I am subject to chance, [and] I must involve myself inexorably in guilt" (Jaspers, 1951/1970a, p. 20; also Ricoeur, 1960/1965). Ultimate situations mark the "boundaries" of human existence, the "limits" of our finitude: They confront us with the "reality of failure"; they are what comes to mind, if only for the moment, when our progress is impeded (if not shattered to its very core) by occurrences (e.g., illness) that disrupt our typical routines, our accustomed habits and relationships with things and with others. When threatened by ultimate situations our everyday and complacent ways of being-in-the-world are bracketed and put into question; we thereby experience the phenomenon of undergoing a "setback" in our lives. For existentialists, however, the setbacks fostered by ultimate situations are more than merely common occurrences whose existential interruptions are best forgotten because time is of the essence, because there is so much to do and so little time to do it that he or she who hesitates is lost. No, say existentialists: Ultimate situations are those happenings that naturally help us to cultivate our sense of the ontological; for they *set us back* to our authentic selves, to our *own* existence, whereby we are called upon to remedy as best as we can the ontological assault that the situations have brought to bare in our lives. As a way of clarifying in more concrete terms what this setback entails and requires, let us consider the following example drawn from the literature of existential psychology and psychiatry (e.g., Boss, 1957/1982; Frankl, 1967, 1946/1984; May, Angel, & Ellenberger, 1958; also see Hyde, 1983b, pp. 151–152).

A person seeking a cure for a perceived psychological problem brings a specific question to a psychoanalytic interview: Is this problem symptomatic of my truth, what I desire to become (and to be) as a human being? This question is being asked by a person who has suffered a setback; it is being asked by a self who, in a moment(s) of self-reflection, had an experience of selfhood whose meaning, at least for the time being, is a source of unforgettable guilt. A struggle is apparent. Truth is up for grabs. This struggle over truth has, in a death-like manner, put an end to a taken for granted habit of living. Death, of course, will prevail in the long run. But what about now? The future is in doubt. The contingency here (which, of course, was there all along) is where the person presently finds himself to be after experiencing the setback of an ultimate situation: He has been set back to his own existence, his own self, his own necessity and possibility. What is yet to come? Who can say for sure?

These questions accompany the person's original question concerning his "truth"; and they perforce admit anxiety: they speak of the future, the "not yet" of the person's life. "What is anxiety? It is the next day" (Kierkegaard, 1848/1939, p. 80; also 1844/1973b); it is the existential and thus ever present condition of not knowing what is to come of one's existence, or when the end will come; and it is the condition that tends to be covered up when all is "going well" with one's everyday habits of living.

What, then, is to be done? Will a "satisfactory" answer to this question dispel the person's anxiety? Perhaps. Will it also dispel the guilt he is experiencing because of his "abnormal" behavior? Again, perhaps. But guilt, like anxiety, is never something that can merely be left behind. Guilt is a condition of existence. As beings who are "condemned to be free" and who are thus always caught up in the process of making choices about the future, we can never escape the guilt that we are. For in choosing and actualizing certain existential possibilities, we are necessarily sacrificing other ones. And since, as selves, we *are* our possibilities, the sacrifice being made here makes us forever guilty of acts of omission (Heidegger, 1927/1962, pp. 325–335).

The setbacks of ultimate situations expose to us our guilt, the contingency and finitude of our existence, and the suffering and struggle that are concomitant with this contingency and finitude. Add to this the anxiety that brings this exposure into sharp focus and it might be easier (i.e., more economical and less threatening) to think about ultimate situations in terms of a somewhat pessimistic saying found on certain paraphernalia popularizing our present day "postmodern condition": "Life is tough and then you die!" Existentialists show some of their own postmodern inclinations in their reaction against the reifying tendencies of modern technological society. Reminding us about the ultimate situations of existence is one of the major ways that they articulate this reaction. This reminder, however, is not intended to produce a doctrine of pessimism; rather, in Sartre's (1957) words, its purpose is to cultivate an "optimistic toughness" (p. 35) in its readers—a toughness that is needed if we are to make "good" use of what the *angst* of ultimate situations reveals: our personal existence, our selves, our authenticity.

By now it should be clear that existentialists see an important relationship existing between a human being's authenticity and the anxiety that accompanies the experience of ultimate situations. Heidegger (1927/1962), for example, speaks of this relationship when he notes that the anxiety over ultimate situations "makes manifest in Dasein its *Being towards* its ownmost potentiality-for-Being—that is, its *Being-free for* the freedom of choosing itself and taking hold of itself. Anxiety brings Dasein face to face with its *Being-free for* . . . the authenticity of its Being, and for this authenticity as a possibility which it always is" (p. 232). In short, anxiety "individualizes" (p. 233) a human being by disclosing to this being its "primordial" condition of being open to the possibilities of Being. Authenticity is this condition of the self's "openness," its "not yet," the "more" of its temporality. Hence, if it is this condition that anxiety discloses, must it not therefore be admitted that the human being is something of a tragic creature? That is, when a human being is placed in a position to realize his or her authenticity, the "dreaded" emotion of anxiety announces its presence. How depressing. Why then bother ourselves about being authentic? Existentialists answer this question by emphasizing that there is another, more positive and life-giving side to the matter.

When anxiety brings us to an awareness of our authenticity it at the same time affords us an opportunity of "rebirth" (Jaspers, 1951/1970a, p. 20). This opportunity takes place in and through a "moment" (*Augenblick*) of vision and decision—a moment that calls upon human beings to face their possibilities with anticipation and conscience, to assume the ethical responsibility of affirming their freedom through resolute choice, and thus to become consciously/willingly/personally (i.e., authentically) involved in the creation of a meaningful existence (Kierkegaard, 1843/1941; Heidegger, 1927/1962, pp. 341–348, 386–389; Schrag, 1961, pp. 132–142). Owing to these uniquely related capabilities we can, like Nietzsche's (1883–1892/1986a) Zarathustra, say "yes" to life in the face of its ultimate situations, its uttermost negativities; we can, by way of a thoughtful and privileged moment, make a life-giving decision that affirms the truth of our power to take charge of our own lives even in the most distressful circumstances (cf. Frankl, 1946/1984; also Marcel, 1956/1968, pp. 28–29).

Of course, writing about this effort in decisive action is much easier than putting it into practice. Each of us is carrying the weight of our personal history, our necessity, when the issue of our authenticity is on the line because of some setback. The burden here can be great. Which of my possibilities have been sacrificed during my history? Which ones have been lost forever? In anticipating my future, which ones can and should be taken over in an act of "repetition" whereby the past can be translated from a burden into a creative possibility? Can I live with the guilt of not having chosen other possibilities? Am I ready for the struggle, the suffering, and the chance that I might fail?

Such questions are directly related to selfhood. "Selfhood is achieved, never simply given" (Schrag, 1961, p. 177); and it is achieved through the act of choice, through the freedom that I am. If this achievement is to be enacted authentically, existentialists contend, then I must assume the responsibility of my freedom of choice. I must choose my own self or others will choose it for me. The options here are as simple as they are important: either to choose or to be chosen, either to achieve integrity through resolute choice or to lose integrity through a retreat from choice. Although the orderly functions of our habits of living can all too easily have us forsake and forget its presence, we cannot escape this either/or, this condition of existence: "As truly as there is a future just so truly is there an either/or" (Kierkegaard, 1843/1959, p. 146).

Our authenticity is always before us, always challenging us (if only "dully") to make the best use of it, no matter how much anxiety must be endured. Existentialists prepare us to meet this challenge by reminding us of its inevitability, by arguing for the personal choice, commitment, and courage that are needed if the challenge is to be dealt with in an authentic manner, and by further reminding us that the challenge of living an authentic existence is a constant task. To exist, we must recall, is to live forever in the midst of ultimate situations. Death, suffering, struggle, chance, and guilt are always there to question any degree of certitude and complacency operating in our lives, in our nature of being on-the-way. The authentic person knows this, accepts it, and takes it seriously while living the commitment of his or her chosen possibilities. To accept and take seriously this knowledge is to be prepared and willing at any moment to question the integrity of one's self: Am I, for example, being a good husband? a good son? a good teacher? a good friend? If not, what should I do? And can I do it? Existentialists would have us ask such questions as a way of promoting our authentic selfhood. But as we shall now see in turning to the final set of related themes, they would also have us question our selfhood for the benefit of others.

Community and Communication

Because so much of what they have to say about authentic existence is rooted in their analysis of the world of the self (the *Eigenwelt*), existentialists are often accused of neglecting the issue of how the individual has a responsibility to form authentic relationships with others in the communal world (the *Mitwelt*) (e.g. see Adorno, 1964/1973; MacIntyre, 1967). This accusation finds some support in a selective perception of a certain strain of existentialist thought—one that is cultivated especially by Kierkegaard, Nietzsche, Heidegger, and Sartre. For example: To read Kierkegaard (1846/1962a, pp. 59–86) on that sociopolitical body known as "the public," or to read Nietzsche (e.g., 1901/1968, pp. 156–162; 1886/1966, pp. 110–114) on that same body but now described as "the herd," is to be given an extremely unflattering view of what happens to the existing self or "individual" when he or she seeks the security of conformity found in the ways and means of communal life. This view gains ontological support with Heidegger's (1927/1962, e.g., pp. 163–168, 210–224) analysis of "publicness," or what he also describes as the everyday world of the "they" (*das Man*, the "anonymous one"). Here one learns that the "everydayness" of Dasein's "being-with-others" is that of "inauthenticity." Existing as a "they–self," Dasein is inauthentic because it has succumbed to the "levelling" process of its community, to the standardizing function of common sense understanding, to the realm of habits, conventions, and customs wherein it is conditioned by others to believe that it "is leading and sustaining a full and genuine 'life' " (p. 222). Looking at this life and the interpersonal relationships that it entails, Sartre (1943/1973) recommends that we conceive the "Other" as being a constant impediment to the performance of our unique possibilities (pp. 340–400).

At first glance, these views of the *Mitwelt* may appear to offer little or no room for speaking about the likelihood and importance of forming authentic relationships with others. Such an assessment, however, would be somewhat unfair. For there exist at least two additional parts to the story being told by existentialists about our being-with-others; both of these parts, when read together, provide the necessary room for addressing the issue of authentic communality.

We began listening to the first of these two parts when discussing the existentialists' reaction to how the technological *Geist* of the modern world conditions us to see ourselves as but a mere assemblance of functions. The danger here is that of sacrificing and forgetting our existential freedom. But this danger, as the existentialists make clear, also extends to our relationships with others. Heidegger (1927/1962, pp. 156–159) is especially perceptive on this point. Drawing from his analysis of Dasein, Heidegger argues that the Other, understood in terms of his or her authenticity, is never merely some "thing-like" instrument or tool that can be used to perform a function for me in light of some "practical concern" (*Besorgen*). To treat the Other in this way is to demonstrate a lack of "personal concern" (*Fürsorge*) for his being, her freedom, their existence; it is, *essentially,* to depersonalize the Other (Schrag, 1961, pp. 41–43). This act of depersonalization is what is being questioned when existentialists speak "unkindly" about our being-with-others. Their solution to the problem brings us to the second part of their additional story about the communal world.

Existentialists readily admit that existing with others is an inescapable condition of one's existence. Even being alone presupposes a being-with-others, for I can be alone only because the Other is not present with me. "So far as Dasein *is* at all, it has Being-with-one-another as its kind of Being" (Heidegger, 1927/1962, p. 163). Owing to this indelible communal character of human existence and to the depersonalization that all too easily influences its nature, life for me and for the Other can indeed become a hell on earth. In order to counter this disconcerting situation, existentialists would have us engage in the challenge of living an authentic existence and helping others to do the same. The responsibility of meeting this challenge begins with the individual who has heard "the call of conscience" (Heidegger, 1927/1962, pp. 317–348) and who has moved beyond the depersonalizing tendencies of the "they" by assuming the personal and ethical responsibility of affirming her freedom through resolute choice. Such an individual is now in the position of taking on the additional responsibility of becoming the "voice" of conscience for others by engaging them in communication and encouraging them to realize their own unique possibilities (pp. 344–345).

Existentialists maintain that the decisive moment of authentic communality takes form in this act of encouragement, in communicating with others about whether or not some chosen course of action is beneficial to all concerned. As an individual struggling to live out the chosen possibilities of an authentic existence, I *can* become a source for the Other's authentic self-realization whereby he would develop a heightened sense of his freedom to choose, to act, and perhaps to change. But I also require the Other as a source of legitimation and, if need be, correction. For in declaring to the Other that my way of being and knowing is good, just, and truthful, there certainly exists the possibility that I may be "wrong." If it is to be authentic, my communication with the Other must not forget this possibility. In and through communication, I must test my selfhood *for* others so that it can in turn be tested *by* others:

> What I gain for myself alone in reflection would — if it were all — be as nothing gained.
> What is not realized in communication is not yet, what is not ultimately grounded in it is without adequate foundation. The truth begins with two.
> (Jaspers, 1952/1970a, p. 124)

How specifically should communication be practiced in order to bring about the reality of an authentic being-with-others? Existentialists answer this question with a certain problem in mind. Jaspers (1932/1970b) directs our attention to the problem when he notes that "I cannot be myself unless the other wants to be himself; I cannot be free unless he is free; I cannot be sure of myself unless I am sure of him. . . . For I do not reach the point of communication by my own action alone; the other's action must match it" (pp. 52–53). If the other's action does not match it, if she, for whatever reason, refuses to be open to my affirmed possibilities, then communication reaches an impasse; hence, the problem (cf. Johnstone, 1970).

Nietzsche (1901/1968) responds to this problem with a question: "How far to acknowledge in one's mind the rule, the commonplace, the petty, good, upright, the average nature, without letting oneself be vulgarized by them?" (p. 493). This question bespeaks Nietzsche's contempt for the "herd" and its tendency to restrict the authentic individual's "innocence of becoming," "creativity," and "will to power." "The tendency of the herd is directed toward standstill and preservation," writes Nietzsche, "there is nothing creative in it" (p. 162). Heidegger, too, is wary of this world of the "they" and its affect on the authentic individual's discourse. Although Heidegger (1949) admits that "Even the essential word, if it is to be understood and so become a possession in common, must make itself ordinary" (p. 275), he argues that the potential truth of the word, when talked out in terms of the common sense understanding of *das Man,* can all too easily be transformed into the language of "idle talk." According to Heidegger (1927/1962), idle talk is inauthentic discourse that "releases one from the task of genuinely understanding," "discourages any new inquiry and any disputation," and encourages people to follow "the route of *gossiping* and *passing the word along*" (pp. 211–214).

Kierkegaard (1846/1971) is equally fearful of this problem; yet he does offer something of a Socratic (and deconstructive) solution with his theory of "indirect" communication. Here the "objective uncertainty" of existence becomes the *modus operandi* for communicating with others in an authentic way: The authentic individual, says Kierkegaard, "is always just as negative as he is positive" (p. 78) about the truth of his world-view and attending actions. He must therefore avoid the solipsistic temptation to convey only the "results" of his personal deliberation (p. 217) and must instead, through acts of maieutic artistry, phrase his "communication in the form of a possibility" so that the recipient is compelled "to face the problem of existing in it" (p. 320). When communication is practiced in this way, according to Kierkegaard, it assumes a "difficult" form—one that challenges public conformity by *"taking away"* the tranquility that preserves such conformity (pp. 245–246). With this challenge comes the need to question the truths of all those who are involved in the ongoing conversation. Jaspers (1932/1970b), in what he terms the "loving struggle" of authentic communication, puts the matter this way: "What I say [to the Other] is intended as a question. I want to hear answers, never just to persuade or to compel. Unlimited response is essential to true communication. When the answer is not promptly forthcoming, it will remain an unforgotten challenge" (p. 61). Similar sentiments about being in authentic communication with others are also shared and developed, for example, by Marcel (1935/1949) in his discussion of the difference between "being" with others and "having" others under one's control, by Merleau-Ponty (1945/1974, pp. 178–199; 1969/1973) in his analysis of "authentic speech," and by Gadamer (1960/1975, pp. 330–447) in his hermeneutic philosophy of "conversation."

This concludes the discussion of the themes of existentialism. The topic of authentic communication may serve as a point of reference for summarizing our progress so far. Existentialists develop this topic in order to clarify how the existing self or individual must take on the ethical responsibility of forming authentic relationships with others—relationships that are meant to breed a communion between "I" and "Thou" (Buber, 1923/1970; see also Arnett, 1986), between people who are willing to take the time for and to assume the risk of being open to the possibilities of others. Nothing less than freedom and truth are at stake here: freedom to seek the truth and to guard against being suffocated by the truth. The "art" of communication, existentialists contend, must serve these ever unfolding ends; it must display the courage of saying "yes" to life's ultimate situations. Borrowing from Nietzsche (1901/1968), one could say that this art "is *worth more* than truth" (p. 451), for without this art and the freedom that fuels its authenticity, there would be no truth, no way of disclosing to others in a passionate, reasonable, and rational manner our emotional involvements with the world.

With this last point we have returned to the place where we began our examination of the themes of existentialism. The next task is to determine how what the existentialists would have us remember about ourselves can be applied to the theory and practice of rhetoric.

EXISTENTIAL RHETORIC

Existentialists tend to stand in the way of anyone who wishes to draw from their themes directives for constructing a favorable theory of rhetoric. In those rare moments when existentialists allow the topic of "rhetoric" (or "oratory") to enter into their discourse, they typically speak of it in less than honorable terms. They tell us, for example, that the practice of rhetoric is an eloquent way of persuading individuals to conform to the "untruth" of the "crowd" or "public" (Kierkegaard, 1846/1971, pp. 16–18; 1846/1962a, pp. 59–67; 1859/1962b, pp. 109–120); that it preserves the downgraded morality of the "herd" (Nietzsche, 1903/1986b; also Blair, 1983); and that it caters to the inauthentic ways of the "they" (Heidegger, 1927/1962, p. 178). Existentialists have this skeptical view of rhetoric partly because they still share certain biases with the philosophical tradition that they stand against and, more importantly for my present purposes, partly because they are radicals, activists at heart (Scott, 1964, p. 275). "In existence, the watchword is always *forward*," writes Kierkegaard (1846/1971, p. 368). Existentialists want people to be faithful to this watchword, to this becoming of existence. They want people to choose, not simply to be chosen; they want people to act, not simply to be acted on or moved; and they want people to create discourse that serves these ends. In short, existentialists want people to be authentic in both word and deed (Gusdorf, 1953/1965).

If existentialists are practicing what they preach (i.e., "authentic communication") when they express such things, then perhaps we can imagine them putting aside their philosophical biases for the moment to become *open to* the suggestion that what they also want is for people *to speak a rhetoric rather than merely allowing themselves to be spoken by a rhetoric*. Here, with their narrow-minded understanding of rhetoric before them, existentialists might ask: Can a theory of rhetoric be constructed to encourage this authentic performance of word and deed, and can we be of any help?

Because a primary goal of this essay is "to keep the conversation going" about existentialism and its potential worth for students of rhetoric, my affirmative answer to the question will be developed so as to take readers beyond what they can already find in the literature of Speech Communication (see footnote 2). I perform this extension by bringing into the conversation at certain points the work of three intellectuals — Hans Blumenberg, Michel Foucault, and Jacques Derrida — whose respective thinking on rhetoric and related matters is playing a significant role in the unfolding of a "postmodern" phenomenon: philosophy's "rhetorical turn." Although these intellectuals, to be sure, are not self-proclaimed "existentialists," my use of their ideas here to help mine the rhetorical potential of the themes of existentialism is intended to suggest that such a proclamation might very well be in order. A case study in rhetoric is also offered to help illustrate the theoretical directives being developed in this section.

Existential Freedom: The Ground of Rhetoric

Existentialists want people to speak a rhetoric rather than merely allowing themselves to be spoken by a rhetoric. To engage in the act of speaking a rhetoric is to be free to do so. It would seem, then, that freedom must be the ground upon which to construct an existentialist theory of rhetoric. The work of Hans Blumenberg provides a way of legitimating this suggestion.

In his essay, "An Anthropological Approach to the Contemporary Significance of Rhetoric," Blumenberg (1971/1987) describes "man" as a "biologically impoverished creature," a "creature of deficiency," a being who, because of this deficiency, must rely on his "actions . . . to take the place of the automatic controls that he lacks or correct those that have acquired an erratic inaccuracy" (p. 433). Blumenberg also maintains that because of this deficiency we can never be sure about whether or not we possess the necessary "definitive evidence" for knowing the "truth" of our reality. For Blumenberg, the necessity of rhetoric emerges out of this biological predicament. He writes that "Lacking definitive evidence and being compelled to act are the prerequisites of the rhetorical situation" (p. 441; cf. Bitzer, 1968). As creatures of deficiency we cannot avoid living in these situations and acting accordingly (i.e., rhetorically). Such action is a practice in survival, a way of holding our own as we struggle to know something about the truth of our situation. But this is not to say that rhetoric and its effects are merely wanting substitutes for the truth. Blumenberg emphasizes this point when he notes that "The antithesis of truth and effect is superficial, because the rhetorical effect is not an alternative that one can choose instead of an insight that one could *also* have, but an alternative to a definitive evidence that one *cannot* have, or cannot have yet, or at any rate cannot have here and now" (p. 436).

Existentialists would not disagree with Blumenberg's description of man as a creature of deficiency, although they certainly would supplement his biological vision of the human condition with an existential one — one that recognizes a more positive dimension of our biologically impoverished state. This dimension is our freedom, our potentiality, our authentic way of being open to the possibilities of Being; in short, it is what Jaspers (1951/1970a) describes as that which defines "man" as being "fundamentally more than he can know about himself" at any point in time (p. 63). For existentialists, human beings are "impoverished" not only because of their biological condition but also because they are always lacking the definitive evidence that would grant them the knowledge of what they are as beings who are always in the process of becoming themselves. But this dimension of their impoverishment, it must be remembered, is at the same time the source of their hope, the source of their actions: Owing to their freedom, human beings can act so as to become more than what they presently know themselves to be.

Blumenberg and existentialists join forces on the topic of human action, and there their wisdom can be shared. Blumenberg helps existentialists to realize that the necessity of rhetoric for human beings extends beyond the boundaries of the "crowd" or "public," the "herd," and the "they." Do not the teachings of existentialism affirm this point? Are not existentialists, themselves, speaking a rhetoric when they remind us of the definitive evidence that we are lacking about ourselves and how we must deal with this situation? "It is rhetoric," writes Blumenberg, "when one suggests to others, as a premise, that it is necessary to think and to act once again—or to do so for the first time ever" (1971/1987, p. 455). Existentialists, it seems, are rhetoricians: they can only retreat to reticence if they deny this fact.

On the other hand, existentialists help Blumenberg to remember that which he seems to forget: that action presupposes freedom. Without freedom the biologically impoverished creature could become nothing more than a conditioned animal destined to go through the "motions" that its conditioning dictates. Or, to put it another way, without freedom human beings would have no hope of speaking a rhetoric that is more than a conditioned response to a rhetoric that has already been spoken for and about them and that may be oppressive in nature. Freedom makes possible the rhetoric that both existentialists and Blumenberg speak. Hence, I think it is fair to say that an existentialist theory of rhetoric would take root in humankind's existential freedom and would proceed from there for the benefit of others—especially those who, if given the opportunity, would want to speak their minds and change their situations "for the better."

Authentic Rhetoric: Of the Self and For the Other (Self)

Existentialists speak a rhetoric in the name of freedom. Their actions must therefore be heard as also speaking on behalf of the "self" and its "authenticity," its condition of being open to (and free for) the possibilities of Being. In and through our authenticity each of us, as selves, exist as a "potentiality-for-Being" *more* than a "they self," *more* than what we are made to be as "subjects" of and for the "crowd" and the "herd." The rhetoric of existentialism is forever reminding us about the importance of taking this "more" seriously. Those who speak this rhetoric do so as selves who, at least for the moment, have moved beyond the depersonalizing tendencies of the "they" and who would have us do the same for the sake of our own authenticity as well as for the purpose of engaging other selves in "authentic communication." Might we say, then, that existentialists are speaking as well as calling for an authentic rhetoric: a rhetoric of the Self and for the Other (Self)?

This way of stating the matter may seem far too archaic and wrong-headed for anyone who has appropriated even a modest amount of the rhetoric of postmodern philosophy. Such a rhetoric is constantly on guard against the spector of "subjectivity" because, according to this rhetoric, the "self," in its historical being, is always a function of the discourse of others. Michel Foucault is one philosopher who has schooled us in this specific understanding of the self. I argue, however, that he is also a philosopher whose practice of criticism exemplifies what is being termed here an authentic rhetoric.

For Foucault, the self of an individual is only that which is configured by and materialized in the body politic, as this body *subjects* its members to certain ways of seeing, speaking, and writing about themselves to further *empower* the body of which they are a part. Ordered to function in this way, the self becomes rhetorically and ideologically situated in its society's "regimes of truth." This being the case, Foucault (1980) argues that "The individual [as subject or self] is an effect of power, and at the same time, or precisely to the extent to which it is that effect, it is the element of its articulation. The individual which power has constituted is at the same time its vehicle" (p. 98).

Foucault offers us a very Nietzschian view of the self, at least as the self is made in the image of the herd. And since Foucault (1988) admitted just before he died that his "entire philosophical development was determined by . . . [his] reading of Heidegger" (p. 250), we might also see Foucault offering us a conception of what Heidegger (1927/1962) terms the "herme-neutical Situation" of the "they-self" (pp. 274–278). Like both Nietzsche and Heidegger, Foucault chose to investigate this reality of the situated self not only to describe it but also to critique its "repressive" regimes of truth so that others could learn how a "transformation" of these regimes might be accomplished to bear better fruit (see Foucault, 1988, pp. 152–156). In their discussion of Foucault's philosophy, Blair and Cooper (1987) correctly characterize this goal of transformation as being an attempt to "enhance the potential for choice and free thought for humankind" (p. 168). Might it be said, then, that Foucault's philosophy is an effort in the creation of an authentic rhetoric, an effort in getting himself and others to speak a rhetoric rather than merely allowing themselves, as subjects of the "herd" and the "they," to be spoken by a rhetoric? Phrasing the question somewhat differently, is not Foucault making use of his self's authenticity, his "potentiality-for-Being" more than a "they-self," so that he can create a rhetoric of the Self and for the Other (Self)? And to raise one additional question along these lines: If others were not capable of realizing their own authenticity, who would Foucault be speaking to when trying to enhance choice and free thought?

If those who have appropriated Foucault's rhetoric want to argue that the self's authenticity is nothing but a discursive effect of the "will to power," then, as they say, more power to them. All that I have been trying to suggest is that Foucault had to be more than what he defined the self to be in order to share with others his thinking on the self; hence, his philosophical project can be used to illustrate what from an existentialist perspective would be termed an effort in the creation of an authentic rhetoric. Rhetorical scholars, I submit, are speaking of such a rhetoric whenever they see fit to identify a rhetorical "touchstone" (Black, 1965; Hyde & Smith, 1979). I do not think that existentialists would object to this specific way of appreciating the matter. I do think, however, that they would want to give the creators of such touchstones as much credit as existentially possible by seeing them as individuals who took on the personal and ethical responsibility of affirming their authenticity, their freedom, through resolute choice and who thereby were able to engage in the struggle of trying to speak a certain kind of rhetoric: not one of the "crowd," the "herd," and the "they," but rather one of the Self and for the Other (Self).

Is such a rhetoric a "pure" creation of some "autonomous" individual? Existentialists would not make such a claim; as indicated earlier, they readily admit that being-with-others is an inescapable condition of one's existence. What an individual is now in his finite freedom carries with it a history that has been influenced by the Other. But an individual's attempt to speak an authentic rhetoric defines an effort in trying to say something *more* about this history than what others are presently saying or not saying about it. Here, the individual puts her self on the line and announces something about the world that, in this particular self's opinion, has yet to be revealed in the vernacular of a community or audience that the individual has chosen to address. This, then, is what a rhetoric of the Self and for the Other (Self) is all about: it seeks to counsel people in the most original performance of freedom of speech in order to direct them in their appreciation of the future.

I now suggest how this existentialist conception of authentic rhetoric can be given further definition by relating it to the themes of emotion, temporality, and truth. This suggestion is developed with the help of Jacques Derrida's philosophical project of "deconstruction." To secure this help I first must say something about how Derrida's project can be seen as an ongoing attempt to cultivate an authentic rhetoric. I say this knowing full well that Derrida (1972/1982a, esp. pp. 63–67) has expressed serious reservations about the whole concept of authenticity, especially as it is developed by Heidegger. As I hope to show, however, Derrida, in a recent defense of his project, allowed the concept of authenticity to become the principal theme of deconstruction. I also hope to show that this move on Derrida's part is one that opens a way for recognizing how authentic rhetoric engages us in an emotional moment of decision whereby we have to make a choice about some existential truth.

Authentic Rhetoric: Making Use of Emotion to Make Time for Truth

One way of making the argument that Derrida's project of deconstruction is an effort in the creation of an authentic rhetoric would be to go the same route with him that I did with Foucault: Like Foucault, Derrida conceives the self as being but an effect of the discourse of others. Of the many different terms that he invents and discusses to make this point, the essential one is what he calls "the play of *différance.*" This play, according to Derrida (1972/1982b), defines the basic economy of language: it is the way in which language functions not only as a semiotic system of differences, of arbitrary and conventionalized signifier/signified relationships and oppositions, but also as a "temporizing" (or "deferring") movement of significations whereby any given semiotic system of meaning, as it takes form, always enters into an "intertextual" relationship with some other system that it is currently transforming.[3] For Derrida, the self is always situated in and comes to "know" itself through this play of *différance;* the self of an existing individual, he therefore maintains, can never be unto itself. For caught up in the play and rhetorical texture of *différance,* the self perpetually finds itself carrying some "trace" of the "other than self," some trace of past systems of meaning that, whether recognized or not, are there with the self as its constant co-authors.

As a deconstructionist, Derrida reads and interprets texts for the purpose of disclosing this coauthorship and any of its "reified and unthinking dogmas." Deconstruction, writes Derrida (1972/1982b), "is not *neutral.* It *intervenes*" (p. 93): through its "unorthodox" reading of writings, it seeks to

---

[3]Derrida's use of the word *"différance"* (as opposed to "difference") is meant to capture this simultaneous "differing" and "deferring" economy of language.

show and tell others that there is necessarily more meaning to texts than meets the eye, especially the eye of a self that knows only how to read and interpret in conformity with "institutionalized critical methods." Moreover, in performing this act of intervention, deconstruction offers itself to others as a way of helping them to realize that "Every culture needs an element of self-interrogation and of distance from itself, if it is to transform itself" (Derrida, 1984, p. 116), if it is to become something different, something other and more than what it presently is under the "official political codes governing reality" (p. 120).

Now, given this admittedly brief (but I hope fair) description of what Derrida is attempting to say and do with his project of deconstruction, could it not be said of him what was said of Foucault: namely, that he is engaged in the existential process of trying to create an authentic rhetoric, of trying to get himself and others to "write" a rhetoric rather than merely allowing themselves, as subjects of some herd-like order, to be "written" by a rhetoric? In other words, is not Derrida making use of his self's authenticity, his "potentiality-for-Being" more than just another indoctrinated reader and writer of texts, so that he can create a rhetoric of freedom, a rhetoric of future possibilities, a rhetoric of the Self and for the Other (Self)?

As noted above, Derrida has taken a stand against the language of authenticity. I thus suspect that he would rather have others see his project on its own terms. That is, deconstruction is but an attempt to further the temporizing movement of the play of *différance* that is always functioning to destabilize, deconstruct, and transform the semiotic systems of meaning that have been constructed by a culture from out of the play of *différance* and that function to stabilize its temporizing movement (Derrida, 1988, p. 147). Indeed, Derrida tells us that the "principal theme" of deconstruction is the "destabilization" characterizing the "intertextuality" of systems of meaning (p. 147). Furthermore, Derrida equates his project of deconstruction with this destabilization, which he defines as "the true source of anxiety" haunting those "conservatives" who seek only the stability of their own meaning systems (p. 147). Is deconstruction, then, an effort in creating anxiety? It would seem so. But what is anxiety? Answering this question in strictly Derridian terms poses a problem; for with these terms one can only say that anxiety is the process wherein some existing individual or self is having the experience of being deconstructed by the temporizing movement of the play of *différance*. This answer, however, begs the question, thereby leaving deconstruction (or that which is an effort in creating anxiety) undefined by its own terms. Deconstruction must therefore be more than what it is willing to admit about itself. Hence, the question must be raised again: What is anxiety? This time, though, let us answer the question in less restrictive terms.

The experience of anxiety is a destabilizing one, to be sure. But this destabilizing experience does not find its "true source" in the temporizing movement of the play of *différance;* rather, as existentialists have shown, anxiety is first made possible by the "objective uncertainty" characterizing a self's temporal existence. Anxiety is the existential experience of coming face to face with *this* uncertainty, with the self's existential condition of being open to and free for the possibilities of Being. In other words, the "true source" of the destabilizing experience of anxiety is a human being's "authenticity," its nature of being "on the way" towards its future, towards that which it is "not yet."

By equating his project of deconstruction with the destabilizing experience of anxiety, Derrida (although he does not admit it) has at the same time allowed for another variable to become part of the equation. Is this to say, then, that the principal theme of deconstruction is perforce the self's "authenticity"? How could it be otherwise? Without this variable there would be nothing: that is, no human beings who, through their capacity to write and speak about their existential condition, bring into concrete existence the play of *différance* so to form meaningful relationships with reality and with each other. We can and often do experience anxiety over the deterioration of these relationships because, with this deterioration, we are brought closer to our "maker." Is this maker God? It certainly is us: we who in and through our authenticity, our being open to the possibilities of Being, have the freedom and the power to *make a difference* for our *own* benefit and for the benefit of *others.*

With his project of deconstruction, Derrida wants such a difference to be made. But like all human beings, he first needs the authenticity of his "self" in order to do it. To deny this existential truth is to commit what might be termed *deconstructive suicide.* Thus, because Derrida is alive and well and continuing "on the way" to do his work, I would again suggest that his project of deconstruction is an effort in the creation of an authentic rhetoric. And this being the case, I would offer one additional and related observation about this project: it must also be an effort in what existentialists might term a "making time for truth." Allow me briefly to explain.

Deconstruction, we have seen, is a rhetorical act of intervention into the discourse of others. It commits this act to destabilize this discourse, its meanings, and thus its purported "truth" claims. Truth is put up for grabs when deconstruction enters the scene and creates anxiety with its alternative readings and interpretations of contextualized truths. Existentially speaking, it might thus be said that deconstruction is its own "ultimate situation," for it seeks to have its readers experience a "setback" in their accustomed habits of interpretation. Here, with this setback, is where the anxiety sought for by deconstruction comes into play—an anxiety made possible by the authenticity of readers who are willing (like it or not) to be *open to* what

Derrida has to say with his own interpretations. Are these interpretations truthful? Certainly not in the sense of a correspondence theory of truth or a Platonic theory of mimesis (Norris, 1987, pp. 52–55). But they are at least being truthful at that most basic existential and rhetorical level of truth-telling where, as Schrag (1986) puts it, truth begins to happen "as the disclosure of possibilities for agreed upon perspectives on seeing the world and acting within it" (p. 187). Raising these possibilities is how deconstruction attempts to make a difference in the lives of others; it is how deconstruction, through the inciting of anxiety, encourages its readers to engage in a "moment of decision" whereby they have to make a choice about meaning and its truth. In short, the rhetoric of deconstruction makes a difference by making time for truth. And it does this by treating us authentically.[4]

But is all this to say that the effort to create an authentic rhetoric must necessarily be related, as in the case of Derrida, to the inciting of anxiety in others? Is anxiety the only emotion that enables the self and the other to speak a rhetoric so that they can make time for truth? Existentialists might feel more comfortable with this second way of stating the question. Although they find anxiety to be *the* emotion having the most *fundamental* relationship with a human being's authenticity, I do not believe that they would go so far as to say that anxiety is the only emotion that can be used by a rhetor to make time for truth. Given their arguments about what constitutes an authentic existence, existentialists should be willing to admit that any emotion warrants recognition as serving this exercise in "reason" (Jaspers, 1935/1973; 1938/1984) as long as the emotion affords others the opportunity for a moment of decision—a moment that, as detailed earlier, calls upon them to face their possibilities with anticipation and conscience, to assume the ethical responsibility of affirming their freedom through resolute choice, and thereby to become consciously/willing/personally (i.e., authentically) involved in the creation of a meaningful existence. Having no explicit and positive theory of rhetoric of their own, however, existentialists never really put themselves on the line with respect to this issue of the rhetorical and reasonable use of emotion.

So far, my way of compensating for this lack of an explicit and positive theory of rhetoric in existentialism has been to suggest how—with the help of Blumenberg, Foucault, and Derrida—an existentialist conception of authentic rhetoric can be given expression. In all of this, theory has had priority over practice. As a way of reversing this priority somewhat, I now bring this second section to a close by turning briefly to a case study in

---

[4]If this conclusion is denied by Derrida and his followers, then how would they justify (politically and ethically) their deconstructive activities? Are those activities just a matter of "free play"? I doubt it.

rhetoric that not only serves to illustrate in concrete terms what has been said so far about an existentialist conception of authentic rhetoric, but also enables one to see how such a rhetoric can make time for truth by using more than the emotion of anxiety. The case is that of the late Jory Graham.

Authentic Rhetoric: On the Way to Reason and Rationality

Jory Graham was a journalist who experienced the setback of an ultimate situation: she was diagnosed as having cancer, had a bilateral mastectomy, and still her cancer metastasized. From 1977 until her death from cancer in 1983, she wrote about her situation in a column, "A Time for Living," which appeared in 50 American newspapers reaching 5½ million readers weekly. She also detailed her experiences in her 1982 book, *In the Company of Others: Understanding the Human Needs of Cancer Patients* (which will be the basis for my discussion here). She did all of this having learned from personal experience that "dying and its anguish are wholly individual" (p. 128). She did all of this having also learned from personal experience that "In truth, cancer comes with something worse than a death sentence: the denial of ourselves as individuals still able to manage our own affairs, direct our own lives, contribute to our households and the lives of others dependent upon us . . ." (pp. 3–4). She did all of this because medical science lacked the definite evidence for determining the cause of cancer and therefore was unable to offer a "guarantee" regarding its cure (p. 6). And she did all of this because, as she put it, "In accepting cancer as the probable cause of my death, I realize that I now have nothing but my life to lose. I am free to speak out, to crusade for the rights of cancer patients everywhere. . . . Yet my voice is nothing if it is not joined by yours" (p. 23).

Graham's crusade was authentic. She was writing at a time when cancer patients were still being spoken by a dominating rhetoric that could be heard from both inside and outside the medical establishment. This rhetoric was deficient in hope and self-determination: it too often spoke of cancer patients only in terms of mortality and morbidity statistics; it told them that they were "*doomed*" (p. 12); it called them "victims" (p. 5); it led others, through fear and mythology, to view them as "pariahs" (p. 4); and it turned them against themselves by condemning them to a world of guilt, self-pity, and emotional isolation (pp. 1–15). "It is terrible enough when others write us off, but catastrophic when we discount ourselves," wrote Graham (p. 117). And she also wrote: "So help me God, I do not know whether the race is for man to conquer cancer or to conquer his feelings about it." (p. 6).

Graham set out to help others conquer their feelings about cancer. She did this by speaking a rhetoric of the Self and for the Other (Self), a rhetoric that interrupted the flow of an already spoken rhetoric in order to make time for truth. Her actions here were twofold: First, she assumed the ethical responsibility of affirming her freedom of choice by engaging in the deconstructive act of being what Sontag (1966; 1978) terms "against interpretation." That is, she sought to destabilize certain reified systems of meaning and "truth" that functioned to marginalize and silence the voice of the so-called "demoralized, pitiful cancer patient" (p. 24). For example, as a way of challenging what Foucault (1963/1975) terms "[t]he *restraint* of clinical discourse" (p. xix), she cited a recent essay in gynecology and obstetrics (Gerbie, 1977) wherein it is said "that the 'proper treatment [for cancer of the vulva] although disfiguring, is not mutilative' " (Graham, 1982, p. 102; Gerbie, 1977, p. 4). After responding to this with the simple and startling question "*Not* mutilative?," and then going on to quote again from the textbook whereby the reader can see in a lengthy passage the sterilized language that is used to define a radical vulvectomy, Graham (1982) added her own voice to the discussion by noting:

> The author is playing with words when he says that the procedure is not mutilative. It is massive amputation, but if it can be successfully denied through word magic, then the physician can dismiss the intensity of his patient's grief when she weeps over what has been done to her (p. 102).

Perhaps one can see from this quotation that Graham had more to say about her topic than what is *not* the case. Whenever she deconstructed a "truth" she also reconstructed a "truth"; and typically these reconstructed truths gave expression to the importance of rehabilitating the emotional life of cancer patients. Listen, for example, to what she tells her fellow cancer patients about developing a "healthy anger" toward their situations:

> Healthy anger gives vitality. It is a glorious sign that we're far from dead. It makes us fight for our jobs — and pride makes us work twice as hard at them. Healthy anger gives us purpose, challenges us to make new decisions, encourages old ideas: to enroll in the courses we've always wanted to take; to embark on the trip we've always wanted to make; to create the journal that is our legacy to our children and our grandchildren . . . (p. 26).

It was such a healthy anger that got Graham to speak her mind in the first place. And this makes perfect sense from an existential, phenomenological point of view. The health of anger, its ability to function in a reasonable and rational manner, shows itself as the emotion gets people to distance themselves mentally from a debilitating situation and, with the advantage of this distance, to transform the situation's present meaning by interpreting (disclosing) it in a way that enhances their self-respect (Solomon, 1976, *passim*). Healthy anger (unlike self-pity, for example) is a "great equalizer" (p. 284): it enables us to take matters into our own hands instead of remaining subservient to the "inappropriate" behavior of others. Moreover, healthy anger makes use of our authenticity, our freedom, our ability to be more than what we are now because, as Graham points out in the above quotation, it "challenges us to make new decisions" and "encourages old ideas." Put in more existentialist terms, healthy anger involves us in the existential process of "repetition"; for, as Schrag (1961) reminds us, "In repetition I take up my past, project it as a future possibility, and thus am able to make an authentic choice with the whole of my being. Repetition makes ethical choices possible" (p. 135) and thereby furthers the development of one's authentic selfhood.

Graham engaged in repetition by first using her anger for her own benefit and then sharing its disclosures with others. In so doing she made time for truth; and in Graham's case, this truth had much to do with the authenticity of a class of people who had been conditioned by a currently spoken rhetoric to forget and forsake their authenticity, their freedom, their existentially sanctioned right to be more than lost members of some "crowd" or some "herd." In using her anger to speak a rhetoric that addressed this right, she sought to fix responsibility, to be a voice of conscience for others, to change a certain set of societal moods, and to move cancer patients and their keepers to action. Although her cancer unfortunately made it all too apparent that she was a "creature of deficiency," her authentic rhetoric was proof that she was also more than that.

Blumenberg (1971/1987) tells us that "Rhetoric is a system not only of soliciting mandates for action but also of putting into effect and defending, both with oneself and before others, a self-conception that is in the process of formation or has been formed" (p. 442). Owing to the success of her rhetoric (at least as indicated by the responses to her column and book), perhaps it can be said that Graham helped to create such a system. Or, borrowing a phrase from John Dewey (1927/1954) perhaps it can be said that she helped to "call a public into being" (p. 27). But dare I make such affirmative use of the terms "system" and "public" when developing an existentialist conception of authentic rhetoric? At least with the case of Jory Graham in mind, I do not believe that existentialists would object at this point. The public that Graham helped to call into being—through the rationality of her anger (and other emotions as well[5]), through her reason,

---

[5]For example, like certain existentialists (e.g., Jaspers, 1932/1970b, pp. 64–66), Graham also emphasized the emotion of "love" as being essential for developing one's authentic selfhood. Now if only existentialists would answer the question: What is the fundamental relationship that exists between love and anxiety?

through her rhetoric—was one that formed a system of meaning and truth that spoke (and still speaks) as directly as possible to the question of what it means to exist as a human being. Given what they stand for, existentialists could only favor such a public, or system, or realm of authentic rhetoric. But, as noted at the beginning of this section, they never directly admit as much. And that creates certain problems that will have to be addressed in the final section of this essay and after we remember some of what has been said so far about the philosophy of existentialism and its relationship to the theory and practice of rhetoric. Throughout this effort in remembrance and critique I will also offer some brief remarks concerning how existentialism enters into a give and take relationship with the other philosophical perspectives being discussed in this book.

REMEMBRANCE AND CRITIQUE

Remembrance

Existentialism is a philosophy of remembrance, a philosophy that is forever reminding us about what it means to exist as a human being. Being reminded of something we necessarily do everyday can be quite annoying. And if we are doing it well, if, as "they" say, we are "really into the swing of things" with our habits of living, why disrupt this momentum and make it difficult by becoming philosophical about "what it all means"?

But who among us is so blessed, so perfect, that he or she will never have to become philosophical about matters of daily existence? Does not the contingency marking such matters guarantee that sooner or later we will find ourselves assuming something of an existentialist perspective on life? Perhaps we should remember:

> The desire to lead a philosophical life springs from the darkness in which the individual finds himself, from his sense of forlornness when he stares without love into the void, from his self-forgetfulness when he feels that he is being consumed by the busyness of the world, when he suddenly wakes up in terror and asks himself: What am I, what am I failing to do, what should I do? (Jaspers, 1951/1970a, p. 121)

Existentialists want to prepare us for answering these questions in an authentic manner. They do this by involving us in a phenomenology of lived existence whereby what has become concealed by our self-forgetfulness is brought into view. This involvement moves us away from the philosophy of idealism and toward the philosophy of social materialism.

For existentialists, idealism is itself a form of self-forgetfulness since, in the spirit of Hegel, it ends up confusing existential being with mental being (the life of the mind) and then further elevates the confusion by proclaiming that the "true" meaning of existence can be captured by the abstract and dialectical thought of reason. Social materialism helps to remedy this confusion by bringing the life of the mind back to where it makes its living: in the interrelated and interdependent regions of the environmental/ biological world (the *Umwelt*) and the communal world (the *Mitwelt*). Here, with Marx and his followers, we learn how the political and economic employment of these two regions by the bourgeoisie can and does diminish the proletariat's livelihood. As witnessed in their critiques of the sociopolitical apparatus of modern technological society, existentialists also have much to say about this dehumanizing and depersonalizing treatment of human beings. When existentialists speak to us about this phenomenon their assessments are informed by their phenomenological appreciation of the *Eigenwelt* or the world of the "self." Marx (1844/1973, pp. 137–139; 1846/1974, pp. 42–48) denied this world any existential status; for him, there is the *Umwelt,* the *Mitwelt,* and nothing else. The existentialist would wonder how the social materialist could be this self-forgetful. More memory is needed.

Existentialists direct us toward an ontological understanding of the self. The self of a human being (Dasein) is its existence, its temporality, its "potentiality-for-Being" its possibilities. The self is the necessity of its past and the possibility of its future. The self is freedom. Existentialists remind us of all of this; they remind us of what we come to face when experiencing the setbacks of ultimate situations. That these setbacks can be the cause of great anxiety for human beings is a crucial fact for existentialists: Anxiety is a self having to face its future after its accustomed habits and relationships with things (in the *Umwelt*) and with others (in the *Mitwelt*) have been deconstructed by the contingency of human existence. Anxiety is a self that has been set back to itself. In short, anxiety "individualizes" a human being by disclosing to this being its *own* authentic existence; hence, if only for a moment, the experience of anxiety serves to certify in a fundamental way the existence of the *Eigenwelt*.

Anxiety and existentialism go hand in hand, at least initially. They both set us on a course whereby we are given the opportunity to see through our self-forgetfulness and to understand something about what it means to exist as a human being. Deconstruction is their modus operandi. Unlike anxiety, however, existentialism performs this operation in a methodical manner; its spokespersons offer us careful descriptions of what can be witnessed as we move away from "being consumed by the busyness of the world" and toward the authenticity of our existence. These descriptions form a rhetoric that defines the themes of existentialism. We must not, however, read this rhetoric as being but an effort in deconstruction. Pragmatism is also a part of the project. When existentialists speak to us about the need to put our authenticity to "good" use by assuming the ethical responsibility of affirming our freedom through resolute choice, they are calling us to responsible action. Here their rhetoric is making a case for the importance of reconstruction. Existentialists deconstruct meaning so that they and others can reconstruct meaning. They do this in the name of freedom. They do this by speaking a rhetoric of the Self and for the Other (Self). They do this by making use of emotion to make time for truth. And they want us to do the same. For they maintain that only by becoming involved in this creative process of authentic communication can we keep alive and legitimate our right to see ourselves as rational beings.

Critique

The case of Jory Graham was presented to suggest how this creative process actually takes form in the world of praxis. With Graham's deconstruction and reconstruction of the life-world of cancer patients we see in concrete terms what it means to speak a rhetoric rather than merely allowing ourselves, as subjects of the "crowd," the "herd," and the "they," to be spoken by a rhetoric. Graham would have us appropriate and preserve the system of meaning and truth that she reconstructed through her rhetoric; she would have us support a public that she helped to produce. Existential-ists could not deny this request without contradicting themselves, for the request is rooted in Graham's having made "good" use of her authenticity by assuming the ethical responsibility of affirming her freedom through resolute choice. In Graham's case, given what she is advocating, it should be more than easy for existentialists to avoid the contradiction (despite their nervousness over "systems" and "publics"). But what about those cases that are not so easy? For example, would existentialists side with those orators who make good use of their authenticity by calling for the legalization of abortion, or would existentialists side with those who also put their authenticity to good use by telling us that abortion must never be legalized because it is an act of murder, plain and simple?

If existentialists want to be "true" to their authenticity, they must make a choice here or others will choose for them. Perhaps they would allow this to happen, but then they would be inauthentic. Or perhaps they would avoid contradicting themselves by *choosing* to argue that both positions are equally satisfactory because each is authentic. Sartre (1957), for example, would certainly be happy with this relativistic approach because he main-tains that "To choose to be this or that is to affirm at the same time the value of what we choose, because we can never choose evil. We always choose the good, and nothing can be good for us without being good for all" (p. 17). But where does this get us, practically speaking?

Existentialists are quite vague when it comes to affirming the kinds of systems of meaning and truth that we ought to produce and preserve. On matters of communication and rhetoric, it is the form, not the content, the process, not the product, the creating, not the preserving, that commands most of their attention and energy. Put another way, existentialists are much more interested in the question of our authenticity than in what our authenticity should be about. The relativism that can be found in existentialist thought because of this committed interest defines existentialism's Achilles heel; critics of the philosophy know it well. Hence, those like Adorno (1964/1973), for example, argue that if the "jargon" of authenticity only tells us that our goodness lies in our freedom of choice, then those who speak this jargon must be condemned for singing "songs of praise" (p. 24) when confronted by realities of misery and destruction brought about by the so-called "authentic" acts of people existing in high and powerful places.

But the "jargon" of authenticity is not as politically and ethically empty as its critics would have us believe. We need only remember existentialism's critique of the ways of modern technological society to confirm this point. When this critique takes form, realism replaces relativism, realities of misery and destruction *are* brought into view so that we can better understand their "truth," and the only songs of praise to be heard are those reminding us about the importance of the reality (truth) of our authenticity and how it grants us the opportunity to be "more" than slaves to some herd mentality. What the content of this "more" ought to be is a question that existentialists only answer in the negative with their critique of technological society; the rest is left up to us, as it must be if existentialists are to be true to the reality of our authenticity.

Is this an invitation to relativism once again? I think it is; although this time the invitation is more selective, or at least more specific. For now we are encouraged to remember, in the face of misery and destruction, that making "good" use of our authenticity is not just a matter of affirming our freedom through resolute choice; we must also become ethically responsible actors by taking seriously how others will be affected by our personal commitments. It is this ethical requirement of authenticity that ends up being brutalized by Heidegger when, in the early 1930s, he narrows his vision of the Other so that he can utter the party line of National Socialism. To be sure, just making "good" use of one's authenticity can be a horrible and unforgiveable mistake.[6]

So let us remember, but not only for the benefit of existentialism: The ethical requirement of authenticity calls the Self toward the Other. In struggling to live out the chosen possibilities of an authentic existence, I must be *open to* the possibilities of others; I must be willing to test my

---

[6]Heidegger's involvement with National Socialism occurs after he moves his philosophical investigations of "Being" beyond his existential analytic of Dasein's authenticity (*Being and Time,* 1927/1962). But the question remains: To what extent did Heidegger's "decision" for National Socialism presuppose his philosophy of existence? Much debate continues to surround this question. See, for example, Löwith (1988); Wolin (1988). Also see Zimmerman (1981, pp. 169–197).

selfhood *for* others so that it can in turn be tested *by* others. I must, as Orr (chapter 4) would have it, show myself to be a critical rationalist. All this is needed to take the test. To pass it, however, requires something more, something that existentialists, for the most part, refuse to cast in a favorable light: the art of rhetoric. Without this art I cannot reach out to the Other, except through the violence of physical force. Without this art I cannot be a "voice of conscience" for the Other; and without this art the Other cannot be a voice of conscience for me. In short, without the art of rhetoric the ethical requirement of authenticity—a requirement that existentialism cannot afford to be without—cannot come into being. Existentialism stripped of rhetoric is bare, indeed. Existentialists do not see it that way. They are very much mistaken.

Conclusion

Blumenberg (1971/1987) makes the point that "Rhetoric teaches us to recognize rhetoric, but it does not teach us to legitimate it" (p. 448). As a philosophy of remembrance, existentialism sends us back to the muck and mire of the contingency of human existence; like rhetoric, it earns its living there. Sometimes it is all too easy to take for granted those who we work with everyday. Moreover, sometimes we only recognize their presence when we notice that they are doing something "wrong." One can only imagine where existentialism would be today if its leading representatives had taken the time to develop a more careful understanding of their fellow worker's being. In this chapter I tried to do just that.

Despite its rather uneducated view of the art of rhetoric, existentialism reveals itself to be a major source of legitimation for the art. Its themes hold the memory of the kinds of things that rhetoric must struggle with on a daily basis. And this memory runs deep—so deep in fact that existentialism becomes a presupposition of all the other philosophies being discussed in this volume. Granted, its attraction to human authenticity can be problematic at times. I am still waiting for an existentialist to tell me specifically how to resolve those types of exigencies (e.g., the abortion issue) that break our hearts and inspire violence. The ethical requirement of authenticity "only" informs us that we are obligated to reach out to others, to speak *with* them, to keep the conversations going for as long as it takes. This "wait and see" outlook, this *ex post actu* attitude, is hard on one's nerves. But it could be worse, much worse in fact. Think about it! What happens when the conversations stop? Where will rhetoric be then? Existentialism legitimates rhetoric. And, yes, rhetoric is quite capable of returning the favor.[7]

---

[7]I wish to express my gratitude to the following individuals who were kind enough to critique earlier versions of this essay: Wesley Avram, Leah Ceccarelli, G. Thomas Goodnight, Richard Lanigan, Stephen O'Leary, Calvin Schrag, and Craig Smith.

REFERENCES

Adorno, T. W. (1973). *The jargon of authenticity* (K. Tarnowski & F. Will, Trans.). Evanston, IL: Northwestern University Press. (Original work published 1964)

Anderson, R. (1963). Kierkegaard's theory of communication. *Speech Monographs, 30,* 1–14.

Aristotle. (1954). *Rhetoric* (W. R. Roberts, Trans.). New York: The Modern Library.

Arnett, R. C. (1986). *Communication and community: Implications of Martin Buber's dialogue.* Carbondale, IL: Southern Illinois University Press.

Baird, A. C. (1962). Speech and the "new" philosophies. *Central States Speech Journal, 13,* 241–246.

Barrett, W. (1962). *Irrational man: A study in existential philosophy.* New York: Anchor Books. (Original work published 1958)

Berger, J. (1965). *The success and failure of Picasso.* Harmondsworth, England: Penguin Books.

Bitzer, L. F. (1968). The rhetorical situation. *Philosophy & Rhetoric, 1,* 1–14.

Black, E. (1965). *Rhetorical criticism: A study in method.* New York: Macmillan.

Blair, C. (1983). Nietzsche's lecture notes on rhetoric: A translation. *Philosophy & Rhetoric, 16,* 94–129.

Blair, C., & Cooper, M. (1987). The humanist turn in Foucault's rhetoric of inquiry. *Quarterly Journal of Speech, 73,* 151–171.

Blumenberg, H. (1987). An anthropological approach to the contemporary significance of rhetoric (R. M. Wallace, Trans.). In K. Baynes, J. Bahman, & T. McCarthy (Eds.), *After philosophy: End or transformation?* (pp. 429–458). Cambridge, MA: MIT Press. (Original work published 1971).

Boss, M. (1982). *Psychoanalysis and daseinsanalysis* (L. B. Lefebre, Trans.). New York: Da Capo. (Original work published 1957)

Brockelman, P. (1985). *Time and self: Phenomenological explorations.* New York: Crossroad Publishing.

Buber, M. (1970). *I and thou* (W. Kaufmann, Trans.). New York: Charles Scribner's Sons. (Original work published 1923)

Bultmann, R. (1957). *The presence of eternity.* New York: Harper & Bros.

Campbell, K. K. (1970). The ontological foundations of rhetorical theory. *Philosophy & Rhetoric, 3,* 97–108.

Campbell, K. K. (1971). The rhetorical implications of the axiology of Jean-Paul Sartre. *Western States Speech Journal, 35,* 155–161.

Camus, A. (1955). *The myth of Sisyphus and other essays.* (J. O'Brien, Trans.). New York: Random House. (Original work published 1942)

Christopherson, M. F. (1963). Speech and the "new" philosophies revisited. *Central States Speech Journal, 14,* 5–11.

Consigny, S. (1977). Rhetoric and madness: Robert Pirsig's inquiry into values. *Southern Speech Communication Journal, 43,* 16–32.

de Beauvoir, S. (1972). *The ethics of ambiguity* (B. Frechtman, Trans.). Secaucus, NJ: Citadel Press. (Original work published 1948)

Derrida, J. (1982a). *Margins of philosophy* (A. Bass, Trans.). Chicago: University of Chicago Press. (Original work published 1972)

Derrida, J. (1982b). *Positions* (A. Bass, Trans.). Chicago: University of Chicago Press. (Original work published 1972)

Derrida, J. (1984). Deconstruction and the other. In R. Kearney (Ed.), *Dialogues with contemporary continental thinkers: The phenomenological heritage.* (pp. 107–126). Manchester: Manchester University Press.

Derrida, J. (1988). Afterword: Toward an ethic of discussion (S. Weber, Trans.). In J.

Derrida, *Limited Inc.* (S. Weber & J. Mehlman, Trans.). (pp. 111-160). Evanston, IL: Northwestern University Press.

Dewey J. (1954). *The public and its problems.* Chicago: Swallow Press.

Dostoevsky, F. (1960). *Notes from underground and the grand inquisitor* (R. E. Matlow, Trans.). New York: E. P. Dutton. (Original work published 1864)

Earle, W. (1976). *Public sorrows & private pleasures.* Bloomington, IN: Indiana University Press.

Foucault, M. (1975). *The birth of the clinic: An archaeology of medical perception* (A. M. S. Smith, Trans.). New York: Vintage Books. (Original work published 1963)

Foucault, M. (1980). *Power/knowledge: Selected interviews and other writings, 1972-1977* (C. Gordon, Ed.; C. Gordon, L. Marshall, J. Mepham, & K. Saper, Trans.). New York: Pantheon.

Foucault, M. (1988). *Politics, philosophy, culture: Interviews and other writings, 1977-1984* (L. D. Kritzman, Ed.; A. Sheridan, J. Harding, D. Parent, A. Baudot, J. Couchman, A. Forster, T. Levin, I. Lorenz, J. O'Higgens, and J. Rahn, Trans.). New York: Routledge.

Frankl, V. E. (1967). *Psychotherapy and existentialism: Selected papers in logotherapy.* New York: Simon & Schuster.

Frankl, V. E. (1984). *Man's search for meaning: An introduction to logotherapy* (I. Lasch, Trans.). New York: Simon & Schuster. (Original work published 1946)

Gadamer, H.-G. (1975). *Truth and method* (G. Barden & J. Cumming, Trans.). New York: Seabury Press. (Original work published 1960)

Gadamer, H.-G. (1983). *Reason in the age of science* (F. G. Lawrence, Trans.). Cambridge, MA: MIT Press. (Original work published 1976)

Gerbie, M. V. (1977). Malignant neoplasms of the vulva. In J. J. Sciarra (Ed.), *Gynecology and obstetrics* (Vol. 1, pp. 1-10). Hagerstown, MD: Harper & Row.

Graham, J. (1982). *In the company of others: Understanding the human needs of cancer patients.* New York: Harcourt Brace Jovanovich.

Guignon, C. (1986). Existentialist ethics. In J. P. DeMarco & R. M. Fox (Eds.), *New directions in ethics* (pp. 73-91). New York: Routledge & Kegan Paul.

Gusdorf, G. (1965). *Speaking (la parole)* (P. Brockelman, Trans.). Evanston, IL: Northwestern University Press. (Original work published 1953)

Hegel, G. W. F. (1951). *The science of logic* (Vols. 1-2) (W. H. Johnston & L. G. Struthers, Trans.). New York: Macmillan. (Original work published 1816)

Hegel, G. W. F. (1967). *The phenomenology of mind* (J. B. Baillie, Trans.). New York: Harper & Row. (Original work published 1807)

Heidegger, M. (1949). Holderlin and the essence of poetry (D. Scott, Trans.). In M. Heidegger, *Existence and being* (pp. 270-291). Chicago: Henry Regnery.

Heidegger, M. (1962). *Being and time* (J. Macquarrie & E. Robinson, Trans.). New York: Harper & Row. (Original work published 1927)

Heidegger, M. (1982). *The basic problems of phenomenology* (A. Hofstadter, Trans.). Bloomington, IN: Indiana University Press. (Original work published 1975)

Heinemann, F. H. (1958). *Existentialism and the modern predicament.* New York: Harper & Row.

Hyde, M. J. (1980). The experience of anxiety: A phenomenological investigation. *Quarterly Journal of Speech, 66,* 140-154.

Hyde, M. J. (1983a). Rhetorically, man dwells: On the making-known function of discourse. *Communication, 7,* 201-220.

Hyde, M. J. (1983b). The hermeneutic phenomenon and the authenticity of discourse. *Visible Language, 17,* 146-162.

Hyde, M. J. (1984). Emotion and human communication: A rhetorical, scientific, and philosophical picture. *Communication Quarterly, 32,* 120-132.

Hyde, M. J. (1986). Treating the patient as a person. *Quarterly Journal of Speech, 72,* 456-469.

Hyde, M. J. (1990). Experts, rhetoric, and the dilemmas of medical technology: Investigating a problem of progressive ideology. In M. Medhurst (Ed.), *Communication and the culture of technology* (pp. 115-136). Pullman, WA: Washington State University Press.

Hyde, M. J., & Smith, C. R. (1979). Hermeneutics and rhetoric: A seen but unobserved relationship. *Quarterly Journal of Speech, 65,* 347-363.

Jaspers, K. (1959). *Man in the modern age* (E. Paul & C. Paul, Trans.). London: Routledge. (Original work published 1931)

Jaspers, K. (1970a). *Way to wisdom* (R. Manheim, Trans.). New Haven, CT: Yale University Press. (Original work published 1951)

Jaspers, K. (1970b). *Philosophy.* Vol. 2. (E. B. Ashton, Trans.). Chicago: University of Chicago Press. (Original work published 1932)

Jaspers, K. (1973). *Reason and existenz.* (W. Earle, Trans.). New York: Noonday Press. (Original work published 1935)

Jaspers, K. (1984). *Philosophy of existence* (R. F. Grabau, Trans.). Philadelphia, PA: University of Pennsylvania Press. (Original work published 1938)

Johnstone, Jr., H. W. (1970). *The problem of the self.* University Park, PA: Pennsylvania State University Press.

Kafka, F. (1968). *The trial* (W. Muir & E. Muir, Trans.). New York: Schocken. (Original work published 1925)

Kierkegaard, S. (1939). *Christian discourses* (W. Lowrie, Trans.). New York: Oxford University Press. (Original work published 1848)

Kierkegaard, S. (1941). *Repetition: An essay in experimental psychology* (W. Lowrie, Trans.). New York: Oxford University Press. (Original work published 1843)

Kierkegaard, S. (1959). *Either/or* (Vol. 2) (D. Swenson & L. Swenson, Trans.). Princeton, NJ: Princeton University Press. (Original work published 1843)

Kierkegaard, S. (1962a). *The present age and Of the difference between a genius and an apostle* (A. Dru, Trans.). New York: Harper & Row. (Original work published 1846)

Kierkegaard, S. (1962b). *The point of view for my work as an author: A report to history and related writings* (B. Nelson, Ed.; W. Lowrie, Trans.). New York: Harper & Row. (Original work published 1859)

Kierkegaard, S. (1971). *Concluding unscientific post-script* (D. F. Swenson & W. Lowrie, Trans.). Princeton, NJ: Princeton University Press. (Original work published 1846)

Kierkegaard, S. (1973a). *Fear and trembling* and *The sickness unto death* (W. Lowrie, Trans.). Princeton, NJ: Princeton University Press. (Original work published 1843/1949)

Kierkegaard, S. (1973b). *The concept of dread* (W. Lowrie, Trans.). Princeton NJ: Princeton University Press. (Original work published 1844)

Lanigan, R. L. (1969). Rhetorical criticism: An interpretation of Maurice Merleau-Ponty. *Philosophy & Rhetoric, 2,* 1-17.

Lanigan, R. L. (1974). Merleau-Ponty, semiology, and the new rhetoric. *Southern Speech Communication Journal, 40,* 127-141.

Löwith, K. (1988). The political implications of Heidegger's existentialism. *New German Critique, 45,* 117-134.

MacIntyre, A. (1967). Existentialism. In P. Edwards (Ed.), *The encyclopedia of philosophy* (Vol. 3, pp. 147-154). New York: Macmillan & The Free Press.

Marcel, G. (1949). *Being and having* (K. Farrer, Trans.). Westminster: Dacre Press. (Original work published 1935)

Marcel, G. (1950). *The mystery of being. Vol 1: Reflection and mystery* (G. Fraser, Trans.). *Vol 2: Faith and reality* (R. Haque, Trans.). Chicago: Henry Regnery.

Marcel, G. (1968). *The philosophy of existentialism* (M. Harari, Trans.). New York: Citadel Press. (Original work published 1956)

Marcel, G. (1978). *Man against mass society* (G. S. Fraser, Trans.). South Bend, IN: Gateway Editions. (Original work published 1947)

Marx, K (1973). *The economic & philosophic manuscripts of 1844* (D. J. Struik, Ed.; M.

Milligan, Trans.). New York: International Publishers. (Original work published 1844)

Marx, K., & Engels, F. (1974). *The German ideology.* (C. J. Arthur, Ed.; W. Lough, C. Dutt, & C. P. Magill, Trans.). New York: International Publishers. (Original work published 1846)

May, R., Angel, E., & Ellenberger, H. F. (Eds.). (1958). *Existence: A new dimension in psychiatry and psychology.* New York: Basic Books.

McGuire, M. (1980). The ethics of rhetoric: The morality of knowledge. *Southern Speech Communication Journal, 45,* 133–148.

Merleau-Ponty, M. (1971). *Sense and non-sense* (H. L. Dreyfus & P. A. Dreyfus, Trans.). Evanston, IL: Northwestern University Press. (Original work published 1948)

Merleau-Ponty M. (1973). *The prose of the world* (J. O'Neill, Trans.). Evanston, IL: Northwestern University Press. (Original work published 1969)

Merleau-Ponty, M. (1974). *Phenomenology of perception* (C. Smith, Trans.). New York: The Humanities Press. (Original work published 1945)

Nietzsche, F. (1966). *Beyond good and evil: Prelude to a philosophy of the future* (W. Kaufmann, Trans.). New York: Vintage Books. (Original work published 1886)

Nietzsche, F. (1968). *The will to power* (W. Kaufmann & R. J. Hollingdale, Trans.). New York: Vintage Books. (Original work published 1901. Revised and expanded edition including 1067 notes published 1906)

Nietzsche, F. (1969). *On the genealogy of morals* (W. Kaufmann & R. J. Hollingdale, Trans.) and *Ecco homo* (W. Kaufmann, Trans.). New York: Vintage Books. (Original work published 1887/1908)

Nietzsche, F. (1971). *Joyful wisdom* (T. Common, Trans.). New York: Frederick Ungar. (Original work published 1882)

Nietzsche, F. (1986a). *Thus spoke Zarathustra* (W. Kaufmann, Trans.). In W. Kaufmann (Ed.), *The portable Nietzsche* (pp. 103–439). New York: Viking Penguin. (Original work published 1883–1892)

Nietzsche, F. (1986b). On truth and lie in an extramoral sense (W. Kaufmann, Trans.). In W. Kaufmann (Ed.), *The portable Nietzsche* (pp. 42–47). New York: Viking Penguin. (Original work published 1903)

Norris, C. (1987). *Derrida.* Cambridge, MA: Harvard University Press.

Ortega y Gasset, J. (1957). *The revolt of the masses* (Trans. anonymous). New York: W. W. Norton. (Original work published 1930)

Pacey, A. (1983). *The culture of technology.* Cambridge, MA: MIT Press.

Poulakos, J. (1974). The components of dialogue. *Western States Speech Journal, 38,* 199–212.

Ricoeur, P. (1965). *Fallible man* (C. Kelbley, Trans.). Chicago: Henry Regnery. (Original work published 1960)

Rorty, R. (1979). *Philosophy and the mirror of nature.* Princeton, NJ: Princeton University Press.

Rosenfield, L. W. (1974). The experience of criticism. *Quarterly Journal of Speech, 60,* 489–496.

Sartre, J.-P. (1948). *The emotions: Outline of a theory* (B. Frechtman, Trans.). New York: Philosophical Library. (Original work published 1939)

Sartre, J.-P. (1949). *Nausea* (L. Alexander, Trans.). Norfolk, CT: New Directions. (Original work published 1938)

Sartre, J.-P. (1957). *Existentialism and human emotions* (B. Frechtman & H. E. Barnes, Trans.). New York: Philosophical Library.

Sartre, J.-P. (1973). *Being and nothingness* (H. E. Barnes, Trans.). New York: Washington Square Press. (Original work published 1943)

Schrag, C. O. (1961). *Existence and freedom: Towards an ontology of human finitude.* Evanston, IL: Northwestern University Press.

Schrag, C. O. (1986). *Communicative Praxis and the space of subjectivity.* Bloomington, IN: Indiana University Press.

Scott, R. L. (1964). Some implications of existentialism for rhetoric. *Central States Speech Journal, 14,* 267–278.

Smith, C. R. (1972). The medieval subjugation and the existential elevation of rhetoric. *Philosophy & Rhetoric, 5,* 159–174.

Smith, C. R. (1985). Martin Heidegger and the dialogue with being. *Central States Speech Journal, 36,* 256–269.

Solomon, R. (1976). *The passions: The myth and nature of human emotion.* New York: Anchor Press/Doubleday.

Sontag, S. (1966). *Against interpretation and other essays.* New York: Farrar, Straus & Giroux.

Sontag, S. (1978). *Illness as metaphor.* New York: Farrar, Straus & Giroux.

Stewart, J. (1986). Speech and human being: A complement to semiotics. *Quarterly Journal of Speech, 72,* 55–73.

Tillich, P. (1951/1957). *Systematic theology.* Vols. 1–2. Chicago: University of Chicago Press.

Wieman, H. N. (1961). Speech in the existential situation. *Quarterly Journal of Speech, 47,* 150–157.

Wild, J. (1955). *The challenge of existentialism.* Bloomington, IN: Indiana University Press.

Wolin, R. (1988). The French Heidegger debate. *New German Critique, 45,* 135–161.

Zimmerman, M. E. (1981). *Eclipse of the self: The development of Heidegger's concept of authenticity.* Athens: Ohio University Press.

Chapter 8

Rhetoric after Deconstruction

James Arnt Aune

In contrast to the other philosophies discussed in this book, deconstruction resists easy summary in propositional form. This resistance does not, as unkind critics would suggest, stem from deconstruction's fundamental incoherence, but from deconstruction's insistence that philosophy is not a set of truths but rather a set of *texts*. There is no such thing as "pragmatism," "idealism," "realism," and such, but only *writing* that bears these labels. What we call "philosophy" is finally a set of material marks on a page, collected by the "authority" of other writings into monuments of something called "Western culture."

At first sight, then, deconstruction bears a superficial similarity to materialism. If philosophy is a material practice of writing, then it loses much of the spiritual authority that it has possessed from Socrates to the present. Although anxious to resist authority in all its guises, deconstruction would resist the idea that there is some primal thing, called matter, to which philosophy is "reducible." To make such a reductive move is to repeat the pattern of all hitherto existing philosophies, to suggest that reality is reducible to some primary substance, whether it be air, water, or fire (in the case of the early Greek cosmologists), the Forms (Plato), Absolute Spirit (Hegel), and so forth.

Deconstruction insists that philosophy, as a practice of writing, sustains itself by breaking up phenomena into fundamental oppositions — essence/appearance, knowledge/opinion, substance/accident — which not only rely upon some primary substance to authorize the oppositions, but which are finally more unstable, less clearly marked, than philosophy would believe. The ultimate inaccessibility of a primary substance (that which, in the etymology of the word itself, "stands beneath" phenomena as a more or less firm foundation) and the ultimately contradictory effort to keep that substance separate from its less fundamental partners stem from philosophy's inability to escape from language itself. This is not to suggest that "language" is a fundamental substance (a philosophic choice made by some varieties of idealism and existentialism), because there is no such thing as "language," but only words and texts which resist assembly into some coherent whole.

Perhaps a better way of illustrating the deconstructionist assault upon conventional notions of philosophy and language is to quote some remarks of Jean Genet which appear in the most representative piece of deconstructionist writing, Jacques Derrida's (1986) *Glas:*

> When one is cunning . . . one can pretend to believe that words do not budge, that their sense is fixed or has budged thanks to us who become, voluntarily, one feigns to believe, gods. As for me, when confronted with the enraged, encaged herd in the dictionary, I know that I have said nothing and will ever say nothing. And the words don't give a fuck. (p. 223)

Genet contrasted the effort of philosophy to fix, in a god-like way, the meanings of words with his own sense of powerlessness before words.

In contrast to the philosophic quest to fix the meanings of words, there is another way of speaking about language and the world in Western culture that has been more conscious of the way in which writing and speaking seem to take on a more or less autonomous status in relation to the material or social world. That way can be called the rhetorical tradition. Interestingly, for our purposes, rhetoric as a textual practice was early on consigned to the secondary or derivative realm of appearance, opinion, or probability by the writers who founded philosophy. It is probably no accident that the widespread revival of rhetorical ways of talking about texts and social practices has appeared at approximately the same time as deconstruction's infiltration of departments of philosophy and literature that have historically denigrated rhetoric.

One possible way of studying how deconstructionist philosophical choices create possibilities for a particular kind of rhetorical theory and criticism is to suggest that deconstruction will seek to invert the traditional hierarchy that places philosophy above rhetoric in the great chain of textual being. The problem with that interpretation of deconstruction is that it repeats the argumentative move that deconstruction criticizes in other philosophies. Establishing "rhetoric" as a foundation for human activity will prove to create the same false bottoms as previous attempts.

This chapter is an investigation into the way in which deconstruction calls into question both philosophy and rhetoric as social practices. Deconstruction calls everything into question, not to find yet another foundation that could reintroduce some form of new authority, but because, if we could try to be honest with ourselves, our communicative practice calls everything into question whether we choose it to or not. I will proceed by first attempting to do something that deconstruction proclaims impossible: reduce deconstructive writing to a set of core concepts; second, suggest how these core concepts might complicate in interesting ways how we write about rhetoric; and, finally, compare and contrast deconstruction with the other philosophies discussed in this book, proposing some limitations of deconstruction. It is a conventional textual practice in the academic essay to prefigure the argumentative moves made by the author, suggesting that the writing that follows is in some way an amplification of something called a "thesis," which is somehow prior to and constitutive of the text itself. Deconstruction would suggest that any thesis that I could present here, at this point on the page, will probably be undercut later on. But let me provisionally write that deconstruction is finally a radically skeptical philosophy, perhaps even a parody of that ruthlessly questioning founder of Western philosophy, Socrates. A sceptical stance toward knowledge and language seems to provide for more possibilities for engaging in the art of rhetoric, while undercutting the sense of prudence or practical wisdom necessary for engaging in rhetoric. I will suggest, more than a little paradoxically, that deconstruction may have more affinities with certain types of conservative political philosophy than with the naughty French radicalism with which it is usually associated. I also need to note, in an aside to the reader that the prose style of what follows will occasionally be annoying, and will strain against the limits imposed by the normal conventions of academic writing. But to do otherwise would be to miss the "point," to blunt the stylus of what is best about deconstructive writing.

DECONSTRUCTION: A PRIMER

We need to back up for a moment. And then back up further than that. The first sentence of this paragraph seems natural enough. Its unfolding in the course of an exposition of key arguments ratifies that sense of temporal progression which we are used to in hearing or reading. The trouble is that this sentence, when examined rigorously, proves to be rather slippery. I have called upon you, the reader, directly, even though I do not know who you are. The first person who will actually read these marks on the page is someone named Richard Cherwitz, but he (and you) know that I am not addressing him directly. But if not, who is this "we" that I have so carelessly addressed? Where, in space and time, are both of us located?

This sort of thing can give the reader a headache, but my purpose here is to suggest a first maxim of deconstruction: *no communication can ever be fully present to itself, for it is always already marked by the play of difference and deferral of meaning which is language.* Speech is always already written. To put it another way, meaning is constituted by difference, not by reference to a material thing or the presence of some real signified, but by the system of signs itself. As Peirce (1958) wrote, a sign

> is anything which determines something else (its *interpretant*) to refer to an object to which itself refers (its *object*) in the same way, the interpretant becoming in turn a sign, and so on *ad infinitum.* (p. 169)

As Culler (1983) wrote "the possibility of endless replication is not an accident that befalls the sign but a constitutive element of its structure, an incompletion without which the sign would be incomplete" (pp. 188–189). Put more simply, reading or interpreting is much like looking up a word in a dictionary. One finds that the definition of that word refers in turn to other words, which (if one is either exceptionally obtuse or persistent) one could continue looking up indefinitely. We may have good reasons for halting the serial displacement of meaning in interpretation (that is, closing the dictionary), but such a halt, usually done for practical reasons such as avoiding boredom or indecision, does not mean that we have exhausted the potential meaning of the word. The meaning of a word, by its own definition, can never be fully present to itself or to its audience. Any appearance of fully present meaning is a fiction much like the "we" that I created in the first line of this section.

Not only is meaning deferred, but it also is constituted by difference. Following Saussure (1959), Derrida saw language as a system of relations and oppositions whose elements must be defined in differential terms. The positive nature of a term is less important than its function in a system. Speakers of a given phoneme may pronounce the same phoneme differently, but so long as they maintain an internal distinction between that phoneme and others they will be intelligible to other speakers. Derrida (1972/1981) developed the implications of the Saussurean notion of difference in this way:

> The play of differences supposes, in effect, syntheses and referrals which forbid at any moment, or in any sense, that a simple element be *present* in and of itself. Whether in the order of spoken or written discourse, no element can function as a sign without referring to another element which itself is simply not present. This interweaving results in each "element"—phoneme or grapheme—being constituted on the basis of the trace within it of the other elements of the chain or system. This interweaving, this textile, is the *text* produced only in the transformation of another text. Nothing, neither among

the elements nor within the system, is anywhere ever simply present or absent. There are only everywhere, differences and traces of traces (p. 26).

Derrida is perhaps vulnerable here to the accusation of confusing the phonological and semantic levels of language, but the extension of the notion of linguistic difference to more general textual difference seems to make "common sense." Something as relatively straightforward as the political ideology of Ronald Reagan does not exist in and of itself. It consists of a set of rhetorical idioms (fierce nationalism, free-market capitalism, a Protestant view of family and work) which are definable only in relation to one another, and by that to which they are opposed. There is a strange way in which someone like Reagan *needs* Communists, Democrats, and feminists to define himself. If they were to disappear, which is presumably the ultimate goal of his political practice, he would disappear, too.

The notions of deferral, difference, and the rejection of presence thus lead deconstruction out of a focus on language which might exclude broader cultural or political questions. A second maxim of deconstruction illustrates the political uses of its view of language: *Pay close attention to gestures of exclusion in texts and metaphysical systems, especially where they are manifested in the construction of binary oppositions in which the second term is seen as a falling away from the presence of the first term.* Examples of such oppositions are speech/writing, literal/figurative, philosophy/rhetoric. I have already suggested that even written language will tend to refer to a nonexistent presence of the reader in order to authorize itself. Writing seems like a poor substitute for direct communion between two people; imagine how much less time and effort and expense it would require if I could just talk to you, the reader, about deconstruction directly. The trouble is, as the first maxim of deconstruction points out, that even such a direct communicative transaction would be much like writing. Our meanings, both to each other and to ourselves, would hardly be more present then than now.

The rejection of ornament upon plain speech, which is implicit in the literal/figurative opposition, and in much of the criticism of rhetoric by philosophers, is unstable, too. To use the term "literal" is to use an implicit, or dead, metaphor, in which the "literal," literally "of the letter," stands in for the pure, unadorned truth of the text. If "literal" is itself a metaphor, then how can it be either prior to or superior to the figurative?

The literal/figurative opposition is in turn similar to the philosophy/rhetoric opposition on which philosophy usually resides. Rhetoric is addressed to particular audiences, playing upon their emotions, usually for unscrupulous ends. Philosophy, on the other hand, has pure motives, and strives as much as possible not to worry about the needs of particular audiences. And yet, because philosophy (at least after Socrates, who did not write his doctrines down) is only accessible in the form of written documents, how can it avoid the need to adapt to present and future audiences? Further, given the institutional character of philosophy — either its role as discourse rewarded by specific people like deans and kings or as discourse referring to previous philosophers — it cannot guarantee its purity of motives. For, if written well — which is to say, rhetorically effective — it will win power and/or fame from particular audiences even if that is not its intention.

Philosophy's insistence upon the priority of the literal, speech-as-full-presence, and philosophy itself is thus revealed to be less easy than it appears. Philosophy seems to need to repress its "written-ness" in order to exist at all. Richard Rorty's (1982) essay on Derrida brings this point out clearly:

> Writing is an unfortunate necessity; what is really wanted is to show, to demonstrate, to point out, to exhibit, to make one's interlocutor stand and gaze before the world. . . . In a mature science, the words in which the investigator "writes up" his results should be as few and transparent as possible. . . . Philosophical writing, for Heidegger as for the Kantians, is really aimed at putting an end to writing. For Derrida, writing always leads to more writing, and more, and still more. (p. 94)

Noting the inevitable collapse of binary oppositions leads to the third maxim of deconstruction: *After noting gestures of exclusion in a text, the deconstructive reader then needs to point out, through a close reading of the figurative structure of the text, how such a gesture of exclusion is logically contradictory.* Derrida's (1967/1976) classic example of such a reading is his study of Rousseau in *Of Grammatology*. Rousseau said that writing is a *supplement* to speech, that is, an addition that is also a falling away, but Rousseau's use of the term supplement in other contexts suggests a contradictory use of the other meaning of supplement as completion. While Rousseau condemned writing as "a destruction of presence and disease of speech" he contradicted himself by defending his own project of writing: "I would love society like others, if I were not sure of showing myself not only at a disadvantage, but as completely different from what I am. The part that I have taken of writing and hiding myself is precisely the one that suits me. If I were present, one would never know what I was worth" (cited in Derrida, 1967/1976, p. 142). Rousseau also described education as a supplement to nature, as if there were some sort of lack in nature that education must fulfill. Further, and more amusingly, Rousseau referred to masturbation as a "dangerous supplement," but his discussion of his love affairs elsewhere suggested that the basic principle of masturbation as self-love which focuses on an imagined, nonpossessable object seems to be repeated in "normal" sexual relationships (Derrida, 1967/1976, pp. 150–157). The undecidable character of the term "supplement" in Rousseau is both a logical contradiction and a necessary component of the otherwise interesting and useful line of argument in his texts. All our speaking and writing involves a fundamental blindness to the consequences of our vocabulary which is nonetheless strangely constitutive of our insight (de Man, 1983).

I have tried to suggest three fundamental maxims, or rules of deconstructive reading:

1. The very nature of language prevents meaning from ever being fully present in any act of communication.
2. Texts (like the larger philosophies or ideologies which they profess to re-present) work by establishing pairs of opposed terms in which one term has priority.
3. These paired terms tend to collapse into one another when one examines their interplay within a text.

RHETORIC AFTER DECONSTRUCTION

"Rhetoric" at times seems to function much like the term "supplement" does in the writings of Rousseau. The term "rhetoric" is like the glue that holds together the various perspectives represented in this book, but I suspect that many readers who have made it thus far are wondering what "rhetoric" is. Philosophers, as we have seen, tend to engage in gestures of exclusion of rhetoric, while still locating audiences, strategically locating themselves in relation to previous writers and texts, and trying to persuade—all of which seem to be consummately rhetorical actions. Yet to locate such persuasive moves seems ultimately to say both everything and nothing. What, finally, does it matter to suggest that all knowing, speaking, and writing is "rhetorical?" Discussions of rhetoric tend to vary in their emphasis upon theory, criticism, and the production of texts. Most people come to the study of rhetoric because they are interested in learning how to engage in certain kinds of persuasive acts: public speaking, debating, writing the argumentative essay, constructing a persuasive campaign. There comes some point in that learning process where "theory" begins to come in: a quest for reducing rhetorical practice to a set of rules that can guide practice. These rules (such as: have a preview statement in a speech introduction, put the weakest of your three arguments in the middle, or "use" more evidence and reasoning with educated and/or hostile audiences) tend to be grounded, implicitly or explicitly, in some sort of larger theory or philosophy of human nature, politics, and language. Thinking philosophically about rhetoric tends to introduce an element of guilt or suspicion into the process. If rhetoric can be used for evil purposes, it may be necessary to speak of it critically, in the hope of immunizing audiences against its effects.

These three fundamental "places" of rhetorical inquiry can be filled up differently, depending on the sort of philosophy of rhetoric one brings to the inquiry. A deconstructionist view of philosophy and rhetoric would tend to focus on the possibilities of reversal of the traditional hierarchical placement of the two terms, not to "privilege" rhetoric but to complicate both types of human practice.

It is probably contradictory to suggest, then, that deconstruction can provide any sort of constructive doctrine for contemporary rhetoric, but it can provide an immensely clarifying stance toward the traditional places of rhetorical inquiry. Deconstruction can help clarify the problems encountered by attempts to make ontological statements about rhetoric, by attempts to elaborate a rational standard which would guide rhetorical practice, and by attempts to privilege a critical stance toward public discourse. Such clarification can occur only in the process of reading some statements about rhetoric closely, following the three maxims that I articulated earlier.

The first problem in talking about rhetoric is what might be called its ontological status: what does it mean to be a human being, and a human being who speaks or writes rhetorically? One way to answer that question is to say that to be human is to engage in "dialogue," that self and other come into being only through the reciprocal process of self-disclosure that is rhetoric. Rhetoric, viewed in this way, is somehow constitutive of what it means to be human. From another perspective, this may say too little and too much, because it does not seem to provide standards by which the meeting of beings in dialogue may be judged. The practice of rhetoric must thus be judged by something outside of the practice.

Here are two texts, the first by Calvin Schrag and the second by James W. Hikins and Kenneth S. Zagacki, which represent the two alternatives I have just discussed. My concern here is not so much with their overall "philosophy" but rather with the texture of their written arguments. Both represent a moment of clarity of revelation in the essays from which they are drawn, where after a long process of weighing arguments and responding to opponents, the reader's patience is rewarded by a statement of truth, a summing up:

> This is the rhetorical moment: the co-disclosure of self and other in a hermeneutic of everyday life textured as an amalgam of discourse and social practices. . . . Rhetoric, thusly understood, is the directedness of discourse to

"our hearers" in our concern with "whatever it is we have to expound to others". . . . Within this space of dialogue, public addresses, deliberation and collaboration, both self and other are disclosed and the meanings embedded in our social practices are made manifest. (Schrag, 1985, p. 170)

The view we have described (rhetorical perspectivism) elaborates specific criteria that, when followed consistently, facilitate epistemologically productive discourse. Rhetorical inquiry can be productive if rhetors: 1) differentiate the relations obtaining among rhetor, extralinguistic phenomena, and tacit audience; 2) draw valid associations between first-person epistemic judgments and derived knowledge; 3) expose their arguments to critical evaluation. Moreover 4) epistemic judgments must be dialectically secured, where rhetors are afforded equal initiative and control over lines of influence (bilateralism); 5) are willing to correct their views, harboring the assumption that the clash of differing ideas is the best means of exposing error and yielding truth; and 6) are willing to risk the possibility that their views (and selves) will be altered as a result of argument. (Hikins & Zagacki; 1988, p. 223)

To read deconstructively the texts signed "Schrag" and "Hikins/Zagacki" is to locate certain points of blindness within their conceptual structure and figuration and to suggest that such blindness is a precondition for their "insight" (see de Man, 1983). Note first that Schrag and Hikins/Zagacki share a common discomfort (if we read them literally): they are writing, but they do not wish to be writing. Despite the differing nuances of Schrag's "dialogue" and Hikins/Zagacki's "clash," both texts presuppose an ideal face-to-face confrontation between self and other. Consider, however, how inefficient a journal article is at providing such an ideal confrontation. It may be efficient at extending the potential space in which such a confrontation may take place, but in the absence of forums that would guarantee multiple confrontations of self and other(s) writing is clearly second best to, say, an oral presentation, debate, or dialogue in front of an audience.

At the same time, if we privilege the moment of self-risk in these texts, we see that writing may be the chief guarantor of this rhetorical virtue. In writing, an argument is frozen in time, made more public than in face-to-face communication, capable of being grafted into other contexts, misinterpreted without a statutory right to reply, even subjected to formalized procedures of institutional evaluation (tenure and promotion) — thus providing a more risky business for the writer than for a speaker of the same statements. The text, too, may continue to "speak" even after the self has disappeared. Since Schrag placed continuing the conversation as a higher value than "exposing error and yielding truth," one would have to say that writing simultaneously guarantees such a continuation in ways that mere orality cannot, and yet violates the ideal of "presence" of self and other which his argument presupposes. Since Hikins/Zagacki presume that the end result of "productive" rhetorical inquiry is silence (the only appropriate response to having confessed one's errors is to contemplate yielded truth quietly), we might say that only writing can guarantee the permanence of truth; yet the conditions for productive rhetorical inquiry must exclude writing.

Violence plays a role similar to that of writing in these texts. Both presuppose a kind of cleared space at the heart of being in which self and other can speak; the two texts differ about whether this ground is to be cleared by dialectic or logic. Yet both would agree that the cleared ground in which communication takes place must exclude violence. Violence, in a way, is the absent term around which the arguments of both texts revolve. The resuscitation of the rhetorical tradition is a response to the violence of this wretched century. Schrag's metaphors of dialogue and disclosure exclude violence on principle, while Hikins/Zagacki's metaphors ("clash," "risk," "altering," "exposing") sublimate violence into speech. Yet one wonders (again, especially in this century) how such exclusions or sublimations could occur other than on a ground cleared by violent action. And despite the best intentions, violence may even intrude into the cleared ground. Presumably a Jew's speech must be dialectically secured even in the presence of a Nazi, or a woman's in the presence of a pornographer. Or — assuming that the Nazi or the pornographer are exceptions that prove the rule — the dialectical/dialogical ground must be secured against their intrusions, either by violence or by the threat of violence. Violence — the very opposite of rhetoric and dialectic — is thus the very condition of their being, at least in any currently available world.

Finally, consider the peculiar status of the privileged term "self" in these texts. It is curious to read discourses exalting self-risk and the embodiment of ideas which are nonetheless written in a code (that of the academic essay) that enforces the effacement of self. It is stretching the bounds of academic courtesy to suggest that at least the Hikins/Zagacki text is grounded in a characteristically male form of ritual combat against its opponents? Note the subtle castration fears lurking behind the innocent metaphors of self-exposure and being "altered." The Hikins/Zagacki text, so concerned with drawing property lines, might also, so to speak, be concerned with measuring *length*. If, as Adrienne Rich (1979) suggested, the very practice of rhetoric is itself grounded in a characteristically male attempt to dominate language and audiences much as males have dominated women and nature, it is no accident that "clash" models of rhetoric should display a subtle fascination with violence. So, too, the idea of approaching the public space of rhetoric as equal partners in dialogue could mean different things to men and women, for whom public and private have been negotiated in different ways under patriarchy.

My invocation of the feminist tradition reveals one way in which deconstructionist philosophical choices ground a particular kind of political rhetoric. While rejecting such previous features of left wing rhetoric as the science/ideology split, economic determinism, and the vanguard party, left deconstruction provides a way of redefining the notion of ideology–critique in rhetorical terms. As Ryan (1982), Spivak (1980, 1985), Glynn (1986), and Warren (1987) argued, deconstruction's focus on gestures of exclusion and the material, institutional character of philosophic writing is useful for grounded a new sort of left politics. From a deconstructive standpoint, the criticism of rhetoric can be seen as "de-sedimentation," as ideology–critique, showing how such constructions as the logic of capitalist economics and the conventions of sexual difference are simply that: *constructions,* not discoveries of some sort of natural law. Ideological discourse is that which represses its own rhetoricity in the name of some master understanding and presence-to-itself beyond history and language. Deconstructionist rhetoric then becomes, as Fredric Jameson (1972) wrote, a sort of militant atheism, ferociously seeking to clear the ground of human interaction of all traces of a transcendental signified (p. 182). Perhaps the best representative of a deconstructionist rhetoric and politics is the American movement known as Critical Legal Studies. Mark Tushnet (1988), perhaps the most philosophically rigorous of the CLS proponents, demonstrates through a series of close readings of the United States Constitution and its interpreters how any formalized system of law or legal interpretation simply fails to provide a coherent grounding for legal practice. This leaves the advocate or judge able to seize on the interpretation of a legal text most congenial to his or her politics and provide the momentary illusion of coherence.

The left wing implications of deconstruction are perhaps obvious, but if examined closely one can find conservative implications, too. I propose a somewhat audacious reading of the deconstructionist position which locates it more closely within the Western rhetorical tradition, which has always found itself at home within a more or less skeptical philosophical perspective. Stated simply, deconstruction teaches us that philosophy taken to extremes makes us unfit for life in the real world, because it enables us to unravel any system of thought. Yet rhetorical practice presumes that the rhetor and audience have found some common ground, some seemingly solid foundation, on which to negotiate meaning. Although deconstruction may undermine the claim to self-sufficiency or self-evidence characteristic of metaphysical systems of thought, deconstruction, in contrast to positivism, Marxism, or other modern attempts at unmasking collective illusions, proclaims no escape from the burdens of textuality. Skepticism is perhaps a more fundamentally Tory stance toward the world than a radical one. Although all traditions may fall apart upon rigorous logical examination, it is an illusion to believe that we can escape from tradition any more than we can escape from textuality.

Perhaps the most coherent discussion of the connection between skepticism and conservative political philosophy is Michael Oakeshott's (1962) *Rationalism in Politics*. Continuing the British tradition of Hume and Burke, which rejected the possibility of abstract human rights in favor of concrete traditions ("the rights of Englishmen"), Oakeshott demonstrated that political life cannot be reduced to rational principle. Political argument always relies on fundamental metaphors: caves, ships of state, Great Beasts, states of nature. The rational plans of political philosophy simply cannot do the work they set out to do:

> In political activity . . . men sail a boundless and bottomless sea; there is neither harbour for shelter nor floor for anchorage, neither starting-place nor appointed destination. The enterprise is to keep afloat on an even keel; the sea is both friend and enemy; and the seamanship consists of using the resources of a traditional manner of behavior in order to make a friend of every hostile occasion. (p. 127)

The sort of knowledge that the effective rhetorician or politician possesses is a tentative one, bound by the constraints of audience and occasion, in which timing and decorum are the fundamental virtues. Put more simply, no abstract system of thought can resist deconstruction, and yet we still go on acting as if we can speak and think coherently. What enables us to do this is tradition, and the short-term tactical maneuvers within and against that tradition that rhetoric enables us to make. Such a realization can lead us either to a sort of romantic or existential despair, or else to an affirmation of the remarkable variety of ways (art, religion, politics) in which human beings have attempted to cover the abyss that yawns beneath them.

By way of a summary of the key principles of deconstruction that I have presented thus far, I want to draw out more explicitly the consequences of conservative skepticism for rhetorical theory and practice.

First, deconstruction reveals an inherent instability in any text or system of thought. This instability usually can be isolated by attending to the warring forces of signification in the text. We can interpret this instability in a way that exalts human creativity, along the lines of McGuire's (1980) exaltation of the Nietzschean Will to Power. Or we can interpret this instability more modestly. Instability or undecidability might, as Jonathan Culler (1983) pointed out, simply be the humanities equivalent of Godel's proof. The fact that Godel demonstrated the incompleteness of mathematics—the impossibility of "constructing a theoretical system within which all true statements of number theory are theorems"—does not lead mathematicians to abandon their work. Why should an acceptance of the provisional and contradictory character of theoretical and critical work in the humanities lead to nihilism? (Culler, 1983, p. 133). It leads to nihilism only if one judges truth by the standards of clarity and coherence characteristic of the canons of modern science. The philosophical justification of rhetorical theory and practice has tended to disappear when absolute systems of knowledge, whether in the form of Christian theology, scientific Marxism, or positivism, have been dominant. When philosophical absolutes disappear, the need for practical systems of reasoning based on probability becomes acute, and the rhetorical tradition at its best (Isocrates, Cicero, Quintilian) becomes the only available alternative. Some commentators (see Nuttal, 1983) argue that deconstruction works only against formalized, absolute systems of philosophy, which it tends to set up as straw men, as if there were no middle ground between absolute knowledge and the abyss of deconstructive undecidability. One is tempted to view deconstruction, then, as a sort of *disappointed hyper-realism or idealism,* which goes too far to extremes when the traditional project of philosophy fails. Still, the recognition of deconstruction as a way of reading and, strangely enough, *conserving* texts may partially meet this objection.

Second, a recognition of the instability of both philosophical and rhetorical practice should lead to a certain humility in matters philosophical. The ancient philosophers made a distinction between philosophy as a way of life and the role of philosophy in the city. I suggested earlier that deconstruction is a sort of parody of the Socratic method. Deconstruction may work best as a sort of Socratic denunciation of the pretensions of modern philosophy, which from its inception has tried to realize itself in the real world. The distinction between ancient and modern philosophy has been made very persuasively by Leo Strauss (1953) and his disciples, including Allan Bloom (1968). Modern philosophy, from the Baconian scientific project, to the Philosophes, to Marx and Mill, has been obsessed with gaining power and ruling the state. All share in common the assumption that speech can be made fully transparent, free from prejudice and passion, resulting in a society in which universal consensus is possible. The deconstruction of the illusion of presence and of the transcendental signified means an end to the hubris of the modern view of philosophy.

This distinction between ancient and modern philosophy's political pretensions helps us see deconstruction in closer relationship to Plato than is usually realized. Plato's objection to rhetoric had more to do with the sophists' assumption that politics was somehow reducible to speech alone (as opposed to wise construction of laws and prudent conduct of the art of war) than with rhetoric's association with the realm of opinion or common sense. As Strauss (1964) and Bloom (1968) demonstrated, that so-called utopia, *The Republic,* is really intended by Plato to show the impossibility of establishing the ideal city other than in speech alone, a realization that serves as a counsel of moderation to the young men who seek to rule the City.

Most of Plato's early dialogues work in what we would now call a deconstructive mode. They seek for a definition of a key concept: courage, temperance, piety, for instance, but end on a note of aporia, or undecidability. Even the *Gorgias,* which people still misread as condemning the art of rhetoric out of hand, ends with a long oration by Socrates that justifies the ethical life in a beautiful myth obviously intended for nonphilosophic audiences.

Plato realized that the attempt to realize philosophy in practice was dangerous both for philosophers and the public, and allowed a place for rhetoric as myth-telling. Socrates' counsel to Crito illustrates the general principles of a Socratic rhetoric more clearly than the somewhat misleading *Phaedrus:* Socrates counsels the rather dull-witted Crito to adopt a sense of piety toward the existing regime, using arguments that Socrates appears to reject elsewhere. The philosophic rhetorician knows how to address his or her rhetoric to different types of souls, counseling piety and patriotism to those unable to follow complex arguments, counseling moderation to the spirited ones best suited to rule the City, and counseling a different sort of life to those few suited to live the life of philosophy.

Despite the conventional argument that Plato was somehow a founder of totalitarianism, Plato's Socrates is remarkably reluctant to engage in political deliberation. Plato parodied forensic rhetoric in the *Apology* and the *Protagoras,* epideictic rhetoric in the *Menexenus,* yet nowhere did Socrates engage directly in deliberative oratory. Plato recognized that the philosophical life, for which few are suited (an observation that is less elitist than the assumption of modern philosophers that the people must be enlightened whether they like it or not), is a quest. For Plato the Ideas were eternal questions rather than established truths. The philosophers must then be protected by the spirited politicians who will lead the city, politicians whose lust for power and for perfection has been tamed by the philosophers. The philosophers also will tend to protect themselves by guarding against the corrosive consequences of their skepticism, scrupulously observing the laws and rituals of the existing regime, and writing carefully in an ambiguous way accessible only to the initiated.

The Straussian interpretation of Plato has some odd affinities to deconstruction. If a philosophical rhetoric needs to guard against destructive uses of its ideas by the uninitiated, perhaps that explains the notoriously complex and seemingly unreadable quality of deconstructionist writing. Derrida and his disciples engage in the same sort of self-restraint counseled by Plato.

Third, after deconstruction, rhetoric emerges as the art that prevents or defends against the corrosive skepticism that philosophy, taken to its logical extremes, would instill in the public. Deconstruction reveals the absurdity of the modern project's quest for fully transparent truth, whether founded on romantic self-expression or on positivistic science. If you start with Bacon and Descartes, you must end with Derrida, who revealed that nihilism was the unacknowledged guest in the house of Western metaphysics all along. Philosophy, in this reading, is always socially subversive, doing violence to everyday life, and the disappearance of the rhetorical tradition has tended to eliminate the social checks on the power of philosophy which the ancients presupposed. Where contemporary discussions of rhetoric seek to supplant philosophy they are at their most misguided, missing the essential role of rhetoric in public life. Without a vital sense of rhetorical theory and practice, philosophy's skepticism is loosed onto the foundations of the City, or, worse, the modern philosophers' dreams of the General Will, the Rational State, the Classless Society, or even the Ideal Speech Situation are constructed in reality instead of in speech. Richard Weaver (1964), who is consistently misread because of common ignorance about Plato's intentions, put the argument quite eloquently:

> Society cannot live without rhetoric. There are some things which the group needs to believe which cannot be demonstrated to everyone rationally. Their acceptance is pressed upon us by a kind of moral imperative arising from the group as a whole. To put them to the test of dialectic alone is to destroy the basis of belief in them and to weaken the cohesiveness of society. (p. 136)

Before moving on to compare and contrast a deconstructionist rhetoric with the other perspectives in this book, I want to summarize the main themes I have tried to articulate. There are at least three types of deconstruction: (a) a method of reading, reducible to rules that focus on the instability of meaning, (b) the search for key oppositions which ground the structure of meaning in the text, and (c) the explanation of how these oppositions tend to subvert the text's intentions. One type of deconstruction uses this sort of reading to advance a sort of decentered leftist politics, ruthlessly criticizing the presumption of institutional authority in all its forms. Another type, which I have tried to describe at length mainly because of its greater affinity with classical political philosophy and rhetoric, offers a different sort of skepticism to the discerning reader.

Derrida's own ironic stance toward Plato, Hegel, Genet, and the other texts he interrogated (Husserl seems to be the only set of texts that he did not approach with a sense of affection) betrays a kind of what Strauss called "erotic" or "zetetic" (needy and questing) skepticism (see Tarcov & Pangle, 1988, pp. 920–921). The dogmatic skepticism of modernity is another sort altogether. Deconstruction as erotic skepticism can preserve the cultural virtues which this century, more than any other, has tried to destroy: the importance of reading, the value of detachment from politics, and a humble acknowledgment of the limitations of human knowledge. Such cultural virtues always went hand in hand with the rhetorical tradition, and it may be the peculiar vocation of deconstruction to clear the ground for the renewal of rhetoric.

IN THE PORTRAIT GALLERY

Three assumptions seem to animate the other chapters in this book: first, that there is somehow (or should be) a linear relationship between a philosophic stance and the theory, criticism, and production of rhetoric; second, that philosophic stances are first and foremost theories of knowledge (as opposed to, say, ethics, aesthetics, and so on); third, that philosophic stances are somehow, if only for convenience, describable in the form of propositions, propositions that exhibit varying degrees of rigor and precision.

Deconstruction calls all three of these assumptions into question, not for the purpose of replacing them with others, but rather to argue that even if these assumptions were true they could not do the work they are intended to do: "authorize" the production and criticism of texts. This is not to say that the various isms that are textualized in friendly competition with each other in this book are somehow false, nor that whoever is writing this particular essay wants to be right. It is rather a matter of making writing, and that form of writing that we call living, more difficult.

Stanley Cavell (1983) talked about the gestures that lie at the base of different ways of writing philosophy. Austin, for instance, cultivated an impression of indifference to speculation and of "common-room wit and superficiality." This gesture, easily mistaken for a sort of dull conservatism, is actually a way of fending off what Austin found most annoying, the mystifying profundity of German philosophy. It is not hard to picture the writer of *How to Do Things with Words* sitting comfortably in a leather chair with a glass of sherry and working a crossword puzzle. Cavell wrote, "Austin was committed to the manners, even the mannerisms, of an English professor the way a French intellectual is committed to seeming brilliant. It is the level at which an American thinker or artist is likely to play dumb, I mean undertake to seem like a hick, uncultivated. These are all the characters in which authority is assumed" (p. 183). As a thought experiment, following Cavell's hint about character, gesture, and philosophic style, I want to reconstruct the sort of gestural moods that lie underneath the competing isms in this book. Each type of philosophizing yields a recognizable "character" to whom it would appeal, a character who enjoys certain kinds of rhetoric, and who is subject to the moral failings and inconsistencies common to human "nature." (I would add, in passing, that this reconstruction of textual gestures has nothing at all to do with the allegedly real people who wrote the essays. I scarcely know most of them, and I do not know the person who has been writing the preceding pages very well, either. He seems to keep writing things that give him a guilty conscience.)

Consider first the pragmatist, the only real American in the bunch, who fits very well Cavell's image of the hick. His rhetorical stance is a bit like Jimmy Stewart in a Frank Capra movie, a bit bewildered and stammering, but inclined to be charitable to other philosophies, regardless of race, creed, or color. He wants things to work, and to work for everybody, and gets angry when bureaucracies or entrenched interests get in the way of doing things. For him, rhetoric is a bit like engineering. He is uninterested in whether fundamental propositions are logically incoherent. In a calculus class, for instance, he wants to solve problems rather than do proofs. He would probably praise the stance of President Kennedy at Yale in 1962: "What is at stake in our economic decisions today is not some grand warfare of rival ideologies which will sweep the country with passion, but the practical management of a modern economy. What we need are not labels and clichés, but more basic discussions of the sophisticated and technical questions involved in keeping a great economic machinery moving ahead" (cited in Gouldner, 1976, p. 250). The pragmatist, however, for all his superficial air of tolerance is secretly rather judgmental of those who disagree with him. To use practice as the foundation of human knowledge is to create a sort of authority that undercuts the putatively inclusive and democratic assumptions that the pragmatist exalts. Like Kennedy himself, the pragmatist has a sense that technical experts, rather than ideologues or the passionate masses, are best suited to control the state.

The idealist, on the other hand, gestures and speaks like a professor, probably a German one. She prefers to be alone, and spends more time in contemplation than in reading, since she wishes to find the authority of her speech in her own mind rather than in a tradition. She seldom balances her checkbook, and tends to be late for class and irresponsible about attending faculty meetings. She has a group of a few students whom she has chosen to carry on her thought, and they secretly collect her table talk and even her discarded drafts. When she lectures, she does not use notes, and seldom looks at her audience. Her favorite speech is Chapman's "Coatesville Address," which accomplished nothing with its immediate audience, but nonetheless captured a truth available for all time. Her secret vice is a desire for power to remake the world in her own image. If mind is the central term in her vocabulary, all that is needed to solve the world's problems is to reconstruct it according to a visionary plan, a plan that may require totalitarian violence for its execution.

The relativist began life as an idealist, impressed by the infinite powers of the human mind, but was horrified by what the 20th century did with rational plans of all sorts, and the more she studied history, the more she saw only philosophers and theologians and politicians red in tooth and claw, and vowed never again to inflict her point of view on another. She, too, is a professor, because that is the only sort of institution that would employ her, other than perhaps the popular music industry. She is an easy grader, although she tends to penalize the fundamentalist Christians and Orthodox Jews in her classes, and particularly enjoys undermining any fixed beliefs that her students may have. This gets her good teacher evaluations, although she tends to drive many students into business or public relations. Her favorite speech is Gorgias' "Encomium on Helen," which she admires for its wit and artificiality. Her secret vice is a sort of indecisiveness. She was killed when the Maoist Revolutionary Youth Brigade and the Students for an Aryan Nation occupied her office during the campus troubles of the 1990s.

The less said about the materialist, the better, because he is fond of quoting Mao's statement that power comes out of the barrel of a gun, and has begun requiring psychosurgery as a prerequisite for his public speaking class. He is fond of locating the various forces (economic, familial, biological) that determine the behavior of his adversaries, but he can never quite seem to explain how his own behavior escapes such forces.

The realist and the critical rationalist are really the same person, except that the critical rationalist gestures more emphatically and is more inclined to hand-wringing at the follies of the present age. He likes Adlai Stevenson most of all, and his presidential candidates always lose elections. He was last seen as a speechwriter for Michael Dukakis in 1988. He is motivated by a desire to make the reasoning, rather than emotional or visionary, aspects of mind central to public discourse, but this desire is founded on a set of noncognitive choices that he cannot articulate easily.

The existentialist is the most easily recognized of all the characters. She has been writing her doctoral dissertation for 10 years, and ekes out a meager existence working at a Burger King. She smokes two packs of Gauloises a day, and has at least 10 scars on each wrist from unsuccessful suicide attempts. She has never been able to speak in public, and tends to reduce rhetoric to lyric poetry, preferably the American confessional poets who died mad or by their own hands: Plath, Berryman, Sexton, Lowell.

Finally, the deconstructionist wears two masks. At times she is the obnoxiously brilliant French professor caricatured by Cavell. Inclined to wear haute couture fashions, she is herself a self-conscious exploiter of current academic fashion. Once an existentialist and a relativist, she is more cheerful than either, and is the highest paid professor in the world. At other times, she wears another mask. She is a little Jewish boy, studying the Torah, knowing (contrary to the philosophers and the rhetoricians) that all has already been answered, and it lies in every jot and tittle of the sacred text. The problem is that we have forgotten how to read. We are in exile, and it is not vouchsafed to us to know when we will return.

My little exercise here in character reconstruction (and, perhaps, assassination), is perhaps less idle than it seems. Surely there is a surface plausibility to the little biographical sketches I have presented (including the assignment of gender to the competing isms), and that means two things: first, that it is hard to contain the disseminating character of language, no matter how we try to keep it within proper bounds, and second, that no matter how much philosophy as a way of writing tries to repress such things as individuality, style, and audience, we still can relate to philosophic texts in much the same way we relate to people. It is possible, as Wayne Booth (1988) recently reminded us in *The Company We Keep* that our relationship to literature — and books in general — is much like our relationship to our friends. Booth imagined himself refuting deconstruction with this observation, but they may have more in common than he believed. For what deconstruction does, and what makes its claim to authority over both philosophy and rhetoric so precarious, is that it resists the possibility of either, by substituting language for the other foundationalisms that it finds so suspect. And it is finally literary language (as a substitute for an elusive sacred scripture) that is the "paradigm" within which deconstruction reads the world.

I have suggested also that each of the philosophic perspectives outlined in this book has a fatal, inherent flaw which blinds its relationship to rhetorical practice. Pragmatism inevitably translates contested issues (ideology, if you will) into matters of technique, which unwittingly creates an authoritative class of experts which undercuts the communal knowledge it privileges. Idealism tries to show us "better versions of ourselves," (to use Weaver's phrase) but falls prey to the temptation to recreate the world in its own image. Materialism exempts itself from its own observations about the world, and is thus unable to explain its own origins. Existentialism cannot articulate the common grounds that would authorize group action, or, if it can, it cannot choose between competing alternatives. Relativism, concerned to resist violence and exalt speech, cannot preserve speech in a time of danger. Realism and critical rationalism cannot speak to the noncognitive side of the human mind, yet rely on noncognitive grounds for acceptance. Deconstruction only wishes to be left alone to read. At least deconstruction is honest.

A final observation leads us back to the moment when something called "philosophy" and something called "rhetoric" began to war with one another and make competing claims upon audiences. If, as I have argued, deconstruction seems like a parody of the Socratic method, perhaps the best way of viewing the implications of deconstruction for rhetoric is to see deconstruction as refusing Athens in favor of Jerusalem (see Handelman, 1982). For if we conceive of language as reducible to *seeing* (consider the visual metaphors that underlie such Greek terms as "idea" or "theory") then philosophy from the beginning wishes to make language disappear. Rhetoric becomes simply the shadow-side of philosophy, the secret armory for philosophy's perennial war against religion and literature. If, on the other hand, we refuse to separate knowing, speaking, acting, and hearing, then we refuse, like the ancient Hebrews, the entire problematic that gives us "rhetoric" and "philosophy" in the first place. How little sense the first book of Genesis makes to the Greek mind, in that the Creator's speech and action are one! Perhaps the best we can do is remain in exile, reading endlessly, trying to see where we got the text of the world wrong in the first place.

REFERENCES

Bloom, A. (1968). *The Republic of Plato*. New York: Basic Books.

Booth, W. (1988). *The company we keep*. Chicago: University of Chicago Press.

Cavell, S. (1983). Politics as opposed to what? In W.J.T. Mitchell (Ed.), *The politics of interpretation* (pp. 181-202). Chicago: University of Chicago Press.

Culler, J. (1983). *On deconstruction*. Ithaca, NY: Cornell University Press.

de Man, P. (1983). *Blindness and insight*. Minneapolis, MN: University of Minnesota Press.

Derrida, J. (1976). *Of grammatology* (G.C. Spivak, Trans.). Baltimore, MD: Johns Hopkins University Press. (Original work published 1967)

Derrida, J. (1981). *Positions* (A. Bass, Trans.). Chicago: University of Chicago Press. (Original work published 1972)

Derrida, J. (1986). *Glas* (J.P. Leavey, Jr., Trans.). Lincoln, NE: University of Nebraska Press. (Original work published 1974)

Glynn, S. (1986). Beyond the symbol: deconstructing social reality. *Southern Speech Communication Journal 51*, 125-141.

Gouldner, A. (1976). *The dialectic of ideology and technology*. New York: Seabury.

Handelman, S. (1982). *The slayers of Moses*. Albany, NY: SUNY Press.

Hikins, J.W., & Zagacki, K.S. (1988). Rhetoric, philosophy, and objectivism: An attenuation of the claims of the rhetoric of inquiry. *Quarterly Journal of Speech, 74*, 201-228.

Jameson, F. (1972). *The prison-house of language*. Princeton, NJ: Princeton University Press.

McGuire, M. (1980). The ethics of rhetoric: The morality of knowledge. *Southern Speech Communication Journal, 45*, 133-148.

Nuttal, A.D. (1983). *A new mimesis: Shakespeare and the representation of reality*. London: Methuen.

Oakeshott, M. (1962). *Rationalism in Politics*. New York: Basic Books.

Peirce, C.S. (1958). *Collected papers, Vol. 2*. Cambridge: Harvard University Press.

Rich, A. (1979). *Toward a woman-centered university. On lies, secrets, and silence* New York: W.W. Norton.

Rorty, R. (1982). *Consequences of pragmatism*. Minneapolis, MN: University of Minnesota Press.

Ryan, M. (1982). *Marxism and deconstruction*. Baltimore, MD: Johns Hopkins University Press.

Saussure, F. de (1959). *Course in general linguistics*. (W. Baskin, Trans.). New York: Philosophical Library.

Schrag, C. (1985). Rhetoric resituated at the end of philosophy. *Quarterly Journal of Speech, 71*, 164–174.

Spivak, G.C. (1980). Revolutions that as yet have no meaning. *Diacritics, 10*, 29–49.

Spivak, G.C. (1985). Reading the world: literary studies in the 1980s. In G.D. Atkins & M.L. Johnson (Eds.), *Writing and reading differently*. Lawrence, KS: University Press of Kansas.

Strauss, L. (1953). *Natural right and history*. Chicago: University of Chicago Press.

Strauss, L. (1964). *The city and man*. Chicago: Rand McNally.

Tarcov, N., & Pangle, T. (1988). Leo Strauss and the history of political philosophy. In L. Strauss & J. Cropsey (Eds.), *The History of Political Philosophy* (pp. 907–938). Chicago: Rand McNally.

Tushnet, M. (1988). *Red, white, and blue: A critical analysis of constitutional law*. Cambridge, MA: Harvard University Press.

Warren, H. (1987). "The truth lies somewhere between the two": Feminist formulations on critical theory and practice. In J. Wenzel (Ed.), *Argument and critical practices* (pp. 103–112). Annandale, VA: Speech Communication Association.

Weaver, R. (1964). *Visions of Order*. Baton Rouge, LA: Louisiana State University Press.

Chapter 9

Rhetoric, Pragmatism, and Practical Wisdom

James A. Mackin, Jr.

Several years ago, a friend of mine who was a chaplain in the Air Force explained to me how he thought a Sunday service should end. He didn't believe in ending with a traditional altar call in which people come forward to contemplate the meaning of their religion at the altar rail. Instead, he felt that the call should be to go into the world outside the doors of the church and try to make it a better place. In the process of trying to improve the world, his congregation would come to understand the meaning of their religion. What the chaplain showed is what I call a pragmatic approach to religion. I call it pragmatic not simply because the attitude demands that our actions should agree with our ideals—idealists have often made that point—but because it insists that we discover meaning in action and not in contemplation of metaphysical essences. A religious belief that does not result in action is not so much hypocritical as it is meaningless. Pragmatism bases itself in an integral relationship between action and meaning.

In a sense, this volume of essays is a more traditional altar call, made by the Church of First Philosophy, asking us to return to the altar to consider the foundations of our practices. The underlying dogma seems to be that we either do derive or should derive our rhetorical theory and practice from our philosophical first principles. However, the pragmatist doubts the rationalistic assumption that our theory and practice derive from our philosophy. Furthermore, even if the assumption were true, the pragmatist doubts that the derivation of theory and practice from philosophy would be a good thing for theory and practice.

By emphasizing action and consequences, pragmatism results in a new approach to the traditional problems of philosophy, an approach that often dismisses these problems as irrelevant to practice. Because it is a different type of approach, pragmatism is not equivalent to philosophical traditions such as materialism and idealism. Some pragmatic philosophers seem to be materialists; Peirce, the founder of pragmatism, was a forthright idealist. What distinguishes the pragmatist, however, is the refusal to privilege materialistic or idealistic intuitions as self-evidently true. Such intuitions serve only as hypotheses that must be tested by their consequences in practice. Even our clear and distinct ideas at times turn out to be humbugs in practice. The pragmatic attitude combines a moderate skepticism about our ideas with a recognition that, on the other hand, many of our ideas do serve us well in practice. Radical skepticism itself is not borne out in practice. There is no generic warrant for doubt; just like belief, doubt requires justification (Rescher, 1969).

The anchoring of philosophy in practice goes counter to the great metaphysical traditions because practice is subject to the vagaries of this world in which actual existents cannot be relied upon. Certain knowledge can only base itself in unchanging essences; this is another dogma of the Church of First Philosophy. From a pragmatic point of view, however, even the search for certainty at the early rosey-fingered dawn of Western philosophical thought arose from the needs of the world of practice. Socrates sought to discover the essence of the Good in order to better know how to act.

After two millenia of apparently fruitless search for essences, pragmatists began to suspect that perhaps we humans were not capable of knowing essences — if there are any such things. Certain developments in the cultural life of Westerners living in the 19th century lent credence to this suspicion. The discoveries of science were providing practical benefits for bourgeois living. Evolution was becoming the foundation of biological theory. Politically, democracy was establishing itself as a practicable form of government. None of these developments supported or were supported by traditional metaphysics of essences. It is not surprising that a new approach to philosophy developed that was more compatible with these cultural developments (Morris, 1970, p. 5). Because pragmatism arose out of these historical circumstances, it has developed its own mode of approach to traditional philosophical problems. In the first part of this essay, I consider that mode of approach in terms of the traditional philosophical categories of epistemology, ontology, and axiology. Before I begin, I must acknowledge that pragmatism does not fit into these categories very well. Nevertheless, by discussing pragmatism in terms of these categories I hope to better illustrate how pragmatism differs from other philosophies. In the second part of this essay, I show the consequences of a pragmatic perspective on rhetorical theory. Pragmatic philosophy has an impact on rhetorical theory not because it offers new first principles but because it insists that we base our theories on inquiry into rhetorical practice and not merely on first principles derived from philosophical dialectic. Finally, in the third part, I consider the implications of this discussion of pragmatic philosophy and rhetorical theory for practical wisdom, which I take to be the overriding concern of the pragmatist.

PRAGMATIC PHILOSOPHY

Epistemology

Epistemology in traditional philosophy is dialectical inquiry into the grounds of human knowing. Pragmatists are uncomfortable with the term "epistemology" because of the Platonic implications of *epistémé*. For Plato, knowledge must be of unchanging essences because knowledge of existing objects would be impossible if such objects are continually in the process of changing (*Theaetetus,* 182–83). Knowledge of the empirical world is the province of the sophist, operating in the darkness of non-being. The philosopher, on the other hand, uses reason to penetrate through to the light shed by the Form of Being (*Sophist,* 254). This light versus dark imagery is not incidental to the Platonic theory of knowledge; the imagery is also the basis of the allegory of the cave and permeates Plato's entire discussion of knowledge in the seventh book of the *Republic*. Such visual imagery early in the history of philosophy led to what Dewey called the "spectator theory of knowledge" (1929, p. 23) and the notion of mind as Glassy Essence or "mirror of nature" (Rorty, 1979, p. 43). On this point of the conceptualization of knowledge and the mind, pragmatists as a whole depart from the philosophic tradition.

Pragmatists return to the practical, empirical world in examining the concept of knowledge. Nevertheless, this return does not lead to logical positivism. Positivism is simply another variant of the spectator theory of knowledge. The early Wittgenstein, for example, sought to explain language as pictures of facts, models of reality (1922/1981). Natural science is then the "totality of true propositions" or pictures of the world (4.1). Pragmatists (and the later Wittgenstein) reject this conceptualization of scientific knowledge as a true picture of an antecedent reality.

The pragmatist can see no reason that humans should necessarily be able to know true pictures of reality, whether one construes reality empirically as knowledge of sense–data or rationally as knowledge of essences. Here the pragmatist draws upon the theory of evolution to suggest that such pictures are not necessary to survival. All that is necessary is that our understanding of our environment be sufficient to guide practical action well enough that the species survives. The measure of theoretical knowledge is found in practice. Peirce, the founder of American pragmatism, observed that accurate knowledge of practical matters, having survival value, could reasonably ensue from natural selection. On the other hand, when it comes to knowledge of essences and deeper meanings, "pleasing and encouraging visions"—illusions and hallucinations—might actually have more survival value (1958/1966, p. 96). In short, the theory of evolution supports the reliability of practical knowledge but does not support the reliability of our clear and distinct ideas.

As Lyne pointed out in Chapter 5 on idealism, our ideas about the nature of reality are very often useful for motivational purposes. However, the process of evolution does not encourage us to believe that we have a faculty of reason that allows us to perceive essences; nor does it encourage us to believe that our pictures of antecedent realities must be correct. For the pragmatist, knowledge is predictive of consequences. To know the truth is to know consequences; this is the import of the often misunderstood statement of William James on the cash-value of truth. "Grant an idea or belief to be true," James writes, "what concrete difference will its being true make in any one's actual life? . . . What, in short, is the truth's cash-value in experiential terms?" (1977, p. 430)

Furthermore, our human experience includes the experience of relationships between events. So, for the pragmatist, truth is "essentially bound up with the way in which one moment in our experience may lead us towards other moments which it will be worth while to have been led to" (James, p. 432). Knowledge becomes an understanding of how events and experiences are related in order to predict and control our experiences. In this way, the pragmatic definition of knowledge finds support in the scientific method.

Science as method presumes that our hypotheses can be tested against reality. Peirce defined reality generally as "that whose characters are independent of what anybody may think them to be" (1958/1966, p. 130). However, reality as a concept, that is, a distinction of thought, must be related to practical action because the "whole function of thought is to produce habits of action" (p. 123). So Peirce provides his famous pragmatic maxim for clarifying concepts:

> Consider what effects, which might conceivably have practical bearings, we conceive the object of our conception to have. Then, our conception of these effects is the whole of our conception of the object. (p. 124)

Following this maxim, Peirce explains that the concept of reality "consists in the peculiar, sensible effects which things partaking of it produce" (p. 131). Scientific investigation takes reality as a hypothesis accounting for the effect of persistence and resistance. Peirce accepts the hypothesis of reality because it has led to scientific successes and because he has no reason to doubt it (p. 108). Dewey distinguishes between reality at large, which he calls "metaphysical reality," and that more specific reality that is the relationship between organism and environment. In Dewey's more limited use of the term, "for ordinary purposes, that is, for practical purposes, the truth and the realness of things are synonyms" (1928, p. 190). Our truths consist of our knowledge of the practical effects of our actions on the reality that is the relationship between organism and environment.

The truths we know are not absolute truths but working truths. Truths that have been warranted by inquiry become part of a funding of truth that guides further inquiry. The notion of warranting assertions by inquiry is an important aspect of pragmatic theories of knowing. Dewey explains that pragmatic warrants depend upon methods because the whole process of knowing is situational. The organism as would-be knower finds itself in a problematic situation. It needs a method for bringing order to the situation (Dewey, 1939a, pp. 581–585). Those methods that most reliably predict consequences provide the best warrants for our assertions because they bring order to the problematic situation. In science, whether a conclusion is to count as knowledge depends on the method used in reaching that conclusion. Dewey extends this importance of method to every field of human endeavor, arguing that the experimental method of science is simply the best example of "intelligent action" that brings order to a disordered situation (p. 583).

For the pragmatist, then, knowledge is instrumental. Prior knowledge consists of warranted assertions that we have found to be reliable and so should be useful in future inquiries. Knowing occurs in the process of inquiry. The method warrants the reliability of that knowledge—that is, it reassures us of the usefulness of the assertion. Truth and knowledge are pragmatic values attributed to assertions because they are useful in solving problems. To say a statement is true is to say that it serves its function well. A collection of such statements comprises a funding that we draw upon in our continuing need to resolve problematic situations. The prior knowledge serves as a source of hypotheses for new problems (Dewey, 1928, p. 182). For the pragmatist, theory derives from and returns to practical action. Theory and practice are never separate because theory serves only to predict effects in practice and so to guide intelligent action.

Because of the melding of theory and *praxis* in pragmatism, "epistemology" is not quite the right term to use for pragmatic theories of knowing. For the pragmatist, the knower is an agent, not merely a spectator. Knowing is an act of inquiry performed by the agent for the purpose of changing an indeterminate situation into a more determinate one. The problem that interests the pragmatist is not how we know or how we know that we know but rather what methods will best solve the problems that occasioned our need to know. Thinking, in the Deweyan sense of inquiry, is not the chief *telos* of the human being; it is simply the human method for coping with the environment. Philosophy would have more to offer humanity in the pragmatist's view if it devoted itself to improving the general methodology of coping.

Ontology

If traditional philosophers are disappointed that pragmatism does not seem to directly address the long-standing problems of epistemology but instead questions the need to bother with those problems, traditionalists will be no more satisfied with pragmatic ontology. Traditional metaphysics treats ontology not as an account of beings but as an account of Being as such. In this vein, ontology consists of the search for the essence of isness. The closest a pragmatist can come to this approach is to examine the nature of beings that we encounter in experience. Perhaps Being shows itself in such an examination, perhaps not. How would one know? What would count as evidence for Being? Or, to apply the pragmatic maxim, what effects does Being have that cannot be accounted for by beings?

Pragmatism in its concern for the beings of experience is thus clearly a naturalistic metaphysics. Santayana (1925) found the whole notion of naturalistic metaphysics to be self-contradictory, and to true believers in the Church of First Philosophy, he may be right. Nevertheless, pragmatists have at the very least made investigations into the nature of Nature. Since the pragmatic project is to reintegrate human activity and the natural environment in which it takes place, ontology for a pragmatist consists of a study of the contents of experience to determine the nature of Nature.

Peirce discerned three separate types of phenomena from his analysis of experience. He refers to these categories as "Firstness," "Secondness," and "Thirdness." In Peirce's usage, Firstness means quality, possibility, chance, or spontaneity; Secondness means reaction, fact, or existence; and Thirdness means mediation, law, habit, universality, generality, or continuity (Morris, 1970, p. 117). Not all pragmatists use Peirce's terms, and no other pragmatist offers as idealistic an ontology as Peirce. Yet the insistence that nature as we know it in practice comprises these different types of phenomena remains entrenched in pragmatism. All pragmatists agree that there are not only qualities (Firstness) and objects (Secondness) but regularized relations between these (Thirdness). Thus both individuality and interconnectedness, chance and regularity, can be discerned in the objects of our experience (Dewey, 1928, p. 21).

Experience itself is simply the interaction between different parts of reality; and, most importantly, the experience is continuous with reality, becoming part of reality itself. An organism interacts with its environment and so experiences it. The experience itself becomes part of the new environment that has been changed by the interaction. Chance and regularity come together in the experience and change occurs. "The conjunction of problematic and determinate characters in nature renders every existence, as well as every idea and human act, an experiment in fact, even though not in design. To be intelligently experimental is but to be conscious of this intersection of natural conditions so as to profit by it instead of being at its mercy" (Dewey, 1928, p. 23).

Consigning the notion of permanent objects to the garbage heap of history, the pragmatist considers every existential object to be an event in practice. What makes some objects seem fixed is the fact that some events occur more slowly than others. "To designate the slower and the regular rhythmic events structure, and more rapid and irregular ones process, is sound practical sense. It expresses the function of one in respect to the other" (Dewey, 1928, p. 25). Structure serves as a Thirdness that combines qualities (Firstness) in such a way that resistance to change (Secondness) is achieved. To treat structure as something fixed and absolute results in either traditional idealism or materialism. Ideal forms are abstractions from structure; matter, such as the atom of Democritus, turns out to be structure at a microscopic level. Both are simply illustrations of slower events that have been hypostatized as fixed and eternal objects. Nature is made up of these various types of events. The objects of our experience are the events constituted by our interaction with other events.

Within this ontology of natural events, what we call "mind" is just another event that has developed naturally in continuity with the other events in nature. Mind is not apart from nature, wondering how to leap the gap, but is a part of nature, experiencing through interaction. From a semiotic point of view, mind is simply our name for the continuing process of signification. As an organism interacts with its environment, it responds to the actions of other organisms. These actions are gestures in the sense that one action leads to another. Growling leads to growling, sniffing leads to sniffing. Signification takes place at a behavioral level; inference becomes possible because a regularity of behavioral responses occurs. When the organism creates a sign to stand for that regularity, signification becomes symbolization and mind exists. So one organism can give a sign to another organism, which interprets that sign to stand for a regular pattern of action (Geiger, 1958, p. 146). Once mind is identified with the process of signification, then "mind is not originally an inner psychic world, nor even the brain inside an organism, but a mode of behavior in which individuals interact with other individuals and the surrounding world through the mediation of language symbols" (Morris, 1970, p. 126). Thinking is that mode of behavior in which one talks to oneself. If we talk to ourselves silently, our actions are "private" and "subjective" simply because the acts of signification cannot be observed by others (p. 127). The concept of self is also a part of the process of symbolizing. Symbolizing makes it possible to speak of oneself as an object and thus to gain self-consciousness. For the pragmatist, mind is a natural event – a mode of experiencing – not a mystical object somehow separated from nature.

Before leaving this discussion of a naturalistic ontology, I should note that the most prominent of current pragmatists believes that the entire pragmatic venture into metaphysics was a mistake. Rorty argues that pragmatic philosophy should not attempt to discuss the traditional problems of philosophy, and he chastens Dewey for having developed a naturalistic metaphysic. For Rorty, metaphysical argument about the nature of existences is unbecoming pragmatists, who ought to limit themselves to criticism of philosophy. Pragmatic philosophers are better seen "as people who work with the history of philosophy and the contemporary effects of those ideas called 'philosophic' upon the rest of culture" (1982, p. 87). Under this definition, pragmatic philosophy is a kind of rhetorical criticism of that particular genre of discourse known as philosophy. Rorty's move is a departure from the earlier pragmatists who found their admittedly hypothetical descriptions of nature to have practical value (James, 1977, pp. 345–362).

Axiology

It should be clear by now that the pragmatic project in each area of philosophy has been to eliminate dualisms such as mind–matter, and knower–known. The perplexing dualism in theories of value has been the apparent opposition between fact and value, "is" and "ought." True to their overall project, pragmatists insist there is no gap between fact and value, that both are interdependent and continuous. The major pragmatic spokesman on issues of value has been Dewey.

Dewey explains that certain of an organism's experiences have qualities that the organism enjoys or appreciates. These qualities belong to the intraorganic events that constitute experience and so are objects in the natural world (1939a, p. 599). Peirce would say that these qualities exist as Firstnesses in nature. The enjoyment or appreciation of such qualities can occur purely by chance; no regularity is necessary for the experiencing of such qualities. However, this type of unique experience is ineffable because signification requires the establishment of regularity. We cannot describe absolutely unique occurrences because we have no symbols with which to describe them. But once having experienced an aesthetic, pleasant, or otherwise enjoyable quality, we will find the lack of that quality to be a problematic situation. So we will seek to discern the regularities that would allow us to bring about a similar experience with the desirable quality. In other words, the chance experience of a desirable quality will lead us to find ways to control events in order to bring about a re-experiencing of that quality.

Dewey's theory of value ties in closely with his theory of aesthetics. For our purposes, we can consider the aesthetic quality of an experience to be a type of good. This quality is something that is undergone, but the work of art is not an undergoing but a doing. The purpose of the doing is to achieve the quality of an undergone experience. This, of course, requires a perception of the relationship between what one does and what one undergoes as a result. The perception of such relationships is the result of intelligent inquiry (Dewey, 1934/1958, p. 45). Art, then, amounts to the act of controlling experience by means of intelligence in order to recreate an undergone quality.

So it is with values in general. An experience undergone is simply good or bad. In this sense, the good cannot be defined because it stands for the family resemblance between ineffable qualities of many different types of experiences. Limiting the meaning of good to those qualities of existential situations that come to be desired means that the good is, as Moore (1903) claimed, indefinable. But that is not the same as to say that the good is a universal quality that is known intuitively. The good is simply a name we give to that category that includes all those qualities of experiences undergone that we would like to repeat. The good cannot be defined because it stands for no essence. In the process of interacting with our environment we, like any other organism, undergo good and bad experiences. At this level, the good is simply a quality, a Firstness that occurs by chance.

Values, on the other hand, do not occur by chance. Values stand in the same relationship to the quality called good that art stands in relationship to the quality called aesthetic. Both are the result of the application of intelligence to our behavior in order to achieve the desired qualitative experience. Valuing is an *act* that involves desiring. "Valuations in the sense of prizing and caring for occur only when it is necessary to bring something into existence which is lacking, or to conserve in existence something which is menaced by outside conditions" (Dewey, 1939b, p. 15). Because the act of valuation takes place only when there is a problem, valuing is a type of inquiry. Goods and desires are a fact of our experience. There is no essential difference between inquiry into these facts and other kinds of facts such as scientific facts. All of these kinds of inquiry are best conducted intelligently.

An intelligent inquiry into a desired end will include a consideration of the means by which such an end may be achieved. Valuation requires appraising means as well as ends. Another dualism—the ends-means dualism — bites the dust. For Dewey (1939b, p. 43), ends and means are a continuum, just as in the physical sciences all effects can be seen as causes. Means become proximate ends that must be achieved before the end-in-view can be achieved. The end-in-view, once achieved, will serve as the means for further ends because it affects future occurrences. Thus means are ends, and ends are means. From this point of view, the problem of the end justifying the means can be clarified. Actions have varied consequences in a continuum of cause and effect. The end-in-view is simply one of the foreseen consequences of an action. We predict consequences through inquiry; that prediction serves as the warrant for the action. In that sense, the end rightly justifies the means. However, intelligent inquiry will predict other consequences of our actions besides that desired consequence that is the end-in-view. When we say that the end does not justify the means, what we are practically saying is that we cannot disregard the other consequences of an action in focusing on the end-in-view (p. 42). Otherwise, we are creating a more problematic situation rather than resolving the problem of the present situation. Intelligent inquiry, that is, good acts of valuing, should help us avoid this kind of shortsightedness.

As in epistemology, inquiries in axiology result in a funding. In epistemology we might choose to call this funding "knowledge." It serves to guide further inquiry. In axiology we could choose to call this funding "values" — the accumulated result of acts of valuing. Values also serve to guide further inquiry. So, from a pragmatic point of view, if we wish to teach "values," what we should teach are those generalized ends–means relationships that have worked well in common situations. However, we should also teach that these values are hypothetical starting points for inquiry into a given concrete situation, not necessarily the answer to be arrived at. We have a tendency to treat values dogmatically rather than hypothetically, just as we have a tendency to treat knowledge as dogma rather than a source of hypotheses for further investigation. To teach values pragmatically is to teach an intelligent process of valuing. Just as science was held back for years because statements of authorities and propositions resulting from dialectical contrast of opinions were taken to be knowledge of preexisting essences instead of being treated as hypotheses to be tested in experience, so our present attempts at valuing may be limited by the same causes. We need not abandon traditional values. Our cultural values often represent an accumulation of human experience. But such values must be tested by their effects in concrete situations. Otherwise, according to the pragmatic maxim, our so-called values are meaningless abstractions that serve only to camouflage our real values that we show by our actions. For the pragmatist, values are not mysterious essences perceived only by the eye of the mind but rather publicly observable motives. They are publicly observable because values direct action and the meaning of the value lies in the potentially observable action it directs.

Values for the pragmatist, as for Aristotle, lie in the realm of practical wisdom, *phronêsis* as opposed to *epistêmê* (*Nichomachean Ethics,* 1139). But as we've seen, the pragmatist, in opposition to Aristotle and the tradition of philosophy, subordinates all philosophical theory, whether epistemological, ontological, or axiological, to the practical effects of that theory. *Theôria* is no longer the highest activity of the human being but simply a part of human praxis — a matter of understanding and anticipating the consequences of our praxis (Dewey, 1929, p. 245). Understanding is a hermeneutic act; it is, as Rorty noted, "a matter of *phronêsis* rather than *epistêmê*" (1979, p. 319). The purpose of philosophy for the pragmatist is an increase in practical wisdom. The aim of the pragmatic philosopher is like the aim of Protagoras, to teach us better ways of living our everyday lives.

A PRAGMATIC THEORY OF RHETORIC

A pragmatic approach to rhetoric cannot be an approach based in some new set of first principles derived from philosophy. For the pragmatist, theory must be based in praxis and should simply be an attempt to account for recurrences (Thirdnesses) in practice in order to better guide future practice. A true believer in the Church of First Philosophy is likely to conceive of rhetoric's function as the search for essences or epistêmê because that is church dogma. Obviously, however, a pragmatic rhetorician has difficulty with the notion of an "epistemic rhetoric." If the concept of epistêmê has not been fruitful in philosophy, why should we be anxious to introduce it into rhetorical theory? A better question for the pragmatist is to ask how rhetoric serves practical wisdom or, as Dewey would have it, intelligent action. If rhetoric has any effect whatsoever, then the consequences of rhetorical action are a changed situation. Ontologically, if the pragmatist holds a metaphysical position, it is that reality is changing as a result of our actions; therefore, rhetoric affects the shape of reality. Rhetorical theory has meaning for the pragmatist only insofar as it helps account for the effects of rhetorical action. For the pragmatist, then, rhetoric is public communication that influences public action.

Pragmatism is compatible with much of contemporary rhetorical theory insofar as theory leads at least indirectly to hypotheses about empirical consequences. The theory that seems to be most directly indebted to a pragmatic outlook is Bitzer's (1968) theory of the rhetorical situation. Dewey's *Theory of Valuation* was an important influence on Bitzer's thought (Patton, 1974, p. 27). Bitzer shares with Dewey the emphasis on problematic situations; he also shares the dubious distinction of often being misunderstood when he is read from another philosophical perspective. Vatz (1973), for example, assumes that Bitzer's perspective requires a realist philosophy of meaning and that the theory is deterministic. He insists that "meaning is not discovered in situations, but *created* by rhetors" (p. 157). Vatz is simply perplexed because he is interpreting a pragmatic approach to rhetoric from his own dualistic point of view in which the rhetor is somehow apart from the situation rather than a part of it.

From the pragmatist's point of view, Bitzer is neither naively realistic nor deterministic (Patton, 1979). To inquire into the situation, according to Bitzer, is to consider rhetoric pragmatically as a moral act that results when interaction between organism and environment creates a problematic situation. Rhetoric, like other forms of moral action from the Deweyan point of view, comes about because of some lack. If things are going smoothly, there is no need for rhetoric. Bitzer is true to Dewey in pointing out that without an exigence, there would be no moral act attempting to change the situation. Salience is simply a matter of determining which factors in the situation are relevant to the problem. Determining salience is thus a matter for inquiry, which, of course, can be done intelligently or not. As a result, the rhetorical response may or may not be fitting. From Bitzer's point of view, rhetoric as a discipline should seek to provide a better method for inquiry into rhetorical situations so that a more appropriate response can be discovered. Bitzer offers a pragmatic definition of rhetoric as a practical art. I suspect that neither Dewey nor Aristotle for that matter would much disagree.

I would not make Aristotle into a pragmatist as a philosopher. Nevertheless, because he considers rhetoric, ethics, and politics to be practical arts, Aristotle's rhetorical theory is in large part commensurate with pragmatism. Rhetoric as a discipline aims at increasing practical wisdom about communication. Both Aristotle and Dewey noted the inseparable relationship between the arts of ethics, politics, and communication (Johnstone, 1980, 1983). Bitzer's (1959) interpretation of the Aristotelian enthymeme incorporates a pragmatic conceptualization of the speech event not as an object but as an interaction between speaker and audience. This conceptualization of speech as interaction seems a natural precursor to his theory of the rhetorical situation. The pragmatic nature of Aristotle's rhetoric further shows itself in the emphasis on general methods that find their specific application in particular cases (*Rhetoric,* 1356b). From a pragmatic point of view, the discipline of rhetoric is an inquiry into empirical regularities (Thirdnesses) in order to better predict and control consequences in actual cases. Following the pragmatic maxim, the meaning of the theoretical concepts is to be found in all possible applications of those concepts in given cases. As a result, concepts like *ethos, logos,* and *pathos* are not useful as standards that define effective rhetoric but as analytical tools that may help predict the effects of a rhetorical act. To define effectiveness as compliance with preexisting standards simply because our theory includes those standards is to defeat the purpose of intelligent inquiry and to halt the progress of the art.

Rhetorical Criticism as Intelligent Inquiry

If Aristotle thought that he was laying down eternal principles of rhetorical practice (and this is not indicated in the text) then the pragmatist disagrees. Aristotle's theory is part of the funding that guides intelligent inquiry into actual rhetorical practices and the consequences of those practices. Intelligent inquiry stands in stark contrast to the practice that Dewey called "judicial criticism" in which the "desire for authoritative standing leads the critic to speak as if he were the attorney for established principles having unquestionable sovereignty" (1934/1958, p. 299). Considering the historical circumstances surrounding the development of departments of speech in the American academy, we can understand why the field of rhetoric in its struggle for respectability appealed to the authority of the ancient writers. But as the discipline began to establish itself, we would expect it to treat classical rhetorical theory as a source of hypotheses, not as judicial standards.

Certainly, we can find ethos, logos, and pathos in effective rhetoric. We can also find ethos, logos, and pathos in rhetoric that has failed miserably. Unless these concepts can be more narrowly defined so that we can distinguish between appeals that succeed and appeals that fail, the pragmatist finds them to be of little use. Of course, the pragmatist would apply the pragmatic maxim not only to neo-Aristotelian criticism but to similar abuses of Burkean theory. Granted that one can find agent, act, scene, agency, and purpose in the rhetorical act, what effect does this configuration have on subsequent public action?

As difficult as the problem of attributing consequences may be, the pragmatist would insist that we address the issue if rhetorical theory is to advance. Too much of theory remains immune to tests of practice. What use is rhetorical theory if it does not help us better predict the consequences of real rhetorical acts? No matter how unpleasant we find the issue to be, rhetoricians must face up to the problem of finding correlations between rhetorical acts and their consequences. If we lack an adequate methodology, then we must begin with an inquiry into possible methods. Experimental methods were favored by Dewey, but experimental methods have their limitations. In controlling the variables we necessarily introduce artificiality into the experimental situation. Artificiality may not be significant when studying something like the conductivity of copper, but it is significant when studying human responses to complex situations. Furthermore, the most important research questions would require unethical manipulation of subjects. Scientific research into human behavior has its own consequences that must be considered in any inquiry into methodology. The value of a given method depends upon all the consequences of that method, not just the end-in-view that is the research question.

When science cannot manipulate the object of study in order to observe the consequences of manipulation, the alternative often used is to manipulate the conditions of observation. Astronomers do not experiment with stars; they experiment with their means of observing stars. They compare their observations of radio waves with observations of light waves, and they compare observations from different reporting points. In this way, astronomers test hypotheses by multiple observations. Criticism of rhetoric can serve the same purpose. Critics first observe the effects of rhetoric on themselves. Then they compare that observation with whatever other data of effects is available. The more observations that are available, the more reliable the results can be. The critic then attempts to explain differences and similarities between observations.

For example, if a former Ku Klux Klan leader conducts a successful political campaign, the critic may want to inquire into his rhetoric. In the process, the critic might find that this candidate's rhetoric lacks salience for the critic, while it clearly resonates with the voters in his district. The critic's experience is part of the data deserving analysis. The critical inquiry aims at explaining these different effects. To increase the funding of knowledge for the inquiry, the critic could conduct research into the findings of other studies of racism. In this case, the critic might hypothesize that fear of becoming a minority makes the voters in this district more susceptible to the candidate's rhetoric about reducing births by mothers on welfare and restricting immigration. This hypothesis may be based on data such as letters to the editor, survey information, and whatever else is available on the subject population. To further test the hypothesis, the critic examines rhetorical artifacts from the candidate's campaign to see if they do contain a pattern of references to the growing numbers of people of other races and religions. If they do, the critic has a reasonable inference. Publishing the inference would continue to test the hypothesis as other trained observers examine the data offered as evidence. The published criticism can then serve as a part of the funding for future inquiries. The funding for the discipline at large includes the results of all intelligent inquiry into the relevant problem, whether the inquiries use quantitative or qualitative methods.

The critical mode of inquiry into correlations lacks the reliability of some other methods, but it is not wholly subjective. The effects of the rhetoric on the critic and other observers are real events that can serve as data. The case is not established beyond a shadow of a doubt, but the critic can claim a degree of warranted assertibility. Having done away with the expectation of absolute certainty in knowledge, the pragmatist accepts varying degrees of reliability dictated by the practical difficulties involved in ascertaining consequences. We do not need certainty to increase the wisdom of our practical decisions. R. J. Reynolds' insistence that science has not yet "proved" a cause–effect relationship between cigarette-smoking and cancer does not affect the wisdom of the decision to quit smoking or to adopt social policies that discourage smoking. Inquiry has produced enough warrant to act. Insisting on certainty is a hangover from Cartesian dualism that serves only to paralyze action.

Rhetoric and Public Consequences

Because pragmatic philosophy conceives of empiricism as including events and their relations with each other, the pragmatic rhetorician seeks to enlarge the conceptualization of rhetorical consequences. The system of relationships within which any act of rhetoric occurs is much larger than the immediate audience of a rhetorical act. Speaker and audience exist within a nexus of social and biological relationships extending even beyond our own planet. The practical state of our discipline may make it impossible for rhetoricians to study all the consequences of a given rhetorical act, but a pragmatic approach would push us into considering many more consequences than we do currently. Attempting to enlarge our definition of consequences may lead to improvements in methods with which to study the larger consequences of rhetorical action. Increased awareness of the larger system of relationships in which rhetoric takes place will improve practical wisdom in both rhetors and audiences.

Again, Bitzer is the rhetorical theorist who has been most Deweyan in his consideration of the relationship between rhetoric and the public. He points out that collective human experience serves as a source of funding for intelligent decisions and actions (1978). If this is true, then this collective, or public, funding is an essential element in the rhetorical situation. For Bitzer, the rhetor serves as a spokesperson for a public, articulating the funded knowledge of that public if the rhetor is to speak competently. The public serves as the authorizing ground of the truths and values in a given rhetorical act. For anyone lacking a Deweyan conception of "public," Bitzer's claims seem normative and even utopian rather than descriptive. Is this not wishful thinking that speakers should always represent the public interest? Clearly, the answer depends on the meaning of "public."

For Dewey (1927/1954), some events are private in nature and others are public. What makes an event public is the fact that its consequences extend beyond those immediately concerned. Actions that affect the welfare of others to such a degree that they must be controlled constitute public acts. So the "public consists of all those who are affected by the indirect consequences of transactions to such an extent that it is deemed necessary to have those consequences systematically cared for" (pp. 15–16). We tend to identify the term public with the state of a fixed community. In fact, there is no unitary public or community but rather a complex relationship of different publics and communities that are more or less stable.

The pragmatic conception of structure as a relative slowness of change may help to explain. Each of us exists in a complex of relationships with others: we belong to schools, businesses, churches, clubs, neighborhoods, and so on ad infinitum. Insofar as each group represents a collection of interests, it constitutes a social system that is going to react as a system to events. Consequences of an event for the members of this group are different from the consequences for those who don't belong to this group because their interests are different. In this way, each of these social groups is, at least potentially, a public. To constitute a public requires some stability (Thirdness) in the patterns of events and consequences. Therefore, a public must have a structure made up of slowly changing events. Obviously, continental geography is very slowly changing; so a group with common interests bounded by geography will be so stable that it will normally evolve into a state. Other interest groups gain stability through institutionalization, which amounts to ritualistic behavior. A few groups have very little long-term stability but gather together ad hoc and cease to exist when a given problem is solved.

Shared knowledge and values contribute to stability because knowledge and values find their meaning in praxis. A shared praxis stabilizes events and consequences. Communities, then, are founded in these shared practices. Yet, because its members also belong to other groups and have other interests, a community does not share all practices. "Public" is simply an aspect of communal life concerned with matters regular and widespread enough to be capable of common management. However, both community and public exist at many different levels of analysis among all these different social groups. This overlapping of communities and publics becomes the source of confusion when we consider the rhetor's role as representative of a public.

Rhetors do speak for a public but not necessarily *the* public. For example, many religious groups believe that they must take action against sin or else they will be found blameworthy by God. They also believe that certain actions, say, the drinking of alcoholic beverages, are per se sinful. Therefore, this group has a public interest within the group to prevent the drinking of alcohol. It follows that a rhetor who competently represents this group will condemn alcohol use. We should not be surprised if the rhetor also seeks to prohibit the use of alcohol within the larger community. Prohibition would make it easier to control alcohol use by members of the group and would supposedly gain them rewards from God for mitigating the evil in the world. However, other communities within the larger community have a public interest in allowing at least moderate drinking of alcohol. From commercial interests who produce alcoholic beverages to people who just enjoy an occasional beer, these publics would also have spokespersons. Other interest groups would find that their interest in issues like separation of church and state were involved. A public debate would engage many rhetors representing many publics.

A pluralistic community must find a way of maintaining stability in the midst of these conflicts between constituent publics. From a pragmatic point of view, rhetoric provides a method for the larger community to strike a balance between stability and adaptability in satisfying the interest of its constituent members. Rhetoric serves as the larger community's means of conducting inquiry into problematic situations. Of course, such inquiry may be more or less intelligent in the pragmatic sense. In the process of arguing for their lesser public interests, each rhetor makes available to the public at large data that may help predict consequences. Even if one disagrees with the prohibitionists, the fact that they hold those values is important to the inquiry. The prohibitionists' prediction of consequences should also be considered and compared to one's own funding of knowledge and values. It is important for the pragmatic purposes of inquiry that all publics be heard so that a more stable consensus can be achieved. In the process of achieving a consensus through rhetoric, a public act of valuation occurs that itself serves as a funding for future ethical decisions. Resolution of problems through inquiry is thus a process of bringing order out of disorder. Rhetoric in the classical tradition of Aristotle, Isocrates, Cicero, and Quintilian has always claimed to serve a public function. The pragmatist agrees because public debate is deliberation at the level of the *polis* and constitutes practical wisdom at that level, just as intelligent deliberation constitutes *phronêsis* at the individual level.

Let us, however, not blind ourselves to the fact that our deliberation is often not intelligent. We often fail to consider relevant facts in our inquiries because we find them unpleasant, and so we end up rationalizing instead of inquiring. So it is with all levels of the public. We do not provide equal access to the public forum because we prejudge some rhetoric as unpleasant. Mass media are both a blessing and a curse. More people receive more information because of mass media, but the media are very selective about what they present. Mediated rhetoric favors the moneyed. Corrupt evangelists have the money to promulgate their views; St. Francis of Assisi would never be heard in this mediated age. As long as all publics are not represented equally, public inquiry is reduced to public rationalizing. The situation becomes worse when we limit our own academic studies of rhetoric to great white male leaders. From the pragmatic perspective, public address as a field should include the study of how publics are and are not represented in public inquiry.

For the pragmatist, the nature of the community depends on the effectiveness of the practical action of all the subsystems that comprise the community. Furthermore, the ability of the community to sustain a domain of public action depends upon the willingness of its members to see their own consubstantiality as a community. Kenneth Burke, of course, has pointed out that rhetoric is the means of obtaining this consubstantiality. For the pragmatist, rhetoric, politics, and ethics are all intertwined in praxis. Public rhetoric can only be understood in terms of the public practices that follow from such rhetoric. Symbols may lead to or substitute for effective action. Therefore, the pragmatic rhetorician's inquiry into public rhetoric requires an assessment of the public praxis that follows from or is displaced by that rhetoric. These public consequences according to the pragmatic maxim determine the significance of rhetorical acts.

In summary then, the pragmatic rhetorician continues the project of Aristotle on a larger scale. Aristotle studied how rhetoric functioned within society. His principles seem to be based on experience and tried in practice. However, the pragmatist takes Aristotle's theory as a starting point for further investigation rather than as a statement of eternal principles of rhetoric. Rhetorical criticism is a form of intelligent inquiry that seeks to find correlations between antecedent rhetorical acts and consequent practices. The purpose of criticism is to increase practical wisdom by both rhetors and audience in their rhetorical praxis. Probable knowledge is all that the inquiry can hope to achieve, but probable knowledge will make our actions more intelligent. The pragmatic rhetorician recognizes that rhetoric is public address, not because of the number of people in the audience but because rhetoric is the method of inquiry for a public. Public action can be based on intelligent inquiry or on rationalizing, depending on how well the community develops a public domain of rhetoric that incorporates all constituent publics. Access to the public arena is thus an important area for inquiry for pragmatic rhetoricians.

What a pragmatic rhetorician will not do is attempt to move the traditional philosophical problems into a rhetorical framework and then claim to have solved them. A pragmatic rhetorician considers philosophy to be a genre of discourse that reflects historical situations and causes changes in practice—in short, a genre of discourse that is rhetorical in its effects. As rhetoric, philosophical discourse is interesting. Philosophy can also serve as a source of ideas that indirectly lead to hypotheses about communication; as such, it is part of the rhetorician's funding of knowledge and values. But doing philosophy is not a rhetorician's project. It may be that the traditional philosophic genre is at an end and that future philosophers will be much more like rhetoricians (Schrag, 1985). If so, the pragmatic rhetorician welcomes them to our field. In the meantime, there is more than enough work in trying to assess the public consequences of discourse to keep us busy on our own project. Even pragmatic philosophy is useful primarily to get rid of those irrelevant questions and critiques raised by traditional philosophers so that we rhetoricians can get to work on our own real problems. But then, that is the purpose of pragmatic philosophy—to return our attention to the problems of everyday life.

THE ISSUE OF PHRONESIS: WHAT DIFFERENCE DOES IT MAKE?

As you wade through the various philosophical and rhetorical theories in this book, you are observing a theological battle in the Church of First Philosophy. If you find yourself asking the question So what? you are asking the question that the pragmatist considers most important. What difference in praxis does a difference in theory cause? That difference in praxis, according to the pragmatic approach, constitutes the meaning of the theoretical concepts. So what have we discovered about these concepts from our meditation in the Church of the First Philosophy? In this final section, I consider the differences these various theories might generate in practice. Finally, I discuss the effects pragmatism itself has had upon praxis in order to show the theoretical deficiencies in American pragmatism that praxis reveals.

Perhaps the position most opposed to pragmatism in current theoretical discourse is realism. This development seems a bit odd since much of current realism, especially perspective realism (see Hikins, chap. 2), is indebted to the empiricism of William James. What distinguishes the two theoretical positions is the kinds of questions one considers important and the certainty one insists upon in the answers. The realist is concerned with the nature of an antecedent reality. Epistemology is important to the realist because epistemology concerns itself with the accuracy of our descriptions of what is really there. Truth, of course, must be correspondence to that reality. In addition, the classical realist insists that we can know some things with certainty. At the heart of the realist approach seems to be the assumption that humans are in some way designed to know antecedent reality. The reality must be antecedent because one cannot know the future with anything like the certainty one has about prior existing realities. What is to come is not yet real. We would expect the realist's rhetorical theory to be especially concerned with the way rhetoric serves to illuminate this antecedent reality.

The pragmatist reverses this emphasis. The pragmatic rhetorician is primarily interested in the consequences of a belief, that is, its impact in the future. A belief that leads to good predictions of future effects is a true belief. Having given up on the notion of certainty, the pragmatist finds the notion of correspondence to an antecedent reality to be of little use. We never escape the process of signification in order to compare our signs with the thing signified, so how can we ever know that our signs correspond to antecedent realities? The ability to predict consequences seems a more useful measure of truth because it helps us to cope with our environment. We may or may not have been designed to know an antecedent reality, but we need the ability to cope in order to survive. All theoretical knowledge of the way things are is simply a funding for hypotheses about what will happen next.

The pragmatist does not disagree with the realist that portions of the world exist independent of human beliefs and actions. The pragmatist simply sets aside that hypothesis as one that can by definition never be supported in experience. What we do know is by definition what we have interacted with. Statements about a hypothetical reality with which we have not yet interacted have no pragmatic truth value. Of course, such statements may have other values; statements about hell and damnation seem to have had motivating value in the great revivals. Belief in a great unknown reality out there has had motivating value for explorers. The pragmatic perspective on rhetoric considers the truth value and other values of rhetorical acts solely in terms of their public consequences, not in terms of their correspondence with some antecedent reality.

Now consider the differences for the practice of the study of rhetoric and public address that the two approaches imply. The realist's approach is always in some sense historical (see Hikins' treatment of "facticity", chap. 2); when we find out what really happened or what really was the case, then we'll have knowledge. Case studies of praxis either stand on their own (presumably, we all should be interested in history for its own sake) or serve to support more abstract theories of reality (this was certainly the case, therefore these rhetorical universals are certainly still the case). The work of academia is thus to develop better histories or better theories. The end of academic praxis is in these ways to accumulate knowledge about the reality of antecedent rhetoric.

The pragmatist agrees that better histories and better theories are desirable. However, the end of academic praxis is not the accumulation of knowledge (*epistémé*) about antecedent rhetoric but the development of practical wisdom (*phronêsis*) for future rhetorical praxis. The rhetorical theories that are the product of academic praxis become true or false as people adapt them for general praxis; they may or may not remain true. Praxis is the cause, the purpose, and the measure of our theories. Phronêsis should be the result. Practical wisdom concerns itself with the past only as a guide for future rhetorical praxis. That there are regularities in human affairs seems a well-supported hypothesis; so case studies and theories are tools for understanding our communicative environment in order to predict how best to interact with it.

Of course, while the pragmatist limits the truth value of academic theories and research to their ability to predict effects in practice, only the most scientistic of pragmatists would deny that theorizing and researching can have other values. A good history has aesthetic value; so does a good theory. A well-formed theory may turn out to have practical benefits that are currently unforeseeable. Theories help us gather and remember otherwise unrelated facts that may serve us well in the future. These other consequences of academic praxis may very well justify research for its own sake.

The strength of realism is its ability to generate workable hypotheses about human interactions. However, in practice the realist often does not accept the hypothetical nature of theoretical observations but instead uses abstraction and dialectic to move further and further away from the praxis that could warrant those observations. Eventually the realist arrives in a mythical world where human reasoning magically corresponds to the transcendent Whatever Is Really There. From a pragmatic perspective, idealism and materialism are simply variations on the theme of the realist's myth. Both make truth claims about the nature of reality that have no pragmatic truth value—that cannot predict a difference in practice. Of course, as Lyne and McGuire have pointed out, idealism and materialism have other values. Believing in a free will may be a good thing for human praxis in general because it may motivate action. Likewise, considering the underlying material causes of social problems may result in better social policies. Both philosophies are of interest, then, because of their rhetorical effects. The rhetorical analyst does well to consider the effects of metaphysical beliefs on a given public, but that pragmatic consideration of effects differs from the idealist's and materialist's founding of rhetorical theory on these beliefs.

In terms of practical effects for rhetorical theory, the approach of the critical rationalist (see Orr, chap. 4) should differ little from the pragmatist. The major difference is in the importance granted to theory. Critical rationalism is a form of skepticism that remains within the philosophical tradition that privileges theory over practice. The unattainable ideal of Absolute Truth still governs critical rationalism, even though the critical rationalist admits that no human knowledge can be proven absolutely true. Again applying the pragmatic maxim, the pragmatist asks what the truth value of the concept of Absolute Truth is, since it clearly has no predictive value for praxis. The pragmatist agrees with the critical rationalist that all our beliefs are hypotheses that may be subject to critical testing but disagrees when the critical rationalist insists that well-supported hypotheses cannot be called true. As long as our rhetorical theory can predict rhetorical practice, why not call it true? Apparently, the difference is that the critical rationalist wants to retain the quest for the Grail of Absolute Truth whereas the pragmatist thinks the quest is a wild goose chase. On the other hand, from a rhetorical perspective, the pragmatist would agree that the motivating value of Absolute Truth is worth investigating.

Absolute Truth no longer seems to be the concern of the existential phenomenologists (see Hyde, chap. 7). Since Husserl, phenomenology appears to have moved further away from the claim to know essences. Yet the desire to have some kind of foundational term on which all theory can be based remains. As a result, the concept of essence still lurks in the background. Reduction of experience to a term like "power" for example is a way of saying that power is the essence of that experience. A common assumption in existentialism is the foundational reality of the self. Kierkegaard's emphasis on the self was a useful and provocative corrective to the concept of mass humanity in Hegel and Marx. Yet concepts like authenticity demand a prior knowledge of self that is not well supported in practice. Attempting to understand ourselves is a continuing part of praxis; we theorize about ourselves in developing guides to action. Existential phenomenology tends to ontologically privilege the concept of self in a way the pragmatist finds unwarranted. On the other hand, in Hyde's discussion (chap. 7) of contemporary Continental writers like Foucault, we find something very like the Deweyan concept of philosophy as cultural criticism and a notion of self as the product of social interaction. Phenomenology seems to be headed toward a congruence of theory and praxis similar to that urged by pragmatism. Unfortunately, serious terminological differences remain because pragmatism and phenomenology are different discourse traditions. I suspect, however, that pragmatic and phenomenological theories of rhetoric have much in common that is hidden by their vocabularies.

Deconstruction is a development within the Continental tradition that also pertains to Dewey's concept of philosophy as cultural criticism. Deconstruction (see Aune, chap. 8) points out the weaknesses in all theoretical discourse by showing the limitations of language. However, the pragmatist would point out that deconstruction itself is dependent on theory—linguistic theory to be precise. It can be a very useful project to use linguistic theory to show the weak links in philosophical theories, especially those metaphysical theories that have extraordinary influence over public policies. But what then? Shall we give up on language because it always contains its own contradictions? Deconstruction is so absorbed with the theoretical level that it seems to miss the fact that language often works very well in practice. If you say "Hand me the green pen" to your friend, she is very likely to hand you the green pen. Deconstruction is useful for deflating the theoretical arrogance of some philosophies and cultural practices. As such, it may serve at times as the beginning of wisdom, but it can never offer phronesis because it does not concern itself with developing positive hypotheses to guide praxis. The difference in emphasis between pragmatism and deconstruction is evidenced by the title of Dewey's book, *Reconstruction in Philosophy* (1948/1957). Perhaps in the hands of feminists and other cultural critics, deconstruction may offer a reconstructive phase that would make it more commensurate with pragmatism.

If pragmatism in recent years has been most opposed by philosophical realism, it has been most often mistakenly allied with relativism (see Brummett, chap. 3). Pragmatism is not relativist because it does not claim that one belief is as good as another. In a given set of historical circumstances, some truth claims account better for effects than others. The pragmatist affirms that better supported claims are true. In addition, within certain historical circumstances one often has to choose between two unsupportable beliefs. Because neither belief has a pragmatic truth value, the better belief is the one that results in the better consequences. In neither case does the pragmatist claim that one belief is as good as another. Relativists, on the other hand, seem to be making a very strange universal claim—that all beliefs are inherently equal. This is a claim that is not only unsupported, it is controverted by practice. Furthermore, the relativist claims to know that all knowledge is relative. The pragmatist wonders how the relativist knows that. Why in this case is the relativist's belief better than the realist's?

Brummett's postmodern relativism (chap. 3) remains subjectivist in its claim that all we know about experience is our own consciousness, even if others shape that consciousness. How do we know that our consciousness is not consciousness of something? If the realist is a true believer in the Church of First Philosophy and the pragmatist is an agnostic, the relativist is an atheist. Both atheists and true believers claim to know something for certain about metaphysical realities; the agnostic simply says that the truth claims of both sides have to date lacked adequate support in experience. The relativist claims to know as an objective truth that we cannot know anything more than our own consciousness; the realist claims to know as an objective truth that we can know the truth about objects external to our consciousness. (Give the realist bonus points for consistency.) The pragmatist asks how you could support either claim in experience.

Both theories can explain the same experiences in practice. Because they account for no differences in practice, both theories have no pragmatic truth value. If one were forced to pick between the two theories, realism seems more useful in practice because no one in practice acts like a relativist. Like the proverbial donkey that starves to death halfway between two sources of food, a true relativist would never be able to choose between two equal beliefs and so would believe nothing. In practice, a donkey would not starve to death; and in practice, people do have grounds for preferring certain beliefs.

As Brummett points out, contemporary relativism tries to avoid these pitfalls by appealing to the concept of the social symbol system — apparently the foundational term of postmodern relativism. This escape from the traditional problems of relativism, however, is achieved only by hypostatizing the process of interaction into an entity that somehow fixes meaning. The pragmatist acknowledges that in communicative practice we can observe regularities of usage and infer that rules of usage exist, but our observation also leads us to the conclusion that these rules underdetermine meaning. The rules do not account for the creativity routinely demonstrated in our interactions.

What the pragmatist sees in this intersubjective variant of relativism is a camouflaged attempt to ground philosophical argument in a new reality, the reality of social meanings. Of course, this new foundation offers a privileged position to rhetoric and so has appeal within the field of communication. From now on it will be the rhetoricians rather than the philosophers or scientists who get to rule on the foundations of our epistemology. The pragmatic rhetorician finds the suasory power of these claims of professional interest, but the pragmatic philosopher would reject the hypostatized foundation of intersubjective meanings for lacking pragmatic truth value.

In general, the problem the pragmatist has with all these other approaches is their tendency to make theory logically prior and superior to praxis. This shows up further in the emphasis on knowledge rather than practical wisdom as the goal of inquiry. For the pragmatist, theory arises out of the needs of praxis. An omniscient being would have no need for theory; it would know the consequences of a given act in every given case. We, however, lack omniscience; so theory derives lessons from past praxis that can be applied with some confidence to future praxis. Theory begins and ends in praxis; its goal is phronêsis, the wisdom that informs practice. A pragmatic turn in the discipline of rhetoric would mean an increased emphasis on improving the practice of rhetoric in our own historical time and place. The question driving rhetorical inquiry for the pragmatist is, How can we do this better?

Some Problems with Pragmatism

If pragmatism aims at practical wisdom, then it is only fair to ask how pragmatism could better practice what it preaches. In practice, pragmatism has revealed some deficiencies of its own. First, the pragmatic meaning of "true" and the pragmatic meaning of "good" have often been confused, resulting in both a loss of usefulness for the term "true" and also a failure to appreciate rhetorical as opposed to logical consequences of utterances. Second, pragmatism has in practice seemed to be reductionistic, scientistic, and behavioristic. Third, pragmatism in practice has often tended to degenerate into a short-term practicalism that masks ideological assumptions.

The confusion of truth and goodness is a confusion of overlapping categories. A good utterance is an utterance that has value for human praxis. Truth is a particular kind of value. All else being equal, a true utterance is a good utterance; but all good utterances are not true utterances. For example, a poem such as "The Walrus and the Carpenter" is a good utterance because its whimsy has good effects on the audience; but it does not have truth value, nor does it claim to. However, a statement like "The planet earth has a roughly spherical shape" has truth value. From such a true statement, one could derive operational hypotheses that will predict consequences—for example, that a great-circle route planned on a sphere will take less time than a straight-line route plotted on a flat map. If a statement makes no difference in our prediction of consequences, it has no truth value. That is why the pragmatist claims that most metaphysical statements have no truth value.

However, the logical interpretants or truth values of statements are not the only interpretants and in a given set of circumstances they may not be the most important. As rhetoricians we should be interested in the power that statements have to motivate regardless of their truth value. Ethically, the rather common circumstance in which it may be advisable not to tell the truth is another example of how other values may be more important than truth values. In such circumstances, one could well argue that a true utterance is not a good utterance.

This confusion of true and good utterances that has bedeviled pragmatism may also account for the charge of reductionism. Because Peirce's maxim reduces the logical truth value of a statement to the practical value of that statement for predicting effects, it seems to reduce human discourse to an arid behaviorism. Peirce himself hoped to make philosophical discourse more scientific by the application of his maxim. Dewey developed his method of inquiry by observing the successes of the scientific method, extracting principles from that method, and applying those principles to other fields. In the process, Dewey contributed greatly to the growth of the social sciences. Pragmatism in the form we know it would probably never have arisen were it not for the scientific climate of the 19th and 20th centuries. Does it follow that pragmatism is necessarily scientistic, behavioristic, and reductionistic? Could pragmatism be humanistic?

The answer depends upon whether one thinks it is scientistic to insist that the truth value of our theories consists solely in their ability to predict effects in praxis. Again, this is not to say that the sole value of our theories lies in that truth value. Parsimony and elegance are nice features of a theory, as well. Some metaphysical theories also may prove to have better social consequences than others. The pragmatist can acknowledge these other values but simply does not confuse these values with truth value, believing it prudent to distinguish between the different values of our utterances.

In order to achieve pragmatic truth value in rhetorical criticism and theory, the pragmatist suggests that a methodical form of inquiry is still a prudent way to proceed simply because it seems to work better in practice. The behaviorist leaning in pragmatic theory is also not a theoretical bias but simply a matter of practice. The pragmatist is not interested in denying the efficacy of human thought; instead the pragmatist emphasizes that thought is important because it results in action that affects others. The problem is that the only human thought we can observe is our own, and we can't observe that very well, so thought does not seem to be a good measure of our theories about the effects of thought.

To say that human thought is for practical purposes unobservable is not to say that it is some mystical entity. If your two best friends go off into another room and talk, their conversation is also unobservable to you. The inability to observe the conversation does not justify denying the existence of the conversation, but it does justify designing a theory that is not dependent on what takes place in that unobserved conversation. The truth value of the theory for practical purposes will depend on its ability to predict what happens after they come out of that closed room. In the same way, statements about other people's minds have no truth value for the pragmatist except insofar as those statements predict differences in observable behavior. If someone claims that you and I think differently but act similarly, the pragmatist finds the claim that we think differently to be empty of truth value.

The pragmatic rhetorician is looking for methods of rhetorical criticism and theorizing that will improve rhetorical practice. If the attempt to improve practice by the most reliable methods available is scientistic, then the pragmatist is scientistic. More likely, it is the tendency of pragmatists in practice to emphasize the logical interpretants, even when analyzing rhetorical discourse, that makes them seem more scientistic than they need be. Yet pragmatism also includes an interest in human values, and the humanistic practice of rhetorical criticism is a means of inquiring into those values. The pragmatist should not object to the methods of rhetorical criticism except when the criticism uses circular logic to justify its own theory instead of offering predictions of real consequences. Pragmatism and humanistic methodology should be compatible.

On the other hand, pragmatism as it is practiced, most noticeably in America, is susceptible to the charge of a different kind of reductionism: not scientistic but capitalistic. Pragmatism is a historicist philosophy (or, perhaps, anti-Philosophy), so it must acknowledge its own historical context. In the context of American society, the practice of pragmatism has often degenerated into an assessment of short-term consequences evaluated on a monetary basis. This development in pragmatism was foreshadowed in the rhetorical choice by William James to represent the pragmatic truth value as the "cash-value" of a belief (1977, p. 430). Many who call themselves pragmatic have taken James' metaphor too literally. Pragmatism offers no justification for privileging short-term financial profit over long-term social welfare; but because short-term profit is more clearly visible than long-term social effects, in practice pragmatism seems to favor the profit motive. In rhetoric, the pragmatic effects of rhetorical acts are often equated with how well the rhetors accomplished their immediate purposes—the cash value of their rhetoric, we might say. In the case of rhetoric and other social practices, the difficulty in ascertaining and correlating long-term effects results in a bias toward those short-term effects that are most easily observed. In American society, we can easily observe events like money exchange, presidential elections, and acts of Congress, and so they tend to be used as criteria for effects. The fund of knowledge that results from such assessments then tends to bias future practice. One could say that such a fund of knowledge is, as a result, ideological.

I cannot offer an escape from ideology for the pragmatist. All I can recommend is humility in recognizing the limitations on our ability to observe situations, rhetorical and otherwise. We do not have an adequate methodology for assessing the long-term consequences of our rhetoric. A few years ago, we did not have a scientific methodology for assessing the long-term consequences of our use of chloro-fluorocarbons, although we knew quite a bit about its short-term effects. Now we have discovered a hole in the ozone layer over the Antarctic. One cannot help wondering what kind of holes we are creating in the rhetorical equivalent of our protective ozone layer. What kind of damage are we doing to our social system with our rhetorical practices while we busy ourselves with short-term assessments of consequences? As difficult as it may be to answer, the question is pragmatic. Finding an answer should be part of the pragmatist's quest for practical wisdom. The pragmatist, of course, does not expect to find the answer inside the Church of First Philosophy. Perhaps it is time to genuflect and quietly exit to the world outside.

REFERENCES

Bitzer, L. F. (1959). Aristotle's enthymeme revisited. *Quarterly Journal of Speech, 45,* 399-408.

Bitzer, L. F. (1968). The rhetorical situation. *Philosophy and Rhetoric, 1,* 1-14.

Bitzer, L. F. (1978). Rhetoric and public knowledge. In D. M. Burks (Ed.), *Rhetoric, philosophy, and literature: An exploration* (pp. 67-93). West Lafayette, IN: Purdue University Press.

Dewey, J. (1928). *The philosophy of John Dewey* (J. Ratner, Ed.). New York: Henry Holt and Company.

Dewey, J. (1929). *The quest for certainty: A study of the relation of knowledge and action.* New York: Minton, Balch & Company.

Dewey, J. (1939a). Experience, knowledge and value: A rejoinder. In P. A. Schilpp (Ed.), *The philosophy of John Dewey* (pp. 517-608). Evanston, IL: Northwestern University.

Dewey, J. (1939b). *Theory of valuation. International encyclopedia of unified science* (Vol. 2, No. 4). Chicago: University of Chicago Press.

Dewey, J. (1957). *Reconstruction in philosophy* (enlarged ed.). Boston: Beacon. (Enlarged edition originally published 1948)

Dewey, J. (1954). *The public and its problems.* Athens, OH: Swallow. (Original work published 1927)

Dewey, J. (1958). *Art as experience.* New York: Capricorn. (Original work published 1934)

Geiger, G. R. (1958). *John Dewey in perspective.* New York: Oxford University Press.

James, W. (1977). *The writings of William James* (J. J. McDermott, Ed.). Chicago: University of Chicago Press.

Johnstone, C. L. (1980). An Aristotelian trilogy: Ethics, rhetoric, politics, and the search for moral truth. *Philosophy and Rhetoric, 13,* 1-24.

Johnstone, C. L. (1983). Dewey, ethics, and rhetoric: Toward a contemporary conception of practical wisdom. *Philosophy and Rhetoric, 16,* 185-207.

Moore, G. E. (1903). *Principia ethica.* Cambridge: Cambridge University Press.

Morris, C. (1970). *The pragmatic movement in American philosophy.* New York: George Braziller.

Patton, J. H. (1974). The contemporary American pulpit as rhetorical situation. Doctoral dissertation, Indiana University, 1974. (University Microfilms No. 74-22, 785)

Patton, J. H. (1979). Causation and creativity in rhetorical situations: Distinctions and implications. *Quarterly Journal of Speech, 65,* 36-55.

Peirce, C.S. (1966). *Selected writings: Values in a universe of chance* (P. Wiener, Ed.). New York: Dover. (Doubleday edition published 1958)

Rescher, N. (1969). The illegitimacy of Cartesian doubt. In *Essays in philosophical analysis* (pp. 309-319). Pittsburgh: University of Pittsburgh Press.

Rorty, R. (1979). *Philosophy and the mirror of nature.* Princeton: Princeton University Press.

Rorty, R. (1982). *Consequences of pragmatism (essays: 1972-1980).* Minneapolis: University of Minnesota Press.

Santayana, G. (1925). Dewey's naturalistic metaphysics. *Journal of Philosophy, 22,* 673-688.

Schrag, C. O. (1985). Rhetoric resituated at the end of philosophy. *Quarterly Journal of Speech, 71,* 164-174.

Vatz, R. E. (1973). The myth of the rhetorical situation. *Philosophy and Rhetoric, 6,* 154-161.

Wittgenstein, L. (1981). *Tractatus logico-philosophicus* (C. K. Ogden, Trans.). London: Routledge and Kegan Paul. (Original work published 1922)

Author Index

Subject Index

S